Decisions and revisions

Philosophical essays on knowledge and value

Decisions and revisions

Philosophical essays
on knowledge and value

ISAAC LEVI

PROFESSOR OF PHILOSOPHY,
COLUMBIA UNIVERSITY

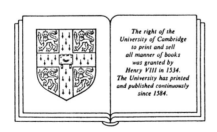

The right of the
University of Cambridge
to print and sell
all manner of books
was granted by
Henry VIII in 1534.
The University has printed
and published continuously
since 1584.

CAMBRIDGE UNIVERSITY PRESS

CAMBRIDGE

LONDON   NEW YORK   NEW ROCHELLE
MELBOURNE   SYDNEY

Published by the Press Syndicate of the University of Cambridge
The Pitt Building, Trumpington Street, Cambridge CB2 1RP
32 East 57th Street, New York, NY 10022, USA
296 Beaconsfield Parade, Middle Park, Melbourne 3206, Australia

© Cambridge University Press 1984

First Published in 1984

Printed in Great Britain at the
University Press, Cambridge

Library of Congress catalogue card number: 83–26355

British Library cataloguing in publication data
Levi, Isaac
Decisions and revisions
1. Knowledge, Theory of
I. Title
121 BD 161
ISBN 0 521 25457 4

N.P.

TO ERNEST NAGEL

Contents

Preface

Scientists must make value judgements. The conduct of their diverse activities requires this of them. The kernel of truth in the contrary claim that scientific inquiries are value-free or value-neutral is more accurately expressed by asserting that scientific interests are autonomous. The values which ought to be promoted in scientific inquiries exhibit features distinctive of scientific as opposed to political, economic, moral or aesthetic deliberations. This way of speaking admits that scientific inquiry is value-laden, that every specific scientific inquiry addresses some problem or family of problems and is, as a consequence, goal-oriented, and that the solution which ought to be adopted from among the strategies available is one which best promotes the goals of inquiry.

To concede the value-laden character of scientific inquiry is not to grant the reducibility of the goals and values of scientific inquiry to moral, political, prudential and aesthetic goals and values. The reconstructed version of value-neutrality I favor denies this reductionist view and insists that scientific inquiries seek or ought to seek to promote values and goals distinctive of the scientific enterprise.

The autonomy of scientific values is compatible with the plurality of human values. Scientists are human beings with personal goals, plans and moral commitments distinct from scientific interests which sometimes compete with the research aims that some human beings also have. Universities, research institutes and other agencies of scientific research have economic, political, educational or other interests distinct from cognitive ones.

But cognitive goals are distinct from moral, political, aesthetic or prudential objectives and may even come into conflict with them. In this sense, conflict between cognitive and other interests can generate moral struggles of the second kind noted by Dewey and Tufts (1932, p. 174) just as surely as can conflicts between competing moral values or between moral values, aesthetic values or life plans.

Insisting on the autonomy of scientific values may be thought to create an untenable dualism between theory and practice. I think not.

That one and the same person or institution may pursue diverse aims and values on different occasions or might be conflicted between different values on the same occasion is generally conceded. There is, to be sure, considerable

ix

controversy concerning how conflict in values is to be understood and addressed. Most of those who write about such conflicts assume that they should be settled (at least ideally speaking) by the time the moment of choice is reached or that they should be settled through choice made at that moment.

In my judgement, such views are mistaken. Rational agents may and sometimes should refuse to resolve the conflicts between the rival aims and values they are committed to uphold even while they are constrained to make a decision. This is one of the main messages of 'Conflict and social agency' (1982e) which is reprinted as chapter 16 of this volume.

No matter how one stands on the question of when conflicts between values should be resolved, we should not deny the existence of such conflicts altogether on the grounds that they presuppose untenable dualisms. Perhaps, we would be hard pressed to draw a precise and general distinction between aesthetic and moral values. Even so, artists are sometimes in conflict between moral commitments and artistic ideals. It would be wrong to deny the existence of such conflict on the grounds that it presupposed an untenable dualism.

The difference between cognitive and other non-cognitive values should not be thought to create a chasm between theory and practice any more or less grand than any other contrast between kinds of values which might come into conflict.

There is a more important point about theory and practice which ought to be emphasized. Once we have acknowledged the value and goal-directed character of scientific inquiry and assessment of evidence, we are in a position to emphasize that criteria for assessing evidence and exercising cognitive options in science share much in common with grounds for evaluating options in other contexts of deliberation. In this respect, there is a unity of theory and practice implied by the view I am considering which could not have been emphasized so readily if we did not acknowledge at the outset a contrast between cognitive and non-cognitive values.

To sustain a view such as this, it is important to explore how a conception of the cognitive values of scientific inquiry combined with a view of rational goal attainment might produce criteria for evaluating potential solutions to problems in various contexts of inquiry. I began considering this question in the late 1950s in a relatively limited way. Subsequently, I have broadened the scope of my reflections in several directions. Over the past two and half decades my views concerning epistemic utility, cognitive decision making and the improvement of knowledge have gone through many minor and some major changes. *Gambling with Truth* (1967a) reports on what was my considered view *circa* 1965 when I completed the manuscript of that book. *The Enterprise of Knowledge* (1980a) is another snapshot of my evolving doctrine as of 1978.

However, from 1960 onwards, I published several articles on epistemic utility and cognitive decision making which fill in many of the gaps in the developments which led in the first instance to (1967a) and then to (1980a). The first series of essays in this collection document various changes in outlook from 1960 to 1978 and may, when taken together with the two books, give a fuller picture of the various considerations which have led to the account of cognitive decision making I favor.

'Must the scientist make value judgements?' (1960a) was written in 1958. It points to the possibility of understanding statistical inferences in particular and scientific inferences in general as cognitive decisions justified in the context of cognitive decision problems relative to epistemic goals. 'On the seriousness of mistakes' (1962) was written in 1959. It proposes a pair of models for decision making in statistics together with epistemic utility functions suited to the models. In this paper, I introduced the notion of a degree of caution understood as reflecting a trade-off between an interest to avoid error and relieve doubt.

These papers were written before I was acquainted with Hempel (1960) and (1962), in which he makes use of epistemic utilities. In my subsequent work, I borrowed his term although I had already used the idea independently of him.

Aside from terminology, there was one other point suggested to me by Hempel's papers – namely that the trade-off between interest in avoiding error and relieving doubt might be clarified by representing the extent to which doubt is relieved by a measure of content or information. I did not think that Hempel had exploited this idea in a useful way. However, it did seem like a good idea to determine whether Popper's ideas on falsifiability and content could be of any help.

With this in mind, I hit upon the idea of trying to interpret Popper's measures of corroboration as discussed in the appendices of (Popper, 1959) as measures of expected epistemic utility which one seeks to maximize in order to determine which of rival hypotheses to accept. I soon realized that this could not be done satisfactorily. I also noticed, however, that the measure $P(x; y) - P(x)$ – which is often taken to be a measure of relevance of y to x – could be represented as an index of expected epistemic utility. Since some of Popper's measures were functions of probabilistic relevance (among other things), I proposed substituting expected epistemic utility as measured by positive relevance as a substitute for Popper's measures of corroboration. These ideas were written up by early 1961 and published as 'Corroboration and rules of acceptance' (Levi, 1963a). My suggested reconstruction of Popper's proposal was clearly unacceptable to Popper and his followers (Michalos, 1966) – much to the detriment, in my judgement, of Popper's own view. I include the paper here, however, not because of its bearing on Popper but because all of the subsequent versions of expected epistemic utility functions I have proposed are generalizations of the idea of probabilistic relevance.

Shortly after writing this paper, I was invited to participate in a symposium of the American Philosophical Association, Eastern Division and, for that purpose, wrote a paper on Hempel's ideas. This paper (1961a) relied on the results of my work on Popper's measures for its main results. Even though it appeared in print before (1963a), it is the derivative of that paper and I have, therefore, omitted it here.

Aside from these gropings for a sensible characterization of epistemic utility, I was concerned to develop a more sophisticated representation of the options in a cognitive decision problem than the representations I had used in my earlier papers. By 1962, I was thinking of inductive inferences as involving the accepting of a hypothesis along with the deductive consequences of that hypothesis and the available background information and evidence. In that way, one could distinguish between sentences accepted as strongest via induction and sentences accepted via induction but not as strongest. Thus, a potential answer to a question or cognitive option could be characterized as the acceptance as strongest via induction of some element of a Boolean algebra consisting of equivalence classes of sentences where equivalence is relative to background information and evidence.

To make this idea work, it was necessary to address Henry Kyburg's argument that if high probability is sufficient for acceptance, the set of accepted sentences should not, in general, be deductively closed. In 1963, I wrote the first draft of (1967a) and worked out to my own satisfaction an account of epistemic utility which, together with the view of cognitive options as cases of acceptance as strongest via induction, yielded a rule of inductive acceptance which rejected the requirement that high probability was either necessary or sufficient for inductive acceptance. This rule preserved deductive closure, assigned a role to indices of caution as determining trade-offs between avoidance of error and relief from doubt or agnosticism and saw expected epistemic utility as a generalized notion of relevance.

Kyburg's point about deductive closure was dramatized for philosophical intuition by the so-called 'lottery paradox'. This paradox became an object of concern among those interested in the epistemological outlook articulated by R. Chisholm (1957). In 'Deductive cogency in inductive inference' (1965a), I took the opportunity to respond to Kyburg's lottery paradox and the reactions expressed in (Lehrer, 1964) and (Sleigh, 1964).

The epistemic utility functions introduced in (1967a) were not the same as the one I considered in connection with my discussion of Popper in (1963a) – although they may be seen as generalizations of it. I did not, however, explain why I had abandoned the earlier proposal, largely because there seemed to be no good reason to discuss technical considerations of this kind for disagreeing with my earlier self when no one else had, so it seemed, joined in the debate. However, while (1967a) was in press, I read an important essay by Jaakko Hintikka and Juhani Pietarinen (1966) in which the proposal I made in (1963a) was introduced independently. This persuaded me that I should write a paper in which I explained systematically why various proposals alternative to those I used in (1967a) ought to be rejected.

While writing 'Information and inference' (1967c), I realized that my characterization of relief from agnosticism in (1967a) had been unnecessarily restrictive. By liberalizing it in certain ways, I was able to think of many more contexts of scientific inference as occasions where the aim is to obtain new information while avoiding error. Due to the vagaries of publication, it appeared in the same year as (1967a), which it supersedes in certain important respects. It remains, in my judgement, the best short statement of the technical details concerning epistemic utility I have written. For this reason, I have included it here.

One of the most insightful critical discussions of my (1967a) appeared as an article by Kenneth Goosens (1976). Goosens raised the question as to how my proposals concerning epistemic utility related to the design of experiments and the evaluation of evidence. I wrote 'Epistemic utility and the evaluation of experiments' (1977) in response to Goosens' paper. Because the relation between epistemic utility and the design of experiments is not discussed in any other publications of mine, it seemed desirable that it be included in this section on epistemic utilities.

Ian Hacking (1967), Richard Jeffrey (1968), Risto Hilpinen (1968) and Ilkka Niiniluoto (1975) all worried about the relativity of my account of inductive acceptance and epistemic utility to a particular set of exclusive and exhaustive hypotheses (the 'ultimate partition'). Although I did not then and do not now see anything objectionable in the relativity, I acknowledged already in (1967a) that there was a problem concerning the conclusions an agent is justified in accepting into evidence via induction when he is committed to recognizing several such partitions as representing problems worthy of being considered.

One of the byproducts of work I began doing in the early 1970s on indeterminate probabilities is an account of indeterminate utilities which can be used to address issues of indeterminacy in epistemic utilities which arise when an investigator is conflicted between different cognitive values without being in a position to resolve the conflict. Utilizing the ideas I was then elaborating in the preparation of my (1980a), I prepared a paper addressing the problems posed by Niiniluoto, in particular. Although some of the material in 'Abduction and demands for information' (1979d) appeared in (1980a), some important technical details were omitted and the order of presentation was substantially modified. For this reason, I have included this paper here.

The papers just reviewed constitute a supplement and commentary on the ideas concerning epistemic utility discussed in (1967a) and (1980a). They are not substitutes for the treatments found in these books; but they should supply some motivational background for issues addressed in them. In the case of (1967*c*), (1977*d*), and (1979*d*), they supply technical details bearing on my current position in a form which cannot be found so explicitly elsewhere.

In the cognitive decision problems discussed in (1967*a*) and (1967*c*), a cognitive option is represented as accepting a sentence as strongest via induction from background information and evidence – i.e., accepting that sentence together with all deductive consequences of that sentence and the background information and evidence. What does 'acceptance' mean in this context? In (1967*a*), I was prepared to discuss several different senses of acceptance (mere acceptance, acceptance as evidence, acceptance for test). However, I saw the problems of acceptance with which I was concerned as ancillary to the problem of revising the system of sentences accepted as evidence. For me, to accept a sentence as evidence was to be certain that it is true, to assign it probability 1 and use it as background information in subsequent investigations. I framed my acceptance rules to handle mere acceptance and not acceptance as evidence on the understanding that rules for mere acceptance concern what should be accepted into evidence were it the case that the problem under consideration and the potential answers identified for that problem the sole issue regarded as worthy of investigation at the time. Hence, I could say that a hypothesis is merely accepted even though it is not accepted as evidence.

My persistence in putting my view in this way derived from two kinds of consideration. In the late 1960s, I still lacked an account of how one should proceed when there is a conflict between the conclusions justified relative to different questions. This issue is the one considered in (1979*d*).

The other problem concerned epistemological fallibilism – the doctrine that each item in a body of knowledge is possibly false. I was wedded to that Peircean view while at the same time committed to the view that scientists do and ought to accept hypotheses into evidence and assign them probability 1. By distinguishing mere acceptance from acceptance as evidence, I was able to say that an agent could recognize the hypotheses he merely accepts as bearing probability less than 1. But this way of speaking generated the appearance of Peircean fallibilism without its substance; for I also wanted to say that scientists do and ought to accept sentences as evidence. An agent who accepts *h* as evidence cannot consistently assign it probability less than 1. Yet, I wanted to say that such acceptance is fallible.

Like everybody else, I was perfectly prepared to say that such acceptance is fallible in the sense that it is revisable; but I took for granted that such revisability committed one to the possibility that what is accepted is false. Admitting that possibility appears to require assigning probability less than 1 to hypotheses other than truths of logic and mathematics. Hence, at most such hypotheses could be accepted as evidence.

In the 1960s, I solved this problem (unwittingly) for myself by remaining in a fog of confusion. By 1971, I had come to realize the incoherence incurred by insisting that sentences accepted as evidence are fallibly so-accepted. To address the difficulty, I proposed to draw a distinction between the fallibility of human knowledge and its corrigibility or revisability. The distinction is simple enough and *prima facie* can be made safe from contradiction. Yet, there seems to have been a pervasive reluctance to make it. In considering this matter, I noticed that two of the most persistent fallibilists, Peirce and Popper, could be understood as having equated fallibilism and corrigibilism due to a shared vision of the ultimate aim of scientific inquiry as being to converge on the true complete story of the world. The explanation is not a causal one. Anyone who has such an aim would find it counterproductive to revise his doctrine if he counted it as certainly true. Rejection of fallibilism brings rejection of corrigibilism in its wake. To escape this predicament, I concluded that one should consider abandoning the Peirce–Popper conception of the ultimate aim of scientific inquiry.

I began reading 'Truth, fallibility and the growth of knowledge' (1983) to diverse audiences in 1971. It was accepted for publication in 1975 but not actually published until 1983. Since it represents the first expression of what I have taken to be an important revision in my thinking and since it seems to me to have a direct bearing on many of the discussions of convergence and truth which have been carried on in the late 1970s and the 1980s, it has been included here.

'Four types of ignorance' (1977c) elaborates further on different senses of belief, knowledge and ignorance I have found useful to consider in my work. It contains a brief discussion of the ramifications of my analysis for John Rawls' arguments from the 'veil of ignorance'.

'Escape from boredom' (1981e) was provoked by the strong exception I took to Richard Rorty's efforts to group the pragmatism of John Dewey together with the views of Martin Heidegger and Ludwig Wittgenstein, and his persistent hostility to science and the notion of truth. I do not include it here, however, because of the polemic against Rorty. Whatever its origin, it does offer a perspective on the way I see the various more technical questions I explore elsewhere which I have not otherwise articulated.

'Serious possibility' (1979c) compares my conception of epistemic possibility with Jaakko Hintikka's conception in his (1962). 'Subjunctives, dispositions and chances' (1977b) restates the view of the relation between objective statistical probability I proposed in (1967a) in the light of the many discussions of modality and propensity interpretations of probability which had emerged in the interim. 'Direct inference' (1977a) focuses attention on Henry Kyburg's important work and its bearing on the interpretation of statistical probability and fundamental issues in statistical inference. It reports on a basic result concerning the relation between Bayesian inference and direct inference which has not been fully appreciated in the literature.

Since 1966, I have insisted on the importance of G. L. S. Shackle's notion of potential surprise and the conception of degrees of belief related to that idea. In this volume, I have taken my latest discussion of Shackle's ideas,

'Potential surprise: its role in inference and decision making' (1980c) and modified it by the addition of material taken from a review of L. J. Cohen's *The Probable and the Provable* (Levi, 1979e).

Although I fancy myself a critic of Bayesian decision theory, some criticisms of Bayesianism have seemed to me less serious than others. A well-known line of criticism has developed out of consideration of puzzles such as 'Newcomb's problem'. In recent years, there has been a growth of a family of related 'causal decision theories' which modify Bayesian decision theory to accommodate features of causal structure alleged to be relevant to rational choice but which Bayesian theory ignores. I continue to believe that my 'Newcomb's many problems' (1975) addresses some decisive objections to such theories and, indeed, did so before others began formulating such theories in an elaborate manner.

Aside from side references, this volume contains no essays focused on what I take to be the main defect in Bayesian doctrine – namely, its insistence that rational agents be committed (at least ideally) to numerically-definite probability judgements and assignments of value or utility. My (1980a) contains a rather extensive proposal for modifying Bayesian doctrine so as to accommodate these complaints and to develop an account of decision making under uncertainty suitable to this proposal. My current work is focused on extending these ideas to contexts where value conflict appears regardless of whether it derives from uncertainty or not.

'Conflict and social agency' (1982e) represents my first published statement of an attempt to extend my ideas concerning individual decision making under uncertainty to social and group decision making. In addition, it contains a treatment of the well-known Allais' paradox.

It is well-known that there is a tension between efforts to promote social welfare and liberal protections of certain rights. In (Sen, 1970), A. K. Sen presented a striking argument which converted this tension into a demonstration of the impossibility of a Paretian liberal. 'Liberty and welfare' (1982b), the final paper in this collection concedes the existence of the tension but insists that there are conditions under which the tension can be broken.

Ernest Nagel has often chided me for misleadingly distinguishing between fallibilism (which I reject) and corrigibilism (which I endorse). He contends that most readers will find it difficult to disassociate the term 'fallibilism' from the view I call 'corrigibilism'.

Even so, Nagel himself contrasts two kinds of fallibilism: that of Peirce and that of Popper. Peircean fallibilism, so Nagel claims, insists that we do have knowledge and that there are no incognizables. On the other hand, settled knowledge might become unsettled and be subject to revision. Popper, on the other hand, denies that science ever achieves knowledge of any matter of fact. Every assertion of science is merely a guess or conjecture. Newton was mistaken in insisting on a distinction between propositions which are settled certainties and hypotheses which are conjectured and in demanding that we treat conjectures differently from certainties. For Popper, hypothesizing is all we ever do.

Although I am on record as disagreeing with Nagel concerning the relation between Peirce and Popper, Nagel's contrast between two kinds of fallibilism corresponds very closely to my distinction between fallibilism (Popperian fallibilism) and corrigibilism (Peircean fallibilism as Nagel understands Peirce). For me, the agreement is far more profound than the disagreement.

At the close of the 'Quest for uncertainty', Nagel comments on a distinction between science and myth drawn by Santayana as follows:

> Although I think with Santayana that myth and science differ, it is well to remember that much that passes as science is indeed myth; and the strength of fallibilism lies in the recognition that continuing effort is required not to confound the two. However, the versions of fallibilism I have been considering (the fallibilisms of Popper and Feyerabend) cannot in the end admit that myth is not the same as science and can often be told apart; and I have tried to show that a fallibilism which leads to such a conclusion is neither coherent nor supported by an adequate analysis of the logic of science.

The projects I have undertaken have sought in their own way to understand how the boundaries between myth and science ought to be revised through inquiry. I owe Ernest Nagel a debt of gratitude for having helped guide me in the direction of this problematic and take this opportunity to show my gratitude by dedicating this volume to him.

New York
June 1983

Part I

Cognitive decision making

1

Must the scientist make value judgements?*†

> The scientific man has above all things to strive at self-elimination in his judgments, to provide an argument which is true for each individual mind as for his own.   KARL PEARSON

Two assumptions implicit in Pearson's characterization of 'the scientific man' have been called into question in recent years: (*a*) At least one major goal of the scientist *qua* scientist is to make judgements – i.e., to accept or reject hypotheses – and to justify his judgements. (*b*) The scientific inquirer is prohibited by the canons of scientific inference from taking his attitudes, preferences, temperament, and values into account when assessing the correctness of his inferences.

One currently held view affirms (*a*) but denies (*b*). This position maintains that the scientist does and, indeed, must make value judgements when choosing between hypotheses. The other position upholds the value-neutrality thesis (*b*) at the expense of the claim that scientific inference issues in the acceptance and rejection of hypotheses (*a*). According to this view, a scientific inquiry does not terminate with the replacement of doubt by belief but with the assignment of probabilities or degrees of confirmation to hypotheses relative to the available evidence.

In this paper, a critical examination of these conflicting conceptions of scientific inference will be undertaken; the *prima facie* tenability of the claim that scientists can, do, and ought to accept and reject hypotheses in accordance with the value-neutrality thesis will be defended; and some indication will be given of the kind of question that must be answered before this plausible view can be converted into a coherent and adequate theory of the relation of values to scientific inference.

1

The tenability of the value-neutrality thesis has been questioned by C. W. Churchman (1948, ch. xv) and R. B. Braithwaite (1955, pp. 250–4) at least insofar as it applies to statistical inference. However, the most explicit

* I wish to acknowledge my debt to Sidney Morgenbesser, whose critical comments in conversation have greatly influenced my thinking on this question, and to Mortimer Kadish and John McLellan, whose reactions to earlier drafts of this paper have helped shape the final result.
† Reprinted from *The Journal of Philosophy* **57** (1960), pp. 345–57.

and sweeping attack against the value-neutrality thesis is to be found in an article by Richard Rudner (1953), who argues that the scientist must make value judgements in drawing any kind of non-deductive inference.

Now I take it that no analysis of what constitutes the method of science would be satisfactory unless it comprised some assertion to the effect that the scientist as scientist accepts or rejects hypotheses.

But if this is so then clearly the scientist as scientist does make value judgements. For, since no scientific hypothesis is ever completely verified, in accepting a hypothesis the scientist must make the decision that the evidence is *sufficiently* strong or that the probability is *sufficiently* high to warrant the acceptance of the hypothesis. Obviously our decision regarding the evidence and respecting how strong is 'strong enough' is going to be a function of the *importance*, in the typically ethical sense, of making a mistake in accepting or rejecting the hypothesis. Thus, to take a crude but easily manageable example, if the hypothesis under consideration were to the effect that a toxic ingredient of a drug was not present in lethal quantity, we would require a relatively high degree of confirmation or confidence before accepting the hypothesis – for the consequences of making a mistake here are exceedingly grave by our moral standards. On the other hand, if, say, our hypothesis stated that, on the basis of a sample, a certain lot of machine stamped belt buckles was not defective, the degree of confidence we should require would be relatively not so high. *How sure we need to be before we accept a hypothesis will depend on how serious a mistake would be* (Rudner, 1953, p. 2).

Rudner's claim is not that values play a role in the scientist's selection of research problems, nor is he arguing that scientists often let their attitudes, values, and temperaments influence their conclusions. These points are relevant to the psychology and sociology of inquiry but not to its logic. Rudner is making an assertion about the requirements imposed upon the inquirer who embraces the goals and the canons of scientific inference.[1] He contends that the scientist in his capacity as a scientist *must* make value judgements even if it is psychologically possible for him to avoid doing so. His argument for this conclusion can be summarized in the following series of statements:

(1) The scientist *qua* scientist accepts or rejects hypotheses.

(2) No amount of evidence ever completely confirms or disconfirms any (empirical) hypothesis but only renders it more or less probable.

(3) As a consequence of (1) and (2), the scientist must decide how high the probability of a hypothesis relative to the evidence must be before he is warranted in accepting it.

(4) The decision required in (3) is a function of how important it will be if a mistake is made in accepting or rejecting a hypothesis.

---

1 The canons of scientific inference can be construed to be normative principles. The value-neutrality thesis does not deny this but does insist that given an initial commitment to these principles, the scientist need not and should not let his values, attitudes, and temperament influence his inferences any further. It is this claim that Rudner appears to deny.

The need for assigning minimum probabilities for accepting and rejecting hypotheses (3) is a deductive consequence of the claim that scientists accept and reject hypotheses (1) and the corrigibility of empirical hypotheses (2). Since (2) is a cardinal tenet of an empiricist philosophy of science and will not be questioned in this paper, the first part of Rudner's argument reduces to the correct claim that if (1) is true (3) is true.

Rudner's rejection of the value-neutrality thesis cannot be justified, however, on the basis of (3) alone. He must show that the assignment of minimum probabilities is a function of the importance of making mistakes (4). But (4) cannot be obtained from (3) without further argument.[2] Rudner attempts to fill the gap by citing illustrations from quality control and appealing to current theories of statistical inference. He believes that the problem of choosing how to act in the face of uncertainty, which is the fundamental problem of quality control, is typical of all scientific inquiry and concludes from this that the importance of making mistakes must be taken into account in all scientific inference.

This argument seems to rest upon certain assumptions adopted more or less explicitly by Rudner and Churchman (1956, p. 248). These assumptions involve the notion of acting on the basis of a hypothesis relative to an objective. To say 'X acts on the basis of H relative to some objective P' is to assert that X carries out action A where A is the best procedure[3] to follow relative to P, given that H is true. The Rudner–Churchman assumptions can now be stated as follows:

(5) To choose to accept a hypothesis H as true (or to believe that H is true) is equivalent to choosing to act on the basis of H relative to some specific objective P.

(6) The degree of confirmation that a hypothesis H must have before one is warranted in choosing to act on the basis of H relative to an objective P is a function of the seriousness of the error relative to P resulting from basing the action on the wrong hypothesis.

Assumption (6) is a version of a principle adopted by Pearson, Neyman, and Wald in their theories of statistical inference. The plausibility of Rudner's argument from quality control (where the problem is how to act on the basis of hypotheses) to (4) is due largely to the reasonableness of this presupposition. However, (6) without (5) will not yield (4).

---

2 Actually Rudner's version of (4) is stronger than mine. According to Rudner, the importance of making a mistake can be construed in 'a typically ethical sense.' In order to simplify the discussion, this rider will be dropped. The importance of making a mistake will be understood to be a function of the values, attitudes, preferences, and temperament of the investigator or group whose interests he serves regardless of the ethical character of these values, etc. Understood in this sense, (4) is still incompatible with the value-neutrality thesis.

3 Perhaps 'A is believed by X to be the best procedure' should replace 'A is the best procedure'. The following discussion does not, however, demand a choice between these two definitions.

Unlike (6), (5) cannot be justified by an appeal to the authority of the statisticians. Not only are these authorities fallible, but some of them have been non-committal regarding the acceptability of (5).[4] Substantial grounds can be offered for praising this exercise of caution.

2

An interesting case against the tenability of (5) has been made by Richard Jeffrey. Jeffrey considers the problem of deciding whether a given batch of polio vaccine is free from active polio virus. The seriousness of the consequences of mistakenly accepting the hypothesis would seem to demand that we confirm the hypothesis to a far higher degree before accepting it than would be the case if we were interested in the quality of a batch of roller skate bearings.

But what determines these consequences? There is nothing in the hypothesis, 'This vaccine is free from active polio virus,' to tell us what the vaccine is *for*, or what would happen if the statement were accepted when false. One naturally assumes that the vaccine is intended for inoculating children, but for all we know from the hypothesis it might be intended for inoculating pet monkeys. One's confidence in the hypothesis might well be high enough to warrant inoculation of monkeys but not of children (Jeffrey, 1956, p. 242).

Jeffrey's point can be reformulated as follows: Action on the basis of a hypothesis H is always relative to an objective P. Consequently if accepting H is identical with acting on the basis of H (5), accepting H in an 'open-ended' situation[5] where there is no specific objective is impossible. But accepting H is possible in open-ended situations, for it is compatible with different and even conflicting objectives. Hence, (5) must be rejected.

In a reply to Jeffrey's paper, Churchman compares Jeffrey's open-ended decision problems to situations that occur in production. Suppose that a manufacturer wishes to place on the market a certain product (rope) that has many different uses. Churchman points out that procedures are available to the manufacturer in terms of which he can single out needs that his product should be designed to meet. He contends that similar procedures must be employed if we are to accept and reject hypotheses intelligibly.

---

4 'The terms "accepting" and "rejecting" a statistical hypothesis are very convenient and are well established. It is important, however, to keep their exact meaning in mind and to discard various additional implications which may be suggested by intuition. Thus, to accept a hypothesis H means only to decide to take action A rather than action B. This does not mean that we necessarily believe that the hypothesis H is true. Also if the application of a rule of inductive behavior "rejects" H, this means only that the rule prescribes action B and does not imply that we believe that H is false.' (Neyman, 1950, 259–260.) In this passage, Neyman does identify accepting a hypothesis H with acting on H. However, he refuses to identify accepting H with believing that H. In effect, therefore, he suspends judgement regarding the truth of (5).
5 This expression is due to Churchman (1956, 248).

In this sense, it is certainly meaningless to talk of *the* acceptance of the hypothesis about the freedom of a vaccine from active polio virus, provided the information has a number of different uses. Even within one business organization one can readily point out that the many uses of information imply many different criteria for the 'acceptance' or 'rejection' of hypotheses (1956, p. 248–9).

Churchman's argument seems to be this: *If* 'accepting a hypothesis *H*' is understood in a sense that makes (5) true, then open-ended decision problems involving the acceptance or rejection of hypotheses can be treated like open-ended production problems. The solvability and, hence, the intelligibility of such problems requires the elimination of the open-endedness.

This true observation does not meet, however, the major point of Jeffrey's objection. Jeffrey's argument attempts to show that in *one* sense of 'accepting a hypothesis' to accept a hypothesis in an open-ended situation is perfectly meaningful and consistent. Consequently, in *that* sense, (5) does not hold.

An easy but cheap victory might be gained at Jeffrey's expense by pointing out that wherever a scientist does not appear to have an objective in mind, nonetheless, one can always be specified – namely, the objective of accepting true answers to questions as true. Accepting a hypothesis *H* would then be equivalent to acting on the basis of *H* relative to that objective.

Resorting to this strategy would be to miss the point of the discussion. To say that accepting a hypothesis is the same as acting on the basis of *H* in order to obtain true answers is tantamount to asserting that accepting *H* is equivalent to accepting *H*. One could not conclude from this alone that the problem of deciding what to believe is on all fours with decision problems in quality control – at least with respect to the value-neutrality thesis. In the latter kind of problem, the objectives are 'practical'; in the former, they are 'theoretical'.

In order to avoid misunderstanding, therefore, an open-ended decision problem will be understood to be a decision problem for which no practical objective has been specified.[6] Consequently, the issue at stake in the debate between Jeffrey and Churchman is whether there is any sense in which a person can meaningfully and consistently be said to accept a hypothesis as true without having a practical objective. The following considerations are offered in favor of an affirmative answer to this question.

(*i*) Many apparently intelligible questions are raised and answered in the sciences for which practical objectives are difficult to specify. What practical

---

6 By a 'theoretical' objective, I shall understand any objective that is concerned with selecting true hypotheses from a given list. A practical objective is one that is not theoretical. This dichotomy overlooks distinctions between ethical, practical, and aesthetic objectives by grouping them together. It also treats many objectives as practical that might legitimately be held to be theoretical. The purpose of the twofold partition of objectives, however, is to avoid a trivial interpretation of (5) while permitting Churchman and Rudner as much leeway as possible in their interpretation of this assumption.

objectives are at stake when an investigator is deciding whether to accept or reject the principle of parity, the hypothesis of an expanding universe, or the claim that Galileo never conducted the Leaning Tower experiment? One could try to show that appearances are deceiving and that practical objectives are always the goals of such decision problems. However, this would be difficult to prove. Furthermore, it would not follow that appearances *must* be deceiving and that practical objectives *must* be operative. Indeed, the cases just cited would normally be considered to be problems of deciding what to accept as or believe to be true regardless of whether practical objectives are involved. This seems to indicate that there is a sense of 'accepting a hypothesis' which is meaningfully applied to choices in open-ended situations.

(*ii*) Even in the case of decision problems where practical objectives are involved, it often seems appropriate to distinguish between acting on the basis of a hypothesis relative to that objective and accepting the hypothesis as true. Suppose that an investor in oil stocks knows that if a certain oil company whose stocks are selling at a low price strikes oil at a certain location, the price of the stock will increase one hundredfold. The investor might buy stock in the company while suspending judgement as to the eventual discovery of oil. Here is a case where one would normally say that a person has acted on the basis of a hypothesis and perhaps was justified in doing so without accepting the hypothesis as true or being warranted in so accepting it.

One could reply by saying that the investor refused to accept the hypothesis because such acceptance would have been tantamount to acting on the basis of the hypothesis of an oil strike relative to some practical objective other than making a profitable investment. However, such an objective would not always be easy to find. Furthermore, the situation would normally be considered a case of action without belief regardless of whether the existence of a practical objective could be shown or not.

(*iii*) There seems to be a sense in which it is possible for a person to believe in the truth of a hypothesis and nonetheless refuse to act on it. He may even be justified in proceeding in this fashion. The Sabin live virus polio vaccine serves as an illustration. The available evidence might warrant belief in the safety and effectiveness of the vaccine without justifying a program of mass inoculation.[7]

---

7 This claim might seem counterintuitive. There is a widely held view that if a person really believes in a hypothesis he should be ready to act on it. This 'put up or shut up' analysis may be understood in two ways: (*a*) belief in *H* implies acting on the basis of *H*, and (*b*) belief in *H* implies that one ought to act on the basis of *H*. R. M. Martin seems to adopt the former view (1959, p. 11). This version of the 'put up or shut up' analysis does not seem adequate to at least one familiar sense of 'accepting a hypothesis'. The very fact that people often think that one ought to act on a hypothesis if one believes it implies that one might not so act. Sense (*b*) of the 'put up or shut up' analysis seems more plausible. Nonetheless it yields results that themselves appear to be counterintuitive. If this thesis demands readiness to act relative to

(*iv*) A plausible case can be made for saying that even when a person is deciding how to act in order to realize a practical objective he will have to accept some statements as true in a sense that does not meet the conditions of (5). The evidence upon which he bases his decisions consists of statements which he accepts as true. He might have to accept the truth of statements asserting the degrees to which various hypotheses are confirmed relative to the available evidence. Finally, he will also have to accept the truth of statements that indicate the best actions relative to his objectives given the truth of various hypotheses.[8]

The considerations just advanced suggest that there is a familiar sense in which a person can meaningfully and consistently accept or reject a hypothesis in an open-ended situation. In that sense, (5) is false and Rudner's argument in favor of (4) and against the value-neutrality thesis fails.

This result need not in itself be fatal to the Churchman–Rudner position. Apologists for this view could admit the meaningfulness of this sense of 'accepting a hypothesis' and deny that the aim of the sciences is (or ought to be) to accept or reject hypotheses in that sense. They might contend that scientific inferences indicate how one ought to act on the basis of hypotheses but not what one ought to believe. The rejection of the value-neutrality thesis would flow quite naturally from this transmutation of scientific inquiry into a quest for normative principles. Oddly enough, however, it is Jeffrey, an apparent defender of the value-neutrality thesis, who denies that scientists accept and reject hypotheses.

3

Jeffrey proposes a conception of the aim and function of science also suggested by Carnap (1950, pp. 205–7) and Hempel (1949, p. 560). According to this view, a scientist does not, or at least should not, accept and reject hypotheses. Instead, he should content himself with assigning degrees of confirmation to hypotheses relative to the available evidence. Anyone who is confronted with a practical decision problem can go to the scientist to ascertain the degrees of confirmation of the relevant hypotheses. He can then utilize this information together with his own estimates of the seriousness of mistakes in order to decide upon a course of action.

One consequence of this view is that all non-deductive inference in science

any objective, then one would not be warranted in accepting a hypothesis as true unless the degree of confirmation approached certainty. For there is always the possibility that some objectives exist relative to which mistakes are so serious as to demand enormously high degrees of confirmation. Such a requirement seems unreasonable. On the other hand, if the objectives relative to which one should be ready to act are restricted in some way, it is difficult to see how the restrictions could be specified without destroying the initial plausibility of the 'put up or shut up' analysis.
8 I owe this observation to Mortimer Kadish.

consists in assigning degrees of confirmation to hypotheses relative to given evidence. Indeed, Carnap (1950, p. 206) defines inductive inference in this way. Hence, if Carnap is correct in maintaining that degrees of confirmation can be ascertained without consideration of values, the Carnap–Hempel–Jeffrey view supports the value-neutrality thesis.[9] However, the value neutrality thesis is upheld at the expense of the claim that scientists accept or reject hypotheses. In this respect, the Carnap–Hempel–Jeffrey view breaks as radically with tradition as does the Braithwaite–Churchman–Rudner position.

In his paper, Jeffrey offers an extremely clever argument to show that scientists can neither accept nor reject hypotheses.

On the Churchman–Braithwaite–Rudner view it is the task of the scientist as such to accept and reject hypotheses in such a way as to maximize the expectation of good for, say a community for which he is acting. On the other hand, our conclusion is that if the scientist is to maximize good he should refrain from accepting or rejecting hypotheses, since he cannot possibly do so in such a way as to optimize every decision which may be made on the basis of those hypotheses. We note that this difficulty cannot be avoided by making acceptance relative to the most stringent possible set of utilities (even if there were some way of determining what that is) because then the choice would be wrong for all less stringent sets. One cannot, by accepting or rejecting the hypothesis about the polio vaccine, do justice both to the problem of the physician and the veterinarian. The conflict can be resolved if the scientist either contents himself with providing them both with a single probability for the hypothesis (whereupon each makes his own decision based on the utilities peculiar to his problem) or if the scientist takes on the job of making a separate decision as to the acceptability of the hypothesis in each case. In any event, we conclude that it is not the business of the scientist as such, least of all of the scientist who works with lawlike hypotheses, to accept or reject hypotheses (Jeffrey, 1956, p. 245).

Jeffrey's argument rests upon two lemmas: (a) if scientists accept and reject hypotheses (1), then they must make value judgements (4); and (b) if (1) is true, then (4) is false. The inevitable conclusion is that (1) is false – i.e., that the scientist neither accepts nor rejects hypotheses.

Jeffrey accepts (a) without any question as having been established by Rudner. His argument for (b) may be paraphrased as follows: Deciding whether to accept or reject a hypothesis is an open-ended decision problem – i.e., there is no practical objective in terms of which seriousness of error can be assessed. Hence, if a scientist decides to accept or reject a hypothesis, he cannot be taking the seriousness of error into account. Consequently, if (1) is true, (4) is false.

9 The difference between this view and the revised version of the Churchman–Rudner position suggested above is that the latter considers the scientist as a formulator of practical policy whereas the former considers him to be an adviser to the policy maker. This difference reflects itself in differing conceptions of non-deductive inference. According to the revised Churchman–Rudner view, the 'conclusion' of a non-deductive inference is a choice of a course of action. According to the Carnap–Hempel–Jeffrey view, the conclusion is an assignment of a degree of confirmation to a hypothesis.

In spite of its persuasive character, Jeffrey's argument breaks down at several points.

(*i*) Rudner's argument for lemma (*a*) has already been shown to hold only if accepting a hypothesis is understood to be meaning*less* in open-ended situations. On the other hand, Jeffrey's argument for (*b*) depends upon the understanding that accepting a hypothesis is meaning*ful* in such cases. Hence, Jeffrey is guilty of equivocation.

(*ii*) Jeffrey's argument from the truth of (1) to the falsity of (4) depends upon the assumption that the decision problem is an open-ended one. An open-ended decision problem has been understood to be one that lacks a *practical* objective. However, such problems may still have a theoretical objective. It is at least an open question whether such an objective can serve as a basis for ascertaining the seriousness of mistakes.

(*iii*) Even if theoretical objectives cannot function in this way, Jeffrey's inference from (1) to the negation of (4) can still be avoided. It has been argued that Jeffrey is correct in asserting and Churchman is wrong in denying that there is a sense of 'accepting a hypothesis' that is meaningful in open-ended situations. This does not mean, however, that this sense of 'accepting a hypothesis' is meaningful *only* in open-ended situations. A person may decide what to believe only in order to believe true statements. But he may wish to believe statements which are true and which have some other desirable characteristic such as simplicity, explanatory power, effectiveness as propaganda, or a consoling emotive connotation. And the sense in which he accepts a statement as true in attempting to realize one of these objectives will be the same sense in which he might accept statements as true in open-ended situations. Again, it is at least an open question whether a scientist *qua* scientist has such a practical objective in accepting and rejecting hypotheses and, hence, has a basis for determining the seriousness of mistakes.

The failure of Jeffrey's argument does not, of course, imply the falsity of his conclusion. Indeed, another argument can be offered for rejecting (1). Whatever may be the merits of the inference from (1) to (4), empiricists are committed to accepting the inference from (1) to (3) – i.e., the inference from the claim that scientists accept and reject hypotheses to the need for assigning minimum probabilities for such acceptance and rejection. How are such minimum probabilities to be assigned? If no plausible alternative to a procedure that takes the values of the investigator into account is available, then (1) entails the rejection of the value-neutrality thesis.

Defenders of the Carnap–Hempel–Jeffrey view might feel that we are in such a predicament. Not wishing to abandon the value-neutrality thesis, they reject the conception of the scientist as one who accepts and rejects hypotheses.[10] However, following this strategy is like crashing into Scylla in

10 Hempel (1949) comes closer to arguing in this way than either Carnap or Jeffrey.

11

order to avoid sinking in Charybdis. As Jeffrey (1956, p. 246) himself admits, the scientific literature suggests that scientists do often accept and reject hypotheses in a sense incompatible with (5). Furthermore, they often appear to feel that it is at least part of their business to do so. Consequently, an attempt to construct a theory of scientific inference based on the assumption that scientists do accept and reject hypotheses seems warranted.

4

The question that remains is whether on this assumption the value-neutrality thesis can be maintained. An answer to this question seems to depend upon determining the manner in which minimum probabilities for accepting and rejecting hypotheses are assigned according to the canons of scientific inference. A study of the procedures for assigning minimum probabilities cannot be undertaken in this paper. Nonetheless, two possible outcomes of such an investigation that would support the value-neutrality thesis are worth mentioning. A consideration of these possibilities will serve to clarify the content of the value-neutrality thesis and to focus attention on the issues that must be settled before an adequate assessment of its merits can be made.

(*A*) The necessity of assigning minimum probabilities for accepting or rejecting hypotheses does not imply that the values, preferences, tempera-ment, etc. of the investigator, or of the group whose interests he serves, determine the assignment of these minima. The minimum probabilities might be functions of syntactical or semantical features of the hypotheses themselves. Indeed, they might not be determined by any identifiable factors at all other than certain rules contained in the canons of inference. These rules might fix the minima in such a way that given the available evidence two different investigators would not be warranted in making different choices among a set of competing hypotheses. If the canons of inference did work in this way, they would embody the value-neutrality thesis.

(*B*) Even if the minimum probabilities were functions of identifiable values, the value-neutrality thesis would not necessarily have to be abandoned. When a scientist commits himself to certain 'scientific' stan-dards of inference, he does, in a sense, commit himself to certain normative principles. He is obligated to accept the validity of certain types of inference and to deny the validity of others. *The values that determine minimum probabilities may be part of this commitment.* In other words, the canons of inference might require of each scientist *qua* scientist that he have the same attitudes, assign the same utilities, or take each mistake with the same degree of seriousness as every other scientist. The canons of inference would, under these circum-stances, be subject to the value-neutrality thesis; for the value-neutrality thesis does not maintain that the scientist *qua* scientist make no value judgements but that given his commitment to the canons of inference he need make no further value judgements in order to decide which hypotheses to accept and which to reject.[11]

Thus, the tenability of the value-neutrality thesis does not depend upon whether minimum probabilities for accepting or rejecting hypotheses are a function of values but upon whether the canons of inference require of each scientist that he assign the same minima as every other scientist.

5

The arguments offered in this paper do not conclusively refute the major theses advanced by Rudner or Jeffrey. However, these arguments have justified further examination of the view that scientists accept or reject hypotheses in accordance with the value-neutrality thesis. In particular, it has been shown that Rudner and Churchman have failed to prove that a scientist must take the seriousness of mistakes into account in order to accept or reject hypotheses where the seriousness of mistakes is relative to practical objectives; it has also been shown that even if Rudner and Churchman were correct, the value-neutrality thesis would not entail Jeffrey's abandonment of the view that scientists accept or reject hypotheses; and, finally, it has been argued that even if scientists must take the seriousness of mistakes or other values into account in determining minimum probabilities, they may still accept or reject hypotheses in accordance with the value-neutrality thesis.

The outcome of this discussion is that the tenability of the value-neutrality thesis depends upon whether the canons of scientific inference dictate assignments of minimum probabilities in such a way as to permit no differences in the assignments made by different investigators to the same set of alternative hypotheses. An answer to this question can only be obtained by a closer examination of the manner in which minimum probabilities are assigned in the sciences. This problem will be the subject of another paper.

11 It should also be clear that the value-neutrality thesis says nothing concerning the rationale for adopting scientific canons of inference but only about the content of these canons.

2

On the seriousness of mistakes*†

Developments in the last thirty years have led some authors to formulate the basic problem of statistics as being rational decision making in the face of uncertainty.[1] This formulation is both suggestive and unclear. On the one hand, it suggests that modern statistical theory can treat from a single viewpoint problems where one must decide *how to act* in the face of uncertainty and problems where one must decide *what to believe* in the face of uncertainty. On the other hand, this formulation raises the question as to whether the unity of viewpoint is due to certain structural similarities between different kinds of problems or whether it is based on a debatable reduction of problems concerning what to believe to practical problems.

Clarification of this last point is of considerable philosophical interest. Applications of statistical procedures are to be found in physics, genetics and the social sciences in contexts where the major objective of inquiry seems to be to accept true propositions as true (i.e., where the problem is to decide what to believe). Statistical procedures are also used in determining insurance rates, in market research, quality control, etc. where the problem is to decide how to act. The fact that similar procedures of inference can be applied to theoretical and practical problems has important implications for any conception of the relations between the theoretical and the technological and policy making aspects of scientific activity. The issue at stake stems from the fact that current statistical theory justifies its procedures by appealing to practical applications of these procedures. Does the application of these same methods to cases where one is deciding what to believe or accept as true imply, therefore, a reduction of the theoretical aspects of science to technology and policy making? This paper is a modest beginning of an attempt to support a negative answer to this question.

* Acknowledgements are due to Professors Ernest Nagel and Sidney Morgenbesser and to Mr John McLellan for their helpful comment, and encouragement.
† Reprinted with the permission of the editor from *Philosophy of Science* **29** (1962), pp. 47–65.
1 For example, H. Chernoff and L. Moses (1959, p. 1) and L. J. Savage (1954, pp. 159–62).

1 Error and the search for truth

Several writers on inductive and statistical inference have questioned the seemingly plausible assumption that scientists attempt to replace doubt by belief. On the one hand, it has been argued (Carnap, 1945–6, pp. 597–8; Hempel, 1949, p. 560; Jeffrey, 1956, p. 242) that scientists never accept or reject hypotheses but merely assign degrees of confirmation to them. These assignments serve as guides to the policy maker in deciding on optimum policies for realizing goals.

Supporters of a second view (Rudner, 1953; Churchman, 1956, pp. 248–9) contend that scientists do accept and reject hypotheses. However, they maintain that belief is to be analyzed behaviorally. According to this position, belief that a proposition P is true is equivalent to acting or being disposed to act on the basis of P. To be sure, belief can be construed as a kind of act and believing or accepting a proposition P as true can be understood to be acting on the basis of P relative to the objective of accepting only true propositions as true. However, supporters of behavioral analysis mean to advance a stronger claim than this. They apparently mean by 'accepting a proposition as true' what statisticians frequently intend by this expression. In this technical sense, 'accepting P' is synonymous with 'acting on the basis of P' where the act that is based on P is defined by the particular decision problem that is being considered. Consequently, the act that would be based on a given proposition P might differ from problem to problem depending upon the objectives to be realized. This means that 'accepting P' has no unique analysis but shifts its meaning from context to context even if the proposition P is the same. Hence, the 'theoretical' objective of accepting only true propositions as true is hopelessly ambiguous.[2]

The view to be adopted in this paper is that scientists do accept and reject hypotheses in a sense different from the technical one just indicated. I do not intend to give an analysis of 'acceptance of a hypothesis' or 'belief' except to say that belief is understood to be qualitative and not a matter of degree.[3] I shall also assume that if a person considers a proposition at all with respect to its truth value he can either believe that it is true, believe that it is false, or suspend judgement.

2 Churchman does maintain that science has a set of long range goals that control the immediate objectives of any inquiry. However, this does not appear to yield any univocal meaning to the notion of accepting a hypothesis unless short range goals are specified. This is explicitly admitted by him in (1956, pp. 248–9). See also Churchman (1948, chs. xiv and xv).
3 In my opinion, an adequate analysis of belief has yet to be offered. However, this paper is not concerned with an analysis of belief but of *warranted* belief. The nature of belief is crucial to an examination of warranted belief only insofar as the *applicability* of the latter concept is concerned, but the assumptions required in order to justify the applicability of a theory of warranted belief need not yield a complete analysis of belief. The only important assumptions that I shall make about belief are those indicated in the paragraph to which this footnote is appended. (Note continues on p. 16.)

To say that scientists accept or reject hypotheses in a sense that satisfies the conditions imposed in the last paragraph hardly suffices as a characterization of even the theoretical aspects of scientific activity. A person who wishes to replace doubt by belief but is indifferent as to whether his belief is true or false would be aiming at a goal that could hardly be called scientific. Presumably a necessary condition for a theoretical objective to be scientific would be that it consist in an attempt to replace doubt by *true* belief.

Attempts to replace doubt by true belief may be divided into two categories:

(*a*) Attempts to seek the truth and nothing but the truth. One objective of this sort is operative in some applications of statistical test procedures in the natural and social sciences. The scientist is confronted with a list of propositions and is informed on either logical or empirical grounds that at least one and only one of the propositions on the list is true. He is then called upon to select the true proposition from this list on the basis of the relevant empirical evidence.

(*b*) Attempts to replace doubt by true belief that are tempered by a concern that one's belief possess certain desirable properties *in addition to* truth. A search for a simple explanation of a given phenomenon is an attempt of this sort. Although I would want to maintain that accepting a certain body of propositions as an explanation of a given phenomenon entails accepting them as true in a non-behavioral sense, it is clear that such acceptance is not an outcome of a quest for the truth and nothing but the truth. Interest in the truth is tempered by other desiderata such as simplicity, explanatory power, etc.

Objectives of types (*a*) and (*b*) are both 'theoretical' in the sense that pursuit of objectives belonging to either category is expected to issue forth in the acceptance or rejection of propositions in a non-behavioral sense. Hence, anyone who claims, as I wish to do, that scientists sometimes pursue objectives of both types is in fundamental disagreement with both those who deny that scientists accept or reject hypotheses in any sense and those who insist that they do so only in a behavioral sense.

It should be observed that my strategy here is similar to one widely used approach to the explication of probability as degree of rational belief. In order for such attempts to have significant application, there must be some sense in which belief admits of degrees warranted or unwarranted. But a subjective theory of probability does not require a precise analysis of degree of belief. As far as I can see, the notion of degree of belief remains quite as obscure as the notion of qualitative belief in spite of the precise analyses offered of subjective probability in recent years. Thus, Savage's criticism of the 'verbalistic' viewpoint that I am defending on grounds of 'vagueness' seems to me to be no more and no less relevant to his own position than it is to mine. Needless to say, by contending that scientists do accept and reject hypotheses in a qualitative sense, I do not mean to deny that they also assign degrees of credibility to hypotheses.

16

In recent years, the attack against the claim that scientists accept and reject hypotheses has been supported by an appeal to certain features of inductive and more specifically statistical inference. The version of this argument that will be presented here is based on a brief advanced by Richard Rudner (1953) in favor of the position that scientists *qua* scientists must make value judgements when deciding whether to accept or reject hypotheses.

Let us suppose that an investigator is called upon to decide which of a given list of propositions (or systems of propositions) to accept. Let us also assume that he cannot know with certainty which of the propositions is true but must work with the probabilities or degrees of confirmation[4] conferred upon these propositions by the available evidence. This means that he must determine the minimum probability or degree of confirmation that a proposition must have before he will consider himself warranted in accepting it as true. According to Rudner, these assignments of minimum probabilities are a function of the values of the investigator (or of the group whose interests he serves) and these values reflect the seriousness with which different types of error are taken.

Implicit in Rudner's argument (and quite explicit in some of Churchman's remarks) is the conclusion that when a scientist accepts (or rejects) a hypothesis he is doing so in a behavioral sense – i.e., he is acting (or refusing to act) on the basis of the hypothesis relative to some practical objective. Otherwise how can the role of value judgements in determining minimum probabilities be explained?

In (Levi, 1960a), I argued that Rudner's contention that scientists must make value judgements is at best misleading. I suggested that when scientists decide to evaluate evidence and the validity of their inferences by scientific standards they are, by their commitment to these standards, making a value judgement. It is at least possible, that such a commitment requires of scientists that they make minimum probability assignments in certain standard ways. Consequently, the value judgements that the scientist must make need not reflect his own interests nor those of the community he serves but may be part of a commitment to handling problems in a scientific manner. And such a possibility is at least consistent with the claim that scientists accept or reject hypotheses in a non-behavioral sense.

One important feature of Rudner's argument, however, was neglected in the earlier paper. According to Rudner, when a scientist assigns minimum probabilities for accepting or rejecting hypotheses, these assignments are functions of the seriousness which he attributes to making different types of error. This claim is not explicitly defended in his paper. Instead, Rudner bases his appeal on statistical theory.

---

4 For those who reject the concept of probability as degree of confirmation, a more complicated statement of the argument would be required.

17

If Rudner is correct in this contention, his argument does not seriously damage the claim that scientists can (and I believe do) rationally accept or reject hypotheses in a non-behavioral sense *provided that such acceptance or rejection is the outcome of attempting to realize objectives of type* (*b*). In other words, Rudner's argument entails that scientists can attempt to replace doubt by true belief only if their interest in the truth is tempered by their concern that the propositions they accept have other desirable properties (simplicity, explanatory power, etc.) as well. They *cannot* rationally seek the truth and nothing but the truth – i.e., attempt objectives of type (*a*).

Let us suppose that an investigator seeks the truth and nothing but the truth – in particular, that he is concerned to select from a given list the one and only proposition that is true regardless of any other properties that it might have. If the investigator is rational, he has undertaken the following obligations: (1) He must not prefer that one proposition on the list be true rather than another. (2) He must consider each possible mistake he might make as serious as any other. If Rudner is correct in saying that in assigning minimum degrees of probability one must discriminate between different errors, condition (2) cannot be satisfied. Hence, a rational investigator cannot seek the truth and nothing but the truth.

On the other hand, if the investigator's interest in the truth is tempered by a concern that the proposition (or propositions) he accepts as true have other desirable properties in addition to truth, he is not obligated to observe conditions (1) or (2). He may prefer accepting as true a simple alleged explanation when it is false (true) rather than a complex one.

Thus, Rudner's argument does not logically preclude a scientist from accepting or rejecting hypotheses (in a non-behavioral sense). Nevertheless, if it is valid, it does prevent the scientist from accepting or rejecting hypotheses as an outcome of a search for the truth and nothing but the truth.

This implication of Rudner's argument alone would give many persons pause before pursuing a defense of the claim that scientists accept or reject hypotheses in a non-behavioral sense; for if scientists cannot rationally accept or reject hypotheses when seeking the truth and nothing but the truth, there are grounds for suspecting that the notion of accepting a hypothesis in a non-behavioral sense might be entirely dispensable in an account of inductive inference. Such suspicions are reinforced by the fact that Rudner's argument appeals to the theory of statistical inference in support of the claim that different errors must be taken with different degrees of seriousness. On the other hand, many of the applications of the methods of statistical inference in the sciences provide the best *prima facie* illustrations of cases where scientists seek the truth and nothing but the truth. Since modern statistical theory seems to call for a behavioral analysis of such cases, the non-behavioralist would appear to be deprived of some of his strongest illustrations of situations where scientists accept and reject hypotheses. Consequently, although Rudner's argument (even if it is valid) does not *entail*

18

the denial of the claim that scientists accept or reject hypotheses in a non-behavioral sense, the fact that it does preclude seeking the truth and nothing but the truth does strongly suggest such a conclusion. For this reason, an examination of the statistical procedures which seem to require discrimination between different errors is vital to a defense of a non-behavioralist point of view.

The remainder of this paper will be devoted to a consideration of two different methods of statistical inference. An explanation will be given of the apparent necessity of taking different mistakes with different degrees of seriousness when these methods are applied. Certain revisions of these methods, or rather their interpretation, which avoid this implication will then be offered. In this way, the beginnings of a rebuttal can be made against the appeal to statistical theory as grounds for denying that scientists can and at least sometimes do seek the truth and nothing but the truth.

2 The Bayes method

The first method of statistical inference that I shall discuss is frequently called 'the Bayes method'. Consider the following illustration.

A candidate for President must decide whether to campaign intensively or only moderately within a given state. Suppose that he is going to base his decision on a poll of voter preference taken two months before election day. The candidate knows that if more than 60 % of the total electorate in the state prefer him to his opponent two months before election day he will capture the state regardless of how he campaigns. He also knows that he will certainly win the state if he campaigns intensively even if 60 % or less of the electorate prefer him two months before election day but that in these circumstances he will surely lose if he campaigns only moderately. Since the candidate must campaign in other states and must allot his time and campaign funds in the most effective manner possible, what campaign strategy should he choose on the basis of the results of his poll?

Let us call the hypothesis that 60 % or less of the electorate prefer the candidate H_1 and the other hypothesis H_2. Let us designate the act of campaigning intensively (which is clearly the best option if H_1 is true) A_1 and the act of campaigning moderately (the best option if H_2 is true) A_2; o_{ij} shall represent the result of adopting A_i when H_j is true. Some of the features of the decision problem confronting the candidate can then be represented by the following matrix.

$$
\begin{array}{ccc}
 & H_1 & H_2 \\
A_1 & o_{11} & o_{12} \\
A_2 & o_{21} & o_{22}
\end{array}
$$

In order to solve the candidate's decision problem by means of the Bayes method, certain additional information must be supplied. In the first place, we must be able to order the candidate's preferences for the various outcomes o_{ij}. Since he would probably prefer winning with only a moderate campaign, o_{22} would appear to be the most favored outcome. Since he would prefer winning to losing, o_{21} would be the least favored outcome. Of the remaining two, o_{11} would be preferred to o_{12} since the candidate would prefer a more to a less efficient victory.

The application of the Bayes method requires that we be able to assign numerical values to these outcomes so that these assignments in some sense measure the value or utility to the candidate of the outcomes.[5] The utility of o_{ij} will be designated u_{ij}. For purposes of illustration, the following utilities will be assigned to the four outcomes: $u_{21} = 0, u_{12} = 0.7, u_{11} = 0.9, u_{22} = 1$.[6] If we represent each outcome by its utility, the matrix looks like this:

$$\begin{array}{ccc} & H_1 & H_2 \\ A_1 & 0.9 & 0.7 \\ A_2 & 0 & 1 \end{array}$$

The information embodied in this matrix not only indicates the values of the various possible outcomes of the two options afforded the candidate but also reflects the preferences of the candidate for each of the alternatives confronting him when one of the two hypotheses is true. Thus, he prefers A_1 to A_2 provided that H_1 is true. Hence, if he knew for certain that H_1 is true, he would choose A_1. However, in general the candidate will not know for certain which of the hypotheses is true. Can he, in a state of uncertainty, construct a rational preference pattern?

The Bayes method gives an answer to this question provided that the candidate knows the probabilities with which the hypotheses are true relative to the available evidence.[7] Such evidence might be obtained from

5 In (1947, ch. 1.3), von Neumann and Morgenstern have constructed a measure of utility which has the following properties: (1) The utility of x is greater than (equal to, less than) y if and only if x is preferred to y (x is indifferent to y, y is preferred to x), (2) the numerical values of utility are unique up to a linear transformation and (3) the expectation of utility of a given act for a given probability distribution over the alternative hypotheses is the value of that act for that probability distribution. This utility measure is applicable only if the decision maker's preferences satisfy certain postulates. I shall assume that such postulates embody conditions for rational preference. Since the von Neumann–Morgenstern utility theory is generally used in the formulation of the Bayes method, to question it would be to criticise the Bayes method at a far more fundamental level than the one on which this discussion is being conducted.

6 I shall always set maximum utility at 1 and minimum utility at 0. This is possible since utility values are unique only up to a linear transformation and in the problems we are considering there will always be maximum and minimum utilities.

7 I would like to be as neutral as possible regarding competing conceptions of probability. However, I shall adopt a distinction between probability as a measure of an empirical property of aggregates and probability as degree of confirmation or rational belief and shall assume the measurability of both. I shall remain noncommital concerning the reducibility of one kind of probability to the other and concerning the intelligibility of the second kind of probability except where it appears necessary to use it (as in the discussion of the Bayes method). Finally, I shall never use probability to mean a measure of confirmation that does not satisfy familiar postulates for probability (e.g., Popper's degree of corroboration).

the poll of the voters. Let the probability of H_1 relative to the available information be p and of H_2 be $1 - p$. Then the value of A_1 relative to these probabilities is the expected utility of A_1: $0.9p + 0.7(1 - p)$.[8] Given a probability p, the prudent candidate will choose the act that has the maximum expected utility. Thus, if p (the probability of H_1) is greater than $\frac{1}{4}$, the candidate should choose A_1.

To sum up: In order to apply the Bayes method, the utilities of the possible outcomes of the available alternatives and the probabilities of the various hypotheses must be known. Given this information, the Bayes method recommends adopting the course of action that maximizes the expected utility.

The example employed in describing the Bayes method illustrates a situation where the problem is to decide what to do in order to realize some 'practical' goal (winning an election). How is the Bayes method to be applied when the problem is to replace doubt by true belief?

As an illustration of this kind of problem, consider the following situation. An experimental psychologist wishes to determine whether a given person has extra-sensory perception or not. He assumes that if the person guesses correctly the colors of cards drawn at random with a frequency greater than 0.6 the subject has ESP. Otherwise the subject lacks ESP. The experimenter's problem is to decide on the basis of a sample of guesses whether H_1 (the long range frequency of correct guesses is 0.6 or less) or H_2 (the long range frequency of guesses is greater than 0.6) is true. A_1 is the act of accepting the hypothesis H_1.

Since the experimenter presumably is interested only in accepting that hypothesis as true which is true, he should consider the possible correct answers o_{11} (accepting H_1 when it is true) and o_{22} (accepting H_2 when it is true) as equally desirable and the corresponding 'mistakes' or 'errors' o_{12} and o_{21} as equally undesirable. These recommendations are a consequence of the conditions laid down for seeking the truth and nothing but the truth in section 1. Consequently, the matrix for this problem will be as follows:

	H_1	H_2
A_1	1	0
A_2	0	1

The Bayes method recommends adopting A_1 if the probability of H_1 is greater than $\frac{1}{2}$ and A_2 if the probability of H_1 is less than $\frac{1}{2}$. Consequently, if the probability of H_2 (that the percentage of correct guesses is greater than 60 and, hence, that the experimental subject has ESP) is 0.51, we would be warranted in accepting H_2 (adopting A_2). Those who are not disturbed by

8 Given exclusive hypotheses H_j, each with a definite probability p_j ($\sum p_j = 1$), the expected utility of the act A_i is $\sum_j u_{ij} p_j$. According to the von Neumann–Morgenstern theory of utility, the expected utility of an act is equal to its utility relative to the given probability distribution (cf. footnote 5).

21

this recommendation may find the following revision of the ESP example suggestive.

Suppose the experimenter is to decide between three hypotheses: H_1 – the frequency of correct guesses is less than 0.4; H_2 – the frequency of correct guesses is in the closed interval (0.4, 0.6); and H_3 – the frequency of correct guesses is greater than 0.6. The act A_i is the act of accepting H_i as true. The matrix for this problem looks as follows:

	H_1	H_2	H_3
A_1	1	0	0
A_2	0	1	0
A_3	0	0	1

Let us assume that the probabilities of H_1, H_2, and H_3 are 0.33, 0.33, and 0.34 respectively. The Bayes method recommends A_3 – accepting the hypothesis that the frequency of correct guesses is greater than 0.6.

The difficulty with both of these illustrations is that the Bayes method recommends accepting a hypothesis as true even if the degree of confirmation or probability of that hypothesis is low. But 'accepting' a hypothesis when its degree of confirmation is low does not seem reasonable unless this acceptance is reduced to action undertaken to realize some objective other than seeking the truth and nothing but the truth.

This difficulty cannot be avoided by discriminating between the values of correct answers and between the losses suffered from different mistakes. On the one hand, such discrimination is not permissible if the problem is to seek the truth and nothing but the truth. On the other hand, although discriminatory utility assignments would raise the probabilities required for accepting some hypotheses, they would lower the probabilities required for accepting others.

These remarks suggest that the Bayes method cannot be applied to situations where the objective is to seek the truth and nothing but the truth. Such a conclusion, however, rests upon the assumption that our formulation of the ESP problem is a fair characterization of this kind of problem. This assumption is false. In all such problems, we have, in addition to the opportunity of accepting one of a set of propositions and rejecting the others, the option of suspending judgement or remaining in doubt. We suspend judgement when we feel that the available evidence does not warrant accepting any one of the available hypotheses.

Let us revise the first (two hypotheses) ESP problem by adding to the available options the act S – suspension of judgement. The matrix will now look like this:

	H_1	H_2
A_1	1	0
A_2	0	1
S	k	k

22

The utility k is the value of the result of suspending judgement when the hypothesis H_i is true. It seems reasonable to suppose that this utility will be the same for all of the hypotheses. Furthermore, the consequences of suspending judgement when H_i is true should not be more valuable than correctly accepting H_i or less valuable than mistakenly rejecting H_i. Hence, $0 \leq k \leq 1$. Furthermore, the minimum probability required before any hypothesis can be accepted will be (according to the Bayes method) equal to k, and if $k < \frac{1}{2}$ the investigator will never suspend judgement (in the two hypotheses problem).

This revision of the ESP problem does seem to overcome the obstacles to the application of the Bayes method. No distinctions are made between the values of correct answers or between the values of mistakes. Furthermore, a high degree of confirmation will be required before *any* hypothesis can justifiably be accepted provided that a sufficiently high value is assigned to k.

At this point, a sceptical reader might object that the value assigned to k is arbitrarily selected. The actual choice of a value for k is controlled by the practical interests of the investigator. For example, the investigator might be inclined to assign a low value to k in the ESP example if he was doing research for a Ph.D. in psychology and had to obtain definite results in order for his research to count as material for a dissertation.

In order to reply to this objection, a digression into the significance of k (the utility of the result of suspending judgement) in the context of the problem of replacing doubt by true belief is in order. Earlier in the paper, the problem of replacing doubt by true belief (which I contend, is one type of problem pursued by scientists) was contrasted with the non-scientific problem of replacing doubt by belief regardless of whether the belief is true or false. Anyone who pursues this kind of problem is a practitioner of a version of Peirce's method of tenacity. The matrix of a two hypotheses problem for such a person would look like this:

	H_1	H_2
A_1	1	1
A_2	1	1
S	0	0

The Bayes method would recommend that the tenacious man should never suspend judgement and that he should choose among the other two alternatives according to any arbitrary procedure regardless of the probabilities assigned to the hypotheses.

A person who seeks the truth and nothing but the truth is also interested in eliminating doubt, but this interest is tempered by his interest in the truth. Unlike the tenacious man he prefers truth to error. However, some truth seekers may be so anxious to obtain an answer that they, like the tenacious man, would avoid suspending judgement at all costs. This means that they would assign a value to k that will guarantee the adoption of one of the other

23

alternatives. (In the two hypotheses problem, $k < \frac{1}{2}$ will do the trick.) Although to say that such truth seekers don't care whether they make mistakes or not would be incorrect, they do not consider avoiding error to be very important at least as compared to the importance of eliminating doubt.

On the other hand, consider the truth seeker who is less anxious about getting an answer. He might assign a value to k that is high enough to guarantee that for some assignments of probability to the hypotheses the Bayes method will recommend suspension of judgement. The chief difference between the first truth seeker and the second is that the latter takes mistakes more seriously in relation to eliminating doubt than does the first. We might describe the situation by saying that both individuals are attempting to replace doubt by true belief but that they exercise different 'degrees of caution' in doing so.

The point of these remarks is that to seek the truth and nothing but the truth is to aim at a complex objective. It is an attempt to eliminate doubt tempered by an interest in finding truth and avoiding error. The interest in avoiding error imposes a restraint upon the desire to eliminate doubt – a restraint that is reflected in the degree of caution exercised by the investigator. Consequently, in order to describe any problem where the goal is to select from a list of propositions the one and only true one, the degree of caution that is to be exercised must be specified. If two different investigators exercise different degrees of caution, they are attempting to solve two different problems. Both problems share much in common – they are both attempts to replace doubt by true belief. The sole difference is in the degree of caution to be exercised.[9]

Now to return to the skeptic's objection. I will concede that the choice of a problem whose goal is to replace doubt by true belief and, as a consequence, the choice of a degree of caution in realizing such a goal can be both influenced and justified by practical considerations. But this does not imply that accepting H or suspending judgement concerning H is to be construed in the technical sense of the statistician in which 'accepting a hypothesis H' changes its meaning from problem to problem even if the hypothesis H remains the same. Indeed, it implies nothing about the possibility or necessity of any kind of behavioristic reduction of belief or suspension of judgement even if such reduction yielded a meaning for 'believing that H' independent of the practical problems involved. Consequently, I do not see how this concession affects any major thesis that I wish to defend in this paper.

9 Whether the two problems are the same or different is a verbal issue. What is important is that any attempt to replace doubt by true belief via rational means requires specification of the degree of caution to be exercised. Without such specification there is no way of knowing to what extent the search for true belief controls the attempt to replace doubt. It is in this sense, that a choice of a degree of caution determines in part the choice of the problem to be solved.

Furthermore, it is an open question whether the degree of caution which the scientist *qua* scientist exercises is one that is imposed on him by the canons of scientific inference regardless of any interests that might motivate or justify his concern with scientific research. In other words, if attempts to replace doubt by true belief are classified according to the degrees of caution to be exercised, there may be only one type of attempt (or, if there is a restricted range of permissible degrees of caution, a set of types) that is legitimately scientific.

The upshot of these remarks is that in applying the Bayes method to the problem of replacing doubt by true belief the scientist does have to reckon with the seriousness of mistakes. However, he does not have to do so in the sense that different mistakes have to be taken with different degrees of seriousness, but only in the sense that the degree of caution that he adopts reflects how serious he considers making *any* mistakes to be in relation to remaining in doubt. If these comments are well taken, the application of the Bayes method to problems where the objective is to find the truth and nothing but the truth does not appear to be impossible. Attempted justifications of behavioral analyses of belief by an appeal to statistical theory are not supported by a consideration of the Bayes method.

3

Although the Bayes method receives considerable attention from contemporary writers on the foundations of statistical inference, it is very rarely used in applications. One reason for this is that probability is usually understood by statisticians to be the measure of some empirical property of aggregates of events – e.g., the frequency with which objects having a certain property appear in a given population. According to this interpretation, the probability of the truth of a proposition is either held to be meaningless or difficult to know. However, such probabilities in general are required in order to apply the Bayes method. Consequently, most of the statistical procedures actually employed are devised so that the *a priori* probabilities of hypothesis and the conditional probabilities of hypotheses relative to observations can be ignored. In this section, I shall discuss one such method of inference. It is the method of significance testing according to the theory advanced by J. Neyman and E. S. Pearson.

Consider our presidential candidate. In order to avoid certain mathematical difficulties irrelevant to the question we are discussing, it will be desirable to sacrifice some of the already questionable realism contained in our description of his problem. We shall assume that he knows for certain that two months before election at least 60 % of the voters in the state favor him. He also knows that if the percentage is only 60 % at that time he will surely lose the state unless he campaigns intensively but that if he does campaign intensively he will win. He also knows that if the percentage is greater than 60 % he will win whether he campaigns intensively or moderately. Let A_1, A_2, and H_2 be as before. H_1, however, is the hypothesis that the percentage of voters preferring the candidate is exactly 60 %.

As in the earlier version of this example, a decision between A_1 and A_2 is to be made on basis of a poll of the electorate. Let us suppose that 1000 voters are polled. Since interrogation of a single individual determines (we shall assume) whether that individual does or does not prefer the candidate, there are 2^{1000} possible outcomes of the poll. Any procedure for deciding whether to adopt A_1 or A_2 on the basis of any given outcome of observation partitions the set of possible outcomes into two sets S_1 and S_2. If the outcome is a member of S_i, the decision procedure recommends adopting A_i. From this point of view, the decision problem is reduced to the question of choosing the 'best' partition (S_1, S_2).

In order to apply the method of significance testing to the problem of formulating a criterion for selecting a 'best' partition, we must distinguish between H_1 and H_2 by selecting one of them to be the hypothesis to be tested (the 'null hypothesis'). The basis of this distinction will be discussed shortly. In our example, H_1 will be the null hypothesis.

Once a null hypothesis has been selected, two other distinctions can be explained. Given a partition of the possible outcomes of observation (S_1, S_2), the set of possible observations recommending acceptance of the null hypothesis is called the 'region of acceptance' and the set recommending rejection of the null hypothesis is called the 'critical region'. In our case, for any partition (S_1, S_2), S_2 is the critical region. The problem of choosing a best partition can now be restated as the problem of choosing a 'best' critical region.

The second distinction is between two types of error: type I error – the result of adopting A_2 when the null hypothesis H_1 is true – and type II error – the result of adopting A_1 when H_2 is true. In terms of this distinction, we are now in a position to state informally the criteria employed in significance testing for choosing a 'best' critical region.

The decision maker must first decide upon the maximum probability of committing a type I error that an acceptable choice of a critical region should permit. He will do this by specifying that an acceptable choice of a critical region will not yield a probability greater than some value k (the 'level of significance' of the test) of adopting A_2 given that H_1 is true.[10] Once

---

10 Strictly speaking, the level of significance is not equivalent to the type I error. This last probability is obtained by multiplying the level of significance (i.e., the probability of an observation falling in the critical region given H_1) by the a priori probability of H_1. Since on the frequency view a priori probabilities are either meaningless or unknown, the most we can say (and this may be too much) is that the highest possible probability of type I error (which obtains when the a priori probability of H_1 is unity) is equal to the level of significance. These comments apply when the null hypothesis is 'simple' – i.e., when it specifies precisely the probability distribution of the population being studied. When the null hypothesis is

the level of significance has been chosen, a restriction has been imposed upon the critical regions that are deemed acceptable. Selection of an acceptable critical region will insure against a probability of making a type I error that is greater than the level of significance. However, these acceptable tests may and in general will differ with respect to the maximum type II error they permit. The Neyman–Pearson theory recommends that the best partition be that acceptable partition which (if it exists) minimizes the maximum type II error.[11]

The chief questions still outstanding in this description of the method of significance testing are: (i) On what grounds is the null hypothesis distinguished from its alternative and (ii) what considerations determine the selection of a level of significance? The usual answer given to the first question is that the null hypothesis is to be selected in such a way that type I error will be more serious than type II error. Thus, in the election example, campaigning moderately when the percentage of favorably disposed voters is 60 % is more serious a mistake than campaigning intensively when this percentage is greater than 60 % (Neyman, 1942, p. 304).

On what grounds is the level of significance introduced and assigned a certain value? I have not been able to find a clear and uniform answer to this question in the literature.[12] However, the illustrations given in discussions of the level of significance suggest that it reflects the differing degrees of seriousness with which type I error is taken in different testing problems. Thus, it seems reasonable to demand a lower level of significance if

'composite', the definition of a significance level has not been a matter of universal agreement. This problem, however, is not central to our discussion. Nonetheless, it should be noted that the hypothesis H_2 of our example is composite. Consequently, without *a priori* probabilities neither the probability of type II error nor the probability of accepting the null hypothesis given that it is false can be computed. What we can do is compute the probability of an observation falling in the region of acceptance given that the percentage of voters favoring the candidate is m for each m greater than 60 % and less than or equal to 100 %. See footnote 11.

11 When the alternative to the null hypothesis is composite (see footnote 14), the Neyman–Pearson theory does not always recommend the above mentioned criterion. However, the criterion is legitimate when the seriousness of different type II errors (i.e., errors resulting from the adoption of A_1 when one of the various probabilities within the range asserted by H_2 obtains) is the same. By maximum type II error in this case is meant the following. Given a test having a specific significance level, the probability of type II error will in general vary for different frequencies in the range permitted by H_2. If there is a maximum or a least upper bound to these probabilities we take that as the maximum possible probability of type II error for the test in question. It is this probability we seek to minimize. See J. Neyman and E. S. Pearson (1932–3, pp. 503–4). It should be emphasized that our concern here is not with the various criteria offered for choosing a 'best' critical region but with certain parts of the conceptual apparatus employed in the Neyman–Pearson theory for formulating such criteria – in particular the distinction between type I and type II error and the notion of a significance level. I have described a criterion solely for expository purposes.

12 Part of the answer is that when decisions are based on small samples, high levels of significance have to be adopted because low levels are mathematically unattainable. But this is by no means a complete answer.

committing type I error will result in loss of life than if it results only in the loss of an election.

The very formulation of the theory of significance testing seems to preclude its application to problems where the goal is to replace doubt by true belief. The distinction between type I and type II error guarantees that different kinds of mistakes will be taken with different degrees of seriousness. Indeed, most expositions of significance testing tend to motivate and to justify its application by means of examples of practical decision problems remote from the search for truth. However, significance tests are widely applied to problems in the natural and social sciences where deciding what to believe would appear to be the primary objective. It seems desirable, therefore, to determine whether significance testing can be reinterpreted so that it can be applied to attempts to replace doubt by true belief without fitting such attempts into behavioral procrustean beds as Rudner seems to do.

One possible reconstruction could be obtained by introducing suspension of judgement as a third alternative. The selection of a test according to this analysis would be tantamount to the choice of a tripartite division of the set of possible outcomes of observation (S_1, S_2, K) into two regions S_i recommending acceptance of the hypotheses H_i and the region K recommending suspension of judgement. Unlike the Bayes method, the method of significance testing is not designed to handle decision problems containing more than two options. Since my concern is to reinterpret the method of significance testing and not to replace it by another procedure, trichotomy tests will not be directly considered here.

Although trichotomy tests will not be examined on their own merits, it will, nonetheless, be useful to explore the possibility of interpreting dichotomous significance tests in terms of trichotomy tests. Such an attempt was actually made by Neyman and Pearson. Unfortunately, their remarks are nothing more than tantalizing suggestions. Nevertheless, in spite of the obscurity of their interpretation, it does serve as a convenient basis on which a more adequate account of the relation between trichotomy tests of the kind mentioned above and significance tests can be constructed.

According to Neyman and Pearson, the region of acceptance S_1 of a significance test (S_1, S_2) is the union of the sets S_1^* and K of some trichotomy test (S_1^*, S_2^*, K).[13] They fail to indicate, however, how one is to construe the act recommended when an observation falls in S_1.

---

13 J. Neyman and E. S. Pearson, 1932–3, p. 493. Other authors have also taken the position that 'accepting the null hypothesis' is not to be taken literally but is to be understood to mean 'not rejecting the null hypothesis'. See, for example, Allen L. Edwards, 1946, p. 281 and R. B. Braithwaite, 1953, pp. 199–201. The remarks made below about the Neyman–Pearson position seem to apply to the views of these authors as well.

One possible answer is that when observations fall within the region of acceptance (outside the critical region), both suspension of judgement and acceptance of the null hypothesis are equally warranted and the investigator is entitled to choose one or the other arbitrarily. This interpretation can be rejected on the grounds that, in general, such a recommendation would be considered irrational. It would amount to saying that if you are not justified in rejecting the null hypothesis you are equally free to accept it or remain in doubt.

Another interpretation that may quickly be eliminated contends that observations in the region of acceptance recommend neither accepting the null hypothesis nor suspending judgement but 'entertaining' the null hypothesis. But even if we acknowledge entertainment of a proposition to be a cognitive state, it is a state that obtains when the question of truth has not been raised. It can hardly be recommended at the termination of an inquiry into the truth of a proposition.

The most plausible interpretation, in my opinion, is the one that maintains that when observations fall outside the critical region suspension of judgement is recommended. In order to justify this proposal, a consideration of the ESP illustration will prove useful.

In order to render the ESP problem parallel to the revised election campaign problem, let us understand by H_1 (the null hypothesis) the proposition that the experimental subject guesses correctly with a frequency of 0.6. The other features of the problem remain the same. If a 5% significance level is adopted and 1000 guesses are observed, the 'best' critical region S_2 according to our criteria will consist of all those possible observations of 1000 guesses in which more than 625 were correct. Thus, if the number of correct guesses is 625 or less in 1000, we are *not* to reject the null hypothesis. But are we to accept it or suspend judgement? Intuitively we should accept the null hypothesis if the number of correct guesses is much smaller than 625 and suspend judgement if it is only slightly smaller. But the only use made of the number of correct guesses in the sample by a significance test is in determining whether the sample does or does not fall within the critical region. Otherwise the number is ignored. Consequently, we cannot incorporate the intuition into the method of significance testing.

In this sense, a significance test of a pair of statistical hypotheses makes less efficient use of the data than a trichotomy test would. In effect, the evidence obtained from the sample that is actually used in a significance test is different from the evidence derived from the same sample that is used in a trichotomy test. From this point of view, it seems plausible to say that if the observed sample falls in the region of 'acceptance' S_1 the significance test recommends suspension of judgement whereas the corresponding trichotomy test might in this case warrant accepting the null hypothesis depending upon whether the observed sample was a member of K or S_1^*. No contradiction arises because the evidence that is actually employed in the two tests is not the same.[14]

This account not only makes sense of the Neyman–Pearson interpretation of significance testing in terms of trichotomy testing, but it also provides a rationale for the distinction between type I and type II error and for assigning a level of significance which renders intelligible the application of significance tests to problems where the objective is to seek the truth and nothing but the truth. According to the proposal just made, the application of a significance test to attempts to seek the truth and nothing but the truth enables us to decide whether to reject the null hypothesis (accept H_2) or suspend judgement. Thus, the choice of a null hypothesis is a selection of a hypothesis that we wish to falsify if we can. An investigator may be motivated and justified in this selection by practical considerations. He may base his choice on a preference for the truth of H_2 to the truth of the null hypothesis. But such preference is irrelevant to the criteria embodied in the significance test for justifying rejection of the null hypothesis. The distinction between type I error and type II error is not a distinction between two different kinds of mistakes (in the sense that a mistake results when a false proposition is accepted as true) but between the result of rejecting the null hypothesis when it is true (type I error) which is a bona fide mistake and the result of suspending judgement when the null hypothesis is false (type II 'error') which is not. Consequently, type II error can be said to be less serious than type I error without violating the requirement that a person seeking the truth and nothing but the truth take all mistakes with equal seriousness.

The level of significance also receives a natural interpretation. As we know, it is the maximum probability of committing a type I error – i.e., a genuine error in the sense that error is accepting a false proposition as true. If we set the level of significance very low, we will not only increase the probability of suspending judgement when the null hypothesis is true but also will in general increase the probability of suspending judgement when it

---

14 If the observations already made warrant suspension of judgement, new observations may be made in an attempt to eliminate this doubt. However, sometimes the same objective can be reached by re-examining the observations already made for relevant information that has previously been ignored. This possibility always exists in significance testing when observations fall outside the critical region. At this point, it might be useful to point out that suspension of judgement is introduced as an option in a different manner than it is in Wald's theory of sequential testing. In this paper, I am suggesting that where one is concerned to replace doubt by true belief suspension of judgement should be considered as a possible 'terminal decision'. In other words, suspension of judgement is not to be equated with a decision to look for further evidence. I do not, of course, mean to imply that when the available evidence warrants suspension of judgement further acquisition of evidence is no longer in order. This may or may not be the case depending upon several factors that are considered in sequential analysis. See A. Wald, 1950, 1.1–1.4.

is false (type II error). In other words, a low significance level reflects the fact that the investigator takes mistakes very seriously relative to suspending judgement. On the other hand, a high significance level indicates that the investigator is anxious to relieve his doubts. Thus, the level of significance can serve as a rough index of the degree of caution exercised in a search for the truth.[15]

4 Conclusion

The outcome of this lengthy discussion is that both the Bayes method and significance testing can be employed in attempts to seek the truth and nothing but the truth without violating the conditions previously laid down for such attempts. Consequently, an appeal to these procedures cannot serve as a basis for contending that statistical procedures warrant an opposite conclusion.

This conclusion raises more questions than it answers. There are many other types of statistical problems besides the testing of the hypotheses – e.g., the problems of point and interval estimation. There are also other methods of statistical inference besides significance testing and the Bayes method – e.g., R. A. Fisher's maximum likelihood method of point estimation and A. Wald's minimax theory. Pending consideration of these problems and procedures no general statement can be made regarding the necessity for distinguishing between different kinds of error in statistical inference. Consequently, Rudner's implicit claim that statistical methods cannot be applied in attempts to seek the truth and nothing but the truth can be considered only partially answered.

Another type of question arises from the rather narrow scope of the paper. The only kind of scientific objective that was considered was that of selecting the one and only true proposition from a given list. Although scientists sometimes attempt such problems, that they take on other endeavors is equally clear. Even when they are concerned to accept and reject hypotheses

---

15 Actually the relation between significance levels and degrees of caution is more complicated than I have indicated above. In the first place, a precise definition of degree of caution is required. If the definition proposed in the discussion of the Bayes method is adopted (where degree of caution was equated with the utility of the outcome of suspending judgement), we have to determine how the utility of suspending judgement is related to significance levels. But this requires founding the theory of significance testing on a decision theory that directly employs utility measures (e.g., the Bayes method or the minimax method). We cannot discuss all of the difficulties connected with this problem. It may be worth pointing out, however, that if the null hypothesis and its alternative are both simple, a likelihood ratio test can be employed as a significance test. But all likelihood ratio tests are Bayes strategies for given *a priori* probability assignments to hypotheses and utility assignments to possible outcomes of the various possible decisions. In particular, if the *a priori* probabilities are fixed, significance level will be inversely proportional to the degree of caution.

in the sense that I have employed, they are not always interested in the truth and nothing but the truth. They often search for systems of statements that are not only true but yield simple explanations. Factors like simplicity could conceivably lead to distinctions in the value placed on different possible correct answers or different possible errors. Can the apparatus of modern decision theory be employed in precise formulations of the various goals of scientific inquiry and in the statement of criteria for judging the adequacy of attempted realizations of these goals?

An examination of this question could shed light on many philosophically interesting problems. It could aid in the assessment of the import of the classical Aristotelian distinction between theory, practice and technology. It could also serve to locate precisely the role of social and personal values and of other subjective and conventional factors in non-deductive inference. Although the limited scope of this paper precludes basing any definite answers on it, some tentative conclusions can be drawn from what has been said.

(1) If the argument of this paper is sound, the application of the Bayes method and the method of significance testing to attempts to replace doubt by true belief is legitimate.[16] This affords ground for the conjecture that no basis can be found in the theory of statistical and more generally of inductive inference for denying a distinction between the theoretical objectives of science where the goal is to determine what to believe or accept as true and practical and technological objectives. A behavioral analysis of belief does not appear necessary in order to employ decision theory in formulating either the goals or the canons of non-deductive inference.

(2) The only place where the canons of non-deductive inference would permit subjective or conventional factors any relevance in attempts to realize the theoretical goal of seeking the truth and nothing but the truth is in the degree of caution exercised by the investigator. (This may not be true, of course, when the objective is to replace doubt by true, simple and explanatorily powerful systems of belief.) It is an open question whether there are limits imposed on the degree of caution that a scientist *qua* scientist can exercise and if so what they are. A clue might be obtained by considering the significance levels that are employed in applications of significance tests of hypotheses in the natural and social sciences. I would also hazard the conjecture that the invidious comparisons frequently made between the results and procedures of the several sciences are partially based on differences in the degrees of caution normally exercised in different disciplines.

---

16 This remark must obviously be qualified by the comment that the legitimacy of the application of both the Bayes method and significance testing depends upon considerations that have not been central to our discussion.

These conjectures are admittedly in need of further examination and development. They are designed to indicate the philosophically interesting issues at stake when an examination of current statistical theory is undertaken and to suggest how the conceptual apparatus of modern decision theory can be brought to bear upon problems that arise when an attempt is made to formulate the objectives of scientific inquiry and the canons of scientific inference.

3

Corroboration and rules of acceptance[†]

According to Popper (1959), 'the doctrine that *degree of corroboration or acceptability cannot be a probability* is one of the most interesting findings in the philosophy of knowledge'. Unfortunately, the debate that raged a few years ago between Popper and the apologists for Carnap made the significance of Popper's thesis depend upon a determination of who had explicated what presystematic concept adequately (Bar-Hillel, Carnap, Popper, 1955–7). Taking Popper's 'finding' to be a gambit in a version of 'button, button, who has the button' hardly makes it 'interesting'. The philosophical importance (if any) of Popper's thesis should be evaluated in terms of the success with which Popper can apply his measure of corroboration to the problems he designed this measure to handle and the philosophical significance of these problems.

Popper's writings offer ample evidence of his intention to formulate rules for accepting and rejecting scientific hypotheses with the aid of his corroboration measures:

Furthermore, the degree of confirmation is supposed to have an influence upon the question whether we should *accept*, or choose, a certain hypothesis x, if only tentatively; a high degree of confirmation is supposed to characterize a hypothesis as 'good' (or 'acceptable'), while a disconfirmed hypothesis is supposed to be 'bad' (Popper, 1959).

This passage not only indicates that Popper considers degree of corroboration relevant to formulating acceptance rules but suggests a general acceptance rule:

Given a set of mutually incompatible hypotheses choose that hypothesis with the maximum degree of corroboration relative to the available evidence.

This rule confers genuine significance on Popper's claim that corroboration is not a probability. He is rejecting any acceptance rules which recommend maximizing probability. (For the duration, we shall assume that probabilities are logical measures à la Jeffreys and Carnap.) He does this without denying relevance to probabilities in formulating rules of acceptance; for degree of corroboration is a function of probability.

[†] Reprinted with the permission of the editor from *The British Journal for the Philosophy of Science* **13** (1963), pp. 307–13.

Obviously the dispute between Carnapians and Popperites has been over the wrong issue. Carnap nowhere claims that scientists maximize probabilities when accepting hypotheses. In point of fact, he denies that scientists accept or reject hypotheses at all (Carnap, 1945–6). He recognizes only two applications of his 'degree of confirmation' (Carnap, 1950):

(1) Assignments of degrees to which evidence confirms (in his sense) hypotheses.
(2) Provision of rules for deciding how to act relative to practical objectives.

If a man is confronted with alternative courses of action and knows the utilities relative to his goals of adopting any one of these policies given that any one of a set of exclusive hypotheses is true, Carnap says that the decision maker ought to maximize expected utility.

Thus, the issue separating Carnap from Popper is not whether scientists do or ought to maximize probability when accepting hypotheses but whether they accept and reject hypotheses at all.[1]

For the remainder of this discussion, Popper's position on this matter will be dogmatically adopted. Our objective is not to question whether scientists accept and reject hypotheses but whether in doing so they do or ought to maximize probability, corroboration, or anything else.

Imagine a hypothetical Carnap who admits that scientists accept and reject hypotheses in accordance with the principle that probabilities ought to be maximized. Such a person might attack Popper's view by turning the tables on Popper's celebrated refutation of Carnap.[2]

Consider a homogeneous die. With Popper let x be the statement 'six will turn up on the next toss' and y the statement 'an even number will turn up'. $\sim x$ is the negation of x. $P(x) = \frac{1}{6}$, $P(\sim x) = \frac{5}{6}$, and $P(y) = \frac{1}{2}$. The probability of x given y is $\frac{1}{3}$ and of $\sim x$ given y is $\frac{2}{3}$. Suppose that a rational gambler is constrained to place an even money bet (assumed equal to utility) on whether a six will or will not turn up on the next toss. The Bayes method (which recommends maximizing expected utility) prescribes betting on $\sim x$ even if the gambler knows that y, which lowers the probability of $\sim x$, is true.

1 Even if Popper had not explicitly stated that degrees of corroboration are to be used to generate acceptance rules, he would have had to do so in order to provide corroboration with philosophical significance. He could not claim that scientists merely assign degrees of corroboration to hypotheses. This view is no more plausible than Carnap's parallel view regarding the 'theoretical' applications of degree of confirmation. Nor could he claim that scientists are guidance counsellors and that degrees of corroboration provide a guide in life. Carnap could do this with logical probabilities; for there are decision theories extant that do provide a basis for using probabilities in determining practical policy. Whatever the merits of these theories, they at least are available for critical scrutiny. No theory is available for utilizing corroboration in practical decision making. Hence, the significance of corroboration must stand or fall with its relevance to the formulation of scientific acceptance rules.
2 For one version see Popper, 1959, p. 390. His example is the one presented with modifications in the text.

Suppose the gambler is not constrained to bet money but is asked to predict whether the next toss will turn up a six or not. He has a disinterested concern to predict correctly – i.e. he is indifferent as to whether a six or some other side turns up. We can say that he assigns equal 'epistemic' utilities to predicting x when x is true and $\sim x$ when $\sim x$ is true and equal utilities to predicting x when x is false and $\sim x$ when $\sim x$ is false. (Greater utilities are to be assigned to potential correct answers than to potential errors.) The Bayes method recommends accepting $\sim x$ on evidence y even though y undermines $\sim x$ in Popper's sense.

Our hypothetical Carnapian might generalize from this example and maintain that scientists always seek the truth and nothing but the truth in the sense that they always assign equal epistemic utilities to potential correct answers and equal but lower epistemic utilities to potential errors. The Bayes method would require that such truth seekers maximize probability; for the probability of x given y would be directly proportional to the expected epistemic utility of accepting x on evidence y.

This 'refutation' of Popper depends upon two important assumptions: (a) that scientists always seek the truth and nothing but the truth when accepting and rejecting hypotheses; and (b) that epistemic utilities can be assigned to potential correct and incorrect answers in accordance with von Neumann–Morgenstern postulates for rational preference or at the very least with postulates which justify maximizing expected epistemic utilities.

Anyone familiar with Popper's writings knows he would reject assumption (a) outright. According to Popper, the scientific importance of a proposition varies with its falsifiability or logical content. Hence, only when the alternative hypotheses from which one is called upon to choose are equal in scientific importance, would Popper admit that the scientist seeks the truth and nothing but the truth. For the sake of the argument we shall agree that Popper is right.

Popper nowhere indicates clearly what stand he would take respecting assumption (b), but he does recognize the notion of scientific importance and attempts to measure it. Moreover, his measure of corroboration is a 'weighting' of scientific importance with probability. Now we can agree with Popper that when scientists accept and reject hypotheses they assign higher 'epistemic utility' to hypotheses with high content than to those with low content. We can also agree that scientists attempt to maximize some weighting of epistemic utility with probability when accepting hypotheses. But we can without contradiction reject the specific kind of weighting embodied in Popper's measure of corroboration. In order to justify maximizing corroboration, we must supplement our agreements with additional assumptions concerning rational preference which together with our initial assumptions entail maximizing corroboration. Unfortunately, Popper fails to offer any such postulates for preference. Instead, he presents 'desiderata' for adequate explications of some presystematic concept of corroboration.[3] Popper's various measures of corroboration undoubtedly explicate the presystematic concept characterized by these desiderata. This fact, however, in no wise supports his thesis that we ought to maximize corroboration any more than one can justify maximizing expected utility by showing that expected utilities satisfy the postulates of an algebra of expectations.

In the remainder of this paper, we shall adopt assumption (b), i.e. a theory of rational 'epistemic' preference based on von Neumann–Morgenstern type postulates (except that we shall use logical instead of frequency or subjective probabilities.) Should Popper balk at this procedure, he is obligated to supply an alternative theory.

Let $P(x, y)$ be the conditional probability of x given y, $C(x, y)$ be the degree of corroboration of x given y, $u(x)$ the utility of accepting x when x is true and $u(x)'$ the utility of accepting x when x is false. Given assumption (b), justification of Popper's recommendation that we maximize corroboration requires that we make $C(x, y)$ equal to the expected epistemic utility of accepting x on evidence y:

(A) $P(x, y)u(x) + P(\sim x, y)u(x)' = C(x, y)$.

If (A) is tenable and scientists do not in general seek the truth and nothing but the truth, $C(x, y)$ obviously cannot be a probability. But is (A) tenable?

A negative answer to this question can be given if we can show that utility functions $u(x)$ and $u(x)'$ which satisfy (A) must violate von Neumann–Morgenstern postulates for preference or any alternative postulates that justify maximizing expected utility. To this much we are committed by assumption (b).

---

3 The remainder of this discussion presupposes familiarity with the discussion in Popper, 1959, pp. 265–81 and pp. 387–419. For purposes of our discussion, the following of Popper's definitions of $C(x, y)$ – the degree of corroboration of x given y – and $E(x, y)$ – the explanatory power of x relative to y – have been used:

$$C(x, y) = E(x, y)(1 + P(x, y)P(x)).$$

$$E(x, y) = \frac{P(y, x) - P(y)}{P(y, x) + P(y)} \quad \text{where } P(y) \neq 0.$$

Popper's conditions of adequacy or desiderata for 'degree of corroboration' are laid down on pp. 400–1. They are reproduced here except for (vi) which is quoted later in the text:

    (i) $C(x, y) \gtreqless 0$ respectively if and only if y supports x, or is independent of x, or undermines x.

    (ii) $-1 = C(\bar{y}, y) \leqq C(x, y) \leqq C(x, x) \leqq 1$

    (iii) $0 \leqq C(x, x) = C(x) = 1 - P(x) \leqq 1$

    (iv) if y entails x, then $C(x, y) = C(x, x) = C(x)$

    (v) if y entails $\bar{x}$, the $C(x, y) = C(\bar{y}, y) = -1$

    (vii) if $C(x) = C(y) \neq 1$, then $C(x, u) \gtreqless C(y, w)$ whenever $P(x, u) \gtreqless P(y, w)$.

    (viii) if x entails y, then: (a) $C(x, y) \geqq 0$; (b) for any given x, $C(x, y)$ and $C(y)$ increase together; and (c) for any given y, $C(x, y)$ and $P(x)$ increase together.

    (ix) if $\bar{x}$ is consistent and entails y, then: (a) $C(x, y) \leqq 0$, (b) for any given x, $C(x, y)$ and $P(y)$ increase together; and (c) for any given y, $C(x, y)$ and $P(x)$ increase together.

Let us consider 'prizes' f, g, h, and i which are preferred in increasing order from left to right. Von Neumann and Morgenstern would assign numerical utilities to these prizes roughly as follows: First, assign numbers F and I to any pair of the prizes – say f and i – subject only to the restriction that the preferred prize i receive the higher number. Second find a gamble with f and i as prizes such that the probability of winning f is p and i is $1 - p$ and such that the gambler is indifferent between taking this gamble or having g for certain. Compute the value G of $pF + (1 - p)I$. Finally, assign G as the utility of g. Repeat the procedure for h.

Among the postulates for preference that a person must satisfy before such utilities can be assigned to his preferences is that for any 'pure' alternative there is a gamble among other alternatives such that the gambler is indifferent as to having the gamble or the alternative. Moreover, it must be assumed that his preferences for the prizes in the gamble have not changed in virtue of being incorporated in the gamble. *But this implies that it must be both possible and rationally legitimate for a person's preference patterns to remain unaltered even if the probabilities of attaining the various prizes change.* A person whose preferences for various prizes change with the chances of attaining them (as in the case of the horse-better who has a penchant for long shots) cannot have his preferences measured by von Neumann–Morgenstern procedures. A theory which requires that preferences change in this way is incompatible with von Neumann–Morgenstern postulates.

Now the 'epistemic' utilities we are attempting to construct are designed to reflect the preferences that scientists ought to have for the various possible correct and incorrect answers available to them when they are called upon to choose among competing hypotheses. The probabilities we propose to use in constructing utility assignments are logical probabilities of the truth and falsity of the various hypotheses on the available evidence. We must do this if we are to use von Neumann–Morgenstern type postulates to justify maximising expected epistemic utility where expectation is a function of logical probabilities. If we made utility assignments to potentially correct answers and errors a function of the evidence – e.g. made the utility of accepting a hypothesis x when it is true vary with the available evidence y – then these utilities would vary with conditional logical probabilities of the hypotheses. Therefore, such utility assignments could not be made in conformity with von Neumann–Morgenstern type postulates. Consequently, we may lay down the following condition of adequacy for epistemic utility assignments:

(I) No rational or scientific assignment of epistemic utilities must require that utilities vary with the available evidence.

It can be shown that if (A) is adopted, the utility functions generated do violate (I). Hence, (A) is untenable on all available theories which support maximizing expected utility. The outcome is that for the present, at any rate,

there is no justification for Popper's contention that scientists ought to maximize corroboration *even if we concede to him that scientists do accept and reject hypotheses and that highly falsifiable propositions are scientifically more important than those with low content.*
The proof of this contention runs as follows:

According to (A): $P(x, y)u(x) + P(\sim x, y)u(x)' = C(x, y)$

If $P(x) \neq 0$, $C(x, y) = \dfrac{P(x, y) - P(x)}{P(x, y) + P(x)}(1 + P(x, y)P(x))$

Let $P(x, z) = P(x)$. Then $C(x, z) = 0$
Hence, $C(x, y) = C(x, y) - C(x, z)$
$$= (P(x, y) - P(x))u(x) + (P(\sim x, y) - P(\sim x)u(x)')$$
$$= (P(x, y) - P(x))(u(x) - u(x)')$$

According to (I), $u(x)$ and $u(x)'$ and, hence, $u(x) - u(x)' = k$ must remain constant through variations in y and $P(x, y)$.

But $k(P(x, y) - P(x)) = C(x, y) = P(x, y) - P(x)\dfrac{(1 + P(x, y/P(x)))}{(P(x, y) + P(x))}$

Hence, $k = \dfrac{1 + P(x, y)P(x)}{P(x, y) + P(x)}$

Hence, the value of k must vary with $P(x, y)$ counter to (I).
The situation is no different when $P(x)$ and $P(x, y)$ are both equal to 0. Here

$$u(x)' = C(x, y) = E(x, y) = \frac{P(y, x) - P(y)}{P(y, x) + P(y)}$$

If we restrict ourselves to cases where $P(x) \neq 0$, it is clear from the proof that the violation of (I) stems from the 'normalization' of $P(x, y) - P(x)$ which yields $C(x, y)$. Had $P(x, y) - P(x)$ been multiplied by a constant factor, the proof of the inadequacy of (A) would not have gone through. Let us choose unity as the factor and write $U(x, y) = P(x, y) - P(x)$. We now propose to consider $U(x, y)$ as the function to be maximized in place of $C(x, y)$.

$P(x, y)u(x) + P(\sim x, y)u(x)' = U(x, y) = P(x, y) - P(x)$.
Let $y = \sim x$. Then $P(x, y) = 0$, $u(x)' = -P(x)$.
Let $y = x$. Then $P(x, y) = 1$, $u(x) = P(\sim x)$.

Putting these values of $u(x)$ and $u(x)'$ back in our original equation:

$$P(x, y)P(\sim x) - P(\sim x, y)P(x) = U(x, y)$$

for constant x and variable y.
The utility assignments $P(\sim x)$ and $-P(x)$ have much to recommend them from Popper's point of view; for they rank the importance of hypotheses with

high content higher than those with low content. Moreover, $U(x, y)$ can be identified with expected epistemic utility of accepting x on evidence y without violating von Neumann–Morgenstern type postulates. And, interestingly enough, almost all of Popper's desiderata for $C(x, y)$ are satisfied by $U(x, y)$. In conclusion, it might be useful to explore this matter somewhat further.

$U(x, y)$ satisfies all of Popper's desiderata save (ii), (v), and (vi). The violations of (ii) and (v) are minor and are due to the fact that $U(\sim x, x) = -P(\sim x)$. Since this violation will have no serious bearing on the hypotheses that are accepted on given evidence, we may ignore it and turn to (vi) which reads as follows:

Let x have a high content – so that $C(x, y)$ approaches $E(x, y)$ – and let y support x. (We may, for example, take y to be the total available empirical evidence.) *Then for any given y, $C(x, y)$ increases with the power of x to explain more and more of the content of y*, and therefore with the *scientific interest* of x (1959, p. 401).

Consider first the case where $P(x)$ and $P(z)$ have positive values very close to 0. (vi) recommends that we choose between x and z on the basis of their likelihoods $P(y, x)$ and $P(y, z)$. When at least one of the ratios $P(x, y)/P(z, y)$ and $P(x)/P(z)$ is very close to unity, maximizing $U(x, y)$ approximates this recommendation very well. In other cases, the approximation is very poor. We may legitimately wonder, however, whether we ought to place the entire burden of our choice on likelihood when there are significant differences in content and conditional probability. Thus, if

$$P(x, y) = 0.0003, \; P(x) = 0.0001, \; P(z, y) = 0.002 \text{ and } P(z) = 0.001, \; U(x, y)$$

will be one-fifth the value of $U(z, y)$ whereas the likelihood of x relative to y will be one and one-half times as large as that of z relative to y and the ratio of $C(x, y)$ to $C(z, y)$ will approximate that very closely. It is not clear that presystematic judgements so strongly recommend choosing x over z that we would be warranted in introducing a desideratum which entails this result.

When the contents of x and z are exactly unity and their conditional probabilities 0 (the typical case with universal hypotheses), $U(x, y) = U(z, y) = 0$, whereas $E(x, y)$ and $E(z, y)$ will frequently have different positive values. Hence, $C(x, y)$ enables us to choose between hypotheses in important cases where $U(x, y)$ fails utterly. In general, the use of the Bayes method with epistemic utilities when choosing among universal hypotheses will result in identifying the expected utility of accepting a universal hypothesis with the utility of accepting such a hypothesis when it is false no matter how we assign these utilities.

This consequence of using the Bayes method might appear to argue against employing it to generate acceptance rules or to criticize Popper's acceptance rule. Several points can be made in response to this objection:

(1) The failure of the Bayes method when logical probabilities and utilities based on logical probabilities are used does not imply that this method will fail when some other probability measure that does permit probabilities greater than 0 for universal hypotheses is used.

(2) Popper's acceptance rule stands in need of justification regardless of the merits of the Bayes method as a tool for criticism.

(3) Given two universal hypotheses x and z both of which entail evidence y, $C(x, y) = C(z, y)$. According to Popper's rule, no decision can be made between x and y. Yet Popper wishes to maintain that in some circumstances we might feel a decision to be warranted (Popper, 1959, pp. 363–77). In order to handle this situation, he introduces comparative measures of content which exhibit 'fine structure' differences in content when measuring content of a hypothesis by means of the prior probability of its negation indicates no such difference. Once Popper is permitted to use such procedures, fine structure measures of $U(x, y)$ should also be permissible. Thus, if $U(x, y)$ is greater than $U(z, y)$ for sufficiently large universes, we might treat $U(x, y)$ as greater in a 'fine structure' sense than $U(z, y)$ for infinite universes even though in such universes $U(x, y) = U(z, y)$.

The upshot is that given the lengths to which Popper is prepared to go to defend his notion of corroboration $U(x, y)$ still has more to recommend it. It takes into account Popper's expressly stated views concerning the scientific importance of hypotheses while weighting such importance with probability in a function the maximization of which is justifiable according to current theories of rational preference. As an extra bonus, $U(x, y)$ satisfies Popper's desiderata to a good approximation save when $P(x) = 0$. Finally, if in this exceptional but important case, we are permitted to use fine structure measures analogous to those Popper uses anyway, we get a qualitative analogue to $U(x, y)$, maximization of which could be supported by a qualitative analogue of the Bayesian approach.

4

Deductive cogency in inductive inference[†]

1 Introduction

Keith Lehrer and R. C. Sleigh (1964) have considered some difficulties lurking in principles laid down by Roderick Chisholm in his book *Perceiving*. The problem raised by Lehrer and Sleigh is not, however, of parochial interest to students of Chisholmian epistemology. The most detailed attempt to come to grips with the problem in recent years is found in Henry Kyburg (1961).[1] In any event, the question is one which must be faced by anyone who takes seriously the idea that at least sometimes investigators have evidence that warrants their accepting sentences as true even though these sentences are not deductive consequences of the evidence.

In Lehrer's presentation, the difficulty arises from two of Chisholm's principles:

P1. S has adequate evidence for h if and only if h is more probable than not on the total evidence of S.

P2. If S has adequate evidence for i and S has adequate evidence for j, then S has adequate evidence for i & j.

If the multiplication rule for conjunction is legislative for probabilities as used in P1, then the probability that i & j will, as a rule, be less than the probability that i and the probability that j. Hence, there will be cases where the probability that i will be greater than the probability that $\sim i$ and the probability that j greater than the probability that $\sim j$ but the probability that i & j less than the probability that $\sim (i$ & $j) -$ i.e., $\sim i \vee \sim j$.

The existence of sentences (or propositions, it does not matter here) i and j having these properties entails the inconsistency of P1 and P2. It suggests two strategies: reject P2 and retain P1 – the approach adopted by Sleigh and, in a more complicated way, by Kyburg; reject P1 while retaining P2 – the view preferred by Lehrer. The position taken here is that both P1 and P2 are wrong, although P2 with some qualifications can be resuscitated.

[†] Reprinted from *The Journal of Philosophy* **57** (1965), pp. 68–77.
1 Reference should be made here to Hempel (1962) and Ehrenfest-Afanassjewa (1958). (I owe the latter reference to M. J. Klein.)

2 High probability

P1 requires that a high probability be necessary and sufficient for rational acceptance. How high the probability must be need not be of concern here as long as it is greater than 0.5 and less than 1. (It will be assumed that a person is sometimes justified in accepting i even when i is not entailed by his evidence.) Lehrer attempts to show that this thesis is untenable by the following sort of argument:

Consider the following definition adopted by Chisholm:

D1. S knows h if and only if S accepts h, S has adequate evidence for h, and h is true.

Suppose now that P2 is rejected and replaced by the following:

P4.   If S knows i and S knows j and accepts i & j, then S knows i & j.

Lehrer argues quite correctly that a contradiction can be obtained from P1, D1, and P4 and the following condition:

There are sentences (propositions) i and j such that

(i) i is more probable than not on the total evidence of S
(ii) j is more probable than not on the total evidence of S
(iii) $\sim i \lor \sim j$ is more probable than i & j on the total evidence of S
(v) S accepts i
(vi) S accepts j
(vii) S accepts i & j
(viii)   Both i and j are true

Lehrer places great emphasis on the fact that this contradiction arises even if Sleigh's strategy of rejecting P2 and accepting P1 is followed:

I wish to argue that even if we do reject P2 the acceptance of P1 will still lead to contradiction. Consequently, I believe that we must reject P1, a somewhat more radical alternative than the one Sleigh proposes (Lehrer, 1964, p. 369).

Recall that, in obtaining his contradiction from P1, Lehrer also appeals to D1 and P4. Now it can easily be shown that rejection of P2 together with D1 and P4 yields the paradoxical result described by Lehrer without the intervention of P1. Hence, a protagonist of P1 could easily claim that P1 is not the guilty party here. Either D1 or P4 is.

The contradiction arises as follows:

From the rejection of P2, it follows that S could be in a position described by the following three conditions:

(i') S has adequate evidence for i
(ii') S has adequate evidence for j
(iii') S lacks adequate evidence for i & j

43

Once conditions (v), (vi), (vii), and ($viii$) assumed to hold by Lehrer (1964, p. 370) are added, D1 and P4 yield a contradiction. No appeal to P1 or probability considerations is necessary.

These considerations suggest that, in the face of D1, P2 and P4 stand or fall together. As a consequence, the difficulties engendered by the multiplication theorem can be escaped only by revision of P1, P2, or both. In order to decide how to proceed further here, it is desirable to determine whether any considerations that do not depend upon direct appeals to the intuitive plausibility of these two principles can be introduced as arbiters.

Consider an illustration often used by Kyburg (e.g. 1963) – to wit, a 1 000 000-ticket lottery that is known to be fair. Here is a case where definite numerical probabilities can be assigned to each of 1 000 000 sentences of the form 'ticket i will win' as well as to their contradictories. For each specific i, 'ticket i will win' bears a probability of 0.000 001, and its contradictory 'ticket i will not win' a probability of 0.999 999.

Chisholm's condition P1 implies that a person confronted with such information would be warranted in accepting 'ticket 1 will not win', 'ticket 2 will not win', et al. This is in conformity with Kyburg's claim: 'It is as rational to accept the hypothesis that ticket i will not win as it is to accept any statistical hypothesis that I can think of' (Kyburg, 1963, p. 463).

Kyburg's (and Chisholm's) thesis must, I submit, be mistaken. If I were asked to predict the outcome of a fair lottery, I would say that it is 'anybody's guess'; and, I suspect, so would most other people. I would defend my decision to suspend judgement not on the grounds that I cannot in principle know with certainty what the outcome of the lottery will be but by an appeal to the information which indicates that the lottery is fair. It is as rational to suspend judgement regarding the outcome of a fair lottery as it is to suspend judgement in any case I can think of.

If my intuition is sound here, a probability greater than 0.5 and less than 1 is sufficient neither for rational acceptance nor for adequate evidence. Consequently, some grounds for rejecting P1 can be afforded without appeal to the contradiction considered by Kyburg, Sleigh, and Lehrer.

3 Deductive cogency

Let K be any set of sentences in a given language L. K will be consistent if no deductive consequence of a finite number of elements in K is of the form $p \& \sim p$. K will be 'deductively closed' if and only if all deductive consequences of any finite subset of K are also members of K. In the subsequent discussion, P2 will be replaced by the following principle:

P5. The set of sentences that S is rationally justified in accepting must be consistent and closed.

Although P2 and P5 are not equivalent, some variant of P2 is a consequence of P5. In any event, the remarks pertaining to P5 should apply *mutatis mutandis* to P2.[2]

Note first that P5 is defective in that its scope is not relativized to total evidence. Clearly the totatity of sentences a person is warranted in accepting throughout his lifetime need not be consistent and closed.

This point is, of course, well-known; and although Chisholm does not explicitly restrict the scope of P2 to a fixed body of total evidence, he manages to take cognizance of it elsewhere. The crucial point here, however, is that the scope of P5 might have to be restricted to sentences accepted under certain conditions in addition to those referring to a fixed body of total evidence. Pending a systematic and adequate account of inductive inference, it would be difficult to anticipate what these other conditions might be in precise detail. Thus, in lieu of P5 it would seem sensible to adopt the following requirement:

P6.   *The Principle of Deductive Cogency*. The set of sentences that S is rationally committed to accept is, *everything else being equal*, a deductively consistent and closed set.

In spite of the *ceteris paribus* clause, the principle of deductive cogency does have teeth. It imposes a *prima facie* obligation on an investigator to accept the deductive consequences of his beliefs unless he can show that certain conditions (such as relevant evidence) are not constant. Moreover, when taken together with the multiplication theorem for probabilities, it rules out the requirement that high (greater than 0.5) probabilities are necessary and sufficient for rational acceptance (provided, of course, that an investigator can accept conclusions not deductively entailed by his evidence).

In the light of these considerations, it would appear that both P1 and P2 have to be rejected. However, P2 (or the stronger claim P5) can be modified by the introduction of a *ceteris paribus* clause in a manner which renders it *prima facie* plausible.

4 Strongest sentences accepted via induction

Consider an investigator who accepts a certain set E of sentences as evidence. As it shall be understood here, this set will include logical truths, and could include as much of set theory, mathematics, appropriate scientific theories, and observation sentences as the occasion requires. The set of evidence sentences E will be expected to be consistent and closed.

Given such a set E, the problem is to ascertain the totality of sentences to whose acceptance the investigator is committed. If that set can in no case be

---

2 Hempel (1962, p. 150) introduces three conditions of adequacy for any system of rules for rational acceptance. P5 corresponds roughly to CR1 and CR2.

anything other than E itself, then no grounds for acceptance are recognized save deducibility from sentences accepted as evidence (or, alternatively, bearing a probability 1 is a necessary and sufficient condition for acceptance). If the conditions for rational acceptance are not so narrowly limited, the set of sentences K whose acceptance is justified relative to E may contain E as a proper subset.

Now cogency requires that the set K be deductively consistent and closed. This means that it can be viewed as the result of selecting some set of sentences T not in E but consistent with it, and taking the deductive consequences of this set and E as the set K. The subsequent discussion will be restricted to cases where the set of sentences T is finite. In that case, there is a sentence c that is the conjunction of those sentences such that the set of deductive consequences of E and c is the set K. c is 'strongest sentence accepted via induction from E'.

Thus, suppose Smith is a political forecaster attempting to predict the outcome of an election in which X, Y, and Z are running. If he predicts that X will win, he is committed to accepting as true the sentences 'X or Y will win', 'X or Y or Z will win', 'X or Z will win', the conjunctions of these sentences with his total evidence, and their deductive consequences. Smith is adding to his 'corpus' not merely a single sentence but a set of sentences.

This explains the disagreement between Smith and Jones, who predicts that either X or Y will win but does not know which. This disagreement is not representable by reference to some sentence i accepted by one but inconsistent with a sentence j accepted by the other. Rather it can be represented either as a difference in the sets of sentences accepted by Smith and Jones or as a difference in the sentences accepted as strongest via induction from the evidence. (Note that the sentences accepted as strongest need not be inconsistent in order for disagreement to arise.)

5 Relevant answers

The pundit Smith of the last section might conceivably have at his disposal evidence warranting a prediction of the order in which X, Y, and Z will place, or regarding whether or not there will be an earthquake in Yugoslavia on election eve. And yet he may be interested only in predicting who will win the election. Although his total evidence warrants accepting as strongest a sentence stronger than 'X will win', he may not do so.

The point being made here is that investigators restrict the conclusions they reach to 'relevant answers'. The order in which the candidates place or the eventuality of an earthquake in Yugoslavia are irrelevant to Smith's problem.

In many cases (of which Smith's problem is an example) it is possible to represent the set of relevant answers as follows:

Let $H_1, H_2, ..., H_n$ be a set of sentences U exclusive and exhaustive relative to E and each consistent with E. Let them be arranged in alphabetical order. Let M be a set of 2^n sentences generated from U as follows:

(i) S is a disjunction of elements of U in which each element of U is a disjunct once and only once and in alphabetical order.

(ii) C is a conjunction of all elements of U in which each element appears as conjunct once and only once and in alphabetical order.

(iii) G is any sentence which is a disjunct of $m\ (1 \leqq m < n)$ elements of U in which each of the m elements is a disjunct one and only one time and in alphabetical order.

The set U will be called the 'ultimate partition' used by the investigator if the investigator recognizes as a relevant answer to his problem accepting as strongest all and only sentences in M, sentences logically equivalent to these, and sentences whose equivalence to elements of M is deducible from E.

Note that the sentence S is deducible from E. Accepting it as strongest via induction is to be understood here as a declaration that the evidence does not warrant anything but deductive consequences of E. The sentence C is inconsistent with E. To accept it as strongest is (given that E is accepted) to contradict oneself.

Thus, Smith might take as his ultimate partition the sentences 'X will win', 'Y will win', and 'Z will win'. Should he do so, the only relevant answers he recognizes would be those eventuating from accepting as strongest one of the following eight sentences:

(a) X or Y or Z will win (S)
(b) X or Y will win
(c) X or Z will win
(d) Y or Z will win
(e) X will win
(f) Y will win
(g) Z will win
(h) X and Y and Z will win (C).

Contrast Smith with Doaks, who takes as his ultimate partition the sentences (e) and (d). The set M in Doaks's case will consist of (a), (d), (e), and the conjunction of (d) and (e) [which is, given E, equivalent to (h)]. Doaks would not consider accepting 'Y will win' as strongest to be a relevant answer to his question, just as Smith would not consider accepting 'X will win, Y place second, and Z third' to be a relevant answer.

Thus, the choice of an ultimate partition can be used to represent commitments as to which sentences are eligible for acceptance as strongest via induction – i.e., which sentences are relevant answers. This method may not prove adequate when infinite ultimate partitions seem called for or when the question is to pick among theories; but complications arising in such cases had best be ignored in the present discussion.

Note that ultimate partitions are used as a device for representing restrictions on relevant answers in the contexts of given questions. They are not intended as a solution of the problem of the grounds on which one set of restrictions is preferable to another. Although there do seem to be situations in which a person may fairly be accused of selecting an inappropriate ultimate partition, it is far from easy to produce criteria for adjudicating such claims. Nonetheless, it seems perfectly clear that investigators do not take all sentences that are consistent but not entailed by their evidence as eligible for acceptance as strongest via induction. And the restrictions are not due solely to limitations of intellect and imagination. Smith might be quite able to consider earthquakes in Yugoslavia and still rule them out as irrelevant to his problem. He might even refuse to consider the order in which the candidates will place.

Once it is conceded that investigators do impose restrictions on answers they consider relevant to their problems and that, on some occasions, these restrictions can be characterized as choices of ultimate partitions, it seems quite plausible to suppose that the scope of the deductive-cogency principle ought to be relativized not only to total evidence E but to the choice of an ultimate partition U. What this means is that an investigator is not obliged to accept the deductive consequences of conclusions reached when using both partitions U and U' even when E remains constant.

Consider, once more, the 1 000 000-ticket lottery. Most people would, it seems, adopt as ultimate the partition consisting of the million sentences of the form 'ticket i will win'. They would recognize that each of these hypotheses bears equal probability with each other one and that, as a consequence, there is no ground for ruling any one of them to be false.

On the other hand, if a person chose to use the ultimate partition consisting of 'ticket 1 will win' and 'ticket 1 will not win', then he might quite reasonably judge that 'ticket 1 will win' ought to be rejected. As far as he is concerned there are only two relevant answers consistent with and not entailed by his evidence (as opposed to the $1\,000\,000 - 2$ in the previous case), and one of these bears a probability overwhelmingly greater than the other. In other words, the plausibility residing in Chisholm's P1 and in the requirement accepted by Kyburg and many others to the effect that a high probability is necessary and sufficient for acceptance stems from its plausibility in the case where the ultimate partition is twofold.

But on the account offered here, this concession is quite compatible with the requirement of deductive cogency. 'Ticket 1 will not win' might be accepted relative to one ultimate partition, 'ticket 2 will not win' relative to a second, and so on. But the conjunction of these sentences and their deductive consequences is not, therefore, justifiably accepted.

The prediction that ticket 1 will not win is relative to the commitment to recognize as relevant answers consistent with but not entailed by the evidence only 'ticket 1 will win' and 'ticket 1 will not win'. The prediction that ticket 2 will not win is relativized to 'ticket 2 will win' and 'ticket 2 will not win'.... The sentence 'Neither ticket 1 nor ticket 2 will win' (which is equivalent, given E, to the disjunction of the remaining 999 998 sentences of the form 'ticket i will win') is an element neither of either ultimate partition nor of the sets M generated by these. To accept it as true is to betray the commitments involved in adopting either one of the two ultimate partitions under consideration. In order to introduce that sentence as a relevant answer, the threefold partition consisting of 'ticket 1 will win', 'ticket 2 will win', and 'neither 1 nor 2 will win' would have to be chosen as ultimate.

As more individual tickets are specified, it is clear that probabilities of the elements of the ultimate partition will tend to equalize until the millionfold ultimate partition relative to which suspension of judgement is appropriate is reached.

Thus far, some brief indication has been given of how the restriction of the scope of deductive cogency to sentences accepted relative to total evidence and an ultimate partition can accommodate both common sense regarding fair lotteries and the intuitions of Chisholm, Kyburg *et al.* In closing, it might be useful to indicate very quickly how probabilities can be related to conditions for rational acceptance according to the scheme proposed here.

Given an n-fold ultimate partition U, there are 2^n distinct 'cognitive options' open to an investigator, represented by accepting as strongest each of the 2^n elements of M (including S and C) generated by U. Each of these options can be represented as a case of rejecting elements belonging to some subset of U. Suspension of judgement would be tantamount to rejecting no elements of U, and self-contradiction (accepting C as strongest) would be rejecting all of them. Now, given U with a definite number n of elements, one might specify a rejection level r such that a necessary and sufficient condition for rejecting an element of U would be that it bear a probability less than r. In order to avoid inconsistency, r could be no greater than $1/n$ but it could very well be less.

Note that the rejection level is applicable only to elements of U – not to other elements of M. Even when an ultimate partition is given, no necessary and sufficient condition for accepting or rejecting elements of M can be stated in terms of an acceptance or rejection level. A rejection level can be stated for elements of U and an acceptance level for the contradictories of these elements.

Observe further that the rejection level depends in part on the number of elements of U. The greater the number of alternatives in the ultimate partition, the lower and more stringent the rejection level proves to be.

The inductive acceptance rule just suggested requires careful scrutiny before its adequacy can be determined. The reason for introducing it here is to indicate how probabilities can be related to rational acceptance and rejection in a manner compatible with the principle of deductive cogency without leading to the view that a probability of 1 is necessary and sufficient for rational acceptance. It also provides some insight into why high probabilities are not sufficient and, perhaps, not necessary for rational acceptance. All of these matters deserve further elaboration and illustration. I intend to consider them further elsewhere.

5
Information and inference*†

1 Inquiry and information

Inquiries are undertaken in science in order to obtain answers to questions.[1] Embodied in any question are more or less exactly specified assumptions regarding the relevance of any proposed answer to the question and a request that from a list of potential answers one be picked which is at once true and informative in the way required by the

* This paper was prompted by stimulating discussions with J. Hintikka and J. Pietarinen during a brief visit to Helsinki. It was written with the support of the John Simon Guggenheim Foundation and the United States–United Kingdom Educational Commission.
† Reprinted with permission of the publishers from *Synthese* **17** (1969), pp. 369–91. Copyright © 1969 by D. Reidel Publishing Company, Dordrecht, Holland.
1 Rudolf Carnap and Karl Popper, among many others, have apparently meant to deny this assertion. More exactly, they have denied the legitimacy of inductive inferences understood as cases of picking one possible answer to a question rather than another on the basis of evidence which does not entail that conclusion. For Carnap, an inductive inference is the assignment of a probability distribution to a list of potential answers on the basis of given evidence. (See Carnap (1950), pp. 205–7, and (1960), pp. 316–18.) Popper's anti-inductivism may be intended merely to deny that one can render acceptance of hypothesis *H* immune from error on the basis of evidence which does not entail *H*. This *may* be all that he means when he says that we accept hypotheses but only 'tentatively' and that there is no form of inference which can justify such acceptance. (See Popper (1962), pp. 54–5.) This thesis is compatible with allowing that we can on some occasions justify accepting such a hypothesis as the correct answer to a given question in the sense that relative to the evidence and the demand for a true and informative answer embodied in the question, *the risk of error is worth taking*. Yet, Popper's anti-inductivism sometimes seems to commit him to rejecting this fallibilistic sort of inductive inference. Thus, he says that tentative acceptance is to be understood as acceptance for purposes of 'further critical discussion'. (See (1962), p. 218 *n*.) Hypotheses are not legitimately accepted as true but only entertained for purposes of testing. We inquire not in order to obtain answers to questions but in order to test possible answers. Testing becomes an end – not a means. This view is a betrayal of fallibilism; for there can be no risk of error in entertaining a hypothesis just as there can be no risk of error in assigning a probability to it. Following Peirce, the position taken in this paper agrees with the first version of anti-inductivism but rejects the second. We are sometimes justified in accepting a conclusion via induction from given evidence even though the evidence does not guarantee the truth of the conclusion. Some grounds for insisting on the importance of inductive acceptance are offered in Levi (1967*a*), ch. I.

question.[2] Consequently, the choice of a conclusion to a given question on given evidence ought ideally to satisfy two desiderata: the answer chosen ought to be true, and the answer ought to supply information of the sort demanded by the question.

Truth, in the sense understood here, is Tarskian truth. Hence, accepting a hypothesis *H* as true relative to evidence *e* which does not entail *H* runs the risk of error even if risks are calculated on the assumption that *e* is true.[3] Risk of error can, indeed, be avoided by refraining from reaching any conclusions save those implied by the evidence. No rational investigator would follow any other course were the sole desideratum to obtain a true answer to a question. It becomes reasonable on occasion to risk error because answers are not only expected to be true but informative as well. The demand for information renders the risk of error worthwhile.

Thus, the notion of information demanded by a question is of critical importance in a systematic account of standards of legitimate inference. Beginning with Karl Popper, several authors have acknowledged the importance of the concept of information; but only a few have attempted to indicate how the demand for information controls the legitimacy of scientific inferences.[4]

Those authors who have engaged in such attempts have all adopted substantially the same approach. Because efforts to obtain true and informative answers to questions resemble decision problems under uncertainty in certain critical respects, they consider criteria for rational inference which can be obtained by adopting some general principle for rational decision making under uncertainty applicable both to 'practical' decision problems and to 'cognitive' decision problems. They supplement this general criterion with a characterization of an 'epistemic utility function' representing the goal of efforts to obtain true and informative answers to questions.[5]

2 I do not mean to suggest that the problem which provides the occasion for an inquiry logically implies certain background assumptions and a list of potential solutions. The identification of the underlying assumptions and potential answers often makes up a considerable portion of an inquiry. But all such activity can be viewed as concerned with reconstructing the problem so as to make it amenable to solution.
3 When *e* is accepted as evidence during a given period *t*, during that period its truth is not subject to any serious doubt. Hence, accepting *e* is not deemed at all risky. Of course, *e* may be false. Moreover, at some later time, its truth may be subject to serious doubt. At that point, *e* should be removed from the evidence and subjected to criticism. Relative to the evidence *f* not subject to question, accepting or rejecting *e* will involve risk of error. However, as long as *e* is accepted as evidence, accepting *e* as true will not be judged as involving error. In sum, all risks are calculated on the assumption that the evidence is true.
4 To my knowledge, the only places where such a program has been discussed at any length are in Hempel (1960) and (1962), Hintikka and Pietarinen (1966) and Levi (1963*a*), (1967*a*), (1969*c*), (1962).
5 Strictly speaking, every distinct inquiry is faced with a different problem to solve and, hence, a different objective. Epistemic utility functions cannot, therefore, be used to characterize a single objective of all such inquiries but rather certain features common to the different objectives of different inquiries.

The general principle for rational decision making is used together with the epistemic utility function to derive criteria for rational inference. The general principle for rational decision making under uncertainty which has almost always been adopted is the Bayesian injunction to maximize expected utility.[6] Objections to this criterion on the grounds that it has an extremely narrow range of direct applicability are well known. But its use does allow for a systematic account of the relations between probabilities (understood as determining fair betting quotients), rational acceptance or belief, confirmation (in the sense in which the best answer to a given question is one bearing maximum confirmation by the evidence), truth and information.

It has generally been assumed that content or information is a semantic feature of hypotheses or a semantic relation between hypotheses and evidence. Moreover, most writers have followed Karl Popper in supposing that the amount of information conveyed by a hypothesis decreases with an increase in either its prior or its posterior probability.[7] The central thesis of this paper is that information demanded by a question has a fundamentally pragmatic component and that information does not decrease with an increase in probability in the sense in which probability determines fair betting quotients.[8]

2 Potential answers

The degree to which a hypothesis is informative depends, at least in part, on the question under consideration. Not every hypothesis expresses a potential answer to that question. Hypotheses about quasars are not potential answers to questions about the atmosphere of Venus. If the demand is for a

6 In Levi (1962), the Neyman–Pearson method for testing statistical hypotheses, which is normally taken to be a criterion for rational decision making ('inductive behavior'), was reconstrued so as to render it applicable to 'cognitive decision problems'.

7 The only explicit exceptions are in Levi (1967a) and (1969c).

8 Thus, those who dismiss the problem of rational belief or acceptance as a pragmatic question are right in their attribution of pragmatic status although they are wrong in their dismissal of the problem. If the logic of science is concerned with purely syntactic and semantic features of scientific knowledge, this paper is not concerned with the logic of science. But the logic of science has no relevance to scientific inquiry unless it sheds light on standards for appraising scientific inferences and other activities involved in scientific inquiry. To demonstrate such applicability, a 'methodology' is required – i.e., a system of normative pragmatic principles.

Many writers tend to equate 'pragmatic' with 'subjective' or 'idiosyncratic'. By assuming that questions of rational acceptance are pragmatic in this sense and, hence, none of their concern, they imply that scientific knowledge and belief is an utterly subjective and idiosyncratic affair. Those who investigate normative, pragmatic acceptance rules adopt a far more optimistic view of the objectivity of scientific knowledge. Whether subjective and idiosyncratic factors control rational belief remains an open question. But by attempting to identify these factors (if there are such) and determining how they objectively control what one ought to believe, the assumption is made that objective factors control rational belief as well.

determination of the percentage of nitrogen in the Venusian atmosphere, statements about the composition of quasars should be viewed as conveying no information at all, simply because they are not relevant potential answers. Or if someone wishes to know which of three candidates X, Y and Z will win an election, the answer that X will come first, Y will come second and Z third conveys no more information than the answer that X will win; for, given the question asked, the order in which the candidates show is irrelevant. To this extent, therefore, information is a function of the question raised and must be considered pragmatic.[9]

But semantic conceptions of information can still be held to have relevance for scientific inference in a somewhat weakened sense. It might be maintained that given a list of potential answers to a question, the informativeness of any item on the list is a function of its semantic properties alone. In order to assess this claim, something more should be said about potential answers.

The first thing to notice is that a potential answer to a given question should not be viewed as accepting a single sentence H as true. If an investigator commits himself to accepting a sentence H on evidence e, he is also committed to accepting all the deductive consequences of H & e. Potential answers to a question are representable by deductively closed sets of sentences which contain as members all sentences accepted as part of the evidence.[10] This set of sentences may be represented by a single sentence (or sentence schema). Thus consider the set K of deductive consequences of H and the evidence e. If K is a potential answer to the question under consideration, adopting that answer can equally well be characterized as a case of accepting the sentence H as strongest sentence obtained via induction from e. H will be said to be 'accepted as strongest'. Of course, any other sentence G such that the evidence e entails that H and G are equivalent will represent the set K equally as well. G and H need not be logically equivalent. As long as the set K' consisting of the deductive consequences of G & e is identical with the set K consisting of the consequences of H & e, the answer afforded by accepting G as strongest and that afforded by accepting H as strongest is the same.

The potential answers to a given question relative to fixed evidence b & e[11] can be represented as follows:

Let U_e be a finite set of sentences H_1, H_2, ..., H_n each consistent with b & e

9 It is possible to entertain the view that questions can be represented by some sort of linguistic entity and that a semantic relation 'the information conveyed by H relative to question Q' can be defined. But even if such a program could be carried out (and that is, to say the least, an open question), it would still remain true that the informativeness of a hypothesis would depend upon which question is under consideration.

10 For a more extended discussion of deductive closure, see Levi (1965a) and (1967a), ch. II.

11 Let b represent the background information available to the investigator at the inception of inquiry and let e represent the new evidence subsequently obtained. (Only cases where b & e is consistent shall be considered.) b & e is then the total available evidence.

such that b & e entails that at least and at most one element of U_e is true.[12] The potential answers to a given question are cases of accepting Boolean combinations of the elements of the 'ultimate partition' U_e as strongest via induction from b & e.[13] There are an infinite number of such Boolean combinations. However, each one will be equivalent given b & e to a member of a set of 2^n sentences M_e generated from U_e (when the elements of U_e are alphabetized) as follows:

(i) S_e is the disjunction of all elements of U_e where each H_i occurs as disjunct once and only once and in alphabetical order.

(ii) C_e is the conjunction of all elements of U_e where each H_i occurs as conjunct once and only once and in alphabetical order.

(iii) G is any disjunction of k ($0 < k < n$) elements of U_e where each disjunct occurs once and only once and in alphabetical order.

Each of these 2^n elements of M_e represents a distinct possible answer to the question characterized by the 'ultimate partition' U_e; and no potential answer is left out.[14] Accepting S_e as strongest is tantamount to accepting all and only deductive consequences of the evidence b & e (i.e., is tantamount to total suspension of judgement) whereas accepting C_e as strongest is tantamount to contradicting the evidence. S_e will not, in general, be a logical truth. However, any logical truth will be equivalent, given b & e, to S_e. Similarly, C_e need not be a logical contradiction. U_e is a subset of M_e. Each element of U_e represents a strongest consistent potential answer to the question under study.

Given the restriction of the list of potential answers to a given question relative to total evidence b & e to elements of a set M_e, the thesis that

12 The restriction to finite cases can be lifted when certain modifications are made; but discussion of infinite ultimate partitions would introduce unnecessary complications into the discussion without substantially altering the main points.

13 The 'initially ultimate partition' U is the ultimate partition at the outset of inquiry when the total evidence is b. As the investigator acquires new information e, some of the elements of U may become incompatible with the total evidence b & e. U_e (the truncated ultimate partition) is obtained from U by deleting such incompatible elements.

14 I do not mean to suggest that to each question there is correlated a unique ultimate partition (even when the evidence is given). The set of potential answers to a given question will depend in part on the genius of the participants in an inquiry. However, at any given stage of inquiry, only a certain set of potential answers will be entertained. I am suggesting that such a set will be representable by a set of sentences M_e generated by an ultimate partition U_e.

In Hintikka and Pietarinen (1966) and Levi (1963a), the potential answers are not explicitly considered. In Hempel (1960) and (1962) and Levi (1962), the potential answers are restricted to elements of U_e and the sentence S_e. This approach is clearly inadequate. If I want to know which of three candidates X, Y and Z will win, I can predict that X or Y will win while suspending judgement as to which will win; and sometimes I will be justified in doing so. Options such as this are neglected in the early papers by Hempel and Levi.

Observe that each of the 2^n potential answers can be represented as a case of rejecting a subset of elements of U_e and taking the deductive consequences.

information demanded by a question is a semantic notion can be rephrased as follows:

(I) Let G be an element of M_e. The information obtained relevant to the question under consideration by accepting G as strongest via induction from b & e is a semantic property of G or a semantic relation holding between G and b & e.

This thesis is adopted in Hempel (1960) and (1962), Levi (1963), and Hintikka and Pietarinen (1966). In these papers, it is accompanied by another assumption generally adopted by writers on semantic information.

(II) Let $p(G, e)$ be the conditional probability of G given b & e and let $p(G)$ be the conditional probability of G given b. The information conveyed by accepting G as strongest via induction from b & e either increases as $p(G, e)$ decreases or as $p(G)$ decreases.[15]

The idea that an informative hypothesis is an improbable one stems from the writings of Karl Popper. It has been almost universally adopted. One of the main points to be made in this paper is that (II) does not hold for information demanded by a question.

It will also be argued that thesis (I) must be abandoned as it stands. The information demanded by a question depends upon what the question demands. Thus, accepting H as strongest via induction from b & e may be a potential answer to two distinct questions where two distinct kinds of information are required. The informativeness of accepting H as strongest will differ with the question under consideration. If this claim is correct, a semanticist substitute for thesis (I) would have to relativize the concept of information to the demands of a question and show how that relativization can be reconstructed semantically. It would be dogmatic to assert that such a weakened version of (I) is impossible; but it is not unreasonable to suspect that prospects for substantiating such a thesis are rather poor.

3 True and informative answers

Given an ultimate partition U_e relative to total evidence b & e, the problem is to select an element of M_e for acceptance as strongest via induction from

---

15 Most writers have assumed that the background information b is a tautology or is reflected in the structure of the 'language' for which the probability measure is defined. Nothing will be lost in the present discussion, however, if b is allowed to represent empirical and theoretical background information as well.

    Probabilities are to be understood to be measures on sentences used to determine fair betting quotients. Thesis (II) will be shown to be untenable regardless of whether the probabilities used to determine fair betting quotients are subjective in the sense that they obey only conditions of coherence or whether they are understood to be logical probabilities or degrees of confirmation in Carnap's sense.

b & e. The answer chosen should ideally be both true and informative. Consequently, the epistemic utility function characterizing the goal of the inquiry can be viewed as a function of two desiderata: truth and information. Each desideratum can itself be represented by an epistemic utility function. Thus, $T(H, t)$ is the utility of accepting H as strongest from b & e when no deductive consequence of b & e & H is false where the sole concern is to obtain a true answer regardless of how informative it is. $T(H, f)$ is the utility of accepting H as strongest from b & e when at least one deductive consequence of b & e & H is false relative to the same objective.[16] The function $T(H, x)$ represents the utility of truth.

Similarly, the utility of information may be represented by a function $C(H, x)$ (where x may be t or f). The C-function is the utility function which would be employed were the objective to obtain an informative answer regardless of whether it was correct or incorrect.

If $V(H, x)$ is a utility function representing the objective of obtaining an answer which is both true and informative, $V(H, x)$ should be some function of $T(H, x)$ and $C(H, x)$.[17] By viewing the matter in this way, it becomes possible to consider conditions which might be imposed on adequate T-functions and C-functions as well as constraints on the manner in which they combine to determine V-functions. Within the framework of such conditions, the properties of the C-function representing the utility of information can be analyzed. On the assumption that any measure of information demanded by a question should be some linear transformation of the C-function[18], this approach provides a vantage point from which proposed measures of information or content can be criticized.

Recall that if G is equivalent given b & e to F, accepting G as strongest via induction from b & e yields the same answer as accepting F as strongest from b & e. Hence, the epistemic utility of accepting G as strongest when it is true (false) should be the same as that of accepting F as strongest no matter which epistemic utility function is employed.

16 In note 3, it was remarked that risks are calculated on the assumption that the total evidence is true. Hence, the truth of H is a necessary and sufficient condition for the correctness of accepting H as strongest via induction from b & e – at least from the point of view of one who accepts b & e as evidence.

17 It should be kept in mind that these three functions are definable only up to a linear transformation; for maximizing expected utility relative to any one of these functions will yield the same results if a linear transformation of the utility function involved is used instead.

18 Remember that we are looking for an analysis of the concept of information which reproduces those features of potential answers rendered epistemically desirable by the demand for an answer to a question. Instead, therefore, of defining a content function and shaping utility functions to its needs, conditions for an adequate utility function for information are presented and measures of content are judged for adequacy in terms of how well they satisfy these conditions.

(A) Let F be in M_e. If G is equivalent given b & e to F,

    1. $T(G, x) = T(F, x)$ (where x is t or f)
    2. $C(G, x) = C(F, x)$
    3. $V(G, x) = V(F, x)$.

Condition (A) rules out any measure of information based on prior probabilities. Consider, for example, cont$(H) = p(\sim H)$. If cont(H) is an adequate measure of information demanded by a question, any linear transformation of it should be substitutable for the C-function. Yet, a logical truth $H \vee \sim H$ is not logically equivalent (in general) to S_e even though it will be equivalent *given* b & e to S_e. Hence, cont$(H \vee \sim H)$ will be 0 even though, in general cont(S_e) is positive. Substituting cont(H) for $C(H, x)$ violates condition (A). The same observation applies to all other measures of information based on prior probabilities (such as inf$(H) = -\log p(H)$).[19]

(B) For every H and G in M_e,

    1. $T(H, t) > T(H, f)$
    2. $T(H, t) = T(G, t)$
    3. $T(H, f) = T(G, f)$.

Condition (B) asserts that when truth is the only desideratum all true answers are to be considered on a par and similarly for all false answers. Moreover, true answers are epistemically preferable to errors. Because $T(H, x)$ is definable only up to a linear transformation, any numerical values a and b can be assigned to $T(H, t)$ and $T(H, f)$ respectively provided only that $a > b$.

Let $ET(H, e)$ be the expected epistemic utility of accepting H as strongest via induction from b & e.

$$ET(H, e) = p(H, e)a + p(\sim H, e)b$$
$$= p(H, e)(a - b) + b.$$

From this formula it is clear that an investigator interested in 'the truth and nothing but the truth' should maximize probability – i.e., pick that element in M_e for acceptance as strongest bearing maximum probability. This would always be S_e. Hence, the truth seeker should never accept any

---

19 Karl Popper is mainly responsible for the view that measures of information are to be pegged to prior probabilities. His view was adopted in Levi (1963a) and Hintikka and Pietarinen (1966). In Hempel (1960) and (1962), the measure $p(\sim H$ & $e) = p(\sim H, e)p(e)$ was adopted as the measure of the utility of information on the grounds that the investigator is concerned with the information added to that afforded by the evidence. Hempel's approach was briefly criticized in Levi (1961a). I no longer think that criticism to be decisive. Indeed, as condition (A) indicates, I now think that Hempel is right in requiring a measure of information added to that afforded by the evidence. There are, however, other objections to his approach which will be considered later on.

conclusion unless it is entailed by his evidence. He should suspend judgement. This result is plainly objectionable.[20]

Truth, therefore, cannot be the only desideratum in scientific inquiry. Risking error becomes reasonable, as was pointed out earlier, because of the demand for information.[21] Observe, however, that the information afforded by accepting a certain answer to a question is independent of whether the answer is correct or incorrect.

(C) For every H in M_e, $C(H, t) = C(H, f)$.

According to condition (C), an investigator who looks for information alone faces no risks. He is well advised to pick an answer bearing maximum information.[22] By way of contrast, the investigator who cares for truth alone has risky options in his choice set. Yet he also has one option (suspension of judgement) which involves no risks and which he should, therefore, select. On the other hand, the investigator interested in both truth and information not only faces risky options but will sometimes find them worth taking.

Let there be n elements in U_e. There are 2^n elements in M_e. Each such element can be accepted correctly or erroneously (with the exceptions of C_e and S_e). Hence, there are $2^{n+1} - 2$ cognitive outcomes to consider when assigning epistemic utilities. Consider then all cases of accepting H as strongest when H is true. Because the truth value is the same in all cases,

---

20 It is not objectionable according to those who endorse the view of Carnap and the second version of Popper mentioned in reference 1 to the effect that inductive inference is never legitimate.

In (1959), pp. 271–2 and elsewhere, Popper observes that maximizing probability leads to less informative hypotheses. If the first interpretation of Popper mentioned in note 1 is adopted and Popper does admit fallibilistic inductive inference, his remarks support the objectionability of maximizing probability as an inductive acceptance rule.

There are several conceptions of the aim of inquiry which could lead to the recommendation to maximize probability. One is 'seeking the truth and nothing but the truth'. Another is looking for probable hypotheses. This objective would be representable by the epistemic utility function $P(H, t) = P(H, f) = p(H, e)$. Relative to this goal, there is no risk of error in picking a conclusion because truth is not a desideratum – only probability. Yet, an investigator seeking probability should follow the same policy as one concerned to obtain true answers (where some of the options do entail risk of error).

In (1967a), p. 102, I contended that seeking the truth and nothing but the truth is the only cognitive objective which yields the prescription that probability be maximized. This claim is clearly erroneous. However, the conclusion based on this contention that 'the aims of scientific inquiry involve desiderata other than truth' (p. 103) is legitimate; for all that is required to support this claim is that seeking the truth and nothing but the truth is sufficient (together with the injunction to maximize expected utility) to warrant maximizing probability and not that it is necessary.

21 'Yet we must also stress that *truth is not the only aim of* science. We want more than mere truth: what we look for is *interesting truth* ....' (Popper (1962), p. 229.)

22 According to the usual view (with which I agree in this respect), C_e is the most informative hypothesis in M_e. Hence, it should receive maximum epistemic utility when information is the sole desideratum. This is not counterintuitive; for one who cares only for information cares nothing for truth.

increments in epistemic utility would be simply increments in the utility of information. This seems to imply that $V(H, t) - V(G, t)$ should equal $C(H, x) - C(G, x)$. By parity of reasoning for the case of all possible outcomes where potential answers are false, $V(H, f) - V(G, f)$ should equal $C(H, x) - C(G, x)$. Observe, however, that the unit for measuring the utility of information is arbitrary. This means that the numerical values for the V-function can remain unaltered for arbitrary changes in the unit for measuring the utility of information. Since no such unit has been selected as a standard, $V(H, t) - V(G, t)$ should be equated with $b_t(C(H, x) - C(G, x))$ where b_t is a positive constant and $V(H, f) - V(G, f)$ should equal b_f for positive b_f. One further requirement can also be imposed. On the assumption that increments in epistemic utility represented by the V-function are increments in the utility of information when the potential answers compared share the same truth value, b_t should equal b_f; for although the scale for the C-function is arbitrary, the choice of a scale should be the same for all possible arguments of that function.

These conclusions are summarized in the following condition:

(D1) If H and G are members of M_e,

(a) $V(H, t) - V(G, t) = b_t(C(H, x) - C(G, x))$, $b_t > 0$
(b) $V(H, f) - V(G, f) = b_f(C(H, x) - C(G, x))$, $b_f > 0$
(c) $b_t = b_f = b$.

(D1) was obtained by dividing the potential outcomes into two subsets: correct answers and errors. It was assumed that when truth value is constant variations in epistemic utility are variations in the utility of information. The set of potential outcomes can also be partitioned into subsets of elements $K_1, K_2, \ldots, K_m$ such that all elements of the same K_i are equally informative but members of different subsets have different informational value. If elements of only one subset are compared, increments in epistemic utility would be increments in the utility of truth value. Thus we could conclude that for any H and G belonging to K_i, $V(H, t) - V(G, f) = a_i(T(H, t) - T(G, f)) = a_i(T(H, t) - T(H, f))$ where a_i is a positive constant of scale. Moreover, the constant of scale should be the same for all subsets K_i.

However, the same result can be obtained with the aid of (D1) by assuming merely that accepting H as strongest is epistemically preferable to accepting it erroneously.

(D2) $V(H, t) - V(H, f) > 0$.

(D1) implies that $V(H, t) - V(H, f) = V(G, t) - V(G, f)$ for any H and G in M_e. (B) implies that $T(H, t) - T(H, f) = T(G, t) - T(G, f) > 0$. Hence, we have the following theorem:

T.1: $V(H, t) - V(H, f) = a(T(H, t) - T(H, f))$ where a is positive and the same for all H in M_e.

We thus have two constants of scale a and b whose role in the representation of the V-function is explored in the following three theorems:

T.2:   (a) $V(H, t) - V(H, f) = a(T(H, t) - T(H, f))$
$$+ b(C(H, x) - C(H, x))$$
       (b) $V(H, t) - V(G, t) = a(T(H, t) - T(G, t))$
$$+ b(C(H, x) - C(G, x))$$
       (c) $V(H, f) - V(G, f) = a(T(H, f) - T(G, f))$
$$+ b(C(H, x) - C(G, x)).$$

From (a) and (c) together with condition (B), we have:

       (d) $V(H, t) - V(G, f)$
$$= a(T(H, t) - T(H, f)) + b(C(H, x) - C(G, x))$$
$$= a(T(H, t) - T(G, f)) + b(C(H, x) - C(G, x)).$$

The results of T.2 may be summarized as follows:

T.3: $V(H, x) - V(G, x) = a(T(H, x) - T(G, x)) + b(C(H, x) - C(G, x))$
T.4:   (a)   Let c be an arbitrary constant which may be set to 0.
          $V(H, x) = aT(H, x) + bC(H, x) + c$
       (b)   Let $\alpha = a/(a + b)$. $V(H, x)$ is a linear transformation of $\alpha T(H, x) + (1 - \alpha)C(H, x)$.

In the preceding discussion, the constants a and b have been understood to be constants of scale. This means that if the units for measuring T-values and C-values are altered (and the units for measuring one set of values can be changed independently of the other), the constants a and b can be modified so that the V-function is unaltered. Suppose, however, that the scales for measuring T-values and for measuring C-values are fixed in some arbitrary way. If the constants a and b are multiplied by the same positive constant, the V-function will be changed by the same positive factor. This transformation does not, however, alter the behavior of the function in any relevant way. It is a mere change in units for measuring V-values. On the other hand, if a and b are altered independently of one another, not only will the V-function be altered, but the new V-function will not be a linear transformation of the old.

This means that the constants a and b have another significance in addition to being scale constants. Once the unit for measuring T-values and C-values is fixed, they function as weights in the weighted sums appearing in T.3 and T.4. Recall that the investigator interested in true and informative answers is concerned to satisfy two desiderata which, when taken separately, tend to pull in different directions. The demand for truth dampens the readiness to risk error for the sake of information, whereas the demand for information reduces concern for risk of error. The pair of constants a and b or the parameter α of T.4 represent the relative importance attached to these conflicting demands. As a and α go to 0, the V-function begins to

COGNITIVE DECISION MAKING

approximate the C-function representing the objective of obtaining information alone. As b goes to 0 or α goes to 1, truth predominates as desideratum. Thus, two investigators interested in true and informative answers might disagree as to the relative weights to be attached to the two desiderata. The one who favored truth more would be relatively reluctant to take risks for the sake of information and in that sense would be more cautious.[23] Although no attempt will be made to fix on a definite method for selecting a pair of constants a and b or parameter α, after introducing another condition certain constraints will be imposed on the choice.

Condition (D2) insured that accepting H as strongest when H is true is epistemically preferable to accepting it as strongest erroneously. (D2) does not preclude, however, some false answers being epistemically preferable to some correct ones. This possibility is taken care of by condition (E).

(E) $V(H, f) < V(G, t)$ for every H and G in M_e.

Condition (E) is consistent with allowing that sometimes the risk of error is worth taking for the sake of information. But it imposes certain definite limits on the relative importance that can be attached to information as compared with truth.

Because M_e is finite, there will be a W in M_e such that $C(W, x)$ is a maximum and an X such that $C(X, x)$ is a minimum. According to the usual theories of utility, these two C-values will be finite. Condition (E) implies (with the aid of T.4) that the following theorems hold:

T.5: $V(W, f) < V(X, t)$
T.6: $(1 - \alpha)/\alpha < (C(W, x) - C(X, x))/(T(X, t) - T(W, f))$.

It is always possible to select units for measuring C-values and T-values so that $C(W, x) - C(X, x) = T(X, t) - T(W, f)$. Relative to such a system of units, the ratio $q = (1 - \alpha)/\alpha$ must be less than unity in order to meet condition (E). Thus, the requirement that no error be preferred to any correct answer does impose a definite restriction on the relative importance which can be attached to information as compared to truth.

It should be mentioned in passing that condition (E) is quite compatible with recognizing the importance of hypotheses known to be false in scientific inquiry. By studying the properties of false hypotheses, other hypotheses eligible for consideration as potential answers to a given question may sometimes be obtained. But the task of devising hypotheses for inclusion among the potential answers is not to be confused with the problem of

---

23 Keep in mind that no significance can be attached to the numerical values of a, b or α unless the units for measuring T-values and C-values are fixed. Thus, if $a = b$ and $\alpha = \frac{1}{2}$, a change in units for the T-function and for the C-function will replace the equalities by inequalities. However, the direction of variation of the parameter α does carry significance independent of a choice of units.

choosing between potential answers in order to obtain a true and informative answer. Condition (E) is proposed for the latter type of problem and not the former.

Let $EV(H, e)$ be the expected epistemic utility of accepting H as strongest via induction from b & e when the investigator is interested in true and informative answers.

T.7:
$$EV(H, e) = p(H, e)\alpha(T(H, t) - T(H, f)) \\ + \alpha T(H, f) + (1 - \alpha)C(H, x)$$

T.8:
If $T(H, t) = 1$ and $T(H, f) = 0$,
$$EV(H, e) = \alpha p(H, e) + (1 - \alpha)C(H, x).$$

Thus, the expected epistemic utility of accepting H as strongest via induction from b & e is a weighted sum of $p(H, e)$ and $C(H, x)$. This does not mean that the objective of inquiry is to obtain answers which are probable and informative rather than true and informative. Probability appears in the expression for the expected epistemic utility function (as it should) and not in the utility function $V(H, x)$.

The measures of information $\text{cont}(H) = p(\sim H)$, $\inf(H) = -\log p(H)$ and all other measures defined in terms of prior probabilities have already been shown to be unsuitable substitutes for the C-function. Hempel (1960, p. 466) has proposed using a function of $p(H, e)$ to determine the utility of information. The function he used is a linear transformation of $\text{cont}(H, e) = p(\sim H, e)$. He defended its adoption on the grounds that the investigator would be looking for the information added by accepting a hypothesis H as strongest to the information afforded by the evidence (1960, pp. 465–6).

The motivation behind Hempel's approach is quite sound. The information demanded by a question should be information not already conveyed by the evidence but only information added to that already available. However, Hempel's own exploitation of this idea runs into difficulties.

According to Hempel, $V(H, t) = C(H, x)$ and $V(H, f) = -C(H, x)$ (1960, p. 466). Consequently, $V(H, f) - V(G, f) = -b_f(C(H, x) - C(G, x))$. This violates clause (b) of condition (D1). Whereas (D1) requires that the utility of false potential answers should be an increasing function of their informativeness, Hempel assumes that it should be a decreasing function. Thus an investigator who is interested in true and informative answers, but who is constrained to choose among answers guaranteed to be false, should, according to Hempel, minimize the informativeness of the answer he chooses. This in itself seems counterintuitive enough to warrant revising Hempel's proposal.[24]

---

24 Hempel's approach has been criticized on substantially the same grounds by Hintikka and Pietarinen (1966), p. 108 (n. 12).

Suppose, however, that Hempel's method of defining the function $V(H, x)$ is modified to meet the requirements of condition (D1). That is, cont(H, e) – which equals $p(\sim H, e)$ – or some linear transformation thereof is substituted for $C(H, x)$.[25]

Then $EV(H, e)$ is, according to T.8, a linear transformation of

(a) $\alpha p(H, e) + (1 - \alpha)p(\sim H, e)$
  $= p(H, e)(2\alpha - 1) + (1 - \alpha).$

Under the conditions of T.8, $T(H, t) = 1$ and $T(H, f) = 0$. Moreover, when $C(H, x) = $ cont$(H, e) = p(\sim H, e)$, C_e is the W of T.5 and T.6 and S_e is the X. Hence, according to T.6, α must be greater than 0.5. Thus, maximizing $EV(H, e)$ as defined by (a) is maximizing a linear transformation of $p(H, e)$ and leads always to recommending that S_e be accepted as strongest. This result has already been found objectionable.[26] Hempel's approach, even when amended to conform with the requirements which have been laid down, does not seem satisfactory.

This argument does not rule out all proposed measures of information which are decreasing functions of $p(H, e)$ but only those which are linear transformations of $p(\sim H, e)$. Thus, inf$(H, e) = -\log p(H, e)$ and $I(H, e) = 1/p(H, e)$ escape the criticisms made thus far. These two functions are objectionable on the grounds that they lead to unbounded epistemic utility functions.[27] There are, however, still other functions not subject to this difficulty or those previously raised. Consider, for example, inf$(H, e, a) = -\log(p(H, e) + a)$ where a is positive. Nothing in the conditions introduced thus far precludes considering them; but there are some additional conditions which do.

4 Information

Recall that accepting some element G in M_e as strongest via induction from b & e is equivalent to rejecting all those elements of U_e incompatible with G given b & e and taking the deductive consequences. Let $H_1, H_2, ..., H_k$ be

25 Since b & e is given, $p(e)$ and $p(\sim e)$ are constants. Hence, $p(\sim H, e)p(e)$ and $p(\sim H, e)p(\sim e)$ are linear transformations of cont$(\sim H, e)$. So is $p(\sim H, e)/p(\sim e)$ which is the utility function actually used by Hempel. From the point of view taken here, all of these representations of the C-function are essentially the same.
26 Thus, maximization of probability is an inductive acceptance rule resulting not only when the investigator cares only for probability or for truth but also for true and informative answers – provided that informative value is a linear transformation of cont(H, e). The argument that maximization of probability is an inappropriate acceptance rule because scientists demand information remains inconclusive unless the notion of information involved is carefully spelled out.
27 If unboundedness does not appear to be a difficulty, a detailed examination of what happens to the V-function when inf(H, e) or $I(H, e)$ is substituted for the C-function in T.4 should be convincing. This exercise will be left to the reader.

those elements of U_e. G is equivalent given b & e to $\sim H_1$ & $\sim H_2$ & $\sim H_3$ & ... & $\sim H_k$ which in turn is equivalent given e to S_e & $\sim H_1$ & $\sim H_2$ & ... & $\sim H_k$. The germ of truth in the idea that information increases with a decrease in probability is found in the view that when an investigator considers which of a list of potential answers to adopt, he would prefer (truth values being equal) answers which rule out more elements of U_e rather than less. Suspension of judgement regarding which element of U_e is true is to be eliminated as far as this is possible.

(F) If G is an element of M_e and H_i is an element of U_e which is a disjunct in G,

$$C(G \ \& \ \sim H_i, x) - C(G, x) > 0.$$

T.9:   For every distinct G and F in M_e, if G is deducible from F & b & e,

$$C(G, x) < C(F, x).$$

Condition (F) introduces a partial ordering of the elements of M_e with respect to the utility of information which makes informativeness an increasing function of deductive power (given the total evidence b & e). Since every measure of information which makes information a decreasing function of probability satisfies this requirement, when only the partial ordering requirement is considered, the utility of information can be viewed as a decreasing function of probability.

But there is another condition which can be imposed upon *increments* of information. Consider any two elements G and G' of M_e which are compatible given b & e with an element H_i of U_e (i.e., in which H_i is a disjunct). Does the increment in utility of information obtained by rejecting H_i in addition to all those elements of U_e incompatible (given b & e) with G differ from the increment obtained in the case of the other element G'? For example, let the problem be to predict whether X, Y or Z will win an election. Is the increase in informational utility obtained by predicting that X or Y will win over predicting that X or Y or Z will win the same as or different from the increment obtained from predicting that X will win over predicting that X or Z will win?

The plausible answer seems to be that rejection of an element of U_e affords the same increment of informational utility no matter how many or which other elements of U_e are also rejected. This requirement is stated in the following condition:

(G) Let G and F be elements of M_e and H_i be an element of U_e which is a disjunct in both G and F. Then

$$C(G \ \& \ \sim H_i, x) - C(G, x) = C(F \ \& \ \sim H_i, x) - C(F, x).$$

65

Def. 1: For every H_i in U_e,
$$K(H_i, e) = C(S_e \& \sim H_i, x) - C(S_e, x)$$
$$= C(\sim H_i, x) - C(S_e, x).$$

T.10: For every H_i and H_j in U_e,
$$C(\sim H_i \& \sim H_j, x) = K(H_i, e) + K(H_j, e) + C(S_e, x).$$

T.11: Let G in M_e be $H_1 \vee H_2 \vee \ldots \vee H_k$,
$$C(\sim G, x) = \sum_{i=1}^{k} K(H_i, e) + C(S_e, x).$$

Def. 2: Let G be as in T.11.
$$K(G, e) = C(\sim G, x) - C(S_e, x).$$

T.12: $K(G, e) = \sum_{i=1}^{k} K(H_i, e).$

T.13: $K(C_e, e) = 0$
$K(S_e, e) = \sum_{i=1}^{n} K(H_i, e)$ where there are n H_i's in U_e.

Def. 3: $M(G, e) = K(G, e)/K(S_e, e).$

Def. 4: $m(H, e)$ is a normalized probability measure defined over all Boolean combinations of elements of U_e if and only if

(i) $m(H_i, e)$ is positive for all H_i's in U_e;
(ii) $m(G, e) = \sum_{i=1}^{k} m(H_i, e)$ where G is equivalent given $b \& e$ to a disjunction of k elements of U_e, $H_1, H_2, \ldots, H_k$;
(iii) If $H_1, H_2, \ldots, H_n$ are all the elements in U_e, $\sum_{i=1}^{n} m(H_i, e) = 1$.

T.14: $M(H, e)$ is a normalized probability measure defined over all Boolean combinations of U_e.

Def. 5: $\text{Cont}(H, e) = M(\sim H, e).$

T:15 $C(H, x)$ is a linear transformation of $\text{Cont}(H, e)$.

Observe that the normalized probability measure $M(H, e)$ has been shown to be a probability only in the sense that it obeys the usual formal requirements of the calculus of probability as applied to sentences. This does not mean that $M(H, e)$ is a probability determining fair betting rates relative to given evidence $b \& e$. Thus, the conditions (A)–(G) do, in a sense, imply that information increases with a decrease in probability; but they do not imply that the probabilities involved are those determining fair betting rates or degrees of confirmation in Carnap's sense. Relative to the total evidence $b \& e$, the investigator is assumed to have selected one normalized probability measure $p(H, e)$ from the family $m(H, e)$ for determining fair betting rates. It does not follow from this that $M(H, e)$, which is used to determine the utility of information, equals $p(H, e)$.

On the other hand, T.14 shows that if the utility of information were to increase with a decrease in $p(H, e)$, $M(H, e)$ would have to equal $p(H, e)$. And T.15 shows that $C(H, x)$ cannot be a linear transformation of $\inf(H, e, a)$, or any other function of $p(H, e)$ which has escaped the strictures previously mentioned, but must be a linear transformation of the objectionable $\text{cont}(H, e) = p(\sim H, e)$. Thus, on the assumption that conditions (A)–(G) are adequate, $M(H, e)$ cannot equal $p(H, e)$ and information cannot increase with a decrease in probability in the sense in which probabilities determine fair betting quotients, degrees of confirmation in Carnap's sense or the like. Thesis (II) has been shown to be untenable.

To avoid misunderstanding, the rejection of thesis (II) does not imply that in no situation and relative to no body of evidence is $M(H, e) = p(H, e)$. Rejection of (II) means only that the equation of $M(H, e)$ and $p(H, e)$ is not a general principle applicable in every situation. After all, there are some problems such that relative to given total evidence b & e, suspension of judgement is warranted. Consider, for example, the case of the 1000 ticket lottery in which the probability that ticket i will win is the same for each i. If the question under consideration is 'Which of the 1000 tickets will be drawn?', the ultimate partition U_e consists of each of the 1000 sentences of the form 'Ticket i will be drawn'. Moreover, each element of U_e is, given the demands of the problem, as informative as any other. In this case, $M(H, e) = p(H, e)$. But, of course, in this case one would expect the justified prediction to be that at least and at most one ticket will be drawn – i.e., to accept S_e as strongest.

Suppose, however, the problem had been to predict whether ticket 1 will win or not. Here the ultimate partition U'_e consists of the two sentences 'ticket 1 will win' and 'ticket 1 will not win'. Moreover, each of these sentences will, *given the demands of the question*, be as informative as the other. In this case, $M(H, e)$ is not equal to $p(H, e)$.[28]

Finally, suppose that the problem is the same as in the first case, but that the evidence indicates rigging of the lottery in favor of ticket 1. Let 'ticket 1 will be drawn' have a probability of 0.4 and the remaining probability be divided equally among the remaining 999 elements of U_e. Assuming that the investigator is not too cautious in the sense discussed earlier, suspension of judgement will no longer be warranted. Indeed, 'ticket 1 will be drawn' might be accepted as strongest. Moreover, $M(H, e)$ will no longer equal $p(H, e)$; for each element of U_e will still have the same M-value as any other. This is no longer true for p-values.

28 Observe that the prediction should be that ticket 1 will not be drawn. This conclusion however, cannot be combined with the conclusion reached relative to the first question or any other questions such as 'Will ticket 2 win or not?' and the deductive consequences taken. The scope of deductive closure is restricted not only to the total evidence but to the question raised. See Levi (1967a), ch. II and (1965a).

The lottery example brings out another important point. Relative to the question 'Which of the 1000 tickets will be drawn?', 'ticket 1 will be drawn' is much more informative than its contradictory. Relative to the question 'Will ticket 1 be drawn?' these two hypotheses are equally informative. Thus, the information conveyed by a hypothesis cannot be taken to be a semantic property of the hypothesis in relation to the evidence. To this extent, thesis (I) must be rejected as well.

A modified version of thesis (I) might conceivably still hold. If questions can be successfully represented by linguistic entities and the information conveyed by a sentence relative not only to evidence $b \& e$ but also to question Q can be reconstructed semantically, a new semantic conception of information relevant to scientific inference would be forthcoming.

Partial headway along these lines can be made in cases where questions are associated with ultimate partitions which are uniquely determinable relative to given evidence.[29] In such cases, presumably, the demands of the question can be met equally as well by accepting one element of the ultimate partition as strongest as it can be accepting another. This is often true, for example, in cases of statistical prediction. If one is asked to predict how many black chips will be drawn from an urn in a given 100-fold sample with replacement, the ultimate partition will consist of 101 sentences of the form 'x draws will show black' where x takes values from 0 to 100. Moreover, accepting any one of these sentences as strongest will meet the demands of the question equally as well as any other. Perhaps, it will prove possible to provide a systematic account of cases of predictive inference, estimation and inductive generalization which is amenable to semantic characterization.

However, in most situations where the problem is to choose between theories or potential explanations, not only is it difficult to determine in any unique way an ultimate partition, but the elements of the ultimate partition will not be equally informative.[30] Due to limitations of imagination and energy, investigators are incapable at any given time of devising an exhaustive list of hypotheses all of which will be potential explanations or potential theories. In order to assure exhaustiveness given the evidence, a 'residual' hypothesis asserting that all other elements of the ultimate partition are false will have to be introduced. Moreover, explanations and theories may differ from one another with respect to simplicity and other factors which an investigator may be seeking in looking for an answer to his question. All of these factors will contribute to a lack of uniformity in the informational values attributed to elements of the ultimate partition; and it

---

29 As the evidence changes, the question may remain the same, even though the ultimate partition changes. However, in situations of the sort envisaged, changes in ultimate partitions will be controlled in a determinate way by changes in the evidence.

30 In Levi (1967a), discussion was restricted to cases where each element of U_e was as informative as any other. This did not seem plausible in the case of choosing among theories. So the scope of discussion was restricted to situations where this condition did obtain.

is far from obvious that such cases can be treated in a purely semantical way.[31]

Thus, if these considerations have any force, the notion of information relevant to scientific inference has a critically pragmatic aspect which cannot be semantically analyzed in ways currently being proposed. This result should occasion neither surprise nor dismay. It is not surprising because the relevance of the concept of information to scientific inference stems from the fact that inferences are drawn in scientific inquiries in order, among other things, to obtain answers which provide information regarding a certain problem. It is to be expected that the kind of information demanded is that appropriate to the question raised. All that has been done here is to attempt to take this banal observation seriously.

Dismay is also out of order. The objectivity of scientific inquiry is not subverted by recognizing the central importance of the pragmatic dimensions of such inquiry. The proposals made here do recognize important objective constraints on the legitimacy of scientific inferences. Relative to total evidence b & e, ultimate partition U_e, an assignment of informational values (which are themselves subject to constraints) to elements of U_e and a judgement regarding the relative importance of truth and information, the proposals made here do yield criteria for assessing the legitimacy of picking one potential answer rather than another. Many writers are prepared to acknowledge the relativity of such criteria to the evidence available to the investigator without judging that objectivity has been betrayed. The proposals mentioned here insist upon other relativities as well. To ignore these relativities will not make them disappear but will, in effect, be an admission that these factors control inference in a highly subjective manner. A far more optimistic view regarding the objectivity of scientific inquiry is adopted by those who recognize the relativities and attempt to ascertain how and to what extent objective constraints can be imposed upon the way these relativities control the legitimacy of scientific inference.

31 In Levi (1967a), I suggested that simplicity, explanatory power, etc. might be desiderata additional to truth and information in certain sorts of cognitive problems. The view I now favor distinguishes two features of information demanded by a question: (a) those features common to all cognitive questions, and (b) those peculiar to each question or to certain kinds of questions. I would now suggest (tentatively) that all cognitive problems have two desiderata: truth and information but that the concept of information has, in all situations, those characteristics mentioned in this paper (subject to qualifications due to the idealization involved in this discussion). Factors such as simplicity do not come in as additional desiderata but as special constraints upon the C-function operative in certain classes of problems. Their influence is reflected in the way C-values are assigned to elements of the ultimate partition (which is a matter that is, to a large extent, left open by the constraints imposed here).

6

Epistemic utility and the evaluation of experiments[†]

1

In a thoughtful and penetrating paper (1976), William K. Goosens undertakes to show that the account of epistemic utilities and criteria for inductive acceptance I proposed in (1967a) as modified in (1967c) runs into serious difficulties when applied to the problem of designing experiments – in particular, when alternative experiments are being evaluated prior to choosing one for implementation.

My previously published remarks on this topic (1967a, ch. IX) were at best fragmentary and not focused on the specific questions Goosens considers. Goosens, therefore, undertakes an examination of the ramifications (if any) of my account of epistemic utility and inductive acceptance for the evaluation of rival experiments. Goosens doubts, in point of fact, that such ramifications can be identified without supplementing my proposals with additional constraints. He does, however, consider one such constraint which, he demonstrates, leads to what he claims to be unacceptable consequences. He acknowledges that I might have good reason for refusing to accept that constraint. However, he then claims that there are too many possible alternatives to contemplate, none of which recommends itself to us.

In this paper, I shall first pose Goosens' problem and identify some assumptions concerning how it ought to be solved which he endorses and which I, for the sake of this argument, shall not question. I shall then review the main features of my account of epistemic utilities relevant to the solution and derive the solution required by combining my theory with the assumptions we share in common. In doing this, it will be demonstrated that no additional constraints need be added to my theory and the assumptions concerning which Goosens and I are in agreement to derive the implications of my theory for the evaluation of alternative experiments. Thus, it will be established that Goosens is wrong in claiming that there are many different ways to extend my theory to apply to this problem. Furthermore, it will be

[†] Reprinted with the permission of the editor from *Philosophy of Science* v. 44 (1977), pp. 368–86. Copyright © 1977 by the Philosophy of Science Association.

shown that the particular constraint used by Goosens in posing difficulties for my proposals in point of fact contradicts these proposals when combined with the assumptions Goosens and I share in common.

Finally, I shall consider whether the correct solution to Goosens' problem according to my theory runs into the same difficulties which the inconsistent version used by Goosens does.

2

At some stage of inquiry, an investigator has as his total knowledge or evidence the 'background knowledge', b, together with all its deductive consequences. The agent is concerned to find out which of a set, U, (the initially ultimate partition) of hypotheses $h_1, h_2, \ldots, h_n$ is true where each h_i is consistent with b and b entails that at least and at most one h_i is true.

One thing the agent might do is to add to his body of evidence of which he is certain at the initial time some sentence, g, equivalent, given b, to a disjunction of some subset of elements of U together with the deductive consequences of b & g which are not entailed by b alone. He might attempt to do so by means of an argument where the only premises or evidence consist of b and its deductive consequences. Should he accept g into his body of knowledge in this way, he would 'accept g as strongest via induction from the evidence b relative to U'.

The agent might, however, follow another procedure. He might devise an experiment X where he knows (as part of the background b) that if X is implemented at least and at most one of the hypotheses $e_1, e_2, \ldots, e_m$ is true and where an e_j describes a possible result of implementing X. The agent implements the experiment. In response to sensory stimulation, he makes the observation report that e_j is true and adds the report to his body of knowledge or evidence so that his total evidence now consists of b & e_j and the deductive consequences. He then adds further information pertinent to the question via induction from b & e_j.

Let w_j be the strongest disjunction in U deducible from b & e_j. w_j is part of the body of knowledge implied by b & e_j. Thus, through taking the deductive consequences of information obtained via the testimony of the senses, the agent has obtained new information pertinent to answering his question. To be sure, w_j may turn out to be the disjunction of all elements of U in which case the agent has obtained no new information pertinent to his question via deduction from new evidence obtained via the testimony of the senses. But sometimes w_j will be a disjunction of a proper subset of U and the agent will have progressed some way towards a full answer to the question.

Once the agent has the total evidence b & e_j, he is then in a position to contemplate further expansion of his body of knowledge via induction from

b & e_j. Since all elements of U inconsistent with b & e_j are, from his new point of view, certainly false, his new ultimate partition U_j will consist only of those elements of U consistent with b & e_j. These are the elements of U concerning whose truth values he suspends judgement. They are, of course, the disjuncts in w_j.

Let g be the element of U_j accepted as strongest via induction from b & e_j. The net result of the agent's implementing the experiment and reaching conclusions both via deduction and via induction from the new evidence is that he has added to b the sentence w_j & g along with the deductive consequences. That is to say, this is the new information he has obtained as answer to his initial question.

The problems of interest to Goosens are these: Should the agent prior to the implementation of any experiment rest content with the conclusions he can reach via induction relative to b or should he conduct an experiment X and add any new pertinent information that may be warranted via deduction and induction from the new data? Moreover, if the agent is able to implement one of several rival experiments, which experiment should he implement?

In (1967a, ch. IX) I did make some remarks pertinent to the first part of this question. Namely, I discussed briefly some aspects of the question as to when an agent should rest content with the evidence already available to him for the purpose of reaching conclusions via induction and when he should inquire further. But the remarks were fragmentary and constitute nothing like a complete answer to Goosens' question. I was primarily concerned to show how G. L. S. Shackle's theory of potential surprise might be used in an interesting way in inquiry to evaluate the weight of evidence or argument in the sense in which, I think, J. M. Keynes understood that notion.

The problem of comparing rival experiments was not even mentioned. I am not sure now what a fully satisfactory answer to this problem should be like. However, the approach favored by Goosens (following I. J. Good, 1967) has some attractive features when correctly deployed. For the sake of this argument, I shall follow Goosens in using this approach.

Goosens reduces the problem of evaluating rival experiments to specifying a function $EZ(X)$ which takes as arguments all the experiments available to the agent – including the option of conducting no experiment at all and reaching conclusions via induction relative to b. The values of the function will, in the present context, represent the epistemic utilities to be assigned to implementing the various experiments. The function induces an ordering on the experiments and the agent should pick an experiment bearing maximum EZ-value.

According to Goosens (1976, pp. 94–5) the first step towards a solution should be to define a function $Z(e_j)$ defined over all possible e_j's for all available experiments. Given any e_j, $Z(e_j)$ is the epistemic utility of coming to

72

know via observation that e_j is true relative to the question under investigation and the information that the appropriate experiment has been conducted and that b is true. Given this function, $EZ(X)$ should be equated with $\sum_{j=1}^{m} P(e_j; b \ \& \ X$ is implemented) $Z(e_j)$ where the e_j's are restricted to those describing possible outcomes of the experiment X. (In the subsequent discussion, I shall delete the tediously pedantic 'X is implemented' from the conditional probability.)

The problem has thus been reduced to that of specifying the function $Z(e_j)$. How is this to be done?

The first step is that the agent should ascertain which of the rival cognitive options in U_j should be chosen by him were he to come to know that $b \ \& \ e_j$ is true. Let that option be accepting g_j as strongest via induction from $b \ \& \ e_j$ relative to U_j. Determining what such a g_j should be is one of the problems the proposals I made in (1967a) and (1967c) were designed to answer. Since this problem needs to be answered in order to determine values for the Z-function, Goosens rightly contends that my account of inductive acceptance does have some sort of bearing on the evaluation of experiments.

Consider then all the relevant ways of expanding a body of knowledge $b \ \& \ e_j$ via induction relative to U_j. These are all representable as cases of accepting some g as strongest via induction from $b \ \& \ e_j$ and relative to U_j where g is a disjunction of a subset of elements of U_j. From the agent's point of view prior to experimentation when he knows only b, each of these options is describable as adding to $b \ w_j$ via deduction and g via induction from $b \ \& \ e_j$. When the agent already knows that e_j is true, it is describable as adding g to $b \ \& \ e_j$ via induction. As long as e_j is fixed, however, the cognitive options represented one way correspond to the cognitive options represented the other way.

For each of the g's determined by U_j, an expected epistemic utility $EV_j(g)$ conditional on $b \ \& \ e_j$ is assigned. I shall consider how this is done according to my theory later on. Given such a function, one can identify those cognitive options for which the EV_j-function gives maximum values. Utilizing a procedure for 'breaking ties' I have proposed (1967a, pp. 84–6), one can identify one of these options by a unique g_j which the agent should accept as strongest via induction from $b \ \& \ e_j$ relative to U_j.

Accepting g_j as strongest via induction from $b \ \& \ e_j$ bears a definite expected epistemic utility $EV_j(g_j)$. Goosens (1976, p. 99) canvasses the idea that this epistemic utility represents the epistemic value to the agent with respect to the question under investigation of having found out via observation of the results of the experiment implemented that e_j is true. He, therefore, suggests tentatively that $Z(e_j)$ be equated with $EV_j(g_j)$.

Until this stage, I have no quarrel (at least for the sake of this discussion) with Goosens' procedure. Moreover, I am prepared to accept part of the assumption implicit in Goosens' equation of $Z(e_j)$ with $EV_j(g_j)$.

In particular, I am prepared to accept the condition that there is an expected epistemic utility function $EV(g; e_j)$ defined all over g's determined by the U_j relative to any fixed e_j and for all e_j's and, moreover, that for any fixed e_j and the function $EV_j(g)$ defined over the g's determined by U_j (and only over this domain), the following conditions hold:

Condition A: $Z(e_j) = EV(g_j; e_j)$

$EV(g; e_j) = a_j EV_j(g) + b_j$

where a_j is positive.

The motivations for condition (A) may be briefly explained as follows. The EV_j-function used to determine an optimal g_j relative to fixed e_j is defined only over a restricted domain – to wit, the consequences of the cognitive options determined by U_j. On the other hand, the EV-function which is to be used to determine Z-values should be defined over the union of all the domains for all EV_j-functions relative to all e_j's and for all experiments. At the same time, the EV-function should be usable relative to fixed e_j to determine an ordering of the cognitive options determined by U_j and relative to b & e_j which is identical with that determined by using the restricted EV_j-function. These two conditions seem to me to capture what is correct in Goosens' assumption that the epistemic utility to be attributed to coming to know that e_j is true should be equated with the expected epistemic utility accruing when e_j is found to be true and the cognitive option of accepting g_j as strongest via induction is implemented. These requirements are expressed by condition (A).

Now we could construct a function EV^* such that $EV^*(g; e_j) = EV_j(g)$ for every j. EV^* would meet the second requirement in condition (A). Should we conclude that it meets the first?

On the basis of what has been said thus far, the matter seems entirely open. We could imagine that there is a function $EV(g; e_j)$ which should be used to determine Z-values in accordance with the first line of condition (A), which meets the second requirement as well but where for different e_j's, the constants of the linear transformations (the a_j's and the b_j's) differ as well.

If this should turn out to be the case, any linear transformation of the *total* EV-function will be guaranteed to give the same evaluation of experiments as the original EV-function itself does. Moreover, only such linear transformations will be guaranteed to do so. But, under the conditions just envisaged, the function $EV^*(g; e_j)$ – though it is a total function – cannot be a linear transformation of the EV-function and, hence, cannot be guaranteed to give the same evaluation of experiments as the original EV-function. On the assumption that the original EV-function is the one to use in determining Z-values and, hence, EZ-values, the EV^*-function cannot consistently be used for the same purpose.

These observations are based on assumptions which Goosens clearly intends to endorse. They follow from the general Bayesian decision theory which he is using in evaluating experiments. What they show is that we

74

cannot leap to the conclusion that $Z(e_j)$ should be equated with $EV^*(g_j; e_j) = EV_j(g_j)$. But they do not show that we cannot make the equation either.

Goosens appears to have understood at least part of the point I am making; for he does acknowledge that I am not compelled by my theory to equate $EV^*(g_j; e_j)$ with $Z(e_j)$ (1976, pp. 99, 107). But he thinks I am not compelled to do so because I am not compelled to identify 'the utility of coming to have evidence' with 'the utility of the act of hypothesis evaluation given that evidence'. Goosens' English formulation is open to many interpretations and I do not quite know what to make of it. I am prepared, for the sake of the argument, to endorse the identification provided this means nothing more than accepting condition (A); but that does not entail equating $EV^*(g_j; e_j)$ with $Z(e_j)$.

Goosens contends that once one refuses to equate $Z(e_j)$ with $EV_j(g_j) = EV^*(g_j; e_j)$, 'the alternative is difficult to criticize, simply because the class of functions possibly measuring the value of coming to have evidence is left indeterminate' (1976, p. 107).

It is, indeed, true that in my previous publications, the epistemic utility functions I proposed defined only the restricted EV_j-functions. Goosens' charge of indeterminacy would be a fair one were it the case that these proposals did not imply that the EV-function should be unique up to a linear transformation. Goosens suggests that my proposals leave this matter indeterminate.

The interesting point is that if condition (A) is adopted (and Goosens is committed to it), it turns out that what I explicitly did say in my previous work does determine an EV-function, unique up to a linear transformation. This is so even though my proposals were not designed with this problem in mind.

Furthermore, it is also demonstrable that the correct EV-function to use in evaluating experiments according to my account of epistemic utility and condition (A) is not a linear transformation of $EV^*(g; e_j) = EV_j(g)$. Thus, my theory prohibits using the only candidate pertinent to my theory which Goosens considers.

Finally, although Goosens is correct in demonstrating that using EV^* in the evaluation of experiments does have what appear to be objectionable consequences, these consequences can be imputed to the fact that this method violates the requirements of my theory. When the correct EV-function is used, it is demonstrable that my theory avoids those consequences which both Goosens and I agree are objectionable.

3

In order to establish the correctness of my claims, it is time to rehearse briefly the proposals I made concerning epistemic utility in (1967a) and (1967c).

I supposed that in the context of an effort to find an answer to a question via induction from the total evidence available, the agent is concerned to promote two desiderata: (i) to avoid error where what counts as an error is based on the assumption that his total evidence is true and is certainly so, and (ii) to obtain new information pertaining to the question under investigation.

Desideratum (i) was represented by an epistemic utility function $T_b(g; x)$ or $T_j(g; x)$ where the variable x takes the two values 'true' and 'false' as follows:

(a) $T_b(g; t) = 1$
$T_b(g; f) = 0$

(b) $T_j(g; t) = 1$
$T_j(g: f) = 0$

The T_b-function given in (a) represents the utility afforded by accepting g as strongest via induction from b relative to U without and with error respectively when the only concern of the agent is to avoid importing error into his body of evidence. The T_j-functions given by (b) are to be understood in the same way except that the total evidence is b & e_j and the ultimate partition U_j.

From the agent's point of view when his total knowledge is $b(b$ & $e_j)$, he imports error by accepting g as strongest via induction if and only if g is false. One might, in some cases, represent g by a conjunction u & v and introduce some notion of partial error resulting when u is true and v false (or vice versa). However, I assumed that when u & v is the strongest conclusion accepted via induction from $b(b$ & $e_j)$, such partial errors are to be assigned the same T-values as total errors.

I represented the second desideratum by another epistemic utility function:

(c) $C_b(g) = 1 - M_b(g)$

(d) $C_j(g) = 1 - M_j(g)$.

The $C_b(C_j)$-function represents the informational value pertinent to the question under investigation afforded by adding g as strongest via induction from $b(b$ & $e_j)$ relative to $U(U_j)$. It represents the agent's 'demands for information'.

I took the $M_b(M_j)$-function to be a normalized probability measure defined over Boolean combinations of elements of $U(U_j)$ and sentences equivalent given $b(b$ & $e_j)$ to such combinations. In addition, I assumed that as long as the agent's evaluations of informational value did not alter from the time his total evidence was b to the time it became b & e_j that the M_b-function and the M_j-function should be related by the following condition:

(e) $M_j(g) = M_b(w_j$ & $g)/M_b(w_j)$.

The motive for (e) is that when the agent knows that b & e_j is true, he knows that w_j is true via deductive closure. In contemplating an induction from b & e_j, he is seeking information to his question additional to that conveyed by w_j which he already knows to be true. This could be represented as follows:

(f) $C_b(w_j \& g) - C_b(w_j)$
$= M_b(w_j) - M_b(w_j \& g)$.

Since the functions I have introduced are intended to be utility functions which are unique up only to linear transformations, when e_j is fixed, as it is when b & e_j is known, $M_b(w_j)$ may serve as a constant for a similarity and, hence, a linear transformation. Dividing (f) by $M_b(w_j)$ yields the right hand side of (d) in virtue of (e).

Thus, (e) represents a conventional decision on my part to measure increments in the utility of information in one way rather than another. I chose this convention for the following reason. It seemed convenient to assign the T_b-functions and T_j-functions the values 1 and 0 although any other pair of values preserving order would have done just as well. It also seemed convenient to restrict the $C_b(C_j)$-values so that the maximum and minimum values possible would be the same as for the T_b-function (T_j-function). Other conventions could have been used provided appropriate adjustments were made in all the formulas I proposed. For better or for worse, I chose these conventions and plainly said so. (1967c, pp. 378–9.)

What was not a matter of convention was the assumption that the utility of information should be measured in terms of increments to the information already afforded by the available evidence. Not only is this condition plausible in its own right, violation of it (as is the practice of Hintikka and Pietarinen (1966) and Hilpinen (1968), leads to untenable consequences as I pointed out in (1967c, p. 374).

Given an appropriate $T_b(T_j)$-function and an appropriate $C_b(C_j)$-function, the epistemic utility function representing the goal of obtaining new error free information pertinent to the question under investigation was characterized by a weighted average as follows:

(g) $V_b(g; t) = \alpha + (1 - \alpha)(1 - M_b(g))$
$V_b(g; f) = (1 - \alpha)(1 - M_b(g))$.

(h) $V_j(g; t) = \alpha + (1 - \alpha)(1 - M_j(g))$
$V_j(g; f) = (1 - \alpha)(1 - M_j(g))$.

Values of α were restricted to the interval from 0.5 to 1. Moreover, as long as the agent did not modify his objectives when acquiring the information that e_j is true, I assumed that the value of α in (h) is the same as that in (g).

Relative to b, the agent was supposed to have a credal state representable by a probability distribution $P(g; b)$ over the elements of U and other hypotheses relevant to the problem. Relative to b & e_j, he was supposed to have a credal state representable by $P(g; b$ & $e_j)$ subject to the conditionalizing requirement that $P(g$ & $e_j; b) = P(g; b$ & $e_j)P(e_j; b)$.

Given this apparatus, relative to $b(b$ & $e_j)$, the expected epistemic utility of accepting g as strongest via induction relative to $U(U_j)$ is as follows:

(i) $\alpha P(g; b) + (1 - \alpha)(1 - M_b(g)) = EV_b(g)$

(j) $\alpha P(g; b$ & $e_j) + (1 - \alpha)(1 - M_j(g)) = EV_j(g)$.

Dividing by α and then subtracting by $q = (1 - \alpha)/\alpha$ yields the following:

(k) $P(g; b) - qM_b(g)$

(l) $P(g; b$ & $e_j) - qM_j(g)$.

(k) and (l) are linear transformations of the left hand sides of (i) and (j) respectively and, hence, rank cognitive options in the same way. I have used them for the purpose of deriving inductive acceptance rules and Goosens employs them when discussing my work. It makes no difference provided care is taken to be consistent in the conventions one uses to represent epistemic utilities. I shall continue to use (i) and (j).

Given total evidence b and ultimate partition U, one can identify those g's whose acceptance as strongest bears a maximum EV_b-value. Among these, g_b is the uniquely weakest one. I recommended that g_b should be accepted as strongest via induction from b relative to U if any expansion via induction is to be made at all.

Similarly, given the total evidence b & e_j, a recommended g_j is identified for acceptance as strongest via induction from b & e_j relative to U_j.

This, in a nutshell, is the theory I proposed in (1967a) and (1967c) for evaluating rival ways of adding new information via induction relative to fixed evidence, a fixed ultimate partition and a fixed value for α.

4

Let us now turn to Goosens' problem. In the light of my theory, what expected epistemic utility function should be used to assign values to the Z-function in conformity with condition (A)? Goosens tries out the idea that we should use EV^* – i.e., the function defined as follows:

(m) $EV^*(g; e_j) = EV_j(g)$.

Values for the EV_j-function are, of course, those given by (j).
Hence, Goosens assumes the following:

(n) $Z(e_j) = EV_j(g)$.

This cannot be right! My V_j-function represents a weighted average of the utility of avoiding error and of obtaining informational value added via induction to that already afforded by the available evidence b & e_j. When the agent is evaluating rival experiments relative to total evidence b and identifies g_j as optimal to accept via induction from b & e_j relative to U_j were he to find out that e_j is true, the total informational value he should impute to finding out that e_j is true should be equal to $C_b(w_j$ & $g_j)$ which is the increment he adds to the information already available in his knowing that b is true. But as we have seen, the V_j-function takes into account only the difference $C_b(w_j$ & $g_j) - C_b(w_j)$. Consequently, (n) ignores the informational benefits accruing from finding out that w_j is true via deduction from b & e_j. Thus, to use (n) would be to contradict the point of view I explicitly endorsed in my previous publications.

More generally, the point of view advanced in my previous work implies that the V-function used to determine the epistemic utilities afforded by implementing experiment X, observing that e_j is true, adding w_j via deduction from b & e_j and g via induction should be representable by a weighted average of $T_b(w_j$ & $g; x)$ and $C_b(w_j$ & $g)$. For remember, we are now concerned to construct an EV-function in order to assign Z-values and, hence, EZ-values for the purpose of evaluating alternative experiments relative to b.

But now we must consider a point which was not explicitly discussed in my previous work. In case both w_j added via deduction from b & e_j and g added via induction are true, we should expect $T_b(w_j$ & $g; t) = 1$ as previously stipulated. The total information added via both deduction and induction is obtained without error and that should be accorded the same T_b-value as would be the case if that information were obtained entirely via induction from b. Consequently, the following must obtain:

(o) $\quad V(w_j$ & $g; t, t) = V_b(w_j$ & $g; t)$
$\qquad\qquad\qquad = \alpha + (1 - \alpha)(1 - M_b(w_j$ & $g))$.

Similarly, the case where as a result both w_j and g are false so that the new information is totally false should be assigned a value equal to $T_b(w_j$ & $g; f) = 0$.

(p) $\quad V(w_j$ & $g; f, f) = V_b(w_j$ & $g; f)$
$\qquad\qquad\qquad = (1 - \alpha)(1 - M_b(w_j$ & $g))$.

What about the case of 'partial error' where w_j is true and g is false? In my previous work where I only considered situations where the total new information added to b was added via induction relative to U, this possibility was not explicitly considered at all. It differs from that case precisely because the part of the new information added without error is added via deduction from b & e_j. Since I did not discuss the evaluation of experiments, I did not consider this possibility at all.

But this possibility becomes important in the current context. The reason is this: The EV-function has a double purpose. For fixed e_j, it is to be used to identify the g_j to be accepted as strongest via induction from b & e_j. By condition (A), when it is used in this capacity it should yield the same result as using the EV_j-function. The EV-function also determines the values of the Z-function.

Now if it is to serve in the former capacity, the following should be clear: what counts as a total error when b & e_j is known obtains if and only if g is false on the assumption that b & e_j is true and, hence, that w_j is true. Therefore, total error relative to b & e_j in accepting g via induction corresponds from the prior point of view to partial error through accepting w_j via deduction and g via induction.

Consequently, the EV-function should be defined as follows:

(q) $EV(g; e_j) = P(g; b \& e_j)V(w_j \& g; t, t) + P(\sim g; b \& e_j)V(w_j \& g; t, f)$.

Here, the V-value for partial error must be used instead of the V-value for total error.

Of course, as far as we have gone, it might turn out that $V(w_j \& g; t, f)$ should equal $V(w_j \& g; f, f) = V_b(w_j \& g; f)$. Once, however, we make full use of condition (A), it is demonstrable that this cannot be so.

If condition (A) holds, (o) implies that the following also obtains:

(r) $V(w_j \& g; t, t) = V_b(w_j \& g; t)$
$= a_j V_j(g; t) + b_j$
$= a_j \alpha + a_j(1 - \alpha)(1 - M_j(g)) + b_j$.

Utilizing (e), (o) and (r), we can solve for a_j and b_j to obtain the following:

(s) $a_j = M_b(w_j)$
$b_j = M_b(\sim w_j)$.

Invoking (s) and condition (A), we know that

(t) $V(w_j \& g; t, f) = a_j V_j(g; f) + b_j$
$= a_j(1 - \alpha)(1 - M_j(g)) + b_j$
$= (1 - \alpha)(M_b(w_j) - M_b(w_j \& g)) + M_b(\sim w_j)$.

(u) $T(w_j \& g; t, f) = M_b(\sim w_j)$
$= C_b(w_j)$.

Thus, partial errors afforded by adding w_j via deduction without error and via induction with error are assigned different epistemic utility from total error. This was not explicitly stated in my previous work. However, it is an implication of the point of view I did advance together with condition (A).

We are now in a position to construct an EV-function. However, here we must be careful. I have pretended thus far that condition (A) holds and claimed that this follows from the general Bayesian approach which Goosens seems to endorse.

This is not, however, strictly speaking so. When the agent contemplates conducting experiment X, making observations and adding the reports made in response to sensory stimulation to his knowledge and evidence, he need not and, in many instances, should not assume at the outset that the information he adds via observation will be true. Consequently, if he thinks his senses are fallible, he will entertain as a possibility that he will report that e_j is true, add it to his evidence together with w_j via deduction and g_j via induction where e_j is false. w_j is false and, hence, g_j is false (for g_j entails w_j). In short, in imputing a value for $Z(e_j)$, the agent will or should take into account the possibility that he will obtain total error.

It is possible to construct an EV-function from the materials provided here which does take this into account and can be used to impute Z-values as required by the first line of condition (A).

Notice, however, that when the agent is concerned to ascertain which g determined by U_j he should accept as strongest via induction on the assumption that b & e_j will be his total evidence, he is asked to make his calculations on the assumption that e_j and, hence, w_j is true. The expected epistemic utilities computed there should not take into account the possibility of total error. The EV-function so computed is as follows:

$$(v) \quad EV(g; e_j) = P(g; b \& e_j)V(w_j \& g; t, t) + P(\sim g; b \& e_j)V(w_j \& g; t, f)$$
$$= M_b(\sim w_j) + \alpha M_b(w_j)P(g; b \& e_j) + (1 - \alpha)(M(w_j)$$
$$- M_b(w_j \& g)).$$

This EV-function is a linear transformation relative to fixed e_j of $EV_j(g)$ as the second line of condition (A) requires. However, it does not satisfy the requirements of the first line as long as the agent regards the testimony of his senses as fallible.

On the other hand, if the agent does consider his observation reports to be perfectly reliable or so nearly so as to warrant neglecting errors of observation, condition (A) will be satisfied or at least approximately satisfied in both parts by the function given by (v).

In effect, I have been assuming that the agent does presume the perfect reliability of his senses in evaluating experiments. In doing so, I have been operating on precisely those assumptions which Good and Goosens following him have at least tacitly employed. With this assumption in place, I have succeeded in identifying an EV-function flowing from my theory which satisfies both conditions specified by (A). Without the assumption, I could have obtained my results by invoking the second line together with a modified version of the first condition. The point would have remained the same: my theory does imply a definite epistemic utility function to use in the context of evaluating experiments provided the general approach to decision making employed by Goosens is accepted.

Let us, for the sake of the argument, continue to assume the perfect reliability of the senses. The question now arises: Is the function EV^* obtained for the same domain as the total EV-function by stipulating that $EV^*(g; e_j) = EV_j(g)$ a linear transformation of the EV-function given by (v)? If it were, it could be used to impute Z-values to the e_j's with equivalent results for the evaluation of experiments as are obtained by using the EV-function. Goosens' first suggested reading of my view would have been fully justified.

To guarantee that EV^* is a linear transformation of the EV-function, a_j must equal $a_{j'}$ and b_j must equal $b_{j'}$ for all e_j and $e_{j'}$ and for all experiments. This will obtain if and only if $M_b(w_j) = M_b(w_{j'})$ in all such comparisons.

This condition will fail even in the case of e_j and $e_{j'}$ relative to the same experiment – at least in many situations. It clearly must fail in any interesting comparison of experiments where e_j describes an outcome of X and $e_{j'}$ describes an outcome of X'. In particular, when a so-called ideal experiment is compared to a less than ideal experiment – where the ideal experiment is such that each possible outcome e_j entails $w_j = h_j$ for one and only one h_j in U and the less than ideal experiment fails to meet this condition – it is clear that the requirement for the function EV to be a linear transformation of EV^* (or vice versa) is not satisfied.

Thus, it follows that it is a mistake to equate $Z(e_j)$ with $EV^*(g_j; e_j) = EV_j(g_j)$ as Goosens initially suggests doing. It is not an open question that it is a mistake if my approach to epistemic utility is adopted.

I place great emphasis on this fact because nowhere in this argument have I taken into account the various conditions of adequacy which Goosens imposes on methods for evaluating experiments. No repairs *ad hoc* or otherwise were made for my theory in order to save it from conflict with these conditions. I simply worked out the implications of the theory for the evaluation of experiments utilizing assumptions which, for the sake of this argument, I share with Goosens. It turns out that the theory has very definite implications for Goosens' problem (counter to what he says) and that they contradict the proposal he suggests.

Because Goosens confused condition (A) with the condition that $Z(e_j)$ equal $EV_j(g_j)$ which is prohibited by condition (A) and the assumptions about how epistemic utility is to be evaluated introduced in my previous work, his subsequent exploration of the extent to which my proposals conform to his conditions of adequacy can carry no weight. Even if the correct EV-function is used and satisfies his conditions of adequacy, it is to be expected that using a function which is not a linear transformation of it will lead to conflicting evaluations and it is not at all surprising that Goosens' conditions of adequacy are violated.

Nonetheless, Goosens' question is an interesting one. Does the correct EV-function satisfy Goosens' conditions of adequacy and, if not, should it be required to do so? This is the problem which should now be examined.

5

Goosens' first set of conditions of adequacy for methods of comparing experiments – the ones which include a condition on so-called 'ideal' experiments – are given below with formulations modified to accommodate to differences in notation:

(R1) *The minimality of the sure experiment:* Let W be an experiment such that conditional on its implementation and relative to b, the outcome e will occur with certainty – i.e., $P(e; b) = 1$. Then for every experiment Y, $EZ(Y) \geqq EZ(W)$.

(R2) *The desirability of further experimentation:* Let XY stand for the joint experiment of doing both experiments X and Y. $EZ(XY) \geqq EZ(Y)$.

(R3) *The maximal preferability of the ideal experiment:* Let X^* be an ideal experiment in the sense that the e_j's in X match one to one with the h_i's in U and such that each e_j entails the corresponding h_i $(w_j = h_i)$. Then for all experiments Y, $EZ(X^*) \geqq EZ(Y)$.

Are these conditions of adequacy acceptable? Not without heavy qualification: (*i*) Suppose the agent's state of subjective probability relative to b is not representable by a numerically precise probability measure. In my opinion, Good's argument in (1967) for (R2) not only does not go through but (R2) goes wrong. I suspect that the other conditions become questionable as well; but I shall not elaborate upon these matters any further. (*ii*) Suppose the agent does not regard the testimony of his senses as perfectly reliable in all situations. Clearly a less than ideal experiment where the testimony of the senses is reliable might be preferable to an ideal experiment where the testimony of the senses is less than reliable. (*iii*) It seems to me that even when an investigator can implement an ideal experiment without side costs, the conclusions he may be justified in reaching relative to what he currently knows via induction might be sufficiently decisive that he considers further investigation and experimentation pointless. This could be so even if the circumstances specified in (*i*) and (*ii*) do not obtain. I am not sure about this remark; but I am inclined to think that a point is reached where enough is enough and that this point can be reached short of obtaining information from an ideal experiment. This hunch guided some of the tentative suggestions I made in (1967*a*) concerning how Shackle's account of potential surprise can be applied in connection with an evaluation of weight of evidence. However, I am not as yet prepared to elaborate on this idea any further but simply put it forth as a doubt.

Nonetheless, I am prepared to concede that if the agent's state of subjective probability is numerically precise, if he assumes throughout the infallibility of his senses and if he thinks it worthwhile at all to compare rival experiments (including the 'sure' or null experiment) rather than to decide without such comparison that 'enough is enough', the agent's evaluations should satisfy Goosens' three requirements. I shall suppose, therefore, that these three conditions are satisfied and that conformity to Goosens' conditions is to be required.

Does the EZ-function determined by the EV-function defined by (v) meet

Goosens' conditions? The answer is that it does. In an appendix to his essay, Goosens proves that if the h_i's are probabilistically independent of the possible ways in which they might be rejected and when the epistemic utilities afforded by the act of implementing an experiment, expanding via deduction by adding the appropriate w_j and then via induction by adding the appropriate g depend only on which of the h_i's is true and the three-step 'act' just described, the conditions (R1), (R2), and (R3) are satisfied. Goosens' proofs are derived from results of I. J. Good (1967a) which hold, incidentally, only on the provisos I specified for Goosens' conditions of adequacy.

Inspection of the epistemic utility values given by (o) and (t) show that they satisfy Goosens' requirements. Hence, my proposals, by Goosens' own arguments, satisfy his requirements.

Now the total function V^* obtained from the V_j's implicit in constructing the function EV^* from the EV_j's which Goosens considers when he equates $Z(e_j)$ with $EV_j(g_j)$ depends for its values not merely on whether g is true or false (or which of the h_i's is true) but also on e_j and the w_j entailed by b & e_j. This is because $V_j(g; x)$ fails to take into account the information added to b via deduction from b & e_j. When that information is fixed as it is when we are comparing rival cognitive options relative to our total evidence, nothing untoward happens. But when we are evaluating experiments, the omission is disastrous. Goosens' demonstration that his three conditions are violated by equating $Z(e_j)$ with $EV^*(g_j; e_j)$ and my proof that they are obeyed by equating $Z(e_j)$ with $EV(g_j; e_j)$ illustrate the point.[1]

---

1 In (1963a), I explored the possibility of construing Popper's corroboration measures as measures of expected epistemic utility. I discovered that this could not be done without implying that the epistemic utility of accepting g as strongest via induction (terminology I did not use at the time) without error and in total error would depend on the available evidence. I took this to be an objection on the grounds that it violates von Neumann–Morgenstern approaches to utility. Actually my formulation was too strong and, it should be apparent, that the epistemic utility functions I eventually proposed in (1967a) and (1967c) do allow epistemic utilities to vary with the evidence. What was crucial was that, in the context of a given decision problem, the agent be in a position to assign utilities to possible consequences in a manner which he would not be obliged to alter due to changes in the probabilities he assigned to these consequences. Alternatively stated, when expected utilities are computed, the utilities and probabilities used should be representable as independent variables neither of which is a function of the other. This cannot be done when Popper's corroboration measures are represented as expected utilities. In (1963a), I suggested using, as an improvement on Popper's approach, the epistemic utility functions subsequently advocated by Hintikka and Pietarinen in (1966) and Hilpinen in (1968). These measures are functions of prior probabilities but can be, nonetheless, regarded as independent of the posterior probabilities used to compute expectations (for the posteriors depend on likelihoods as well as priors). In (1967c), I explained the objections to this approach which led me to abandon the idea when I wrote (1967a) and why, therefore, the view advanced in Hilpinen (1968) and Hintikka and Pietarinen (1966) seems to me to be untenable.

The proposals I made in (1967a) and (1967c) do yield V_j-functions which are relative to the total evidence but are not functions of the credal or expectation determining probabilities.

Goosens' diagnosis of the troubles with using $Z(e_j) = EV^*(g_j; e_j) = EV_j(g_j)$ is that epistemic utility is made to depend on the evidence. The diagnosis is correct as far as it goes but it does

Goosens introduces yet another set of conditions of adequacy (conditions on 'efficiency'). I am not sure I even understand the content of these conditions. They seem to me to be ambiguous. Instead of attempting to interpret them here, let me say a few remarks concerning what I think the main import of his discussion of efficiency is. Goosens, I conjecture, takes the position that in evaluating experiments we should be able to do so without having any cognitive or, for that matter, practical objective in mind. There should be some way of doing so which is neutral between the diverse aims of different investigators or scientific communities and which, in this sense, can give an 'objective' appraisal of experiments relative to the background *b*.

It should be obvious to everyone that I reject that point of view. I do not believe that there is any useful reason for conducting an experiment except when the agent has some end in view. The very arguments of I. J. Good which Goosens uses at some stages of his discussion are predicated on the same point of view. Even if one rejects the view I advance that one can identify objectives which are characteristically cognitive or scientific, it seems to me that no experimentation is worthwhile unless one has some other sort of aim in mind.

I know of no way of proving to Goosens or to anyone else who shares what I think his view is that I am right, and I shall not attempt to muster whatever poor arguments are available to me to support it. But it is worth emphasizing that, given that I take this position, it is question begging to attempt to refute my proposals by conditions of adequacy which seem to rest on a contrary view. It would be all too easy to refute anything by elevating one's own theses to conditions of adequacy. I suspect that when the ambiguities in Goosens' conditions are sorted out, my proposals do violate them; but, unlike the case

not go deep enough. The dependency is vicious because the information and epistemic utility afforded by adding w_j via deduction from the data b & e_j to the initial background b is not taken into account. When this mistake is made, it then appears that if the same g is the g_j for b & e_j and the $g_{j'}$ for b & $e_{j'}$ the epistemic utility of accepting g as strongest without error (with error) is different due to differences in the evidence. But the same consequence should, so it seems, be assigned the same epistemic utility throughout. Observe, however, that, relative to b, the two consequences are not the same. One is a case of adding w_j & g to b and the other of adding $w_{j'}$ & g to b. On the assumption that there is a difference in epistemic utility added via deduction and that added via induction, the dependency on the evidence ceases to be vicious. What is mistaken is neglecting the informational value obtained by adding new information via deduction from the new evidence.

Once this mistake is corrected by using *EV*-values instead of *EV**-values to determine *Z*-values, it becomes clear that any vicious dependencies on evidence are circumvented. The values of $V(w_j$ & $g; x, y)$ are determined by the truth values of w_j and g alone which is sufficient for Goosens' conditions (R1), (R2), and (R3).

It is amusing to note that Goosens cites the advantages of the Hintikka–Pietarinen–Hilpinen approach in connection with conditions (R1), (R2), and (R3) because it avoids dependence on the evidence in determining epistemic utility. This observation parallels the move I made in (1963*a*). We have come nearly (but not, I hope, quite) full circle. None-theless, Goosens rejects the Hintikka–Pietarinen–Hilpinen approach for the reasons cited in (1967*c*).

of his first set of conditions, that can scarcely be decisive concerning the fundamental issues over which we apparently differ.

In spite of these negative remarks, I wish to reiterate my high regard for this fine paper. Goosens has asked worthwhile questions concerning the ramifications of my proposals. He has developed his own competent and responsible examination of these questions with the cautious good sense to recognize that his arguments are not decisive. I am grateful to Goosens for having posed a serious challenge to my theory. Although I myself am not convinced that we have, as yet, a satisfactory account of design of experiments, I think my theory does successfully meet his challenge.

7

Abduction and demands for information[†]

1 Cognitive states

The main preoccupation of students of the growth of knowledge should be to explore criteria for evaluating revisions of cognitive states of rational agents.

Any bearer of propositional attitudes or decision maker whose attitudes may appropriately be appraised with regard to coherence or consistency qualifies as an agent. Thus, not only persons but families, corporations and communities of scientific investigators may be agents and have cognitive states.

My concern now, however, is not with who or what is a bearer of cognitive states. If we are to consider improvements in knowledge, we should have some view of what is to count as a change in knowledge or cognitive state. Discussions of the growth of knowledge deriving from Popper, Kuhn and other critics of that mythological creature, the received view of philosophy of science, have paid scant attention to what it is that changes and improves or deteriorates when scientific or any other sort of knowledge changes.

Of course, students of both 'foundationalist' and 'naturalist' epistemologies often provide characterizations of knowledge and, by implication, states of knowledge. Looking backwards, they hope to distinguish between those elements of current belief or doctrine which qualify as knowledge from those which do not by reference to how they were acquired. But just because one acquired a belief in a dubious manner does not imply that one should jettison it in order to improve one's knowledge state. Nor, indeed, need it be necessary to appreciate how one could have obtained a correct belief legitimately in order for that belief to be as solid a citizen in one's doctrine as it could be. Pedigree may sometimes be relevant to the improvement of knowledge but only occasionally so.

Thus, we must consider how pedigree epistemologists (i.e., foundationalists and naturalists) characterize belief states rather than knowledge states. And here we find little attention to characterizations which provide us

[†] Reprinted with some modifications with the permission of the editors of *Acta Fennica Philosophica* from 'Abduction and demands for information', *The Logic and Epistemology of Scientific Change* edited by I. Niiniluoto and R. Tuomela, North Holland for Societas Philosophica Fennica (1979), pp. 405–29.

with some understanding as to why we should be interested in improving cognitive states so construed.

I stand with John Dewey who thought of human knowledge as a 'resource' for inquiry and deliberation. I wish to furnish an account of cognitive states according to which X's cognitive state at a given time serves as a resource at that time in X's practical deliberations and his theoretical inquiries. (See Levi, 1976a, 1980a, and 1983b.)

I suggest that cognitive states be taken as serving as standards for evaluating truth value bearing hypotheses with respect to serious possibility and credal probability. To explain this, restrict attention to truth value bearing hypotheses expressible in some suitably regimented first order language L.

Agent X's corpus of knowledge or evidence $K_{X,t}$ at t is representable by all sentences in L expressing hypotheses whose falsity X is committed at t to discounting as not seriously possible. X need not be capable of identifying all such items explicitly. He need not possess the superhuman abilities to store information and make computations required for such explicit identification nor need he have the mental or social good health also required for that purpose.

Nonetheless, rational X should be committed at time t to evaluations of all truth value bearing hypotheses within his conceptual purview with respect to serious possibility. Whether X is able to identify his commitments explicitly or not, his corpus $K_{X,t}$ consists of all hypotheses he is committed to regarding as not possibly false in the sense of serious possibility which guides deliberation and inquiry.

A potential corpus of knowledge or evidence or a potential standard for serious possibility K expressible in L should meet the following requirements:

(i) K should be deductively closed.

(ii) K should contain all sentences in L which belong to the urcorpus UK where UK meets the following conditions:

(a) UK contains all truths of first order logic expressible in L.

(b) UK contains all set theoretical and mathematical truths expressible in L.

I do not mean to specify exhaustively the contents of UK. If one potential corpus is a proper subset of another, it is weaker than the other in that it allows more hypotheses to be serious possibilities. UK is the weakest such potential corpus. To be committed to that corpus is to be committed to a 'state of maximal ignorance' insofar as hypotheses expressible in L are concerned. I do not wish to decide here what such a state should be.

It is customary to regard hypotheses as logically possible when they are logically consistent. But I see no point in using 'logically possible' for this purpose when we already have 'logically consistent'. I suggest, therefore, that we construe a hypothesis to be logically possible when it is seriously possible relative to the state of maximal ignorance. Of course, this obtains if and only if the hypothesis is consistent with the urcorpus. But this interpretation of logical possibility relates it to the conception of serious possibility which, I claim, has an important role in deliberation and inquiry.

To explain this role would require an account of rational decision making. An account of my views on these matters may be gleaned from (Levi, 1974, 1977b, and 1980a). For the present, it may suffice to note that when X considers hypotheses concerning the consequences of the options feasible for him, he considers only hypotheses whose truth is seriously possible according to him – i.e., hypotheses consistent with what he takes for granted, assumes true or accepts as evidence.

Just as X is committed to evaluations of truth value bearing hypotheses with respect to serious or personal possibility, so too he is committed to evaluations of such hypotheses with respect to credal or personal probability. Indeed, evaluations with respect to personal probability are introduced to make finer discriminations among hypotheses judged possibly true.

X's *credal state* (i.e., his system of evaluations with respect to credal or personal probability) should be representable by a non-empty set B of real valued functions of the form $Q(h; e)$ defined for all e consistent with K such that for fixed e consistent with K, $Q(h; e)$ is non negative, finitely additive and where if $K, e \vdash h$, $Q(h; e) = 1$. Furthermore, for $e \& f$ consistent with K, $Q(h \& f; e) = Q(h; f \& e) \cdot Q(f; e)$. Finally, B satisfies a convexity condition: if B_e is the set of Q-functions in B restricted by specifying the fixed value e as the second argument for each function, for every e consistent with K, B_e is convex.

To complete this brief account of X's cognitive state, the notion of a *confirmational commitment* is also required. At t, X is committed to a rule specifying for each potential corpus the credal state X should endorse relative to that corpus. The function $C_{X,t}(K)$ should meet the requirement of confirmational conditionalization which I have formulated in (1974, 1977b, and 1980a).

If X is committed to such a rule, it follows immediately that his confirmational commitment $C_{X,t}$, corpus $K_{X,t}$ and credal state $B_{X,t}$ must satisfy the following requirement: $C_{X,t}(K_{X,t}) = B_{X,t}$. This is the principle of *total knowledge* or *total evidence*. Once it is granted that X should be committed to a rule for selecting a credal state relative to diverse potential corpora, this principle is entirely trivial.

What is nontrivial is the adoption of the confirmational commitment to be used together with the principle of total evidence to determine one's credal state. This seems to me to be the chief kernel of truth in A. J. Ayer's critique of the total evidence requirement (Ayer, 1957).

Of course, someone might wonder why X should be saddled with a commitment to a rule of the sort being considered. I cannot offer any argument to determine decisively that he should. However, the assumption is a very weak one. I have not assumed that X should be wedded to a specific confirmational commitment. I have not assumed that he should be committed to the same commitment all the time. Nor have I assumed that the commitment specifies numerically precise credal states for each potential corpus. To the contrary, these credal states could all be maximally indeterminate.

Near trivial though it may be, however, the total knowledge requirement establishes a link between the three components of a cognitive state additional to the conditions imposed on the three components separately.

An account of the improvement or the growth of knowledge ought to focus attention on the rational revision of cognitive states construed in the manner briefly outlined here. This account links cognitive states with deliberation and inquiry through a theory of rational choice. Cognitive states become resources for inquiry and deliberation. A study of how they ought to be improved becomes an account of how such resources are to be bettered. When reading Popper, Kuhn, or Feyerabend, one often wonders why one should care about the growth of knowledge altogether. On the account I am suggesting of what constitutes a cognitive state, an answer is, for better or for worse, forthcoming: cognitive states provide guidance in deliberation and inquiry. It matters, therefore, how we revise them.

As long as X holds faithful to his confirmational commitment, revisions of credal state depend on revisions of corpora of knowledge or evidence. To the extent that rational agents should conform to the dictates of confirmational tenacity, an account of the revision of credal states reduces to an account of the revision of bodies of knowledge.

Confirmational tenacity, however, is not always warranted and an account of the revision of confirmational commitments is also needed. But criteria for the revision of confirmational commitments are parasitic on criteria for the revision of bodies of knowledge. The question, however, is too complicated and I shall not deal with it here. Yet, if I am right, the lynchpin of an account of the revision of cognitive states is an account of the revision of knowledge. (See Levi, 1980a, ch. 13.)

All legitimate revisions of knowledge, so I claim, are either contractions or expansions or sequences of these as I have argued in Levi, 1980a and 1983b. Shifting from K_1 to K_2 is a *contraction* if K_1 contains K_2 and is an *expansion* if K_2 contains K_1. I shall not discuss contractions here.

Legitimate expansions fall into two broad categories: *routine* or *noninferential* expansions and *deliberate, inferential* or *inductive* expansions.

Routine expansion is the result of implementing a program, to which the agent is committed beforehand, for using the testimony of the senses or of other agents as inputs where the outputs are expansions. The agent lets the input determine how he expands his corpus. He does not decide on the basis of the total information available to him which of rival expansions of his corpus is best. To proceed in the latter fashion is to expand deliberately, inferentially or inductively.

One sort of routine is an observational routine. In response to sensory stimulation, men make observation reports. Making an observation report that h is an episodic propositional attitude sometimes manifested in verbal utterance but by no means necessarily so. Whatever the psychological or physiological processes involved might be, reporting that h is true should not be confused with adding h to the corpus of knowledge or evidence. The reports which X makes in response to sensory stimulation depend on his sensory apparatus, past training, and his body of knowledge in ways I do not pretend to understand. If his responses are perfectly reliable in some domain, for every sentence within that domain which X reports true, that sentence is true. If X were to know this to be so, he would be justified in training himself so that he will routinely respond to his making observation reports that h by expanding his corpus through adding h to the corpus along with the deductive consequences. At least, he will commit himself to this practice.

Of course, it is well known that the senses are rarely perfectly reliable. Sometimes, however, X will know that a given observational routine involves a systematic error (due, for example, to defective depth perception). In such cases, X might modify the routine by adding correction g to his corpus when he reports that h.

But, as with any measuring apparatus, relying on the senses involves random error. Consequently, in adopting routines for expansion via observation, X will typically have to rest content with using routines for which the error probabilities (where 'probability' = 'chance' = 'statistical probability') are sufficiently low although not necessarily 0.

Routine expansion via observation is supplemented by routine expansion through the reports of others. Once more the merits of a routine of this sort depend on correcting it for systematic error and evaluating random errors.

There are other sorts of routine decision making besides routine expansion. Observation reports or the testimony of others can be used as inputs in programs whose outputs are 'decisions' of various sorts. Neyman and Pearson undertook to develop a statistical theory providing accounts of procedures for using such inputs in routine decision making. We often think of Neyman's conception of inductive behavior as focusing on statistical decision making. But it is somewhat narrower than that. Neyman's conception concerns routine statistical decision making where the agent utilizes the same program over and over again for letting the outcome of some stochastic process decide for him what policy to follow. It is important to understand this: On the one hand, decision making according to Neyman and Pearson differs from deliberate decision making where one evaluates rival policies utilizing the total evidence available as evidence and not as input into a program (this is the sort of decision making dealt with by

Bayesians) and, on the other hand, just as criteria for legitimate deliberate decision making can be applied in cognitive as well as practical contexts, so can criteria for routine decision making.

Thus, I think the contrast between inductive behavior and inductive inference is rather misleading. Neyman's contrast is between routine decision making and deliberate decision making.

Of course, evaluation of rival routines is itself a piece of deliberate decision making. Consequently, one cannot dispense with the need for an account of deliberate decision making. Nor, for that matter, can one dispense with routine decision making. The difficult problem is to identify their respective domains of applicability. This difficulty carries over to the special case where we are concerned with the expansion of a corpus of knowledge. To what extent should we seek to restrict expansion to routine expansion and to what extent should we provide for deliberate or inductive expansion?

Followers of the Neyman–Pearson–Wald approach tend to view many kinds of problems in statistics, such as the estimation of parameters, as problems of routine expansion or routine practical decision making. In my opinion, many of these problems should be regarded as cases of deliberate, inferential or inductive expansion. This disagreement derives from differences in cognitive, ethical, and political values. (Levi, 1980a, ch. 17.)

In any case, I contend that there is at present and always will be a wide scope for deliberate inductive expansion. In the remaining portions of this paper, I shall discuss certain aspects of inductive expansion.

2 Potential answers

Efforts at expansion begin with the agent demanding some kind of information not already available in his corpus of evidence. At the outset, the investigator might not be very clear concerning the kind of information he is seeking and his first task will be to convert his 'indeterminate situation' (to borrow and modify a term of Dewey's (1938, ch. VI)) to a determinate one where he can identify what his 'cognitive options' are or, equivalently, identify a list of potential answers to his question.

Abductive logic furnishes criteria for evaluating proposed potential answers to a given question to determine whether, given the demands for information and the available knowledge, they are, indeed, potential answers.

Some aspects of the process of abduction cannot be regulated by an abductive logic in any general and systematic manner. Clearly the subject matter of the investigation is of critical relevance to whether a putative potential answer is, indeed, one. Abduction exercises little control over this. On the other hand, there are some aspects of abduction which can be dealt with systematically in a relatively context independent manner.

92

In particular, we may insist that a set of potential answers expressible in language L and relative to corpus K be representable in the following manner:

(a) An ultimate partition U of sentences in L exclusive and exhaustive relative to K is given where each element of U is consistent with K.

(b) A potential answer relative to U and K is adding to the corpus K sentences in the set $K_g - K$ where K_g is the result of adding g to K and forming the deductive closure and where, given the truth of all members of K, g is true if and only if some element of a specified subset of U is true. (When U is non-countably infinite, we may wish to restrict attention to measurable subsets of U.)

In the subsequent discussion, I shall consider only finite U. However, in cases of estimation of the value of a real valued parameter, U will be non-countably infinite and it is important, therefore, to take such situations seriously in a fully general treatment.

The g in K_g is a strongest sentence added to the evidence via induction. We can always represent a potential answer by such a sentence rather than by $K - K_g$. The two modes of representation are equivalent as both are to the representation by the expanded corpus K_g.

The set of potential answers is determined by the ultimate partition U. At various stages of the process of abduction the investigator will have different ultimate partitions.

In many cases, at the beginning of inquiry, X may have no idea of what he takes to be a potential answer. At least, so we might say in ordinary language. In the systematic presentation I am proposing, there are indeed potential answers. The ultimate partition contains exactly one element or, more accurately, one equivalence class of elements. Any item in K is itself the sole element of U. The set of potential answers consist of accepting that element as strongest (i.e., refusing to modify K at all) and of contradicting oneself.

Relative to such a U, the two options are, in effect, not to expand at all but to remain in suspense and to expand into contradiction. The latter is deliberate courting of error. The former yields no new information. In this sense, the situation is indeterminate given the demands for information. X should seek a more determinate U. In the interim, needless to say, he should not expand at all.

Subsequently X might identify hypotheses $h_1, h_2, ..., h_{n-1}$ whose acceptance as strongest would add new information to his corpus gratifying his demand for information. The h_j's are all consistent with K and no more than one is true given that all items in K are true. However, such a set does not qualify as an ultimate partition unless it is exhaustive given K. It is trivial that such a set can be made exhaustive by introducing the hypothesis h_n that the first $n - 1$ alternatives are false.

To be sure, the residual hypothesis (to use Shackle's (1961, p. 49) phrase) may fail to gratify X's demands for information very well. If X wishes to know who killed Cock Robin where he already knows that some one individual did so, he will be satisfied with the answer 'The Cook did it' or 'The Butler did it' – provided they are true. But the answer 'Neither the Butler nor the Cook did it' may seem too indeterminate to fully satisfy X's demand for information – even when true.

Similarly X may seek a theory to explain phenomena in some domain and succeed in identifying T_1 and T_2. Relative to K, they are exclusive and consistent but not exhaustive. To form an ultimate partition, a residual hypothesis asserting the falsity of both T_1 and T_2 will be required. But rejecting both theories (and thereby accepting the residual hypothesis) is a cognitive option – i.e., a potential answer – and, hence, should be taken into consideration. This is so even though the residual hypothesis has little explanatory merit.

At a given stage of inquiry when X's corpus is K and his ultimate partition is U, X will often be able to take some element of U – say h_j – and repartition it – e.g., into h_j & $f \lor h_j$ & $\sim f$. However, neither of these alternatives represents a potential answer gratifying X's demands for information any better than accepting h_j as strongest does.

To be sure, for some elements of U, X might wish that he could find a way of repartitioning them into hypotheses which do satisfy his demands for information better. This is so in the case of so called residual hypotheses. But in the context in which U is X's ultimate partition, no such repartitioning of U has been devised. Both Schick and Niiniluoto seem to think of my ultimate partitions as being always perfectly determinate in the sense that given X's demands for information, he regards further repartitioning under all circumstances as pointless.[1] That is not my understanding of ultimate partitions. The elements of X's ultimate partition at a given stage of inquiry

---

1 Schick (1970) and Niiniluoto (1975). That is to say, these authors take exception to my views relative to an interpretation of ultimate partitions in this way. It is on this interpretation that it should be objectionable to insist that ultimate partitions be exhaustive. Schick correctly objects. Niiniluoto introduces a distinction between open and closed questions. For closed questions, he writes 'we are in a position to give an effective method of enumerating or of building the potential answers' (1975), p. 275. His subsequent argument to the effect that inquiries are concerned with open questions does not, however, seem to me to proceed on this construal of open questions. In a case of estimating the value of a real valued parameter, the ultimate partition is a set of real numbers in some interval and the potential answers are representable by Lebesgue measurable subsets. But this characterization does not put us in a position to effectively enumerate the potential answers. Yet, I suspect Niiniluoto would consider the question closed. Niiniluoto seems to mean that an open question is one where the set of propositions eligible for acceptance as strongest form an 'atomless' Boolean or σ-algebra. That is to say, he maintains that in such inquiries there are no strongest consistent potential answers. I am inclined to think he is mistaken about this and that his thinking otherwise derives from a confusion between this thesis and the true observation that scientific inquiry is a non-terminating process. But even if he is right and I am wrong about this, this

consist of those hypotheses whose acceptance as strongest represent strongest consistent potential answers given X's demands for information and his current ability to identify potential answers gratifying demands for information. Perhaps, X should continue to pursue the process of abduction and refine his partition by constructing new potential answers. But pending such efforts, the ultimate partition he has is the only one he has relevant to the question under investigation.

In other words, I do not think that X's ultimate partition is always perfectly determinate relative to his demands for information in the sense that he regards it as pointless to seek any sort of partition of any item in the ultimate partition.

Some situations come close to satisfying the requirements of perfect determinateness given the demands for information. Estimating the value of a parameter known to be binomial is generally a perfectly determinate one; for U consists of all real values between 0 and 1. A point estimate of any of these values would gratify the demand for information so well that no additional information would be called for.

But in other cases such as looking for a theoretical systematization of some domain, we are often stuck with some unavoidable measure of indeterminacy. In such cases, there will be need to include a relatively indeterminate residual hypothesis in the ultimate partition.

Under these circumstances, the investigator must decide when to stop the process of devising and refining and rendering more determinate his ultimate partition and consider the evaluation of rival potential answers from among those identified. I have no counsel to give here except the obvious – to wit, that termination of the abduction process depends on the wit of the investigator, the cost of deliberation in money and effort and the extent of indeterminacy in the ultimate partition already available. Finally, it should be noted that even if X has decided to terminate abduction, he may, after the evaluation of the available potential answers in the light of his evidence or in the light of new evidence obtained from further experimentation, comes to the conclusion that he should accept the residual hypothesis into his corpus.

In that event, X will have excellent reason to re-open the abductory process and seek to carve up the residual hypothesis into more determinate potential answers.

---

does not touch my proposals. An ultimate partition for me represents the set of strongest consistent potential answers available to the agent at the given stage of inquiry and not the strongest consistent potential answers which in some obscurely defined sense are 'in principle' available. Of course, even here it is entertainable that some sets of potential answers for some problems can be identified which are characterized by atomless Boolean or σ-algebras. The procedures I have devised do not cover such cases and I am not clear in detail how to proceed with such cases. However, I think real problems rarely present themselves in that form – if they ever do.

One further aspect of my characterization of potential answers deserves emphasis.

The potential answers consist not only of cases of accepting elements of U as strongest via induction and of accepting the disjunction of all elements of U as strongest – i.e., of total suspension of judgement. There are intermediate forms of suspension of judgement.

Neither Hempel nor I gave consideration to such intermediate forms in our early work on cognitive decision making and inductive expansion (Hempel, 1960, 1962, and Levi, 1960a, 1962).

Even today there is a tendency to overlook the obligation to consider all possible modes of suspension of judgement between elements of an ultimate partition. Sometimes the topic of point estimation is discussed as if, in point estimation, the only cognitive options are accepting the strongest point estimates of parameters. This absurdity is one (though not the only) source of the tendency to draw a distinction between point and interval estimation. Insofar as estimation is a topic in inductive expansion, there is no interesting distinction between the problem of point and interval estimation. The ultimate partition consists of point estimates. Interval estimates represent various sorts of suspension of judgement.

3 Epistemic utility

Ever since writing (Levi, 1962), I have defended the idea that the proximate goals of diverse efforts to expand a corpus of knowledge share a common concern: the acquisition of error-free information. Goals of this type involve a conflict between two different desiderata: the concern to avoid error and the concern to obtain new information or 'relieve agnosticism'.

In (Levi, 1967a), I proposed representing these two desiderata by distinct epistemic utility functions. $T(g; x)$ represents the epistemic utility of accepting g as strongest via induction in the interest of avoiding error. When g is true so that $x = t$, $T(g; t) = 1$. When g is false, $T(g; f) = 0$. (The T-function can be any linear transformation of the one just specified but this particular one is convenient to use.)

$C(g; t) = C(g; f) = C(g)$ represents the epistemic utility of accepting g as strongest via induction in the interest of obtaining new information regardless of truth value. I assume that $C(g) = 1 - M(g)$ for some M-function which is a finitely additive, non-negative and normalized probability measure over the Boolean algebra generated by U. Once more, any linear transformation of $C(g)$ will serve; but $C(g)$ itself is convenient to use.

To suppose that $C(g) = 1 - M(g)$ rather than $1/M(g)$ or $-\log M(g)$ is to assume that increments in informational utility afforded by rejecting a given element of U are the same regardless of how many other and which other elements of U are rejected. Thus, the choice of a measure of informational value from among these candidates is by no means a matter of complete indifference. The choice makes a difference both to the rules of acceptance and rejection one obtains and to the conception of the aims of efforts at expansion one is formulating. I cannot prove that my view is (in some unspecified sense) the correct one; but I believe it yields more attractive results than the alternatives.

In (Levi, 1967a and 1967c), I assumed that the epistemic utility function $V(g; x)$ representing the quest for error free information is a weighted average $\alpha T(g; x) + (1 - \alpha)C(g)$ where α is restricted to values from $\frac{1}{2}$ to 1 in order to secure that no error is preferred to any correct answer.

When $q = (1 - \alpha)/\alpha$, it can be shown that if X's credal state for the elements of U is representable by a single Q-function, the injunction to maximize expected utility combined with the advice to suspend judgement between all hypotheses whose acceptance as strongest is optimal yields the rule that X should reject all and only elements of U meeting the condition that $Q(h) < qM(h)$.

Although I did offer arguments for the assumption that the V-function should be a weighted average of the T-function and the C-function, the entire matter can be viewed from a more general perspective by exploiting arguments advanced by John Harsanyi (1955) in discussing conditions on legitimate ways of representing social utility functions as depending on utility functions representing the preferences of individual members of society. Harsanyi assumes that the social utility function satisfies the requirements of a von Neumann–Morgenstern utility as to the utility functions representing the individual preferences of members of society. He also assumes that if two prospects, states or hypotheses are indifferent according to every individual in society, they are indifferent from the social point of view as well. From these fairly (but not totally) benign assumptions, Harsanyi deduces the result that the social utility function must be a weighted average of the utility functions for the individuals.

Our problem here is not that of determining a social utility function as a function of individual utility functions. Rather it is to take seriously a point which Harsanyi fails to consider – namely, that individuals have preferences or values which are in tension due to commitments to conflicting desiderata or value systems. Hence, it will often be the case that an individual's system of preferences may be thought of as represented by a utility function which is itself a function of other utility functions each of which represents a desideratum or interest he is committed to taking into account in his deliberations.

The formal requirements introduced by Harsanyi apply with as much plausibility to the relation between utility functions representing desiderata and the utility function representing the 'resolution' of the 'conflict' between them as it does to the determination of social utility functions in terms of individual utility functions. Such a resolution becomes a weighted average of

97

or a linear transformation of such a weighted average of the utility functions representing the desiderata.

This, of course, is precisely the view of the matter I took concerning epistemic utility functions in (1967a) and (1967c). The V-function is a resolution of a conflict between the desire to avoid error represented by the T-function and the demand for new information represented by the C-function. Caution or boldness is manifested by the choice of a method of weighing the two desiderata.

Thus far, I have merely restated ideas concerning epistemic utility I have advanced elsewhere.

Consider, however, that both in cognitive and practical decision making, agents may have to take decisions without being in a position to resolve conflicts between diverse desiderata. Jacob may have to decide whether to marry Rachel, Leah or Zilpah (but only one of these) wishing to marry a beautiful woman who is also a cordon bleu cook. But it may turn out that Rachel is prettier than Zilpah who is, in turn, prettier than Leah whereas Leah cooks better than Zilpah who cooks better than Rachel. Jacob's values may be in conflict and he may have to make a decision without the opportunity to resolve the conflict.

In such situations, agent X's goals and values are not representable by a utility function unique up to a linear transformation. His goals and values should be represented by a set G of utility functions where G is both closed under positive linear transformations and is convex. Each distinct weighted average of the utility functions representing desiderata is a different potential resolution of the conflict between the desiderata which he has not as yet ruled out of consideration. Because X may fail to rule out all but one function (unique up to a positive linear transformation), his conflict may be unresolved and his utilities indeterminate – just as I have suggested probabilities may be.

In (Levi, 1974), I have outlined an account of rational choice for cases where credal probability judgement goes indeterminate which may be readily extended to cases where utilities go indeterminate.

It is entirely entertainable that rational X may be in conflict due to diverse demands for information which lead to different evaluations of cognitive options. Such conflicts can be represented by convex sets of epistemic utility functions over pertinent consequences of pertinent cognitive options.

Similarly X's credal state can go indeterminate.

In such cases, if the ultimate partition is given, the decision theory I favor recommends accepting as strongest via induction the disjunction of all hypotheses acceptable as strongest via induction when expected epistemic utility is computed using some permissible Q-function in B and some permissible epistemic utility function $V(g; x)$ from the permissible set.

Given a fixed ultimate partition U and, hence, a definite set of cognitive options, conflict in epistemic utility functions can arise in two distinct ways:

due to conflict concerning the index of boldness $q = (1 - \alpha)/\alpha$ to be used and due to the M-function to be endorsed. A somewhat more complex form of conflict arises due to conflict in the ultimate partition to be used. I shall consider each of these three matters in turn.

4 Boldness

Suppose the corpus K, ultimate partition U and M-function are fixed. The sole conflict concerns the value of q. It is trivial that the weighted average of two V-functions differing only in the value of q must be another V-function for which q takes a value intermediate between the initial pair of values. The criteria of rational choice described above imply that rational X should reject all and only those elements of U which, for every permissible Q-function, are such that $Q(h) < qM(h)$ for the lowest value of q in the range of values of q permitted. In other words, when in doubt as to how bold or cautious to be, adopt the maximum degree of caution or minimum degree of boldness among those under consideration.

5 Information

Suppose there is no conflict in the degree of boldness exercised or in the ultimate partition. What about conflict in the choice of M-function? In my early work on epistemic utility, I attempted to devise procedures for avoiding such conflicts. In a paper in which I undertook to reconstruct Popper's measures of corroboration as measures of expected epistemic utility, I came to the conclusion that such a reconstruction could not be achieved but that if one used the so called 'prior' probability – i.e., the unconditional Q-distribution according to one's confirmational commitment relative to the corpus of background knowledge or relative to the urcorpus – for each element of U, one obtained the so called relevance function $Q(h; e) - Q(h)$ as a measure of expected epistemic utility (Levi, 1963).

This measure was subsequently endorsed by Hintikka and Pietarinen (1966). Both Hilpinen (1968) and Niiniluoto (1975) have argued for the use of a prior probability as determining M-values.

This procedure, however, violates an elementary equivalence condition. If g and g' are equivalent given K, accepting g as strongest to add to K should represent the same potential expansion strategy or potential answer as accepting g' as strongest – even if g and g' are not logically equivalent and, hence, do not or need not bear the same prior probability relative to the urcorpus or the 'background knowledge'. Consequently, using prior probability to determine M-values either violates this equivalence requirement or leads to unresolved ambiguities. Should one use the prior probability for g or g'? There seems no clear answer.

In (Levi, 1967a), I followed another strategy. I recommended always using an M-function assigning equal values to all elements of U.

I believe this method appropriate to certain kinds of demands for information. Hence, some of the applications made of this approach in (Levi, 1967a) continue to seem correct to me. However, as I emphasized in (Levi, 1967a), the procedure is limited in scope of applicability. In particular, in situations where the ultimate partition is highly indeterminate due to the need to introduce a residual hypothesis – as, for example, when X is able to identify one or two rival theories and must introduce a residual hypothesis which is not itself a theory into the ultimate partition – not all elements of U are of equal informational value.

Even if Popper's own methods for evaluating informational value through falsifiability are open to question, he is surely right in suggesting that the residual hypothesis is less informative (and, hence, has higher M-value) than the alternatives.

In (Levi, 1967a), I suggested that the appropriate epistemic utility function should be a weighted average of the T-function, the C-function and other functions representing the utility of simplicity, explanatory power and the like. I abandoned this view in (Levi, 1967c) along with the requirement that the M-function assign equal values to all elements of the ultimate partition.

Since (Levi, 1967c), I view choice between theories as cases where the epistemic utility function remains a weighted average of a T-function and C-function alone but where the C-function and the M-function determining the C-function take into account considerations of simplicity, explanatory power and other features of elements of the ultimate partition which do not depend on truth or probability of truth. Consequently, ever since I wrote (1967c), I have not thought of the choice of an ultimate partition as uniquely determining the M-function. Hence, it is possible, according to my view, for conflicts between demands for information to be conflicts between different M-functions even when the ultimate partition is fixed.

For example, X might be conflicted as to whether he takes theories allowing for action at a distance to bear higher explanatory and, hence, informational value than those which insist on contact action or whether he rates theories the other way around. This could lead to his endorsing as permissible M-functions several quite different functions. I now suggest that X should consider as permissible all potential resolutions of conflict – i.e., all weighted averages of the M-functions in conflict. That is to say, X should do so pending resolution of the conflict.

The upshot is that X should reject all and only those elements of U such that $Q(h) < qM(h)$ for all pairs consisting of a permissible Q-function in B and a permissible M-function.

100

Sometimes, however, the conflict between M-functions will be so severe that this method will lead to extremely weak conclusions. What should be done?

At this point, reference to the regulative ideals directing inquiry becomes pertinent. An M-function is an expression of a demand for new information in a specific context of inquiry. More specifically, it is an evaluation of potential answers with respect to how well they gratify demands for information.

When demands for information become controversial, this conflict is in turn often a manifestation of a conflict between different regulative ideals each of which specifies directions for worthwhile research. In recent times, such regulative ideals have been called paradigms or research programs. There are elaborate discussions concerning the structure of such ideals and how conflicts between them are adjudicated. In my opinion, these discussions do little to connect the choice of a research program or a paradigm to an account of how potential answers to a given question are to be evaluated in the context of a given inquiry relative to given background knowledge to determine an optimal revision of such knowledge. Yet, without such an account, no number of novels culled from the history of science will make much sense of the question as to how research programs or paradigms or other regulative ideals are modified.

Suppose that potential answer T_1 explains phenomena in some domain with the aid of a principle of action at a distance while T_2 invokes contact action alone. The ultimate partition consists of these alternatives and a residual R. R will obviously bear a higher M-value than the other two elements of the ultimate partition. X might, however, be in conflict concerning the explanatory adequacy of T_1 as compared to that of T_2.

One way of resolving the conflict would be to reflect on the relative merits of regulative ideals which rank contact action explanations and action at a distance explanations so differently.

But there is another way of proceeding. Sometimes the investigator can collect more data and perform more experiments. These may yield verdicts which are decisive even in the presence of conflict. Sufficient data might be obtained to warrant rejecting T_1 and not T_2 no matter what M-function among the permissible ones is employed.

I do not say that continuing inquiry will always lead to such a result. Perhaps we cannot always avoid appealing to a political process in dealing with regulative ideals. I myself am not sure how far one can go in resolving conflicts in demands for information in an objective manner.

But even if one has to concede something to political epistemology, the concession need not be disastrous for the objectivity of scientific inquiry; for it will often be the case that disagreements over research programs, paradigms and the like play less of a role in deciding the outcome of specific inquiries than many contemporary writers appear to believe.

Reaching definite conclusions may require more research and experimentation when conflict in demands for information and, hence, conflict in regulative ideals such as research programs or paradigms is rife; but, as in politics, so too in science a liberal approach can be successfully pursued only if we are prepared to pay the costs of deliberation and inquiry. This, as I understand it, is implicit in the views of liberals of pragmatist persuasion who follow John Dewey.

6 Ultimate partitions

Partition U^* (relative to K) is a *refinement* of U (also relative to K) if and only if every element of U is either an element of U^* or is equivalent given K to a disjunction of elements of U^* but U is not identical with U^* (or each element of U equivalent given K to an element of U^*).

Shifting from U to U^* is enlarging the set of potential expansion strategies or potential answers while preserving all potential answers relative to U.

Suppose X contemplates such a shift and wishes to avoid a revision of his initial assessments of epistemic utility relative to U. Only if such revision is not made can we say that X's demands for information have not been modified by the shift.

Under these circumstances, for every g which is a Boolean combination of elements of U and, hence, also of elements of U^*, $V^*(g; x) = V(g; x)$. What remains unsettled is how epistemic utilities are assigned to cases of accepting h as strongest where h is a Boolean combination of elements of U^* but not of elements of U.

One possibility is that V^* is an extension of the V-function to the Boolean combinations of U^* obtained by extending the T-function in the obvious way and extending the M-function in one of the infinitely many ways available.

Should X adopt such a V^*, this implies that he thinks the new list of potential answers renders his problem or situation more determinate relative to his demands for information. Thus, if the shift from U to U^* results from X's identifying a new theory and 'carves it out of' the residual hypothesis, he might continue to assign the theories already identified the M-values initially assigned and continue to evaluate the residual hypothesis in the same way. The innovation will be to apportion the M-value attributed to the old residual hypothesis to the new theory and the new residual hypothesis.

In such a case, a shift from U to U^* is, given the demands for information, an advance in clarity and determinateness. X's failure to make the shift previously derives from his lack of wit or energy or because the costs of the effort of inventing new hypotheses were too great under the prevailing circumstances.

A shift from U to U^* does not always yield potential answers of greater informational value. More accurately, let h be a Boolean combination of elements of U^* which is not a Boolean combination of elements of U. There is a unique Boolean combination $g = g(h)$ of elements of U (up to equivalence given K) which is the strongest such combination entailed by h (given K). As far as X is concerned, accepting h as strongest via induction bears epistemic utility $V(g; t)$ when g is true and $V(g; f)$ when g is false.

Thus, if X is interested in finding out who killed Cock Robin, accepting as strongest that the Butler did and Jimmy Carter will be elected to a second term as President of the United States has the same epistemic utility as accepting as strongest that the Butler killed Cock Robin.

When U and U^* are related in this fashion, the shift from U to U^* preserves X's initial demand for information – as in the previous case – but *fails to render it more determinate.*

Sometimes a shift from U to U^* renders the demand for information more determinate in part and partially fails to do so. This happens when the shift can be decomposed into two non-vacuous shifts: from U to refinement U' which renders the demand for information more determinate followed by a shift from U' to U^* which fails to render the demand for information still more determinate.

Notice that if the shift from U to U^* is of the second kind (where there is total failure to render the demand more determinate), then provided one always chooses the weakest of optimal cognitive options the prescription favored relative to U^* will coincide with the one favored relative to U. If the shift is of the third kind, the prescription favored relative to U^* will coincide with the one favored according to U'. If the shift is of the first kind, the prescription favored according to U^* will not necessarily be favored relative to U.

On the other hand, no revision of ultimate partition due to refinement where the demands for information are preserved can lead to rejecting elements of U relative to U^* which went unrejected when U was used as the ultimate partition.

Thus far, I have considered only cases where X has shifted his ultimate partition by refinement where he has only one demand for information and where he, therefore, preserves it.

Suppose, however, that X regards two or more lines of inquiry as worth pursuing and has identified an ultimate partition U_1 with associated V_1 and M_1 and another ultimate partition U_2 with associated V_2 and M_2. (Where there are more than two such demands for information the problems remain substantially the same. To simplify, I suppose the degree of boldness exercised is the same in both cases.)

Let U^* be the *combination* of U_1 and U_2 in the sense of Niiniluoto (1975, p. 268). That is to say, U^* contains all conjunctions of elements of U_1 and U_2 consistent with K. It is, therefore, a refinement of both U_1 and U_2. X is committed to regarding all consistent ways of implementing jointly those expansion strategies available relative to both problems as cognitive options and, in addition, all methods for suspending judgement between these not recognized according to either inquiry separately.

Under these circumstances, X should consider ways of shifting from U_1 to U^* which preserve the demands for information appropriate to that partition and do the same for the shift from U_2 to U^*. Depending on the character of each demand, each shift will be regarded as rendering the demand in question more determinate, failing totally to do so or partially doing so and partially not. In any case, we shall have two epistemic utility functions V_1^* and V_2^*. X is committed to the demand expressed by both of these. There is a conflict in utility which if utterly unresolved yields a system of epistemic values represented by the convex hull of the two epistemic utility functions. (Notice that X might regard more than one extension of V_1 as permissible and likewise for V_2. In that case, the convex hull of all such extensions is to be considered.)

Sometimes it will be possible for X to reduce the amount of conflict by adjusting his demands for information. Sometimes the conclusions which might be reached without such adjustment are sufficiently definite to render it unimportant for X to do so.

I cannot offer a further system of prescriptions here. It is worth noting, however, that conclusions warranted relative to the convex hull of V_1^* and V_2^* cannot lead to rejecting elements of U_1 or elements of U_2 which go unrejected relative to U_1 and U_2 respectively when these are considered as ultimate partitions.

Moreover, there is one important class of cases where the conclusions prescribed even when conflict goes unresolved are identical with those which would be prescribed if one considered the conclusion recommended relative to U_1 and V_1, the conclusion recommended relative to U_2 and V_2 and jointly implemented them.

Such cases arise when all conjunctions consisting of one element of U_1 and one element of U_2 are consistent with K and where U^* fails totally to render either U_1 or U_2 more determinate. In that case, it can be demonstrated that the conclusion warranted relative to U^* relative to every weighted average of V_1^* and V_2^* which assigns positive weights to both is the same as the conclusion obtained by directly pooling the conclusions obtained relative to U_1 and relative to U_2.

Now cases like this arise when X is concerned with inquiries into questions pertaining to subject matters which satisfy certain requirements of logical independence and where demands for information are also taken to be quite independent of one another – e.g., in being interested in who killed Cock Robin and in whether Jimmy Carter will be re-elected President of the United States. Many (but by no means all) inquiries in science meet such requirements so that, at least for the moment, diverse investigators do not have to worry about conflicts in their conclusions due to differences in ultimate partitions.

This account connects determinacy in a situation approximately according to Dewey with the investigator's diverse demands for information and through that with his diverse commitments to research programs and paradigms between which he may or may not be conflicted. It articulates with more system than I have offered in the past how conclusions warranted via induction from an available corpus of knowledge depend upon the potential answers identified for given questions.

This account differs from the approach in (Levi, 1967a) in two respects:

(1) As explained previously, I abandoned the idea that each element of an ultimate partition bear equal informational value over a decade ago.

(2) The second difference is in precision and clarity and not a basic difference in approach. I have never recommended that X is justified in accepting into his corpus conclusions warranted relative to different ultimate partitions and demands for information when they conflict. To the contrary, I suggested that when such conflict arises, the conflicting conclusions should not be added to the corpus but further investigation should be undertaken.

In the light of these explicit disclaimers on my part, the complaints of Hacking (1967), Jeffrey (1968), Hilpinen (1968), and Niiniluoto (1975, pp. 281–90) that my approach renders acceptance too sensitive to the choice of ultimate partitions seem to me to be beside the point.

Nonetheless, my previous account is defective because it fails to give a prescription as to what X should do when matters are left in abeyance. Should he refuse to expand at all or should he be entitled to add some new information although not all that he would have been entitled to add had there been no conflict?

My proposals in this essay attempt to answer these questions.

In so doing, I have not eliminated sensitivity of my acceptance rules to ultimate partitions and M-functions. It remains conceivable on my view that h should be rejected relative to U_1 and M_1 and accepted relative to U_2 and M_2. This is anathema according to Hilpinen (1968, p. 101) and Niiniluoto (1975, pp. 281–90). Of course, I do not recommend adding both h and $\sim h$ to the body of knowledge or evidence.[2] In that sense, it is anathema to me too.

But instead of seeing such situations as generating difficulties for my account of inductive inference, I conclude that such predicaments are to be expected to arise simply because conflicts in demands for information ought to be expected to take place with great frequency.

2 Levi (1967a), pp. 149–54. I would now modify the disclaimer on p. 151 that 'it is doubtful whether such a criterion is needed' where the criterion concerns what is a legitimate question. I still doubt whether necessary and sufficient context independent conditions can be specified. But I do think it important to relate concerns regarding what is a question worthy of investigation with research programs and the like.

When such conflicts arise, we must 'come to terms' with them. I have just attempted to outline part of a formal account of such 'coming to terms'.

Hilpinen and Niiniluoto, as well as Hacking and Jeffrey, apparently would prefer a scheme where there is no need to come to terms with conflicts of this sort at all.

I cheerfully acknowledge that I am a wishy-washy liberal in epistemology as in politics. But even wishy-washy liberals do not have to pretend that conflict is non-existent. To the contrary, they should be as emphatic as revolutionaries and anarchists in acknowledging its presence. But they should assume that one can come to terms with such conflict in a less dramatic and flamboyant and in a more reasoned fashion than many of our contemporary anarchists and revolutionaries seem to allow.

Part II

Knowledge and ignorance

8

Truth, fallibility and the growth of knowledge*†

> In scientific inquiry, the criterion of what is taken to be settled, or to be knowledge, is being *so* settled that it is available as a resource in further inquiry: not being settled in such a way as not to be subject to revision in further inquiry.   JOHN DEWEY, *Logic*, p. 9

1

According to a familiar story, beliefs qualify as knowledge only if they can be justified on the basis of impeccable first premises via equally immaculate first principles. The story has no truth to it. Centuries of criticism suggest that our interesting beliefs are born on the wrong side of the blanket.

Fixating on the pedigrees of our beliefs is unlikely to be helpful in any case. We use our beliefs as resources for inquiry and deliberation. That is to say, we assume the truth of our beliefs as premises in justifying our decisions and in justifying revisions of these beliefs. When they are so used, a question of justification does not arise. We may, indeed, be concerned to justify a revision of our assumptions either by adding items to them or removing others from them. But the premises used in such justifications are precisely the assumptions endorsed prior to such modification. These assumptions, while they are themselves being used as premises, do not stand in need of justification.

From the point of view of X (who may be a person or group acting in concert such as a scientific community) at time *t*, there is no relevant

* Earlier versions of this paper were read at Rutgers University, Case Western Reserve University, Rockefeller University, Cambridge University, the London School of Economics and before the British Society for the Philosophy of Science. This version has been presented at the University of Michigan, the University of Pittsburgh and at Boston University. Work on a longer version was partially supported by NSF grant GS 28922. The work was carried out while I was a Visiting Scholar at Leckhampton, Corpus Christi, Cambridge University.

   (Added in September, 1981). Since I submitted this essay and the replies to Margalit and Scheffler in 1975, I have published another and later version of the same ideas as the first three chapters of my book, *The Enterprise of Knowledge* (Cambridge, Mass. MIT Press, 1980). Because this essay has not been altered since 1975, wherever the later discussion differs from this one (as it does on some points of detail), the version found in my book should be understood as representing my current views.

† Reprinted with the permission of the publisher from *Language, Logic and Method* edited by R. S. Cohen and M. W. Wartofsky, Dordrecht: Reidel, pp. 153–74. Copyright © 1983 by D. Reidel Publishing Company.

distinction to be made between what X fully believes at t and what he knows at t. Whether his beliefs are truths of logic or physics; whether they are theories, laws, statistical claims or observation reports, in believing them, X takes for granted that they are true, that the logical possibility of error infecting all but logical truths believed by him is not to be taken seriously, and that, regardless of the origins or modes of acquisition of these beliefs, all of them are certainly true. Hence, from X's point of view at t, all of his beliefs at t are true, infallibly true (in the sense that they could not possibly be false in any respect to be taken seriously) and certainly true. Under the circumstances, from X's point of view, his beliefs possess all the qualifications they need to be accorded the honorific status of knowledge.

2

The thesis of infallibilism I am advancing ought to be distinguished from other doctrines which I do not advocate:

(1) I do not claim that there are sources of information such as the Delphic Oracle, the Pope, Stalin or sensory stimulation which never breed error. The testimony of our senses and even of competent authorities is eminently fallible in that it is sometimes false.

(2) I do not claim that X should regard his past convictions or future beliefs as free from error any more than he should allow that the views of those with whom he disagrees are free from error.

(3) I am not objecting to the vacuous version of fallibilism which informs us that it is logically possible that any extralogical statement we believe to be true is false.

(4) I have no quarrel with those who insist that human knowledge is corrigible – i.e., sometimes legitimately subject to revision. On the contrary, I am a rabid corrigibilist and contend that the major context in which a question of justification of epistemological significance arises concerns the conditions under which X is justified, from his initial point of view, in revising his body of beliefs or knowledge.

The doctrine of infallibilism I espouse is a consequence of a conception of the way a corpus of knowledge should be used as a resource for inquiry and deliberation. We are not concerned merely to affirm our beliefs upon interrogation. Our beliefs guide our conduct by furnishing a criterion for distinguishing between logical possibilities which are serious and logical possibilities which for *all* practical and theoretical purposes may be utterly ignored. In ignoring such logical possibilities, we set the risk of error involved in acting as though they were false at 0. In this sense, we are certain that they are false. Thus, what we know or believe is, from our point of view, not only infallibly true but certainly true as well.

110

If X is offered a gamble on the outcome of a toss of a coin, he may consider it possible that, on a toss, the coin will land heads, that it will land tails or, even, that it will land on its edge. But X will normally consider it utterly impossible that the coin will take off in the direction of Alpha Centauri or that, as the coin is tossed, the earth will explode. From his point of view, his belief that the earth will not explode is infallible in the sense which is primarily relevant to any decisions he may have to take for which the appraisals of results of tossing the coin are relevant.

Some authors seem to say that X should not, strictly speaking, regard these eventualities as utterly impossible and certainly false. X should assign a positive, albeit minuscule, probability to the logical possibility that the earth will explode on the toss.[1]

I can find no contradiction in this view. It is, nonetheless, untenable. Let X be offered a gamble where he wins one cent regardless of whether the coin lands heads or tails. He has the choice of accepting the gamble (in which case the coin will be tossed) or refusing it (in which case it will not). Should X reject the gamble on the grounds that the earth might explode? Let us reduce the size of the prize from one cent to any arbitrarily small fraction of a cent. Is there a positive greatest lower bound to the value of the prize at which X should reject the bet rather than accept it for fear that the earth might explode? Those who tell us that X should take the logical possibility that the earth will explode seriously seem to suggest that there should be. I submit that those who endorse this position recommend neurosis – not rationality.

X's corpus of knowledge serves not only to distinguish what is a serious possibility from what is not in the conduct of deliberations aimed at reaching a decision in order to promote some ethical, political, economic or other practical aim. It does the same in the context of investigations concerned with modifying X's corpus of knowledge in order to obtain new explanatory theories, to make predictions, to correct errors in the old corpus and to pursue other theoretical endeavors. It is widely conceded that hypotheses can be tested only relative to a body of 'background knowledge'. Such background knowledge serves to define the possible outcomes of testing which need to be taken into account and delimit the rivals to the hypothesis being subjected to test.

Thus, X's corpus serves as his criterion for distinguishing the seriously possible from what is not and the certain from the merely possible both in theoretical inquiry and practical deliberation. I submit that there is no double standard here. We should not regard our knowledge as infallible for practical purposes but fallible in the context of scientific inquiry. To do so would be to re-open the traditional gulf between theory and practice which pragmatists have been concerned to close.

1 This, I take it, is the view expressed by R. C. Jeffrey in (1965, pp. 156, 160–1 and 168–70).

111

3

Peirce condemned infallibilism for placing obstacles in the path of inquiry. Popper has followed him in this. Both Peirce and Popper seem to hold that if, from X's point of view, his knowledge is infallible, he can have no good reason for revising it. Infallibility presupposes incorrigibility.

One conclusion which both Peirce and Popper drew from their endorsement of fallibilism is that the standards for distinguishing serious from nonserious possibilities are, indeed, different for theory and for practice. Peirce is quite emphatic on this point:

We *believe* the proposition we are ready to act upon. *Full belief* is willingness to act upon the proposition in vital crises, *opinion* is willingness to act upon it in relatively insignificant affairs. But pure science has nothing at all to do with *action*. The propositions it accepts, it merely writes in the list of premisses it proposes to use. Nothing is *vital* for science; nothing can be. Its accepted propositions, therefore, are but opinions at most; and the whole list is provisional. The scientific man is not in the least wedded to his conclusions. He risks nothing upon them. He stands ready to abandon one or all as soon as experience opposes them. Some of them, I grant, he is in the habit of calling *established truths*; but that merely means propositions to which no competent man today demurs . . . (Peirce, 1931, p. 347).

Thus, pure theoretical knowledge, or science, has nothing directly to say concerning practical matters, nothing even applicable at all to vital crises. Theory is applicable to minor practical affairs; but matters of vital importance must be left to sentiment, that is, to instinct (Peirce, 1931, p. 348).

In these passages and those which follow, Peirce makes several observations with which I do not quarrel. He insists that the goals of pure science ought to be distinguished from those of deliberations aimed at realizing moral, political, economic or other practical ends. He denies that scientific knowledge alone is sufficient to guide practical conduct. He insists on the corrigibility of scientific knowledge. My objection is to his further contention that the standards of certainty and possibility which apply in practical deliberation are not and ought not to be the same as those which apply in scientific research. Peirce denies that any of the conclusions of scientific inquiry should be accorded the status of full belief where by 'full belief' he means certainty in the sense relevant to practical deliberation. On the other hand, he does not deny that scientists propose to use the conclusions they accept at the moment as premises in subsequent inquiries involving the testing of hypotheses and the designing of experiments. But when they are used in this way, they are being used as standards of certainty and possibility. The implication seems to be that the standards for certainty and possibility employed in scientific inquiry differ from the corresponding standards used in practical deliberation.

I wish to defend a view which denies this gulf between theory and practice. What is taken to be infallible for purposes of guiding conduct should on this

TRUTH, FALLIBILITY AND THE GROWTH OF KNOWLEDGE

view, coincide as far as is humanly feasible, with the conclusion of scientific inquiry. To sustain this position, I must deny that infallibility presupposes incorrigibility or that infallibilism is the obstructionist doctrine Peirce took it to be.[2] In adopting a corpus of knowledge as a standard for distinguishing serious possibilities from logical possibilities to be discounted – for the time being – as impossible for all practical and theoretical purposes, X can still consistently recognize that occasions might and, indeed, will arise where he will have good reason for revising his corpus of knowledge.

To sustain this position, I must show how X could have such good reasons. I shall not attempt to offer a complete answer here. To do so would entail furnishing a systematic account of criteria for revising and improving knowledge. In this essay, I shall try only to outline the general shape which, in my opinion, such a systematic account ought to take and, thereby, to bring some of the issues involved into somewhat sharper focus.

4

A potential corpus of knowledge expressible in a language L is a set K of sentences in L satisfying the following conditions:

(i) K is deductively closed.

(ii) K contains the set UK which is deductively closed and contains all logical truths, set theoretical truths and mathematical truths expressible in L along with any other sentences in L which are regarded obligatory items in any potential corpus and, in that sense, incorrigible.[3]

2   In (Levi, 1970, pp. 197–9) I styled myself a fallibilist like Peirce but insisted that fallibilism is consistent with allowing that rational men may be certain of extralogical statements. I did this by equating fallibilism with corrigibilism. I now think my remarks on this score were confused. The issue is not the verbal one as to whether 'fallible' should be used interchangeably with 'corrigible'. It is rather whether claims taken to be settled as resources for inquiry and deliberation in determining what is seriously possible and what is not can legitimately be opened for revision. Peirce and Popper seem to have denied that they could and, hence, denied that any scientific investigator is ever entitled to take extralogical, extra set theoretical and extramathematical statements as infallibly true in the sense that he refuses to take seriously the possibility that they are false. In this particular respect, their views seem to coincide with those of Carnap and Jeffrey. In the past, I did not fully appreciate the extent of Peirce's agreement with Carnap and Jeffrey on this score and his disagreement with the view I mean to advocate. To give expression to the disagreement with Peirce, Popper and Quine on this matter, I call my view 'infallibilist'.

3   When I say that X adopts a potential corpus as his corpus at t, I mean that X's beliefs at t and the beliefs to which he is committed at t by his beliefs at t for inquiry and deliberation are expressible by the elements of a potential corpus K in L insofar as they are expressible in L at all.

When X adopts K in L as his corpus at t, he is committed to using it as a standard for distinguishing between those sentences in L (or paraphrasable into L) which are possibly false and those which are not. In addition, the corpus adopted commits X to a definition of 'true in L' which characterizes the sense in which he seeks to avoid error when undertaking modifications of his beliefs or knowledge expressible in L. (Note continues on p. 114.)

113

KNOWLEDGE AND IGNORANCE

Let L_1 be a language containing (1) sufficient logic and set theory and descriptions of expressions of L to supply a syntax for L and, if L is added to (1), to supply a definition of 'true in L'; (2) designators for times and agents and means of expressing information such as 'K is X's corpus at t'; and (3) all sentences in L.

S_1 is the sublanguage of L_1 consisting of (1) and (3). S_2 is the sublanguage of L_1 consisting of (1) and (2).

Let T be the deductively closed set in S_1 which furnishes the standard Tarskian definition of 'true in L' in L_1. For any potential K in L, let $T(K)$ be the set of sentences in L_1 which are the deductive consequences of T, K and 'All sentences in K are true in L'.

The Principle of Total Knowledge with respect to Truth in L

If X adopts K as his corpus in L at t, X's definition of 'true in L' for use in explicating the principle that error should be avoided is given by $T(K)$.

This principle can be reformulated by saying that X's corpus expressible in the language L_1 at time t when K is the corpus expressible in L contains the set $T(K)$.

Let $W(K)$ be the set of maximally consistent extensions of potential K in L. h in L is possibly true in L according to K if and only if there is a w in $W(K)$ such that h is an element of w. h is infallibly (necessarily) true in L according to K if and only if h is a member of every w in $W(K)$.

The Principle of Total Knowledge with respect to possibility

h is possibly true in L for X at t if and only if h is a member of some w in $W(K)$ where K is X's corpus in L at t.

I shall suppose that X's corpus expressible in L_1 at t contains sentences specifying for each h in L whether it is a member of a w in $W(K)$ for every potential K. The second principle, in effect, stipulates that if X adopts K as his corpus in L at time t, he also endorses in his corpus expressible in L a sentence 'h is possible in L if and only if h is possible in L according to K'.

Finally, I shall suppose that X's corpus expressible in L_1 at t contains the statement 'X's corpus expressible in L at t is K' when X's corpus expressible in L at t is K. Otherwise X's corpus expressible in L_1 at t contains information about X's corpus at other times as well as information about the corpora of other agents at various times.

I have allowed the inconsistent corpus in L – i.e., the set of all sentences in L – to be a potential corpus. The reason is that sometimes a rational X will legitimately modify his corpus so that it becomes inconsistent. X might, for example, make an observation and as a result add information to his corpus contradicting what is already in it. The result is contradiction.

When K is inconsistent, so will $T(K)$ be and, hence, so will the corpus expressible in L_1. This means that the truth definition furnished by $T(K)$ will be useless for characterizing X's aims in attempting to avoid error.

This is an excellent reason for X to seek to withdraw from an inconsistent corpus. It also provides an excellent excuse for ceasing to be concerned with X's corpus of knowledge expressible in S_1 – i.e., that portion of X's corpus of knowledge expressible in L_1 which is expressible in S_1 but not in S_2. The point is that the knowledge expressible in S_1 furnishes X's definition of 'true in L' which, as we have seen, is useless to X when his corpus is inconsistent. Moreover, it is a positive nuisance; for X will still be considering how to modify his inconsistent corpus and will need means for expressing that his current corpus in L is inconsistent and that shifting this way or that will eliminate the inconsistency. To do this by means of the corpus expressible in L_1 will be ineffectual since that corpus is inconsistent. Hence, I suggest that X retreat to the corpus expressible in L_2 consisting of the deductive consequences of X's knowledge of the syntax of L, his knowledge concerning which potential corpus is his corpus at t and at other times and his knowledge of the corpora of others.

Notice that when X's corpus is inconsistent, his standard for distinguishing possibility from infallibility collapses. As I have formulated the information about possibility in X's corpus in L_1, that information can be expressed in S_2. Hence, when X's corpus in L is inconsistent, his

114

In imposing the deductive closure requirement, I gloss over differences between what X explicitly or consciously identifies as part of the potential corpus he adopts as his own at a given time and other items X is committed to counting as infallibly and certainly true. Moreover, I deliberately ignore the sorts of changes in knowledge which occur due to the proof of new theorems. I do not mean to deny that in some important sense mathematicians discover new knowledge. I mean only to exclude changes of that kind from the scope of this discussion.

In a similar spirit, I do not mean to say that removal of logical, set theoretical or mathematical truths from the urcorpus UK is unconditionally illegitimate but only that changes of knowledge of this sort are beyond the scope of this discussion. The only sorts of shifts in knowledge to be considered here are shifts from corpora satisfying (i) and (ii) to others satisfying the same requirements.

Armed with these qualifications, the shifts or revisions of corpora of knowledge which are feasible can be distinguished into four kinds:

(i) *Expansions* where a shift is made from K_1 to a stronger corpus K_2 obtained by adding a sentence e (or set of sentences) and forming the deductive closure.

corpus in S_2 will contain information implying that every sentence in L is infallibly true and, moreover, that it is infallibly false as well. There will be no contradiction in the corpus. The appearance of inconsistency derives from standard principles of modal logic which apply only relative to consistent corpora.

It is important to keep distinct the different perspectives from which avoiding an inconsistent corpus is desirable. From X's point of view, when X has a consistent corpus and Y does not, Y's corpus contains error. Hence, Y should shift away from inconsistency.

This, however, is not a reason X can offer to Y; for X is invoking his own definition of 'true in L'. When Y has an inconsistent corpus, Y lacks a usable definition and, hence, cannot be committed to holding that his corpus contains error. Rather he will wish to shift to a new corpus precisely because his current corpus is useless as a standard for distinguishing the seriously possible from the seriously impossible and for defining error. X can, of course, point this out to Y if X is concerned to persuade Y why Y should shift to a new corpus; but this reason has no relevance to X's own appraisal of Y's corpus.

Every time X modifies his corpus expressible in L, his definition of 'true in L' is modified as well. So is his definition of 'possibly true in L'. However, 'true in L' is not equivalent to 'is known' or 'is known by X at t'. If X knows at t that h, then h is true in L. But the converse does not hold unless X's corpus in L is a maximally consistent set of sentences in L. This will not, in general, be the case when L is rich enough to express a substantial portion of X's knowledge. 'Infallibly true in L' is equivalent to 'is known by X at t' and is, in this sense, an epistemic predicate.

When X and Y adopt different corpora in L, their definitions of 'true in L' do differ. What this means is that they 'judge truth' differently in inquiries where they are concerned to avoid error. It does not mean that X and Y speak or use different languages or conceptual schemes in any respect which precludes their identifying the respects in which they agree or disagree with one another. I offer no account here of the conditions under which X's beliefs agree or differ with Y's or of translation from one language to another. My concern is rather with adopting a standardized way of representing X's beliefs at a given time and changes in such beliefs which will be useful in a systematic discussion of revisions of beliefs or knowledge.

(*ii*) *Contractions* where a shift is made from K_1 to a weaker K_2 (i.e., where K_1 is an expansion of K_2).

(*iii*) *Replacements* where a shift is made from a consistent K_1 containing h to a consistent K_2 containing $\sim$.

(*iv*) *Residual Shifts* which are none of the other three types.

The problem before us boils down to this: At t_1 when X's corpus is K_1, he is committed to counting all items in K_1 as certainly and infallibly true. How, from his point of view, could he ever be in a situation where he would be justified in revising his corpus by expansion, by contraction, by replacement or by a residual shift? I shall explore each of these four topics in turn.

5

Expansions may be assigned to one of two categories: (*a*) inferential expansions and (*b*) routine expansions.

Suppose that X's corpus at t is $K_{X,t}$. $K_{X,t}$ contains theories, laws, statistical claims and singular statements including data obtained via the testimony of his senses and the testimony of other agents. X is concerned to answer some question or find answers for some system of questions. For each such question, he has identified a system of potential answers. A potential answer is an expansion strategy – i.e., a way of adding new information to X's corpus which will somehow meet the demands for information implicit in the question or questions relative to which it is a potential answer.

Thus, an investigator wishing to identify the value of some parameter may regard any point estimate as a potential answer or any conclusion asserting that the true value falls in some interval or union of such intervals. Or X may be concerned to decide whether to add theory T_1 to his corpus, to reject it or, perhaps, to remain in suspense and continue inquiry further.

Given the demands of his question and the potential answers he has identified, X should attempt to justify, relative to what is already in his corpus, adopting one potential answer rather than another. The expansion strategy adopted on this basis is, when implemented, an inferential expansion. It is sometimes called an inductive or non-deductive inference.

In routine expansion, X does not choose one from a list of rival potential answers. He may not, indeed, have identified any such list. Rather he lets the selection depend on the outcome of a stochastic process. The situation is analogous in some respects to deciding whether to turn right or left at a fork in the road on the basis of a toss of a coin. There is, to be sure, an important difference. The outcome of tossing the coin does not depend on which of the forks in the road will lead the person to his destination. When X lets a stochastic process decide for him how he shall expand his corpus, he does assume, in doing so, that the chance or statistical probability of expanding without committing an error by letting the stochastic process decide is quite

116

high and that the chance that he will add h rather than $\sim h$ depends on which of these hypotheses is true.

Thus, X may ask Y whether h is true or false and let Y's response determine whether X adds h, $\sim h$ or neither into his corpus. Alternatively, X may make an observation and let the report he affirms in response to sensory stimulation determine what statements will be added to his corpus to be used in subsequent inquiry.[4] In the first case, X trusts Y as a reliable authority or witness as to the truth value of h. In the second case, X trusts his own senses.

Why should anyone expand his corpus? The short answer is to obtain new information. The demand for information will vary from context to context and will often itself be motivated by different considerations. Sometimes new information is important for the resolution of a practical decision problem. Sometimes it is relevant to a scientific inquiry aimed at systematic explanation of some subject matter.

Whatever the demand for information might be, the concern to obtain new information should be tempered by another consideration. In non-trivial expansion, information not contained in $K_{X,t}$ is added to it. From X's

---

4 The response X makes in response to sensory stimulation is the formation of a propositional attitude which I shall call 'making an observation report'. If X reports that h in response to sensory stimulation, however, he need not add h to his corpus of knowledge. To report that h is not to incorporate h into one's standard for discriminating serious from non-serious possibilities in subsequent inquiry and deliberation.

Reporting that h is an outcome of a trial of some kind (e.g., stimulation of X's sense organs under conditions C). The process is stochastic in that the chance of obtaining an outcome of that kind on a trial of that kind is, in general, less than one. Moreover, if the kind of outcome is described as reporting a sentence h or a sentence which is an instance of a given schema when that sentence is true, the chance will also, in general, be less than one.

In making observations, X typically lets the outcome of such a random experiment decide what he will add to his corpus. Typically he does so as a matter of habit. But often, especially in carefully designed experimental situations, the circumstances under which he will let the outcome render a verdict are circumscribed. If X knows that making observations on a foggy night have a great chance of yielding false reports, he will refuse to follow the practice of letting such observations determine what he will add to his corpus.

The sentence added to X's corpus via an observation routine is not inferred from what is already in his corpus (including knowledge of the error probability of the routine) and information concerning the response made to sensory stimulation. Rather X is committed prior to observation to the practice or routine of letting the application of the routine legislate what he will add. Being so committed, the actual implementation of the routine is not an inference at all.

The structure of expansion via observation is similar, according to the account I am proposing, to statistical decisionmaking on the Neyman–Pearson model. According to the 'forward look' advocated by followers of the Neyman–Pearson school, an investigator plans beforehand which outcomes of an experiment will lead to rejection of a 'null hypothesis' and which will not. The probability of error (and other 'operating characteristics' such as the power of the test) are determined beforehand and the plan evaluated on the basis of this information. This procedure stands in contrast to the approach invoking the 'backward look' where one assesses whether one should reject the null hypothesis relative to a body of knowledge including information about the outcome of the experiment.

point of view at t, that information is possibly false in the serious sense. Hence, any expansion which promises new information bears a risk of importing error as well. A scientifically responsible X should be concerned that the new information he obtains be free of error. Strictly speaking, therefore, the immediate or proximate objective of X is not to obtain new information but to obtain new error-free information.

Given this view of the proximate aims of efforts to expand a corpus of knowledge, the problem before us is how expansion could ever be justified. Prior to expansion, X regards everything in his corpus as infallibly and certainly true. Hypotheses not in his corpus but consistent with it are merely probable and eminently fallible – i.e., possibly false. Hence, for X to add h to his corpus is for him to add a fallible item to his corpus – counter to the claim that what is in his corpus is infallible.

This objection presupposes that possibility or infallibility belong to sentences or propositions independently of their membership in X's corpus of knowledge. This may be so for logical possibility and various other sorts of possibility which have been discussed. But it is simply false in the case of the sort of epistemic possibility relevant to the conduct of inquiry and deliberation which has been discussed here. When X modifies his corpus of knowledge, what is, from his point of view, infallible changes as well. From X's point of view prior to expansion, adding h to his corpus is, indeed, a possible source of error. Accepting h is fallible *ex ante*. It is, however, infallible *ex post*. Once X has adopted h as an item in his corpus and shifted his point of view, h becomes infallible in the context of subsequent deliberation and inquiry.

There is, however, a more serious objection to expansion. From X's point of view at t, h is possibly false and merely probable. Adding h to his corpus entails a risk of error. Refusing to expand at all incurs no risk whatsoever. Surely the latter option must always be preferable to expansion.

Recall, however, that in considering expansion strategies, X is concerned not only to avoid error but to obtain new information. The promise of obtaining new information is a risk-inducing factor which may sometimes (though not always) compensate X, from his initial point of view, for the risk he is incurring. As long as the proximate aim is not merely to avoid error but to obtain error-free information, X will sometimes be justified in incurring risks for the sake of new information.

6

The ways in which informational benefits and risks of error are traded off against one another differ in routine expansion and inferential expansion. In routine expansion, X is committed before expansion to letting some stochastic process select for him the items he is to add to his corpus. He does not wait until the process has come to an end and then decide, depending on the outcome, whether to carry through with the routine.

Thus, if in response to sensory stimulation, X makes an observation report inconsistent with what is already in his corpus and, hence, certainly false from the point of view he adopted prior to carrying out the observation routine, he is committed to carry through and add the report to his corpus. This is so even though the result is to convert his corpus into an inconsistent one.

Carrying the routine through in this way is not to trample on the desideratum of avoiding error. In following the routine, X respects the desideratum by taking care to employ a routine which, as far as he knows, is reliable. That is to say, X adopts a routine for which the statistical probability of error is fairly small. How small is fairly small? That depends on how fecund the routine is in furnishing new information.

What is true of expansion via observation holds also for expansion via appeal to the testimony of others. Both sorts of routine expansion have the capacity to breed contradiction even though following the routines is in keeping with the demand that serious efforts be made to avoid error.

The situation is different in the case of inferential expansion. X does not let some stochastic process like the testimony of his senses or of witnesses decide for him what items he will add to his corpus of knowledge. Rather, he compares rival expansion strategies with respect both to risk of error entailed and informational benefits promised and, relative to the information already available in his corpus (including information already gathered by observation and other routines), determines which strategy yields the best tradeoff. Given that X wishes to avoid error, he should refuse to regard as optimal any option which will, for certain, import error. No amount of informational benefit can be worth that risk. Hence, in inferential expansion, contradiction cannot legitimately be imported into X's corpus.

According to this account, reports added to a corpus via observation are not distinguishable from theories, laws, statistical assumptions or predictions with respect to certainty or infallibility. All items in X's corpus are, from X's point of view, equally certain and infallible. Nor are observation reports especially distinguished with respect to corrigibility. Observation reports are distinguished by the way they gain admission into a corpus. Expanding via observation (like expanding via the testimony of others) is capable of injecting contradiction into a corpus. This trait is not to be counted a virtue. To the contrary, it is a defect of observation routines in particular and all modes of routine expansion in general that they can breed error and, indeed, contradict our most cherished theories. We put up with the defects because of the information to be gained by consulting our senses. We ought not, however, make a virtue out of our necessity, as some empiricists are prone to do, and maintain that the senses are the ultimate arbiter of what should and should not be in a corpus of knowledge. There is no such ultimate arbiter.

119

KNOWLEDGE AND IGNORANCE

7

In seeking to expand his corpus, X is or should be concerned to avoid error. What does 'error' mean in this context? Given that X's corpus at t expressible in language L is to be expanded, such expansion avoids error if no sentence in L which is false is added. Thus, we require a definition of 'false in L' or 'true in L'. 'True in L' may be defined relative to a set of assumptions in a corpus expressible in a metalanguage along Tarskian lines. My contention is that the definition of 'true in L' relevant here is relative to assumptions which logically imply that all sentences in $K_{X,t}$ are true in L. That is to say, it is relative to such a truth definition that X is concerned to avoid error in expanding his corpus $K_{X,t}$.

Thus, the truth and error which figure in the aims of expansion are of the sort which Quine claims we judge 'as earnestly and absolutely as can be' within 'our own total evolving doctrine' (Quine, 1960, p. 25). I mean, however, to say rather more than Quine. We not only judge truth earnestly but seek to avoid error in modifying that evolving doctrine and we do so employing conceptions of truth and error relativized to that very doctrine. That avoidance of error, in this sense, can be a desideratum directing the improvement of knowledge is a point which neither Quine nor other major figures in the pragmatist tradition have taken seriously.

In attempting to expand his corpus of knowledge in order to obtain new error-free information, X will often have to identify potential answers relevant to his question. Sometimes the task is trivial. In others – especially when X is looking for a theory to systematize some subject matter – considerable genius may be required. However, once potential answers are proposed for that status, it is often important to consider whether they are potential answers to the question under consideration and how well they gratify the demands for information occasioned by the question when issues of truth value are set aside.

Such appraisals of expansion strategies may to some extent be regulated by criteria which apply to a diversity of situations. They correspond, at least roughly, to what Peirce calls principles of abduction.

At least on some occasions, Peirce does not regard abduction as a way of fixing beliefs – i.e., of adding new items to a corpus of knowledge to be used as premises in subsequent inquiry. Rather it is a way of identifying potential answers to the question under investigation.

It is to be remarked that, in pure abduction, it can never be justifiable to accept the hypothesis otherwise than as an interrogation. But as long as that condition is observed, no positive falsity is to be feared (Peirce, 1950, p. 154).

As Peirce notes, the 'conclusion' of an abduction can entail no error; for such a conclusion is the mere entertaining of an hypothesis for further test, scrutiny and inquiry. By way of contrast, in inductive inference (i.e., inferential expansion), an erstwhile hypothesis is added to a corpus of

120

knowledge and its status as hypothesis is stripped from it. It becomes a settled assumption qualifying as evidence in subsequent investigations. To make this inductive inference does entail a risk of error.

Thus, in the context of abduction, the only factors which need to be taken into account in appraising would-be potential answers are their informational virtues. In inquiries where the aim is to add theories to the corpus which will furnish systematic explanations in some domain, good potential answers are good potential explainers possessing such virtues as generality and simplicity. Neither the truth values of the potential explainers nor their probabilities are relevant. Hence, there is no need to suppose the informationally attractive hypotheses are true or are likely to be true. We need not, in particular, postulate the simplicity of nature. To do so would, in any case, be dubious. This is not only because of the ambiguity and subjectivity of our notions of simplicity. Even in situations where widely shared criteria for assessing simplicity can be invoked such as in some curve-fitting cases, it is simply not the case that simpler hypotheses are more probable. Relative to data represented by two points, it is no more probable that the true hypothesis is linear than that it is circular. Fortunately, in the context of abduction we do not have to suppose otherwise. Probability is irrelevant in the context of abduction.

Induction or inferential expansion is an entirely different story. Granted that the informational desiderata relevant to assessing the quality of hypotheses as potential answers continue to be relevant in a context where the concern is to choose a potential answer for addition to a corpus of knowledge, inferential expansion does entail risking error for the sake of the information promised.

Consequently, anyone who claims that the same criteria which are relevant to abduction control the legitimacy of inductions so that the distinction between abduction and induction is, at best, a matter of degree, appears to be committed to embracing one of the following two alternatives:

(i) Hypotheses which are informationally attractive – e.g., because they are simple – are more probably true than those which are not.

(ii) Avoidance of error is not a desideratum of efforts at expansion.

I have rejected both of these alternatives. Hence, I am committed to rejecting points of view which see abduction and induction as modes of inference which vary only in degree.

If I understand them correctly, Quine and Ullian disagree:

Calling a belief a hypothesis says nothing as to what the belief is about, how firmly it is held, or how well founded it is. Calling it a hypothesis suggests rather what sort of reason we have for adopting or entertaining it. A man adopts or entertains a hypothesis because it would explain, if it were true, some things he already believes. Its evidence is seen in its consequences (Quine and Ullian, 1970, p. 43).

121

The reasons, according to Quine and Ullian, for 'adopting or entertaining' a hypothesis are those which render it a good *potential* explanation of what the investigator already believes. It appears that these reasons are reasons for identifying hypotheses as potential answers at the abductive phase – for 'entertaining' them. But Quine and Ullian hold that these very same reasons or sorts of reasons are grounds for adopting hypotheses as premisses or as beliefs. In any case, Quine and Ullian subsequently quite explicitly state that induction is but a species of 'framing hypotheses' (1970, p. 55). Thus, Quine and Ullian do appear to hold that the same informational desiderata which control the appraisal of hypotheses as potential answers control without additional supplement the selection of one of a list of potential answers as a conclusion to be used as a resource in subsequent inquiry. If I understand them right, they are faced with the dilemma of assuming dubious claims such as the simplicity of nature or denying that avoidance of error is a desideratum of inquiry. In 'On Simple Hypotheses of a Complex World' Quine registers some scepticism as to the claim that nature is simple (Quine, 1966, pp. 242–5 and Quine and Ullian, 1970, p. 46). It seems to be the case that for Quine and Ullian, avoidance of error (except, perhaps, for avoiding contradictions) is not a desideratum of induction any more than it is for abduction.

On the view I advocate, avoidance of error is relevant to induction though not to abduction. This means that hypotheses which earn high marks when informational desiderata alone are taken into account may, nonetheless, fail to gain admission into X's corpus because the risk of error entailed by such expansion is too great. In other situations, simplicity may be a sufficient inducement to incur risks.

Thus, we do more than judge truth earnestly and seriously relative to our evolving doctrine. Our judgements of truth define for us our aims in revising our doctrine insofar as we are concerned to avoid error. Since our conception of error changes with revisions of our evolving doctrine, it follows that revisions of doctrine yield modifications of our aims in subsequent inquiries.

8

Contraction is the inverse of expansion. X shifts from an initial corpus K_1 whose elements are, for him, infallibly and certainly true to a corpus K_2 which is a proper subset of K_1. He ceases to believe or know items he initially believed. He shifts the status of some statements from infallibly and certainly true resources for inquiry to possibly false and merely probable hypotheses.

What justification could X have from his initial point of view for removing items he regards as certainly and infallibly true from that status?

Notice that X's concern to avoid error is no obstacle to such contraction;

for in contraction X cannot import error into his corpus. To do that, he would have to add items to his corpus.

The trouble with contraction is that it entails a deliberate loss of information which, from his initial point of view, X counts as certainly and infallibly true. *Prima facie* this is counterproductive since X is presumably concerned to obtain more information and not to shed it. What could justify deliberately surrendering information?

If X detected inconsistency in his initial corpus, he would have excellent reason to contract. An inconsistent corpus fails as a standard of possibility. That even an X so ideally rational that he avoids mistakes of computation and memory could have an inconsistent corpus is clear; for X might legitimately expand into an inconsistent corpus either by observation or relying on the testimony of others. Observations sometimes contradict our most cherished theories and men whose authority we respect sometimes disagree with us. The result is pressure to contract.

When such a need arises, it then becomes a problem to decide on a contraction strategy. The considerations ingredient in evaluating alternatives cannot be explored in detail here. It is important, however, to emphasize one point.

In evaluating contraction strategies, we will be led to make discriminations between those items in the corpus to be contracted which are more vulnerable to removal from the corpus and those which are not. In this sense, we can talk of differences within the corpus with respect to grades of corrigibility. It is tempting to correlate these grades of corrigibility with grades of certainty or probability. According to the view I advocate, that would be a mistake. All items in the initial corpus K_1 which is to be contracted are, from X's initial point of view, certainly and infallibly true. They all bear probability 1.[5]

In contraction, the aim ought to be to minimize the loss of information or important information suffered subject to the constraint that the considerations (such as the detection of inconsistency) which generated the need to contract are met. Thus, discriminations between items in a corpus with respect to removability or corrigibility are a function of informational value and not of probability of truth.

5 Strictly speaking, this is so only when the corpus to be contracted is consistent. When contraction is occasioned by the need to remove inconsistency, probabilities are not defined for sentences in L relative to the initial, inconsistent corpus and, as we noted in note 3, the standard of possibility and infallibility breaks down as well. The main point, nonetheless, stands; for it remains the case that no discrimination can be made between sentences in an inconsistent corpus with respect to certainty and infallibility – even though they may differ from one another with respect to revisability or corrigibility. Moreover, in contracting an inconsistent corpus there is no risk of error involved. However, the investigator is still in a position to evaluate the information lost by adopting one contraction strategy rather than another. He can do so on the basis of information in his corpus expressible in the language S_2 for which he does have a consistent corpus.

In cases where two or more contraction strategies will prove equally optimal, it will generally be sensible to implement all them. Thus, if a theory firmly ensconced in the initial corpus is contradicted by new data, we may throw the theory out of the corpus and construe it as hypothesis. But to take it to be a hypothesis and not certainly false, the observation reports obtained via an observation routine will have to be questioned as well. It will be desirable to check on the observations as well as the theory.

The conflict of data with a theory already established in a corpus of knowledge ought not to be confused with the conflict of data with a theory which is a potential answer not yet incorporated into the corpus. In the latter case, the verdict of the data is typically much more decisive and the conclusion that the theory is false is added to the corpus of knowledge.

When the theory is not a hypothesis but a settled assumption, the data which conflict with it could not be construed as the outcome of a test for the theory; for one never tests assumptions taken for granted as knowledge while they are so taken but only when they are removed from the corpus of knowledge and cast into doubt.

Thus, Michelson's first experiments were not conducted to test Newtonian mechanics, Maxwell's electromagnetic theory or the ether hypothesis. He took these for granted as background knowledge. Michelson was concerned to test a hypothesis of Stokes concerning the motion of the ether surrounding the earth relative to the earth (Whittaker, 1960, pp. 386–7 and 390–1). When Lorentz subsequently noticed that Stokes' hypothesis conflicted with mechanics and electromagnetic theory, Michelson's results were recognized to have generated a conflict within the settled scientific corpus. Not only were various items in that corpus subject to scrutiny but so were Michelson's results.

Contradiction is one good reason for attempting to contract. There are others. Sometimes the initial corpus contains T_1. T_2 is inconsistent with T_1. From X's initial point of view, it is certainly false. On the other hand, T_2 may be superior in all other respects for furnishing systematic explanations of some domain. For example, X might recognize the superior explanatory virtues of statistical mechanics even though he is certain that it is false and that classical thermodynamics is true.

In such a case, X might remove T_1 from his corpus in order to give T_2 a hearing without begging any questions. To contract in this case is not to reject T_1 as false but to shift to a position where judgement is suspended between T_1 and T_2 so that investigations can be undertaken to decide whether T_1 should be reinstated in X's corpus via subsequent expansion, T_2 should take T_1's place or another candidate considered.

Whatever the details of the story I am outlining might be, as outlined the story indicates how an investigator who initially regarded T_1 to be certainly and infallibly true could acquire good reason for revising his judgement. The doctrine of infallibilism is no obstacle to justifying, at least sometimes, the contraction of a corpus of knowledge.

9

We have not as yet faced the most serious objection to the contention that the rejection of fallibilism is consistent with the advocacy of corrigibilism. The most impressive revisions of scientific knowledge have arisen in situations where one theory is replaced by another which contradicts it. Indeed, these are the sorts of revisions which have most fascinated anarchists like Feyerabend or revolutionists like Kuhn. In such cases, it seems as though from X's initial point of view when he adopts T_1, replacement of T_1 by T_2 inconsistent with T_1 involves the deliberate substitution of a theory X is certain is false for one he is certain is true. That is to say, this is so if X regards his initial assumption of T_1 as certainly and infallibly true. Given that X is concerned to avoid error, such a presumption of infallibility would render it irrational for X to undertake the replacement. Authors like Feyerabend and Kuhn conclude that replacements are not subject to control by the desideratum that error be avoided. Peirce and Popper conclude that infallibilism is untenable.

Observe, however, that replacement can be regarded, for purposes of analysis, as a contraction followed by an expansion. First, X contracts by removing T_1 from his corpus in order to give T_2 a hearing. Subsequent investigation leads to expansion by adding T_2. The net effect is replacement. Yet, each step can be rationalized in keeping with the claim that at each stage the corpus adopted is considered infallible and with the desideratum that error be avoided.

This approach is, in my opinion, entirely sound. But one important objection demands consideration. Sometimes X will know prior to contraction that if he contracts by removing T_1, the contracted corpus will furnish ample warrant for subsequently adding T_2. From X's initial point of view, he knows that contraction will lead to his subsequent incorporation of a theory into his corpus which is certainly false. It appears as though our difficulties with replacement have not been eliminated after all.

Thus, if X contemplates removing classical thermodynamics from his corpus after the experiments of Svedberg and Perrin on Brownian motion have been conducted and reported, he may anticipate that he will then be justified in endorsing statistical mechanics. If he is initially certain that statistical mechanics is false, it appears that he would be foolish to contract because he would deliberately put himself in a predicament where he will import error into his corpus.

To come to grips with this objection, we must examine more closely the sense in which avoidance of error is a desideratum in scientific inquiry.

According to a view endorsed both by Peirce and Popper, the ultimate aim of inquiry is to obtain a true and maximally consistent story of the world. The aim is an ultimate aim in the sense that specific inquiries with their own proximate goals are undertaken in order to realize immediate objectives which will promote this ultimate aim.

Clearly, if X regards his initial corpus containing T_1 to be infallible and knows that removing T_1 will certainly lead to his subsequent incorporation of the false T_2, from his initial point of view, contraction will frustrate the long-run goal of coming closer to the truth.

This difficulty does not arise if X is not certain at the outset that T_1 is true. If X regards T_1 as possibly false and T_2 as possibly true at the outset, replacing T_1 by T_2 cannot qualify as deliberately replacing truth with error.

Thus, Popper endorses fallibilism and retains his vision of getting closer to the truth as the ultimate aim of scientific inquiry.

Of course, Popper's view has its own troubles. If at the outset both T_1 and T_2 are serious possibilities and remain so after T_1 is replaced by T_2, what, after all, has happened when one theory replaces another? I am afraid I cannot give a coherent report of Popper's view on this score. Apparently T_2 replaces T_1 in the sense that it is rated as more worthy of being subject to serious test. But if our proximate aim is merely to accept hypotheses for purposes of testing them and somehow this concern is seen to promote the long-run aim of obtaining the true complete story of the world (in a manner which remains a mystery to me), then truth or avoidance of error may be an important desideratum in the long run. It has no importance, however, in the proximate aims of inquiry. If testworthiness is what we are after, we need not concern ourselves with the truth values of our hypotheses or with avoiding error.

Thus, Popper's view succeeds in placing truth on a pedestal remote from the immediate concerns of inquiry.

Furthermore, by insisting on the fallibility of human knowledge, both Peirce and Popper render mysterious how the fruits of scientific inquiry are to be used in practical deliberation to guide our conduct and in subsequent scientific inquiry in the revision of knowledge.

The doctrine of infallibilism, by way of contrast, is able to provide a clear characterization of how knowledge identifies the space of serious possibilities for practical decision-makers and scientific investigators without requiring a double standard for theory and practice. And infallibilism does not lead (as Peirce feared) to dogmatic obstruction of the course of inquiry. To the contrary, it is fallibilism together with the doctrine that getting closer to the truth is the ultimate aim of inquiry which renders knowledge irrelevant to practice and truth irrelevant to the revision of knowledge.

Infallibilism is compatible, indeed, congenial with a non-dogmatic and corrigibilist epistemology – provided that we turn our backs on the view that getting closer to the truth is the ultimate aim of inquiry. Abandoning this

126

ideal is not to deny that truth matters. It is rather to extol the virtues of myopia. Avoidance of error is an invariant feature of the *proximate* goals of specific inquiries. When X modifies his corpus by removing T_1, he should be concerned to avoid error in making this modification. He should not be concerned with whether subsequent modifications based on his contracted corpus will lead to error.

Once X has contracted his corpus, his concern to avoid error should be based on judgements of truth and error relative to his contracted corpus. Relative to that corpus, T_2 is possibly true. Adding T_2 is not, from X's point of view after adopting the contracted corpus, to incorporate certain error. X will be justified in adding T_2 provided that the risk of error – as judged relative to the contracted corpus – is sufficiently small to be compensated for by the informational benefits promised by adding T_2.

Once this is understood, residual shifts can be analyzed into sequences of contractions and expansions just as replacements can. On this view, the task of a revisionist epistemology reduces to exploring the criteria for legitimate expansion and legitimate contraction.

Thus, knowledge is revisable. Avoidance of error is an important desideratum in revision. Yet, knowledge is infallible in a sense important to understanding how such knowledge guides our conduct and directs scientific efforts to improve our knowledge.

I suspect that we may go further and wonder whether corrigibilism can coherently be defended at all without insisting on the infallibility of human knowledge. That, however, is another story. My aim has been only to show that infallibilism is consistent with corrigibilism and a view which respects avoidance of error is an important desideratum for science.

9

Four types of ignorance[†]

According to his own lights, X is ignorant of the truth value of h if and only if both the truth and falsity of h are serious possibilities from his point of view. Thus experimenter X is ignorant concerning the superiority of therapy A over therapy B when it is possible as far as he knows that therapy A is superior and it is also possible that it is not. Alternatively stated, X is ignorant if he suspends judgement concerning the truth values of these alternatives.

Similarly, investor Y is ignorant concerning the yield of a given portfolio of stocks and bonds when several hypotheses specifying different yields are possibly true, as far as he is concerned, no two of them are possibly both true, and at least one of them must be true.

In these cases and countless others, possibility is what I call 'serious' possibility according to an agent at a time.[1] Perhaps it would be helpful to call it subjective possibility in analogy to subjective probability. Evaluations of truth-value-bearing hypotheses with respect to probability are evaluations with respect to a factor which determines risks and expectations in a sense best understood by reference to decision theories where risk and expectation are fundamental, as for example in 'Bayesian' decision theories, which enjoin rational agents to maximize expected utility.

It is axiomatic in such theories that rational agents may assign subjective probability other than 0 to hypothesis h only if the truth of h is a serious possibility according to X – i.e., only if the truth of h is a serious or subjective possibility according to X.

Hence, if the truth of h is not a serious possibility according to X at time t, X should assign h a subjective probability of 0 and assign $\sim h$ a subjective probability of 1 – i.e., X should be certain that h is false. When that happens, X is not ignorant of the truth value of h in the sense under consideration. He *knows* (at least from his own point of view) that h is false or, at least, is committed to knowing, taking for granted as a settled assumption, or accepting as evidence, that $\sim h$ is true. (I speak of commitment here to bypass the fact that X may not have a perfect memory, be a perfect calculator, or be

† Reprinted with the permission of the editor from *Social Research* v. 44 (1977), pp. 745–56.
1 The 'agent' need not be an individual person but could be a corporate person such as a family corporation or parliament.

in perfect emotional health so that he will fail to live up to all of his commitments.)

Let $K_{X,t}$ be the set of assumptions X is committed to accepting as evidence at time t. The truth of h is (or should be) a serious possibility according to X at t if and only if the truth of h is consistent with $K_{X,t}$. X is ignorant of the truth of h at t if and only if both h and $\sim h$ are consistent with $K_{X,t}$.

We might as well let $K_{X,t}$ consist of all hypotheses whose falsity is inconsistent with $K_{X,t}$ so that the corpus or body of assumptions accepted as evidence is deductively closed. Given some formal language L, all sets of sentences in L eligible for adoption as 'standards for serious possibility' or 'potential corpora of knowledge or evidence' may be characterized as deductively closed sets in L which contain all logical truths in L.

We can, therefore, introduce the notion of serious possibility relative to a potential corpus K. Moreover, potential corpora can be partially ordered by the set inclusion relation. K' is weaker than K if and only if K' is a proper subset of K. In that event, K' allows more hypotheses to be serious possibilities than does K. The weakest potential corpus is the corpus of logical truths UK. h is logically possible if and only if it is consistent with UK.

To adopt UK as one's standard for serious possibility is in an important sense to be in a maximal state of ignorance; for then one is committed to a view where one is ignorant of the truth value of every extralogical hypothesis.

When h and $\sim h$ are both serious possibilities from X's point of view, he shall be said to be *modally ignorant*.

In real life, men do not adopt cognitive stances representable as extreme states of modal ignorance where all logical possibilities are serious possibilities. On the other hand, no one ever endorses as his corpus of knowledge or evidence (his standard for serious possibility) a maximally consistent set.

In deliberation and in inquiry, men find themselves in a state of modal ignorance in some respects and free of modal ignorance in others.

Thus an investor is normally ignorant concerning the consequences of choosing a given portfolio, but he will not be utterly ignorant. He will regard several hypotheses as possibly true and be quite certain that others are false. How should he evaluate the portfolio when comparing it with other portfolios about whose consequences he is ignorant in the same way?

The Bayesian answer is to assign personal, subjective, or credal probabilities to alternative seriously possible hypotheses representable by a numerical function obeying the requirements of the calculus of probabilities. These probabilities are used as weights to compute expected utilities for each of the investment policies. The investor should then pick an option so as to maximize expected utility.

Many Bayesians seem to think that there is sense of ignorance other than modal ignorance. Suppose that X is modally ignorant of the truth of h in the sense that both h and $\sim h$ are serious possibilities according to his point of view. X might adopt a 'credal state' – i.e., a mode of evaluating hypotheses with respect to credal probability – which assigns h a probability $Q(h)$ equal to $1 - 0.000\,001$. Had X been certain of the truth of h, he would have adopted $Q(h) = 1$. He would (under certain typical circumstances) have ruled out the truth of $\sim h$ as being a serious possibility. If he were considering an option and h and $\sim h$ were hypotheses concerning the consequences of choosing the option, the expected utility of the option when $Q(h) = 0.999\,999$ would be marginally different from the expected utility when $Q(h) = 1$. Hence, so the argument runs, it is rather misleading to suppose that X is ignorant concerning the truth of h when he is modally ignorant, given that his state of credal probability judgement is as just indicated.

From this point of view, X is ignorant concerning the truth of h if and only if h is as probable as its negation – i.e., if and only if $Q(h) = 0.5$.

Consider, however, a coin that is tossed 1000 times. There are 2^n distinct hypotheses which are possibly true concerning the sequence in which that coin lands heads and tails. X may be modally ignorant concerning what that sequence is. But consider the sequence consisting of heads on every odd toss and tails on every even toss. That has a probability of $\frac{1}{2}^n$. Its negation has a probability of $1 - \frac{1}{2}^n$. On the view under consideration, X is most decidedly not ignorant as to the truth of the hypotheses that the coin will land heads on every odd toss and tails on every even toss. Indeed, if one considers any hypothesis concerning the exact sequence of heads and tails, X is not ignorant concerning its truth in the new sense. There appears to be something bizarre about this view of states of ignorance.

Those who wish to characterize states of ignorance probabilistically have suggested that X is ignorant in this case after all because he assigns equal probability to all hypotheses specifying the exact sequence of heads and tails.

Such characterizations of ignorance in probabilistic terms, however, are sensitive to the 'partition' being used – i.e., the set U of hypotheses exclusive and exhaustive relative to K and each element of which is consistent with K. We can say that X is probabilistically ignorant relative to U and K if and only if every element of U is assigned equal probability with every other. Thus X is indeed probabilistically ignorant concerning the truth of h when he assigns it a value of $\frac{1}{2}$ provided that such ignorance is relative to U consisting of h and $\sim h$. But at the same time, such a credal state is incompatible with probabilistic ignorance concerning h relative to another partition.

Whatever partition U may be used, probabilistic ignorance presupposes modal ignorance; for X must be modally ignorant concerning the truth of each and every element of U to be probabilistically ignorant.

Authors like Laplace have been criticized for having advocated the view that being in a state of modal ignorance concerning elements of some partition U is sufficient for probabilistic ignorance. Whether Laplace or any other author of stature actually endorsed such principles of insufficient reason understood in that manner is at least debatable. At any rate, it is customary to point out the inconsistency of proceeding in such a fashion.

There is, however, no inconsistency in speaking of being in a state of ignorance concerning hypotheses equivalent given K to Boolean combinations of elements of a partition U if and only if each element of U bears equal probability.

Many Bayesian statisticians speak of states of ignorance of this sort, and sometimes such notions of ignorance are exploited in other contexts as well.

An interesting example of this is John Harsanyi's use of this probabilistic conception of ignorance as a way to arrive at welfare judgements. Harsanyi contends that to make a moral judgement concerning the merits of rival social states for societies containing n individuals, X should consider each of the social states and evaluate the expected utility that would accrue to him if that social state were realized while he was probabilistically ignorant as to which individual he was (so that U consists of n distinct hypotheses as to which individual X is in that social state and the probability of each element of U is $1/n$) (Harsanyi, 1955, pp. 3–4).

Harsanyi understood, of course, that in real life X will rarely if ever be in such a state of ignorance with respect to his situation in the society in which he lives or concerning what his situation would be in a society alternative to the prevailing one. Yet he thought that evaluating alternative social arrangements in a manner which gains moral authority requires the sort of impersonal appraisal which X might achieve by considering how he would evaluate social arrangements were he in a state of ignorance.

It should be apparent that the ignorance involved cannot be merely modal ignorance (although such ignorance would be required); for being in a given state of modal ignorance may very well be consistent with being in diverse states of probability judgement. Harsanyi thought that the appropriate state of ignorance needed to secure the impersonal appraisal required for moral judgement is probabilistic ignorance.

Thus our efforts to distinguish between different views of what constitutes a state of ignorance amounts to rather more than an elaboration of entries in some philosophically sophisticated lexicon. In Harsanyi's case, his conception of ignorance is critical to his assessment of the conditions under which moral judgements concerning social welfare may be made.

Consider, however, the often registered complaint that Bayesians like Harsanyi impose on rational agents the unreasonable demand that they be committed to a credal state representable by a single probability measure. This demand is blatantly absurd when it is coupled with the view that there are no objective criteria (no principles of inductive logic) which can be conjoined with contextual considerations to prescribe the choice of some definite measure in any particular context. The currently fashionable personalist view insists that a rational agent, if he endorses a single probability measure, does so arbitrarily in the sense that he lacks sufficient basis for selecting that measure over others (although he may have good reason for restricting his choice to some subset of the set of all probability measures). The same fashionable personalist view then urges the arbitrary choice.

There is an alternative view of rationality which allows a rational agent to be wise and suspend judgement when he has no warrant for choosing one way rather than another and can refrain from making a choice. Should we not urge rational agents to remain in a state of suspense between alternative distributions when there is no basis for choosing between them?

In that case, a credal state would not be represented by a single Q-function but by a set of Q-functions, and a given set would represent a state of ignorance of some kind (Levi, 1974). Given, in particular, a partition U relative to K regarding which X is modally ignorant, X is *probabilistically ignorant in the extreme sense* if and only if he has not ruled out any distribution over U obeying the requirements of the calculus of probabilities relative to K.

Suppose that X knows that he has feasible options, $A_1, A_2, ..., A_n$ and that given any option A_i at least and at most one of the possibly true hypotheses $o_{i1}, o_{i2}, ..., o_{imi}$ is true if A_i is chosen, and finally, let u_{ij} be the utility assigned o_{ij}. Consider now all the Q-functions obeying the requirements of the calculus of probabilities which assign values to $Q(o_{ij}; A_i$ is chosen) for every i and j. X is, so we shall assume, in a state of extreme probabilistic ignorance in the sense that he is committed to a credal state allowing all such Q-functions.

Bayesians might object that there is no clear way to recommend what X should do in such a situation.

That, however, is not quite so. X can at least state that he should not choose an A_i unless there is some Q-function in the set B such that the expected utility for A_i is a maximum. This could eliminate some options from consideration. And among those options which survive, X could claim that he should endorse one bearing the highest security level as the maximin principle requires.

Such a view of rational choice is at least implicit in the decision theory outlined by C. A. B. Smith to accompany his account of indeterminate probability judgement.[2] And there are cases where such a view makes considerable sense.

Many authors, including Harsanyi, contend that when maximin is used in this manner an option is picked which is a Bayes solution according to some Q-function. They contend therefore that in using maximin X is willy-nilly endorsing a numerically precise credal state. Moreover, maximin prescribes using the most pessimistic credal state (Harsanyi, 1975).

2 For references to Smith and others who have explored indeterminate probability, see Levi, 1974.

Criticisms such as this are blatantly question-begging. If X has a credal state in which he suspends judgement between rival Q-functions and identifies those options which are Bayes solutions, he has exhausted his resources for appraising the options available to him utilizing his judgements of credal probability. He is then going to seek other criteria – distinct from maximizing expected utility – for selecting an option from among those which passed the test of expected utility. The option he selects is obviously going to be one which has passed the test of expected utility and hence bears maximum expected utility according to at least one Q-function in B. To infer from this that X is committed to one of the Q-functions which determines the option chosen to bear maximum expected utility is to presuppose what is subject to dispute – namely, that X is committed to a credal state represented by a numerically precise probability distribution.

Such question-begging is commonplace among contemporary Bayesians and prevents some authors such as Harsanyi from taking seriously notions such as extreme probabilistic ignorance.

John Rawls, like Harsanyi, thinks that impersonal appraisals of social states of the sort required to make moral judgements concerning just distributions can be obtained by considering counterfactual evaluations of the social states one would choose were one in a state of ignorance. However, unlike Harsanyi, Rawls takes the state of ignorance not to be a state of probabilistic ignorance but a state of extreme probabilistic ignorance (Rawls, 1971, pp. 150–75).

An interesting aspect of this difference is that Rawls derives a different appraisal of distributions than does Harsanyi. Thus it appears that, within the framework of so-called 'contractarian' views of social justice, one source of controversy ought to be concerning what constitutes a state of ignorance.

This, however, is somewhat misleading; for the issue is not so much what we mean by a state of ignorance but rather which of the two senses (or some alternative) is the appropriate one to use in deriving impersonal moral appraisals of rival distributions of social benefits.

But once we appreciate this point, we may begin to wonder whether contractarian approaches get us anywhere after all. I see no obvious way in which an appeal to self-evidence or, if not that, to some cogent purely epistemological consideration will decide which of the two senses of ignorance will be better suited to the making of appraisals of social states of the impersonal kind required by Harsanyi and Rawls. Linguistic reflections on the ordinary meaning of ignorance will not help. What on earth would ordinary language have to say to us here? Shall we consult moral intuitions? Should we consider the consequences of one approach rather than another for social policy? I shall not enter into these and other issues. What should be apparent is that the evaluation of rival criteria for appraising distributions with respect to equity cannot rely on contractarian considerations alone. Moreover, once one begins to reflect on the additional considerations which might be required to render a verdict, the suspicion arises that contractarian considerations might not be required at all.

Suppose X is concerned neither with social policy nor with individual decision making but with revising his body of evidence or standard for serious possibility. In particular, he may be concerned to add new information to K to answer some particular question. One way he may expand his corpus by accepting new information *into* evidence is through making observation reports. Another way might be through some mode of inductive inference.

In inductive inference, we may suppose that X has some sort of criterion or rule for evaluating rival potential answers to a question relative to his initial corpus K to determine what should be added to K via induction.

I have suggested elsewhere that the set of potential answers may be represented by identifying a partition U relative to K with respect to which X is modally ignorant (Levi, 1967a). Given any g equivalent given K to a disjunction of elements of U, accepting g into evidence as strongest via induction from K is adding g to K along with all deductive consequences of K and g. To do this is, of course, to reject all elements of U inconsistent with K and g. Hence, we can formulate the acceptance rule employed as a rejection rule.

We can, in point of fact, regard X, prior to revising his corpus via induction, as considering in a preliminary manner the conclusions he would reach relative to each rule in a family of rules belonging to a caution-dependent set. Such a set is characterized by a parameter k such that, for each potential answer g, there is a value $k(h)$ which is the maximum value of the parameter for which h goes unrejected unless h is inconsistent with K, in which case h is rejected relative to all values of k (whose values might be restricted to the range from 0 to some maximum – say 1).

As an example of caution-dependent rules, consider the rule which recommends rejecting an element of U if and only if the highest Q value assigned that element according to X's credal state B is less than k/n where U contains n elements. I do not recommend this rule, but it is useful for illustrative purposes.

There will be some elements of U which avoid rejection for all values of k and others which avoid rejection for some but not for all. We can say that those which avoid rejection for all values of k are not tentatively disbelieved or rejected at all. The negation (given K) of the disjunction of all such unrejected elements of U can be said to be tentatively believed or accepted.

To be tentatively or preliminarily accepted in this sense is not to be accepted as evidence in the initial corpus or even to be worthy of being accepted into evidence. It is, however, to pass an important hurdle toward being accepted into evidence. Another hurdle would be to be justifiably acceptable in this manner for lower values of k.

Now if $k(h)$ is less than the maximum of 1, we can say that h is rejected and, indeed, rejected to a positive degree. Its degree of rejection, disbelief, or, in the language of G. L. S. Shackle, potential surprise is equal to $1 - k(h)$.[3] The degree of tentative acceptance or belief that h is equal to $1 - k(\sim h)$.

An interesting feature of Shackle's measure $y(h) = 1 - k(h)$ for potential surprise is that: (i) at least one element of U must bear 0 surprise; (ii) several and indeed all elements of U may bear 0 surprise; and (iii) $y(h \vee g) = \min(y(h), y(g))$. These properties are in violation of the conditions on probabilistic measures.

Another interesting feature is that we can introduce a new non-probabilistic notion of a state of ignorance relative to U. A Shackle-like state of ignorance is one where each element of U bears 0 degree of potential surprise or disbelief. Since $b(h)$, the degree of relief that h, equals $y(\sim h)$, such a state of ignorance amounts to assigning each element of U 0 b-value.

In a Shackle-like state of ignorance, no element of U is rejected even tentatively. Hence, relative to the initial corpus K not only is X in a state of modal ignorance but, no matter what value of k he uses, he has no warrant for revising K so as to alleviate that state of modal ignorance. Hence, insofar as he is engaged in inquiry in order to remove that ignorance, he may require the acquisition of new information via observation and the answering of other questions via induction before he returns to the question under consideration.

How does Shackle-like ignorance relate to probabilistic ignorance of the sort canvassed previously? The answer depends on the sort of caution-dependent rejection rule one uses.

The rule used purely for illustrative purposes can be exploited to draw some morals.

It is necessary and sufficient to be in a Shackle-like state of ignorance for elements of U that the upper probability for each element of U be no less than $1/n$. This will hold, of course, when each element of U bears the definite and unique Q-value of $1/n$. It will also obtain when all coherent probability distributions over elements of U are members of B. And it will hold in a great many other cases as well. Thus Shackle-like ignorance is implied by probabilistic ignorance in the weak sense, in the extreme sense, and by other sorts of credal states.

The last three senses of ignorance canvassed here presuppose the first – to wit, modal ignorance. For the rest, the uses to which weak and extreme probabilistic ignorance can be put are rather different from those to which Shackle-like ignorance can be adapted. Finally, it is doubtful whether there is much purpose in attempting to fix on any one of these senses as the 'correct' meaning of ignorance. All of these notions have their uses. It is rather more important to identify them and evaluate their significance for deliberation and inquiry than it is to engage in verbal disputes.

3 See Levi, 1967a, ch. 8, for references to Shackle.

10
Escape from boredom: edification according to Rorty*†

Richard Rorty sings in the antifoundationalist chorus. His song equates the rise of foundationalist epistemology with the professionalization of philosophy. The discordant notes he finds in the foundationalist score become, as a consequence, subversive of philosophy as an autonomous discipline.

Nonetheless, the most salient feature of Rorty's recent book, *Philosophy and the Mirror of Nature*, is that it is by a professional philosopher, for professional philosophers and about the future of philosophy as a profession. The early chapters of the book are polished pieces of professional philosophical prose addressed to issues which have provoked interest in recent years among members of academic philosophy departments. They represent efforts to undermine foundationalist epistemology even in some of its currently fashionable guises as philosophy of language. Although Rorty disavows the intention of replacing epistemology with a professionalizable alternative, he allays fears of unemployment by asserting that there will continue to be philosophy departments and that there is no danger of philosophy coming to an end. He even suggests an activity for philosophers to engage in when not teaching the great thinkers of the past. They might practice hermeneutics by engaging in edifying conversations with advocates of incommensurable viewpoints or participants in incommensurable discourses.

Little importance ought to be attached to speculation about the future of philosophy. And opposition to foundationalism ought to be the philosophical equivalent of resistance to sin – although it is a regrettable sociological fact that it is not. We should stop talking about turning our backs on foundationalism and start turning our backs.

But what should we do when turning our backs? Rorty thinks we should engage in edifying efforts to bridge the gulf between incommensurables. In my view, there are no incommensurable abysses worth bridging.

---

* David Weissman first drew my attention to the centrality of the concern with boredom in Rorty's view. Frederic Schick made some constructive editorial suggestions. In no other respects are Weissman or Schick to be held accountable for what I have written.
† Reprinted with the permission of the editors from *Canadian Journal of Philosophy*, v. 11, no. 4 (1981), pp. 589–601.

Rorty follows Kuhn in taking normal science to be a practice of solving problems relative to a 'consensus about what counts as a good explanation of the phenomena and about what it would take for a problem to be solved' (Rorty, 1980, p. 320). In revolutionary science, new problems and paradigms of explanation are introduced. In normal science, 'everybody agrees on how to evaluate everything everybody else says'. This is not so in revolutionary science.

Rorty proposes generalizing this contrast rendering it applicable not only to inquiry concerned with explaining and describing the way the world is but also to moral and political reflection and artistic judgement.

Thus, in revolutionary situations, rival points of view (concerning the truth or falsity of scientific theories, the propriety of political arrangements or the aesthetic qualities of works of art) are incommensurable in the sense they are incapable of being 'brought under a set of rules which will tell us how rational agreement can be reached on what would settle the issue on every point where statements seem to conflict' (Rorty, 1980, p. 316).

Prima facie, when one finds oneself in a controversy of the sort Rorty describes as revolutionary, the obstacle to the very feasibility of subsequent inquiry or deliberation leading to 'rational agreement' is that the issues under dispute presuppose conflicting approaches to the conduct of inquiry. Under such circumstances, the sensible thing to do is to identify those assumptions and procedures which are noncontroversial in the context of the controversy and move to a point of view where only these assumptions and procedures are taken for granted in the inquiry, deliberation or discourse. Once this is done, judgement should be suspended concerning the issues under dispute pending further inquiry aimed at identifying which of the rival positions ought to be adopted.

If this is not done but the parties to a controversy remain committed to the points under dispute, they must perforce beg the question when arguing against their opponents. Under these circumstances, it is obvious that the dispute is incapable of being 'brought under a set of rules which will tell how rational agreement can be reached'.

Controversies where questions are begged are as common as blackberries. Sometimes such question-begging is wilful. Sometimes it derives from failures of understanding. No doubt it is often helpful to have some mediator facilitate the process of understanding – at least in those cases where it is desirable that inquiry be carried on in a non-question-begging manner to resolve the points under controversy.

But it is not always sensible to suspend judgement in the face of disagreement in order to give other views a hearing. Feyerabend to the contrary notwithstanding, it is silly to give a serious hearing to every fool proposal that comes along. Indeed, it is an interesting and important question when one should and should not open up one's mind to rival points

137

of view concerning the truth of scientific theories, the rightness or wrongness of actions, the legitimacy of political constitutions or the qualities of works of art. It is just as indefensible to answer 'always' as 'never'; and no alternative context independent principle applicable on all occasions and regardless of the nature of the dispute and its participants will prove better.

In any case, if there is no point in opening up one's mind to a rival point of view on some occasion, the need for the services of a hermeneutical mediator can scarcely be urgent. On the other hand, if it is desirable to inquire on some matter in a non-question-begging manner, one is not doing hermeneutics as Rorty apparently conceives it. Hermeneuticists 'converse' with advocates of rival 'discourses' 'whose paths through life have fallen together, united by civility rather than by a common goal, much less by a common ground' (Rorty, 1980, p. 318). Practitioners of hermeneutics 'keep conversations going' so that participants in different ways of life might come to some agreement or at least to fruitful disagreement (Rorty, 1980, pp. 317–18). But mediation is not the goal of the enterprise. The edification provided by participation in hermeneutical activity enables us to redescribe ourselves in new and interesting ways and 'redescribing ourselves is the most important thing we can do' (Rorty, 1980, pp. 358–9).

From the educational as opposed to the epistemological or technological point of view, the way things are said is more important than the possession of truths (Rorty, 1980, p. 394).

Whether hermeneuticists are envisaged as conceptual fixers facilitating comprehension or as entertainers multiplying the numbers of ways we might describe ourselves, the point for Rorty is not to enable agents to move to a position where they can inquire without prejudicing the issue under dispute.

In any case, refusal to suspend judgement does not make a controversy revolutionary in a Kuhnian sense. Even in normal science, occasions arise when investigators refuse to open up their minds to rival viewpoints and suspend judgement concerning the points under dispute.

As I understand Kuhn, when rival points of view are incommensurable, judgement cannot be suspended on the points under dispute even when one desires to do so. The question 'Which side are you on?' cannot be avoided even for the duration of an inquiry. There is no hiding or straddling of fences.

When rival viewpoints are commensurable, there is no obstacle to suspension of judgement pending the outcome of inquiry. Rorty appears to think this is feasible within the framework of some practice or way of life with its codified or codifiable procedures for engaging in inquiries to resolve unsettled issues; but once one faces a confrontation with practitioners of another way of life, there is no way to address the matter without insisting on working by one's own rules or converting to the other side.

138

Rorty appears to think it is a good thing to become familiar with diverse incommensurable ways of life or discourses. Intellectual travel is somehow good for the soul, although it is far from clear why Rorty thinks so. But there is no way, even in principle, in which conflicts between incommensurable outlooks can be evaluated from 'neutral', non-question-begging vantage points.

Following Kuhn, Rorty correctly observes that identifying a dispute as between incommensurable alternatives does not preclude X understanding Y even when his interpretation of Y's doctrine is from his conflicting viewpoint. But given such understanding, either X stands pat or undergoes a revolutionary conversion.

Rorty also emphasizes, as does Kuhn, that making comparisons of incommensurable viewpoints is feasible. Thus, according to Kuhn, incommensurable theories can be compared with respect to how well they agree with the available observations and experiments, with respect to their scope, simplicity and their fruitfulness. Nevertheless, when the controversy is in a revolutionary context, the manner in which these desiderata are weighed will diverge as will the detailed specification of the desiderata themselves (Rorty, 1980, p. 327).

I do not understand myself why difficulties over weighing rival desiderata should preclude commensurability. If the point under dispute is how to weight the desiderata and no resolution specifying a unique weighting is in sight, then one should suspend judgement between all verdicts not unanimously ruled out by weighting schemes which have not themselves been eliminated.

Nor does the failure to resolve the controversy over how to weight the desiderata doom the dispute to remain in a state of suspense forever. As was insisted by one of Rorty's heroes (the only one also on my list), John Dewey, one way of dealing with an unresolved conflict in values is by acquiring sufficient data through inquiry so as to render one solution optimal according to all desiderata or by finding some new option having this property. Proceeding in this manner will often prove feasible (whether in science, ethics, politics or art) even if the conflict concerning weighting of desiderata remains unresolved.

These maneuvers for sidestepping conflicts in weighting desiderata are applicable in what Rorty would consider to be 'normal' and non-revolutionary inquiry.[1] Hence, the fact that conflicts over incommensurables involve differences over weighting desiderata cannot suffice to explain why such revolutionary disputes differ from normal ones.

Thus, we are thrown back on the conclusion that the distinguishing mark of revolutionary controversy is that judgement cannot be suspended pending further inquiry.

1 See Levi (1980a, pp. 180–2) and (1979d), reprinted in this volume.

139

Rorty links the denial of a distinction between revolutionary and normal controversy with a commitment to foundationalism.

The holistic, antifoundationalist, pragmatist treatments of knowledge which we find in Dewey, Wittgenstein, Quine, Sellars and Davidson are almost equally offensive to many philosophers precisely because they abandon the quest for commensuration and are thus 'relativist' (Rorty, 1980, p. 317).

Rorty fails to explain why, in order to 'commensurate' rival viewpoints one must appeal to ground which is neutral not merely for the controversy under investigation but for all inquiries. Dewey did not endorse this assumption. Insofar as Quine focuses on Neurath's metaphor of rebuilding ships at sea, he also avoids doing so. Rejection of foundationalism need not be accompanied by a commitment to incommensurability.

To the contrary, antifoundationalism appears to be far more congenial with the denial of incommensurability. According to those who distinguish revisions of doctrine turning on changes in conceptual framework from non-conceptual changes, controversies over conceptual revision cannot be grounded in a neutral framework relative to which the rival conceptual framework may be assessed without begging questions. Those who are addicted to conceptual frameworks tend to think that everyone should be an addict. We cannot do without conceptual frameworks. We cannot be non-committal respecting conceptual matters. But if we reject the distinction between conceptual and non-conceptual changes, at least one basis for distinguishing the commensurable from the incommensurable is rejected as well.

Rorty rejects a distinction between conceptual and non-conceptual changes (Rorty, 1980, ch. 6). But his own contrast between normal and revolutionary changes in doctrine does not differ in important respects from the distinction he rejects. At least I can discern no relevant respect in which someone changing conceptual frameworks proceeds differently from someone being converted from one viewpoint to another incommensurable with it except that those who follow Rorty would refuse to call the latter changes in conceptual frameworks.[2]

I do not know how to prove the non-existence of incommensurables. But even if it could be shown that judgement may always be suspended without begging questions, there is no guarantee that enough will survive in the way

2 Rorty does worry about the difference between conceptual shifts and revolutionary shifts (note 1, p. 316) but nowhere comes to terms with the main point – namely, that revolutionary shifts, like conceptual shifts, are changes of doctrine which cannot be assessed from a 'neutral' point of view. I suspect that his failure to address this point stems from his confusion of the feasibility of moving to a point of view neutral for the issues under scrutiny with the feasibility of moving to a point of view neutral for all controversies.

of non-controversial assumptions and methods to secure resolution in a reasonable and definite manner.

However, like Peirce (and Dewey who follows Peirce in this), we may always hope that proceeding with inquiry will yield the resources for resolving disputes. To rule out in advance of inquiry the possibility of resolution by insisting that it involves a choice between incommensurables is to place roadblocks in the path of inquiry. Talk of incommensurability may be congenial with the outlooks of assorted hermeneuticists, existentialists and phenomenologists. I do not know. But, Rorty to the contrary notwithstanding, such talk is alien not only to the antifoundationalist and pragmatist Peirce but to the antifoundationalist and pragmatist Dewey as well.

Rorty's distance from pragmatism (for which in its Deweyite form he professes much admiration) emerges even more emphatically when he seeks to exploit his insistence on revolutionary changes in science to argue against the physical sciences as the paradigm of knowledge.

Rorty apparently thinks that in normal science, the available repertoire of background assumptions, routines and canons of procedure serves as an 'algorithm' for deciding between rival solutions to a problem (Rorty, 1980, p. 322). Algorithms for decision are usually understood to be effective or recursive criteria for deciding whether something satisfies some condition or other. To my knowledge, few serious writers since the 1930s have maintained that the decision problem for physics could be solved affirmatively. Certainly after it was shown that it could not be solved for first order predicate logic, skepticism on this score was rampant so that Kuhn's questioning 'whether philosophy of science could construct an algorithm for choice among scientific theories' is scarcely an innovative line of doubt.

Of course, neither Kuhn nor Rorty meant what their words are normally used to say. Unfortunately it is far from clear what they did mean to say. I conjecture that they are denying the existence of an effective criterion for deciding whether given assumptions justify favoring one theory over another. Kuhn's contention that in the case of theory choice, decisions require weighing competing valuations of the rival theories, where the values (such as simplicity) and the weighings depend upon the particular context of inquiry, does undercut the idea that the appraisal of scientific arguments may be settled by an algorithm checking whether the rival hypotheses bear appropriate relations of support, confirmation or corroboration.

But this observation is not original with Kuhn. Nor does it entail the distinction between revolutionary and normal science. The absence of such algorithms is perfectly normal. According to current statistical theory, normal efforts to test a statistical hypothesis need to take into account not only the data of experimentation and the hypothesis being tested but the alternatives to that hypothesis. Moreover, trade-offs between competing desiderata need to be made and are manifested in the specification of such factors as significance levels. Thus, the absence of 'algorithms for choice' cuts across all scientific inquiry and cannot be confined to allegedly 'revolutionary' choices.[3]

Rorty contends that the absence of such algorithms for choice casts doubt as to 'whether epistemology could, starting from science, work its way outward to the rest of culture by discovering the common ground of as much human discourse as could be thought of as 'cognitive' or 'rational' (Rorty, 1980, pp. 322–3). According to Rorty, Kuhn has shown us that controversies in the sciences do not differ 'in kind' from controversies in politics, morals, art criticism and the like. Because scientific controversies derive not only from disagreements concerning what is the case but from differences in values – including cognitive values – scientific inquiry is no more disinterested than moral or political deliberation (Rorty, 1980, p. 331).

Rorty's observation contains an important germ of truth – even if it is misleadingly stated.

Any specific scientific inquiry is goal or problem oriented. What is an optimal solution depends on the nature of the problem and, hence, on the aims and values of the inquiry. In these respects, scientific inquiry resembles practical deliberation. As I have urged for some time, this suggests that the canons for rational goal attainment applicable in practical deliberation aimed at choosing policy to promote moral, economic, political or other practical goals and the canons for rational goal attainment applicable in inquiry aimed at realizing cognitive goals ought to be the same.

Such a view allows for recognition of 'the fundamental unity of the structure of common sense and science' (Dewey, 1938, p. 79) which Dewey insisted should be recognized. On the other hand, we are not compelled to adopt the 'reductive' view which assimilates the cognitive aims of scientific inquiry to the aims of common sense inquiries focused on 'use and enjoyment'.

This position is congenial with antifoundationalism without recommending the 'which-side-are-you-on' mentality which Rorty and Kuhn seem to share.

To deny incommensurability is not to recommend suspension of judgement on every occasion where controversy arises but merely to remind us that suspension of judgement is an option. More to the point, it is to insist that if we do choose sides, we should do so in a manner which can be justified in a non-question-begging manner from a basis which is neutral not vis à vis all controversies but relative to the issue under consideration.

---

3 In (Levi, 1962, pp. 47–65), I suggested that the choice of caution levels in statistical testing reflected a trade-off between the urge to remove doubt and to avoid error. This idea was, elaborated and extended to scientific inquiry generally in (1967a) and (1967c, pp. 387–91) in 1967. The relations between my views on these matters and Kuhn's rather later observations about trade-offs are discussed in chapter 3 of (Levi, 1980a).

Once this is understood, we may, perhaps, be in a position to encourage respect for truth as a desideratum for scientific inquiry along with the other desiderata on the Kuhnian list. We can do so without assuming glassy essences seeking to mirror an undescribed reality or to mimic the opinions of some objectively privileged omniscient mind. Truth or avoidance of error is as judged relative to our evolving doctrine.

Of course, if all we do is judge truth as earnestly and as seriously as can be relative to the evolving doctrine, life would become a boring cocktail party. But if we regard the evolving doctrine as a resource in inquiry as Dewey did, we may take such earnest judgements as the standard relative to which we discount some hypotheses as not possibly true and others as serious possibilities. In this way, our earnest and serious judgements will play an important role in guiding our conduct whether we are engaged in scientific inquiry, in moral, political or other practical deliberation or in artistic creation.[4]

Furthermore, when in scientific inquiry we seek to develop the evolving doctrine further, we may seek to avoid error in the sense of error generated by a Tarskian apparatus on the assumption prior to revision that all items in the initial state of the doctrine are true.

Avoidance of error in this sense could not be a desideratum where the shift is from one theory to another incommensurable with it. If T_1 is the theory in the initial version of the evolving doctrine, to substitute T_2 for it would be to replace certain truth with certain error.

On the other hand, if it is feasible first to modify the doctrine by suspending judgement between T_1 and T_2 (such a move incurs loss of information but imports no error) and then judge truth relative to the new weakened doctrine, one can take the risk of error into account in rendering a verdict between the rival theories. Sometimes the risk to be incurred by choosing sides will be worth taking and sometimes not. And sometimes, when the risk is worth taking, T_2 will be adopted so that the net effect is a replacement of T_1 by T_2.

By insisting that some (and, indeed, the important) revisions of doctrine involve shifts from T_1 to incommensurable T_2, Rorty following Kuhn has an excuse for ignoring risk of error in such cases (had he ever thought of the matter in the first place). He can argue that investigators cannot suspend judgement between the rivals so as to appraise risk of error in a non-question-begging manner.

Thus, Rorty is in a position to claim that even in science truth does not matter – even in the sense in which talk of truth involves no appeal to glassy essences mirroring the world.

Neither Kuhn nor Rorty has offered the slightest basis for supposing that incommensurability ever has obtained or does obtain. To be sure, there are

4 Some ramifications of this view are discussed in the first three chapters of Levi (1980a).

plenty of cases where agents have refused to suspend judgement concerning points under dispute. Sometimes they were right to do so and sometimes not. Bellarmine, for better or worse, clearly refused to open up his mind; but this shopworn example does not establish incommensurability – i.e., that suspension of judgement was not feasible. Whatever may have happened in the past, to assume in some context in advance of inquiry that a controversy concerns incommensurable alternatives is to place roadblocks in the path of inquiry.

Thus, we should avoid Rorty's confusion of anticommensurabilism with antifoundationalism, antirepresentationalism and opposition to glassy essences and any of these with opposition to recognizing truth as an important desideratum in inquiry.

Scientific inquiry, like moral, political and other practical deliberation and like artistic creation, is goal-oriented; and we should agree with Dewey that the structure of inquiries aimed at realizing ends of diverse kinds should exhibit similar features to be recognized as rational. In these respects, there is nothing different 'in kind' between scientific inquiry and deliberation in ethics, politics or the arts.

But there are important differences between these activities with respect to the ends they pursue and how they contribute to the realization of ends other than the ones which constitute their proximate objectives. The fruits of scientific inquiry are more than ornaments to be admired and appreciated. They serve as resources for further information gathering inquiry, as standards for judging possibility in guiding policy and furnishing technologies useful for policy and for the arts. It matters critically that the results of scientific inquiry be free of error not only for the sake of science but for other 'ways of life' as well.

Furthermore, as Dewey emphatically insisted, it is through the application of scientific methods of inquiry (methods, by the way, which are not fixed but are open to revision through inquiry itself) that we can expect to enhance our capacities for use and enjoyment not only as consumers but as artists and students of Man (Dewey, 1938, p. 78). To suppose, as Rorty suggests, that we should turn to edifying discourses of a hermeneutical character which give priority to 'the way things are said' over 'possession of truths' is to kid ourselves and to take a view diametrically opposed to Dewey's.

Arguing for the autonomy of science with respect to the characteristic aims of scientific inquiry and for the importance of the values it promotes (as well as its products) for other important human activities is not suggesting that morals, politics or art are parasitic on science or that the current scientific institutions are or ought to be immune from serious criticism. To the contrary, insofar as public support has tended to create powerful special interest groups among scientists, we should be as suspicious of them as we are of other special interest groups. And, of course, judgement as to which problems are worth investigating are and should be controlled by moral, political, economic, and artistic interests as well cognitive interests in obtaining error-free information. But as Dewey insisted, our moral, political, economic, and artistic values should themselves be subject to critical control in inquiries which bear marks of rationality similar to those exhibited by properly conducted scientific inquiries.

On the one hand the outstanding problem of our civilization is set by the fact that common sense in its content, its 'world' and methods, is a house divided against itself. It consists in part, and that part the most vital, of regulative meanings and procedures that antedate the rise of experimental science in its conclusions and methods. In another part, it is what it is because of application of science. This cleavage marks every phase and aspect of modern life: religious, economic, political, legal, and even artistic.

The essence of this split is put in evidence by those who condemn the 'modern' and who hold that the only solution of the chaos in civilization is to revert to the intellectual beliefs and methods that were authoritative in past ages, as well as by radicals and 'revolutionaries'. Between the two stand the multitude that is confused and insecure. It is for this reason that it is here affirmed that the basic problem of present culture and associated living is that of effecting integration where division now exists. The problem cannot be solved apart from a unified logical method of attack and procedure. The attainment of unified methods means that the fundamental unity of the structure of inquiry in common sense and science be recognized, their difference being one in the problems with which they are directly concerned, not their logics. It is not urged that the attainment of a unified logic, a theory of inquiry, will resolve the split in our beliefs and our procedures. But it is affirmed that it will not be resolved without it (Dewey, 1938, pp. 78–9).

If Dewey's hopes could be realized, there would be nothing special about science in one important respect. It would share a 'unified logical method of attack and procedure' with other 'ways of life'.

To be sure, Dewey does not assume that science would share with 'common sense' a system of assumptions and criteria capable without supplementation of resolving every controversy or difficulty which might arise. Those respects in which the logical method of attack and procedure is the same in scientific inquiry, in legal, moral, and political deliberation and in artistic endeavor are far too weak for such purposes. The method must be supplemented by additional assumptions and rules, by special objectives which differentiate branches of scientific inquiry from one another and these from activities focused on problems of 'use and enjoyment'.

Even when some discipline or 'way of life' is characterized by these supplementary aims, procedures, and assumptions, there need be no pretense that these methods can resolve all problems which the discipline might seek to confront. Furthermore, there is no claim that these aims, procedures, and assumptions are fixed and immune from criticism from within the ongoing activity of that discipline, way of life or 'discourse'.

Even more crucially, different institutions, 'ways of life', or what have you

145

with different objectives and which are relatively autonomous in the sense that they often pursue their interests without interfering in the business of others sometimes do come into conflict. If a shared concern to resolve the dispute is justified, as it often may be, the methods of attack and procedure involving a willingness to suspend judgement over conflicting issues in order to pursue further inquiry in a non-question-begging manner may lead to modifications in one or another way of life. The results of scientific or technological inquiry may impose limits on or enhance our capacity to realize certain artistic values. Conversely our interest in realizing certain aesthetic values may redirect our priorities among topics to be subjected to close scientific investigation.

Rorty envisages scientific institutions, like other social institutions, as constituted somehow by relatively rigid aims and procedures whose undermining would destroy these institutions.

As I understand Dewey, not only should we avoid organizing our scientific institutions in this manner, we should modify other social institutions in order to minimize their fragility. Institutions (whether of science or anything else) which are organized along the liberal lines envisaged by Dewey are capable of entertaining serious criticism in a piecemeal non-revolutionary fashion.

Rorty presupposes that each way of life has its own normal discourse codifiable by its own epistemology. He also appreciates (correctly I think) the vulnerability of such ways of life to change. Combining Rorty's founda-tionalism in the small with the vulnerability of institutions to change implies that revolutions should be expected.

It is also easy to see how someone bored with life on his particular ship at sea might enjoy and, indeed, appreciate uplift from an intimation of what life might be like if he jumped ship; and the more ships one jumps in fantasy, the more intense the desire to do it again. Hence, the importance of edifying hermeneutical conversations in Rorty's scheme of things.

I for one continue to urge and hope for a different and more liberal vision both of scientific inquiry and other aspects of human life where the distinction between what is normal and revolutionary is blurred if not obliterated and where urges to Marcusean grand refusals are resisted.

To say this is not to suggest that life should always be filled with solemn and earnest inquiry. There is a critical role for play; but play should not be confused with business, for 'that way madness lies'.

11
Serious possibility*†

1 Credal states

Strict Bayesians emphasize the importance of the evaluation of truth value bearing hypotheses with respect to subjective or credal probability for both practical deliberation and scientific inquiry. According to strict Bayesians, agent X's *credal state* $B_{X,t}$ for hypotheses expressible in language L containing neither modal nor epistemic operators or predicates is representable by a function $Q(h; e)$ from sentences in L to real numbers satisfying the following conditions.

(1) $Q(h; e)$ takes all $h \in L$ in the first argument place and all and only $e \in L$ such that the truth of e is a serious possibility according to X at t. The value of the function is non-negative, real and finite for every such pair $(h; e)$.

(2) If the falsity of $e \equiv e'$ and $h \equiv h'$ is not a serious possibility according to X at t, $Q(h; e) = Q(h'; e')$.

(3) If the falsity of $e \supset h$ is not a serious possibility according to X at t, $Q(h; e) = 1$.

(4) If the falsity of $e \supset \sim(h \& f)$ is not a serious possibility according to X at t, $Q(h \lor f; e) = Q(h; e) + Q(f; e)$.

(5) $Q(h \& f; e) = Q(h; f \& e)Q(f; e)$.

Agent X need not be a person but could be a group or institution. But whether X is a person or group, we cannot expect X to be capable of adopting a credal state for hypotheses expressible in L satisfying these conditions on all occasions. Emotional or sociological disturbances, failure of personal or group memory and lack of computational facility are among the factors which will normally prevent X from satisfying the requirements just prescribed. In real life, X will normally fail to be ideally situated.

* I wish to thank Charles Parsons for having saved me from some errors. In spite of his gentle benevolence, however, I have resisted his efforts to save me from others.
† Reprinted with the permission of the publisher from *Essays in Honour of Jaakko Hintikka*, Dordrecht: Reidel (1979), pp. 219–36. Copyright © 1979 by D. Reidel Publishing Company, Dordrecht, Holland.

Nonetheless, we may prescribe that X conform to the prescriptions for an ideally situated agent insofar as he is able. In this sense, we may suppose that less than ideally situated X should be committed to a credal state representable by a Q-function satisfying the conditions just specified even though he may excusably fail to live up to his commitments. It is such a commitment which I shall take to be X's credal state.

Even so, it seems to me that the demands imposed by strict Bayesians on ideally situated agents are excessive. I shall not argue the point here, but it seems to me that ideally situated agents are not only permitted to have credal states representable as sets of more than one Q-function satisfying the conditions (1)–(5) but that under suitable circumstances they are obliged to adopt such credal states. But whether $B_{X,t}$ is representable by a single Q-function or by a non-empty set of such functions (satisfying a convexity condition), the conditions (1)–(5) presuppose that X is committed to evaluating all truth value bearing hypotheses expressible in L with respect to serious possibility in a manner which meets the following conditions:

(6) The sentences in L are partitioned into those belonging to the *corpus* $K_{X,t}$ and those which do not where $h \in K_{X,t}$ if and only if the falsity of h is not a serious possibility according to X at t.

(7) $K_{X,t}$ is deductively closed in L.

(8) $K_{X,t}$ contains the *urcorpus* UK for L
  (a) UK is deductively closed
  (b) UK contains all truths of first order logic, set theory and mathematics expressible in L
  (c) UK contains all other incorrigible hypotheses expressible in L.

If $e \in K_{X,t}$, $Q(h; e) = Q(h)$. Hence, $Q(e; e) = Q(e) = 1$ and $Q(\sim e) = 0$. On the other hand, if $Q(\sim e) = 0$, it does not follow that $e \in K_{X,t}$ and, hence, it does not follow that the falsity of e is not a serious possibility according to X at t.

X's corpus $K_{X,t}$ at time t is his *standard for serious possibility at t*. All and only hypotheses consistent with $K_{X,t}$ are serious possibilities according to X at t.

2 Confirmational commitments

At t, X is committed to a corpus $K_{X,t}$ and credal state $B_{X,t}$ for hypotheses expressible in L which together satisfy conditions (1)–(8). But there are many pairs (K, B) other than $(K_{X,t}, B_{X,t})$ which meet these requirements. Any such pair is a *potential corpus cum credal state*.

I shall assume that at time t, ideally situated and rational X adopts a rule stipulating for each potential corpus K what the credal state should be in the eventuality that X adopts K as his standard for serious possibility. Less than ideally situated but rational X is committed to some such rule. Such a rule is representable as a function $C(K) = B$. Let $C_{X,t}$ be the function to which X is committed at t (his *confirmational commitment at t*). (K, B) is *accessible to X at t* if and only if $C_{X,t}(K) = B$. Clearly $(K_{X,t}, B_{X,t})$ should be accessible to X at t. That is to say, $C_{X,t}(K_{X,t}) = B_{X,t}$.

Let $K \subseteq K'$ where K' is obtained from K by adding e consistent with K and forming the deductive closure. If X should change from K to K', he has *expanded* his corpus. If he shifts from K' to K, he has *contracted* his corpus.

Let both (K, B) and (K', B') satisfy (1)–(8).

B' is the *conditionalization* of B with respect to K and K' if and only if for every $Q \in B$ there is a $Q' \in B'$ and for every $Q' \in B'$ there is a $Q \in B$ such that for all h in L and all f in L consistent with K', $Q'(h; f) = Q(h; f \& e)$.

The principle of *confirmational conditionalization* stipulates that X's confirmational commitment be a function C such that $C(K')$ must be the conditionalization of $C(K)$ with respect to K and K'.

Setting aside minor technicalities, all consistent potential corpora are expansions of UK. Given (UK, B_{uk}) accessible according to X at t for the urcorpus UK, the confirmational commitment is uniquely determined for all other potential corpora.

Confirmational conditionalization does not by itself regulate revisions of credal state over time. It is a condition on a rule to which X is committed at t for revising his credal states with respect to revisions in his evaluations of hypotheses with respect to serious possibility. If X lives up to his commitments as a rational agent and has no good reasons for revising his confirmational commitment over time, revisions in his credal state will manifest his endorsement of confirmational conditionalization.

Thus, if X expands his corpus by shifting from K to K' while keeping his confirmational commitment constant, the shift from B to B' will be a *temporal credal conditionalization*. Should X shift from K' to K, the corresponding shift from B' to B will be an *inverse temporal credal conditionalization*. If, however, X revises his confirmational commitment in the interim, the shift in credal state need not be either a temporal credal conditionalization or its inverse.

Many authors have characterized legitimate changes in credal state as conforming to temporal credal conditionalization. Doing so presupposes that confirmational commitments should never be revised and that all revisions of corpus are expansions. In my opinion, the untenability of both assumptions is obvious. The obviousness of these absurdities has been masked, so it seems, by a failure on the part of those who have discussed conditionalization to distinguish carefully between confirmational conditionalization, temporal credal conditionalization and inverse temporal credal conditionalization.

3 Consistency and possibility

h (in L) is seriously possible according to X at t if and only if h is consistent with X's corpus or standard for serious possibility $K_{X,t}$ at t. This suggests that we can also consider a notion of serious possibility relative to potential corpus K. h is a serious possibility relative to K if and only if h is consistent with K.

In this case, the relativity of serious possibility to X's cognitive state at t is replaced by a relativity to a potential corpus K. Observe, however, that the importance of serious possibility relative to K depends on the fact that K is a corpus which an agent is capable of adopting as his standard for serious possibility and the agent may wish to calculate how he would evaluate hypotheses expressible in L with respect to serious possibility were he to adopt K as his corpus.

Thus, we must not automatically suppose that every time one can construct a notion of A-consistency – i.e., consistency with some set of sentences – we have a useful notion of A-possibility – i.e., serious possibility relative to A. The set A may not qualify as a potential corpus and even if it does, it may not be a potential corpus which agents are likely to endorse. In that case, there is no useful purpose in having a notion of A-possibility additional to the notion of A-consistency.

To illustrate, consider the notion of logical possibility. Some authors construe this to be equivalent to logical consistency – i.e., consistency with the truths of first order logic – perhaps, including identity.

However, if L is sufficiently rich, the set of such logical truths is not a potential corpus. A rational agent should be committed to a corpus containing these logical truths but much more as well. The weakest potential corpus UK should be substantially stronger. Consequently, there is little point in considering how serious possibility should be evaluated relative to the set of first order logical truths. Of course, the notion of logical consistency is of first rate importance. But there is no need to have another term 'logical possibility'.

We can make 'logical possibility' do work for us if we equate it with consistency with the weakest potential corpus UK; for we are often interested in how serious possibility should be evaluated in case UK is adopted as the standard for serious possibility. Indeed, there are many authors who think rational men should always endorse UK as the standard for serious possibility insofar as they are able. But even if we do not follow such an extreme view, we may be interested in how X evaluates hypotheses with respect to serious possibility in a state of modal ignorance.

One sort of evaluation of hypotheses with respect to serious possibility often invoked is relative to a corpus which is a specified transformation of the currently adopted corpus. Thus, if X is prepared to affirm 'if h were the case, g would be the case', he is evaluating the falsity of g as not being a serious possibility relative to a corpus obtained from $K_{X,t}$ by first removing $\sim h$ in a manner which yields a minimal loss of informational value and then adding h. That is to say, $\sim g$ is inconsistent with the corpus obtained from $K_{X,t}$ in this fashion.

On other occasions, serious possibility is evaluated relative to a corpus

150

described in a manner which makes no reference to its relation to $K_{X,t}$. This is true of logical possibility construed as consistency with UK.

In the philosophical literature, we often hear talk of physical possibility, psychological possibility and the like where we mean consistency with the laws of physics, psychology and the like.

Now the deductive closure of UK and the true laws of physics expressible in L does, indeed, qualify as a potential corpus in the sense covered by conditions (6)–(8). However, it is far from clear that there is any interesting basis for evaluating hypotheses with respect to serious possibility relative to such a corpus.

Not only is it highly unlikely that any agent will ever adopt a corpus containing all the true laws of physics, it is even more unlikely that such an agent would ever endorse a corpus containing only the true laws of physics (in addition to items in UK). And it is obscure to me why one should wish to evaluate serious possibility relative to such a corpus.

To be sure, there is an interesting notion of physical possibility. If I were asked to run a four minute mile at a track meet, I might declare that it is physically impossible for me to do so. I am not thereby claiming that 'Levi will run a four minute mile at the meet' is inconsistent with the true laws of physics. Indeed, I think it is consistent with the true laws of physics. The claim is that I lack the physical ability to run the race in four minutes.

If I know that I lack this ability, I shall, indeed, regard the truth of 'Levi will run a four minute mile at the meet' as not a serious possibility. But even if I did believe that I had the ability, I might appraise the truth of the sentence as not being a serious possibility. I might know, for example, that I will not enter the race at all. Or, alternatively, I might know that I did run the race but failed to run a four minute mile even though I was capable of doing so.

In this discussion, I focus on various types of possibility parasitic on the notion of serious possibility and not on notions of ability, constraint and disposition. There are, indeed, useful notions of physical possibility, psychological possibility, economic possibility and technological possibility; but they concern abilities of various kinds and have little to do with consistency with the laws of physics, psychology, economics and (heaven help us!) technology.

4 Knowledge and belief

Consider any proportional attitude or activity such as knowing, believing, desiring or choosing. Given such an attitude A, let $A_{X,t}$ be the set of hypotheses expressible in L such that X A's these hypotheses true at time t.

As before, we have a notion of A-consistency readily available to us. Should we also introduce a notion of A-possibility?

If the attitude A is that of evaluating the falsity of hypotheses as not being

151

serious possibilities, then $A_{X,t}$ is the corpus $K_{X,t}$. On the other hand, the set of hypotheses desired true does not serve as X's standard for serious possibility and, indeed, does not qualify as a potential corpus.

What about the set of hypotheses X knows at t to be true or the set of hypotheses X believes at t to be true?

Presystematically, knowledge and belief are highly ambiguous notions. Any proposal for explicating them ought to recognize the need to select from this abundance of riches and should keep in mind the purpose for which a selection is made.

The concern here is with how knowledge and belief ought to function as relevant factors in practical deliberation and scientific inquiry. The thesis advanced here is that, in at least one important sense, partial belief is explicated in terms of credal probability and that our full beliefs when taken together with their deductive consequences constitute our standard serious possibility.

On this view, 'X fully believes that h' does not imply that X has a maximal degree of introspectible conviction that h or that X is disposed to a maximally intense affirmative response to interrogation as to the truth of h. With due apologies to Hume and Quine, the relevance of conceptions of belief such as these to deliberation and inquiry remain obscure.

Hintikka distinguishes between what X knows at t and what X fully believes at t. Corresponding to the distinction between knowledge and belief, Hintikka recognizes two notions of possibility: possibility for all that X knows and compatibility with everything X believes.

I do not quarrel with the introduction of a body of knowledge and a body of belief and speaking of consistency relative to the one set and relative to the other. Nor does it really matter that Hintikka talks of possibility in the one case and compatibility in the other.

What I am concerned about is this: Should X's body of knowledge serve as his standard for serious possibility? Should his body of full beliefs? Or, perhaps, neither should.

X should be urged to avoid a double standard for serious possibility. Hence, if neither X's corpus of knowledge nor body of beliefs has the exclusive right to be X's standard, neither corpus should serve as the standard at all. In that event, it becomes unclear what relevance either knowledge or belief have for deliberation and inquiry and what point there is in speaking of epistemic or doxastic possibility.

These considerations present us with a dilemma. On the one hand, there is the ancient philosophical tradition of distinguishing between knowledge and belief to uphold. On the other hand, if we identify either X's body of knowledge or X's body of belief as his standard for serious possibility, we remain with the problem of determining what the relevance of the corpus which has not been identified as X's standard for serious possibility is as far as deliberation and inquiry are concerned.

To avoid the dilemma, I propose that we distinguish between X's point of view at t and the point of view of a third party Y who contemplates X's propositional attitudes.

From X's point of view at t, all items in his standard for serious possibility $K_{X,t}$ are infallibly true. That is to say, if $h \in K_{X,t}$, the falsity of h is not a serious possibility according to X at t.

I contend that under these conditions X fully believes that h is true and, moreover, is committed to the view that whatever he believes true at t is true.

I also think it appropriate to say that from X's point of view at t, X knows all items in $K_{X,t}$ to be true so that $K_{X,t}$ qualifies as X's corpus of knowledge at t. I also call $K_{X,t}$ X's corpus of evidence at t. If $h \in K_{X,t}$, X accepts h as evidence at t.

Terminology is unimportant. What is crucial is that, from X's point of view, there is no interesting distinction between what X knows and what X believes. The philosophical tradition which suggests otherwise is based on an illicit transfer of a distinction which has some value from Y's point of view at t' when appraising X's cognitive state at t to the case where X at t contemplates his own cognitive state at t.

While assessing X's corpus $K_{X,t}$, Y is committed to his own corpus $K_{Y,t'}$ expressible in L and to a corpus $K_{Y,t'}^1$ expressible in the meta-language $L_1 \supseteq L$. In general, $K_{X,t} \neq K_{Y,t'}$. $K_{Y,t'}$ will contain items inconsistent with $K_{X,t}$. Y is committed (in L_1) to assuming that such beliefs belonging to X's corpus are false beliefs and not knowledge.

Of course, Y will also identify items in X's corpus expressible in L which belong to his corpus expressible in L. $K_{X,t} \cap K_{Y,t'}$ should be deductively closed and contain UK. From Y's point of view, all items in L which Y knows to be false but which belong to $K_{X,t}$ should be removed from X's standard for serious possibility at t. Should that standard be restricted to $K_{X,t} \cap K_{Y,t'}$?

$K_{X,t} \cap K_{Y,t'}$ should, from Y's point of view, be contained in X's standard for serious possibility at t but need not coincide with it.

First, Y might identify h as an element of $K_{X,t}$ even though neither $h \in K_{Y,t'}$ nor $h \notin K_{Y,t'}$. From Y's point of view, it is a serious possibility that X knows that h. However, Y does not know that X knows that h.

Second, Y might assume, in his metacorpus $K_{Y,t'}^1$, that there is a true sentence in $K_{X,t}$ which is not in $K_{Y,t'}$. In this case, not only is it, from Y's point of view at t', a serious possibility that X knows something Y does not know but Y knows this to be the case.

Thus, Y may usefully distinguish between what X knows and what X believes without saddling either himself or X with a double standard for serious possibility. However, X at t cannot distinguish in the same way between what he knows and what he fully believes at t. His predicament is similar to what Y's would be were Y in perfect agreement with X.

Perhaps, someone who is prepared to concede that from X's point of view his corpus of beliefs and corpus of true beliefs are indistinguishable will,

153

nonetheless, insist on a distinction between X's corpus of true beliefs and his corpus of knowledge.

This objection rests on a confusion of knowing with coming to know.

At t, X may contemplate adding new information to his current corpus $K_{X,t}$. One appropriate potential expansion strategy might be to add g to $K_{X,t}$ and form the deductive closure $K_{X,t}^g$. From X's point of view prior to expansion, it is a serious possibility that g is true and also that it is false. Thus, implementing the strategy might lead to importation of error or it may fail to do so. If error is imported, X would come to believe that g falsely. It would not be an instance of coming to know the items in $K_{X,t}^g - K_{X,t}$ even when they are true.

Suppose, however, that g is true so that implementation of the expansion strategy is error free. Would X then come to know all items in $K_{X,t}^g - K_{X,t}$? Not unless he was justified in choosing that expansion strategy over the alternatives available to him.

Thus, from X's point of view in the context of inquiry concerned with evaluating expansion strategies, the distinction between coming to believe without error and coming to know is an important and intelligible one.

Suppose, however, X has implemented an expansion strategy and has shifted to the new corpus $K_{X,t}^g = K_{X,t'}$. From X's vantage point prior to expansion when his corpus was $K_{X,t}$, X may not have been justified in implementing this strategy. Hence, from that vantage point, the shift is not an instance of coming to know. However, once X has implemented the strategy, he has a new standard for serious possibility. All items in $K_{X,t'}$ are then judged to be true, infallibly true and certainly true. There are no invidious distinctions between them due to the way they gained admittance into his corpus. From X's new point of view at t' all items in $K_{X,t'}$ qualify as objects of his knowledge regardless of pedigree. He draws no distinction between what he truly believes at t' and what he knows at t'.

The serious point lurking behind the verbal byplay is that questions of justification of belief arise in the context of revising a standard for serious possibility either by adding new items to a corpus (expansion) or removing items (contraction). Unless we are considering a context where alternative strategies for revision are contemplated, there is no point in talking about justification of belief or of drawing distinctions between true belief and knowledge.

5 Modal realism

'The truth of h in L is seriously possible according to X at t' bears a truth value. It describes X as having a propositional attitude – namely as appraising the truth of h to be a serious possibility.

Furthermore, rational X evaluates only truth value bearing hypotheses with respect to serious possibility. Presumably, therefore, h has a truth value.

154

What about X's evaluation of the truth of h as a serious possibility? Does it have a truth value? Clearly some propositional attitudes have truth values and others do not. Believings have truth values. Desirings do not.

One can, to be sure, claim that desirings have truth values after all. One might claim that X desires that h be true if and only if X believes that the truth of h is desirable. In this way, 'the truth of h is desirable' is taken itself to be a truth value bearing hypothesis. The truth of that hypothesis is, given that X believes it true, a necessary and sufficient condition for the truth of X's belief and, hence, for the truth of X's desiring that h be true.

Of course, those who adopt this strategy are confronted with the task of offering some account of desirability of a proposition's being true where 'It is desirable that h is true' is not equivalent to 'X desires that h be true' or 'It is desirable that h be true according to X'. If there are good reasons for pursuing the strategy, the task must be faced. I do not know of such good reasons and regard the maneuver as an illustration of an incursion into gratuitous metaphysics.

Thus, in my opinion, believings do (at least sometimes) bear truth values while desirings do not. What about evaluations of hypotheses with respect to serious possibility? I contend that they are more like desirings than like believings.

Recall that we are concerned here not with X's beliefs about what his evaluations of hypotheses with respect to serious possibility are or with his beliefs about what the evaluations of other agents are but with his evaluations. The claim is that these evaluations lack truth values.

If they do have truth values, they presumably are to be construed as cases of believing truth value bearing hypotheses of some kind to be true. We are thus supposed to construe 'It is seriously possible that h according to X at t' as equivalent to 'X believes at t that it is objectively possible that h' where 'It is objectively possible that h' is not itself a description of X's evaluations of hypotheses with respect to serious possibility or a description of anyone else's.

Anyone who endorses such a modal realist view of appraisals of hypotheses with respect to serious possibility faces the task of explicating the notion of the objective possibility of truth value bearing hypotheses. As in the case of desiring, so here I find the realist maneuver unnecessary and the incursion into metaphysics gratuitous. Moreover, there is yet another complication.

Let L^m be an extension of the language L obtained by adding a new modal operator '$\Diamond$' for objective possibility. If evaluations of hypotheses expressible in L with respect to serious possibility have truth values in the sense just indicated, there should be some interpretation of the modal operator such that the following condition obtains:

(I) It is seriously possible that h according to X at t (where $h \in L$) if and only if X fully believes at t that $\Diamond h$ – i.e., if and only if '$\Diamond h$' is in X's corpus at t expressible in L^m.

155

It is not seriously possible that h according to X at t if and only if X fully believes at t that $\sim\Diamond h$.

Let h be a sentence in L. Either h is in X's corpus at t expressible in L, $\sim h$ is in that corpus or neither h nor $\sim h$ is in the corpus. In the first and the third case, '$\Diamond h$' is in X's corpus at t expressible in L^m. In the second case, '$\sim\Diamond h$' is in X's corpus at t expressible in L^m. These results are secured by condition (I).

Thus, X's corpus expressible in L^m at t must contain either '$\Diamond h$' or '$\sim\Diamond h$'. X cannot suspend judgement between these rival alternatives. In my opinion, this is unacceptable. X should not be compelled to make up his mind in all cases concerning the truth values of hypotheses purportedly describing objective conditions.

If someone persists in endorsing *de dicto* realistically construed possibility statements in L^m, the following weakening of (I) might be adopted.

(II) If the truth of h is a serious possibility at t according to X, then X fully believes that $\Diamond h$ at t.
If X fully believes that $\sim\Diamond h$ at t, the truth of h is not a serious possibility according to X at t.

(II) fails to yield necessary and sufficient conditions for the truth of X's evaluations of hypotheses expressible in L with respect to serious possibility. We might try to obtain such truth conditions by substituting some other truth value bearing propositional attitude for full belief in the condition (I). Let that propositional attitude be accepting hypotheses in some sense where X may accept h, accept $\sim h$ (reject h) or do neither. Not only would we have to determine what significance is to be given to the notion of acceptance thus introduced but we would still face the predicament that X should either accept $\Diamond h$ or reject it.

Thus, if the only motive for introducing truth value bearing modal statements is in order to specify truth conditions for appraisals of truth value bearing hypotheses with respect to serious possibility, the motive is insufficient. Evaluations of hypotheses with respect to serious possibility lack truth values.

None of this should be surprising. X's credal state – i.e., his system of appraisals of truth value bearing hypotheses in L with respect to credal probability lacks truth value in just the same way.

Suppose to the contrary that such appraisal has truth value. That is to say, if X assigns h degree of credence r, he fully believes that h is objectively probable (in some sense) to degree r.

Consider now a situation where X suspends judgement as to whether the degree of objective probability that h is 0.4 or 0.6. Let y be his degree of credence that the objective probability is 0.4 and $1 - y$ that the objective probability is 0.6. X's degree of credence that h is, under these circumstances, equal to $0.4y + (1 - y)0.6$. As long as y is positive and less than 1, X's degree of credence that h must be different from 0.4 and from 0.6. But this means that X must fully believe that the degree of credence is different from 0.4 and from 0.6 counter to the assumption that he is in suspense between these two rivals.

I have been arguing that categorical evaluations of hypotheses expressible in L with respect to serious possibility lack truth values. But if the system of evaluations adopted by X at t lacks a truth value, so do alternative systems. Consequently, conditional appraisals of hypotheses with respect to serious possibility also lack truth values. This suggests that open and counterfactual conditionals construed as expressions of such hypothetical appraisals are neither true nor false.

Jaakko Hintikka has insisted that possible worlds alternative to the actual one are to be described by means of counterfactual conditionals. David Lewis proceeds in the reverse fashion and specifies a semantics for subjunctive conditionals in terms of possible world semantics. Both views imply that subjunctive conditionals have truth values and, moreover, that the truth conditions make no reference to the subjective states of the utterers (except, of course, insofar as such subjective states are described in antecedents or consequents of such conditionals).

On my view, counterfactuals have truth values only insofar as they are construed as descriptions of the agent's conditional evaluations with respect to serious possibility. The appraisals themselves lack truth values and, as a consequence, so do the conditionals construed as expressions of such appraisals.

Hintikka must have in mind some alternative conception of how subjunctive conditionals are to be construed than the construal I favor here. Neither he nor Lewis nor any other modal realist has, to my knowledge, established an alternative construal which bears the relevance to deliberation and inquiry which evaluations with respect to serious possibility both categorical and hypothetical have.

I cannot prove conclusively that realistically construed notions of *de dicto* modality both conditional and categorical are *verdoppelte Metaphysik*. But the onus is on those who deny this to explain why the introduction of such conceptions is not gratuitous insofar as we are concerned with questions pertaining to epistemology, scientific inquiry and practical deliberation.

6 Truth

Quine contends that we judge truth as earnestly and as seriously as can be relative to our evolving doctrine. I construe him as claiming that we 'judge' truth on the assumption that all items in our corpus are true. With this much I agree.

But, for Quine, to judge that h is true seems to amount to little more than declaring that h is true as earnestly and as seriously as can be. My contention is that in seeking to improve our evolving doctrine, we seek to avoid error where error and truth are judged relative to the very same evolving doctrine.

I do not believe that Quine intended to make this sort of claim. Indeed, there is ample evidence to indicate that avoidance of error is never a desideratum for him in inquiry and deliberation.

If agent X is to have the sort of aims I urge upon him, it seems clear that he is at least committed to the view that all items in his corpus $K_{X,t}$ expressible in L are true in L. But this assumption is most conveniently construed as expressible in X's corpus $K^1_{X,t}$ at t expressible in a metalanguage L_1 rich enough to specify truth conditions for sentences in L. I follow the practice of letting L_1 contain L and, hence, letting $K^1_{X,t}$ contain $K_{X,t}$.

7 Knowing that one knows and that one does not know

Suppose $h \in K_{X,t}$. Should X be committed to including this information in his corpus $K^1_{X,t}$?

Remember that an affirmative answer does not entail insistence that rational X be consciously or explicitly aware of the contents of his corpus expressible in L. But we may insist that insofar as limitations of computational facility, memory, emotional instability and the like do not prevent him, he should know which items expressible in L belong to $K_{X,t}$.

Suppose X is offered a gamble on the truth of the hypothesis that the integer in the billionth place in the decimal expansion of pi is 9. X is committed to assuming the truth of that hypothesis or assuming the truth of its negation. That is so because either the hypothesis or its negation is entailed by the urcorpus and, hence, by X's corpus.

Hence, X is committed to assigning the hypothesis the degree of credence 0 or the degree of credence 1.

Yet, X may not be in a position to carry out the calculations required to identify his commitments. He may not, therefore, be able to evaluate the gamble in accordance with the dictates of the credal state to which he is committed.

Decision theories of the sort for which accounts of credal states and appraisals of serious possibility like mine are designed to provide an underpinning cannot pretend to offer wise counsel for such predicaments. Some second best criterion for choice may have to be invoked.

Nonetheless, it does not seem sensible to jettison an account of rational decision making designed for ideally situated agents because predicaments such as this can and will arise.

To the contrary, it seems preferable to obtain a clear view of the demands imposed on ideally situated agents so that we can help ordinary agents approximate the behavior of ideally situated agents.

In the example just cited, X does not know what is in his corpus. Yet, it seems clear that he should know if he is able.

If, for the moment, we overlook the fact that Hintikka treats 'X knows that' as an operator whereas I treat it as a metalinguistic predicate, there appears to be substantial agreement between us concerning the propriety of endorsing the requirement that if X knows that h, he should know that he knows that h.

Suppose, however, that $h \notin K_{X,t}$. Should X know this? Hintikka answers in the negative. I disagree.

If $h \notin K_{X,t}$, then we still need to consider X's credal state for h and $\sim h$. Suppose that both h and $\sim h$ are not members of $K_{X,t}$. That is to say, both are serious possibilities. Suppose further that $B_{X,t}$ contains exactly one numerical assignment for $\sim h$ say, x. $Q(\sim h) = 1 - x$. If X were confronted with a decision where the payoffs for rival options depended on the truth values of h and $\sim h$ but did not know the value of x, he would be suffering from disabilities similar to those facing the agent offered a gamble on a hypothesis about the integral value in the billionth place in the decimal expansion of pi. An ideally situated agent would not be in such a predicament and we are considering requirements imposed on such ideally situated agents.

Now if x is different from 0 or 1, X is committed to the view that neither h nor $\sim h$ belongs in $K_{X,t}$. It is but a small step from this observation to the conclusion that if $h \in K_{X,t}$, X is committed to knowing this.

Following this approach does not incur commitment to the claim that an effective decision procedure exists for membership in X's corpus in L. An ideally situated agent should be able to know what is and what is not in his corpus; but this does not imply that membership in his corpus expressible in L must be effectively decidable.

Hintikka represents X's cognitive state in a language L^k containing iterable epistemic operators. He adopts as an epistemic logic a variant of $S4$. If I were to represent X's cognitive state in such a language L^k, the underlying epistemic logic I would employ would be a variant of $S5$.

Someone might wonder why I objected previously to evaluations of hypotheses with respect to serious possibility being construed as beliefs as to the truth of statements of objective possibility on the grounds that X would be obliged to be opinionated about objective modality while I am prepared to insist that X should be opinionated as to what is and what is not in his corpus expressible in L.

I have already explained that in requiring that X be opinionated as to what he knows, I am concerned only with X's commitments. Insofar as X fails or is incapable of living up to these commitments, he will be incapable of using his standard for serious possibility effectively in deliberation and inquiry.

Suppose, however, that X is ideally situated in this regard and is capable of living up to the requirement that he be opinionated concerning what he knows. He should then be in a position to use his standard for serious possibility for hypotheses expressible in L in deliberation and inquiry. This is so whether X's evaluation of h as a serious possibility is equated with X's assuming that it is objectively possible that h or X's evaluation is not regarded as bearing a truth value at all.

Thus, the requirement that X be opinionated concerning the contents of his corpus expressible in L is motivated by the fact that failure to satisfy this condition weakens the effectiveness of X's corpus expressible in L as a standard for serious possibility useful in deliberation and inquiry. Considerations such as this serve as an excuse for requiring ideally situated X to be opinionated in this way.

No such excuse exists for being so opinionated concerning hypotheses about objective possibility – assuming such hypotheses to be intelligible. That is to say, there is no excuse for our obligating ideally situated X to be opinionated in this way. In my opinion, we should always allow X the option of suspending judgement between rival hypotheses – unless there is some countervailing consideration.

8 Quantifying in

I have not considered the appeal which Hintikka and others who adopt similar approaches make to the virtues of appealing to possible worlds semantics in dealing with quantification into epistemic contexts.

Keep in mind, however, that I am concerned with corpora of knowledge as standards for serious possibility and with the revision of such standards.

My thesis is that only truth value bearing hypotheses are evaluated by agents with respect to serious possibility. This thesis is companion to the thesis that only truth value bearing hypotheses are evaluated by agents with respect to credal probability. I know of no problem in decision theory or scientific inquiry where evaluations of either sort are required to be *de re*.

If this thesis is correct, X's standard for serious possibility or corpus of knowledge is representable by a set of sentences containing no modal operators. A change in X's knowledge is representable by a change in the set of sentences known to be true.

No doubt it will be objected that this view is a dogmatic and cavalier dismissal of linguistic evidence to the effect that we do quantify into epistemic contexts – evidence which even Quine acknowledges.

The kernel of truth in this charge is located in the same place as the kernel of truth in the charge that I ignore the distinction between knowledge and belief.

Recall the important differences noted between X's point of view when assessing his corpus and X's point of view when assessing X's corpus. From X's point of view, there is no difference between what he knows and what he fully believes (at present). From Y's point of view, only a subset of X's corpus constitutes knowledge.

160

We have also just noted that an ideally situated X is committed to an identification of each h in L as belonging to $K_{X,t}$ or its complement. But even an ideally situated Y need not know of every sentence in L whether it is in X's corpus or not. On the other hand, Y may have information that X's corpus contains some sentence in L satisfying conditions C without Y having in his corpus a sentence 'X's corpus contains h and h satisfies C' where 'h' is a standard designator for a sentence in L.

Thus, Y may assume that X knows who killed Cock Robin. That is to say, Y knows that X's corpus contains a true sentence which qualifies as a potential answer to the question 'Who killed Cock Robin?'

In my view, this sort of story can be told in all cases where it is alleged that X's evaluations with respect to serious possibility are *de re*.

9 Conclusion

Hintikka's work on epistemic and doxastic logic has pioneered in efforts to understand relations between modality and cognitive attitudes. By focusing attention on the role of evaluations of hypotheses with respect to serious possibility and credal probability in deliberation and inquiry, the conclusions I have reached tend to conflict rather strongly with Hintikka's ideas.

Hintikka and those who share his views may, perhaps, be able to respond to the difficulties I have raised from my quasi-Bayesian viewpoint. Hintikka himself is after all very much interested in probability judgement. It would be worthwhile to understand his approach to integrating judgements of possibility and judgements of probability. My rather desultory comments will have served their purpose if they provoke Hintikka to some discussion of these matters.

Part III

Chance and surprise

12

Subjunctives, dispositions and chances[†]

1

X says 'It is probable that h' and Y says 'It is improbable that h'. No doubt X and Y disagree in some ways. In particular, they disagree in the way they evaluate h with respect to credal (or personal) probability to be used in practical deliberation and scientific inquiry in computing expectations.

This disagreement between X and Y with respect to the way in which they evaluate credal probability may be attributable to a disagreement between them as to the truth values of some statements which one or the other uses as evidence warranting his evaluation of h with respect to credal probability.

Notice, however, that X and Y will not disagree concerning the truth value of h. Their utterances indicate that neither of them assign probability 1 or 0 to h and, hence, that both X and Y suspend judgement concerning its truth value.

More to the point, X and Y do not disagree as to the truth value of X's utterance 'It is probable that h'. That utterance is either (a) elliptical for 'X's assignment of credal probability to h at time t is high' or (b) is not a truth value bearing assertion at all but is an expression of X's assignment of high credal probability to h at t.

'Probability' and cognate terms do occur in contexts of other kinds as well. Thus, 'The probability of heads on a toss of coin a is 0.5' is neither a description of X's credal state nor an expression of it. Moreover, it bears a truth value and purports to describe coin a.

X might, at some time, endorse some criterion for deciding the credal probabilities which should be assigned to h relative to various bodies of evidence or knowledge which he or someone else could come to endorse. Given his commitment to such a criterion, he might wish to indicate that according to that criterion the credal probability which should be assigned to h relative to a body of knowledge consisting of truths of logic (set theory and mathematics) and an extralogical e (together with the deductive

[†] Reprinted with permission of the publisher from *Synthese* 34 (1977), pp. 423–55. Copyright © 1977 by D. Reidel Publishing Company, Dordrecht, Holland.

consequences of these) is high. To do this, he might say 'The probability of h relative to e is high'.[1]

Suppose X utters 'It is possible that h is true'. Y utters 'It is impossible that h is true'. X and Y disagree in their evaluations of the modality of h just as in the previous example they differed in their evaluations of h with respect to credal probability. Moreover, this disagreement could have important ramifications for their approaches to practical deliberation and scientific inquiry. In designing an experiment, Y will not plan for the truth of h; for, according to Y, the truth of h is not a serious possibility. If he is offered a bet where he wins if h is false, then regardless of the payoff promised if h is true he will accept the gamble. X will not proceed in this manner.

Imagine a situation where coin a is about to be tossed. Both X and Y consider it seriously possible that the coin will land heads. They also hold it seriously possible that it will land tails. They may even regard it to be seriously possible that it will land on its edge. Consider, however, the sentence h asserting that coin a will fly off to Alpha Centauri. Y does not consider the truth of h a serious possibility. X does. Most of us, I trust, would agree with Y – even though there are many philosophers who profess a different point of view according to which all sentences (in a given language L) consistent with logic (set theory and mathematics) are seriously possible.

The crucial point for present purposes is, however, that whether we side with X or with Y there is no dispute over the truth value of 'It is possible that h'. That sentence is either (a) elliptical for 'h is possible for X at t' or (b) is an expression of X's evaluation of h and, as such, lacks a truth value.

X and Y do, to be sure, have a disagreement concerning the truth value of h. Y evaluates h as impossible on the grounds that h is false. That is to say, he assumes as part of his body of knowledge or evidence that h is false and appeals to this as a warrant for his appraisal of h with respect to modality. X makes no such assumption. He either assumes as evidence that h is true or suspends judgement between h and not $\sim h$. In general, h is possible for X at t if and only if h is consistent with X's body of knowledge (or full beliefs) at t. Hence, disagreements between X and Y with respect to their appraisals of modality will reveal differences in their evaluations of hypotheses with respect to truth value.

Of course, even at t, X can recognize that h is possible relative to some corpus other than the one to which he is currently committed. The statement 'h is possible relative to K' does bear a truth value and need not be construed as a description of the cognitive state of any person or group of persons. However, in forming policy and in scientific inquiry, X will appraise possibility relative to his corpus at t or, at any rate, should do so (Levi, 1983a).

---

1 The criterion for determining the appropriate 'credal state' for each potential corpus of knowledge corresponds approximately to what Carnap has called 'credibility'. I call such a criterion or rule a 'confirmational commitment'. For further discussion of confirmational commitments, see Levi (1974).

There are other contexts where possibility is predicated not of sentences or propositions but of actions or other sorts of events. Thus, it may be economically possible for X to purchase a house but not for Y to do so. Here we are not declaring that 'X purchases a house' is possibly true. Rather we are declaring that purchasing a house is economically feasible for X at t. I shall not directly consider such uses of 'is possible' here.

It is a regrettable contemporary fashion to suppose that statements of the type 'h is possible' bear truth values without being descriptions of the cognitive states of agents or groups of agents at given times. Such objective statements of modality are interpreted with the aid of a realistically construed possible world semantics.

I do not understand such objective statements of modality very well nor have I been helped by possible world semantics. I do not wish, however, to present my intellectual limitations as an objection to modal realism. My chief complaint is that no one has made out a serious case that conceptions of objective modality have any useful role in the illumination of the results of scientific inquiry or to the understanding of the methods of scientific inquiry or practical deliberation.

Yet, appraisals of statements with respect to serious possibility and impossibility (i.e., with respect to modality epistemologically construed) are clearly relevant to inquiry and deliberation. For this reason, it seems far more charitable to construe those who make judgements of modality as making evaluations which could have some relevance for their conduct than to become diverted by the fantasies of modal realism.

In the remaining portions of this paper, I shall outline how I think subjunctive conditionals should be construed within the framework of this approach and, with this as background, restate some views I have already advanced elsewhere concerning dispositions and chances.

2

Let L be some first order language. By X's *corpus of knowledge expressible in L* at time t, I mean that set of sentences in L whose falsity X is committed at t to discounting as a serious possibility.

The word 'committed' should be emphasized. $K_{X,t}$ will consist not only of those sentences in L representing full beliefs X can explicitly and consciously identify as his beliefs at t. X may not recognize h as a deductive consequence of sentences he believes true. Yet, he is committed to the truth of h and, hence, h should be included in $K_{X,t}$. Moreover, even though X may not be versed in logic, set theory or mathematics, I shall say that he is committed to all logical, set theoretical and mathematical truths expressible in L. He is not, however, committed to all sentences which are true in L.

On this view, every h in L whose truth is seriously possible for X at t is so if and only if h is consistent with $K_{X,t}$. Thus, X's corpus of knowledge at t is X's standard for serious possibility at t and becomes, in this way, a relevant resource for him to use in inquiry and deliberation.

X's corpus $K_{X,t}$ expressible in L is part of a hierarchy of corpora expressible in a sequence of languages $L, L_1, L_2, \ldots$ each containing its predecessor and enough additional apparatus to furnish a truth definition for its predecessor language. Moreover, given X's corpus $K_{X,t}^i$ expressible in L_i, X's corpus $K_{X,t}^{i+1}$ expressible in L_{i+1} should meet some further conditions. It should not only contain $K_{X,t}^i$, it should contain 'All sentences in $K_{X,t}^i$ are true in L_i'. It should contain 'h is in $K_{X,t}^i$' if and only if h is in $K_{X,t}^i$.

Given a more ample characterization of this hierarchy, a specification of the contents of $K_{X,t}$ should determine at least part of the contents of higher level corpora. Insofar as we are concerned with X's corpora of knowledge expressible in L, we can leave these higher corpora out of account.

From X's point of view at t, every item in his corpus $K_{X,t}$ is infallibly true in L. That is to say the falsity of any such item is not a serious possibility for him at that time. This does not mean that he accords infallibility to all items in bodies of knowledge he previously endorsed in this way or items in bodies of knowledge he will endorse in the future in this way. Nor does he have to accord such infallibility to items in Y's corpus (except, of course, to the extent that Y agrees with X). Nor does my thesis imply that if h is in X's corpus at t he is committed to its incorrigibility – i.e., immunity from removal from his corpus at some later time (Levi, 1983b).

There are quite good reasons which X might have at time t when his corpus is $K_{X,t}$ for removing h from his corpus even though in doing so he will be removing from his standard for serious possibility some item which, at t, is infallibly true for him. Sometimes X will detect inconsistency in his corpus and recognize that, as a consequence, $K_{X,t}$ breaks down as a standard for serious possibility. Clearly, contracting his corpus by removing items from it makes good sense in such cases.

On other occasions, more relevant to our present concerns, $K_{X,t}$ entails the falsity of some sentence h. From X's point of view, it is impossible that h. Yet, h may be a theory which has the properties of a good explanatory theory for some domain (whatever those properties might be). Even though h is infallibly and certainly false for X at t, he may wish to give it a hearing because of the informational value he imputes to it due to its explanatory virtues. To give h a hearing is to shift to a new corpus (i.e., a new standard for serious possibility) relative to which it is seriously possible that h is true. That is to say, X may have good reason to open his mind by suspending judgement between h and statements conflicting with it in $K_{X,t}$ in order to explore the question of the truth value of h without begging any questions.

As far as X is concerned, contracting his corpus in this way does not entail any risk of importing error into his corpus. From his point of view at t, every item in $K_{X,t}$ is certainly and infallibly true. Moreover, contraction does not involve importing any new sentences into his corpus at all. Clearly, there can be no question of importing error. X does, however, suffer a loss of information. He will be warranted in suffering such a loss if and only if the informational value imputed to h due to its explanatory (or other informational) virtues render giving it a hearing sufficient compensation for this loss (Levi, 1983b).

X's contracting from $K_{X,t}$ to a new corpus K_1 (which is a proper subset of $K_{X,t}$) to give h a hearing is a shift from one deductively closed set of sentences to a deductively closed subset (in L) subject to the constraint that relative to K_1 h is a serious possibility. In general, there will be several contraction strategies satisfying the constraint. These alternative strategies will normally differ from one another with respect to the losses of informational value incurred. The general principle which should guide the choice of one contraction strategy from those available should be that such loss of information be minimized subject to the constraint that h be given a hearing. When two or more such contraction strategies minimize the loss of informational value, X should contract in a manner which implements both strategies.

Informational value is construed as independent of truth value and as partially dependent on the demands of the inquiries which X regards as worth pursuing at the time. Thus, the simplicity, explanatory power, and the subject matter of the hypotheses contribute to their informational value. There is one important context independent condition. If K_1 and K_1' are two alternative contractions of $K_{X,t}$ and K_1 is a subset of K_1', shifting to K_1 cannot incur a smaller loss of informational value than shifting to K_1'.

One implication of this account of contraction requires emphasis. In a context where X is concerned to contract $K_{X,t}$ to give h a hearing, some assumptions in his corpus are more vulnerable to removal than others. The vulnerability or corrigibility of any such assumption g does *not* depend on the evidential support X has for g at t, his judgement of its credal probability, plausibility or the like. All items in $K_{X,t}$ bear credal probability 1 for X at t. X's total evidence in L consists of all items in $K_{X,t}$ – including g. Hence, all items in that corpus are, as far as X is concerned, fully supported by his evidence. There is no basis for discriminating between items in his corpus with respect to credal probability or evidential support.

Degrees of corrigibility or vulnerability to revision depend on losses of informational value incurred by the various available contraction strategies subject to the constraint that h be given a hearing (Levi, 1983b).

For example, sentences in $K_{X,t}$ which X counts as lawlike are less vulnerable to removal, as a general rule, than accidental generalizations. This is not due to the availability of better inductive backing for the lawlike sentences but because giving up lawlike sentences incurs greater loss in explanatory power than giving up accidental generalizations.

The only other form of revision of a corpus of knowledge which, in my opinion, is legitimate is a shift from $K_{X,t}$ to a deductively closed set K_1

containing $K_{X,t}$. This mode of revision is 'expansion'. It occurs when X adds observation reports to his corpus or the testimony of witnesses. It also occurs via inductive inference when X adds some ertswhile hypothesis h to his corpus $K_{X,t}$ together with the deductive consequences and, hence, obtains K_1. Unlike contraction, expansion does incur a risk that error will be imported. From X's point of view prior to expansion, adding h to his corpus (where h is not entailed by $K_{X,t}$) involves a serious possibility of adding some false sentence to his corpus. X could be induced legitimately to risk the error only if the informational value obtained by adding h compensated for the risk of error incurred (Levi, 1967a, 1967c, 1980a, 1983b).

I shall not elaborate on expansion or contraction any further but shall exploit the remarks made thus far to sketch an account of subjunctive conditionals epistemologically construed.

3

X's assessments of sentences with respect to serious possibility are relative to his corpus $K_{X,t}$. Occasions arise, however, where X may be interested in calculating evaluations of possibility relative to other corpora – e.g., the set of logical truths. Of particular interest are situations where X considers evaluations of modality relative to some corpus obtained from $K_{X,t}$ by a sequence of contractions and expansions.

Consider a situation where $K_{X,t}$ contains $\sim h$. Let K_1 be obtainable from $K_{X,t}$ by removing $\sim h$ in a manner which minimizes the loss of information incurred. K_2 is obtained from K_1 by adding h and forming the deductive closure. X may wish to ascertain the modality of g relative to K_2 even though at the time of evaluation X has not revised his corpus $K_{X,t}$ at all and, from his point of view, $\sim h$ is true, certainly true and infallibly so.

As I understand them, counterfactual conditionals are used to make just such evaluations. Thus, if K_2 entails the truth of g, X is entitled to assert 'If h were true, g would be true'. If K_2 does not entail g, X is entitled to assert 'If h were true, g could yet be false'.

Sometimes X may be interested in another sort of modal evaluation. $K_{X,t}$ does not entail h and it does not entail $\sim h$. At t, X suspends judgement regarding the truth of h. Both h and $\sim h$ are serious possibilities for him at that time. Let K_3 be obtainable from $K_{X,t}$ by adding h and forming the deductive closure. X may wish to evaluate the modality of g relative to K_3 even though at t his corpus is $K_{X,t}$.

In such a situation, X can express the impossibility of g's being false relative to K_3 by saying 'Should h be true, g would also be true'.

It is of some small interest to note that the modal appraisal expressed by such an open conditional can also be indicated by X's asserting 'Either $\sim h$ or g' in a context where it is clear that X is suspending judgement as to the truth of h and to the truth of g. X also has the option of asserting the truth of the

170

indicative conditional (construed as a material conditional) when the context indicates his suspension of judgement as to the truth of h and of g.

Suppose that at time t, X was convinced that Oswald alone killed Kennedy and, hence, that no one else did and that somebody did. Somebody proposes a hypothesis about Kennedy's death which contradicts X's convictions because it posits that someone other than Oswald killed Kennedy. It can account for phenomena otherwise unexplained and, yet, can explain much that X's view at t can explain. It is worthy of a hearing. Hence, at t', X contracts in order to give 'Someone other than Oswald killed Kennedy' a hearing. As a consequence, he must give up 'Oswald killed Kennedy'. But he is not compelled to surrender 'Someone killed Kennedy'. Indeed, he would be foolish to do so; for he would lose informational value unnecessarily.

Once he has contracted, X can express his new evaluations of serious possibility in many ways. He might say 'Should it turn out that Oswald did not kill Kennedy, someone else must have killed him'. Alternatively, he might assert 'Either Oswald killed Kennedy or someone else did'. Equivalently, he could assert the truth of the indicative conditional (which is here a material conditional) 'If Oswald did not kill Kennedy, someone else did'. Of course, this material conditional was in X's corpus when he endorsed 'Oswald killed Kennedy'. But in a context where X is contracting by removing this last statement, he may wish to emphasize that he continues to endorse the material conditional and, in so doing, he reveals his new modal evaluations.

I imagine that this scenario fits rather well the circumstances of many who lost confidence in the report of the Warren Commission. But there are other ways in which the faith might be lost. X might be prepared to give a hearing to the hypothesis that Kennedy died of natural causes or that he did not die at all but is now living comfortably in seclusion in Costa Rica. Having contracted to give this rather bizarre alternative a hearing, X might say 'Either Oswald killed Kennedy or no one did'. Alternatively he might say 'If Oswald did not kill Kennedy, no one did'.

When $K_{X,t}$ contains (and, hence, entails) h, the falsity of h is not a serious possibility for X at t. X need not, however, express his modal evaluation of g in unconditional form by saying that g must be true. If he is concerned to persuade someone else of the propriety of his modal appraisal, he might assert the factual conditional 'Since h is true, g must be true as well'.

Returning to the important case of counterfactual conditionals, it is normally taken for granted that the hypothetical contraction should be one where the constraint is to give the indicative version of the antecedent of the counterfactual a serious hearing. But sometimes this is not clear. Thus, in a subjunctive beginning 'If Oswald had not killed Kennedy, ...', it is clear that the contraction from $K_{X,t}$ to K_1 requires removing 'Oswald killed Kennedy'. It is not always clear without further specification of the context

CHANCE AND SURPRISE

whether 'Someone other than Oswald killed Kennedy', 'No one killed Kennedy' or both of these alternatives should be given a hearing as well. Thus, if X asserts 'If Oswald had not killed Kennedy, Johnson would never have been President', it is apparent that X has implicitly imported into the antecedent of the counterfactual the stipulation that no one killed Kennedy and that he did not die in Dallas. On the other hand, if X asserts, 'If Oswald had not killed Kennedy, the information as to who did kill him would not have been concealed from the public', X has implicitly included in the antecedent the supposition that someone other than Oswald did kill Kennedy. Finally, X might assert, 'If Oswald had not killed Kennedy, someone else would have'. In that case, the constraint on contraction is removal of 'Oswald killed Kennedy'. In making the counterfactual assertion, X has indicated that in contracting to K_1 he has refused to remove 'Kennedy was killed by someone'. Presumably the loss of information incurred by removing this statement is judged greater than removing 'No one other than Oswald killed Kennedy'.

It seems to me that X could at t be prepared to assert all three of these counterfactuals. I take it that this does not reveal incoherence in his modal appraisals. Rather it reveals the elliptical character of some counterfactual judgements. Observe, however, that I am not claiming that we can handle the question of cotenability in this way. The ellipsis to which I refer is in the specification of the constraint on the contraction step from $K_{X,t}$ to K_1 – i.e., in the specification of the hypothesis to be given a hearing in contraction. As shall be explained shortly, cotenability is handled according to the proposal made here in terms of evaluations of losses of information incurred by alternative contraction strategies satisfying the constraint.

I do not pretend to exhaust all the ways in which modal evaluations are expressed in English or to have captured all the nuances in those cases I have considered. My current concern is not linguistics but modal evaluation as it bears on the conduct of inquiry and deliberation. My contention is that we make modal evaluations which discriminate serious possibilities from impossibilities in the sense explained previously. Conditional modal evaluations should be construed in a similar fashion. Whatever correct English usage may be, my thesis is that modal statements are not truth value bearing statements at all unless they are intended to be statements of a biographical sort. Insofar as modal statements are not descriptions of the cognitive state of speakers, modal statements are not, strictly speaking, statements at all. They lack truth values. No one can suspend judgement as to their truth. No one can assign credal probabilities to them.

Thus, I can assign credal probability of 0.5 to the hypothesis that on the next toss coin a will land heads. I do not assign any credal probability to 'It is possible that coin a will land heads on the next toss'. Nor do I assign any credal probability to 'If coin a were to be tossed 1000 times in the next day, it could land heads 359 times'. Advocates of the use of a realistically construed

172

possible world semantics for interpreting modal sentences or, more generally, advocates of the view that modal sentences are truth value bearing objective statements seem committed to assigning credal probabilities to such statements. In my opinion, such a view is fraught with troubles. I shall not attempt, however, to elaborate on this here. It is worth noting, however, that introducing objective modalities does not remove the need for making appraisals of serious possibility in deliberation and inquiry. Nor is it clear that introducing such objective modalities helps in understanding such epistemological modalities. This is a theme to which I shall return later.

Views such as this have, of course, been advanced in various forms before.[2] There are, however, two respects in which the account I have been proposing here is somewhat novel. (1) I have required that modal evaluations be relative to a corpus obtainable from $K_{X,t}$ by a sequence of contractions and expansions. To my knowledge, most other authors have not insisted that the transformation of $K_{X,t}$ to the corpus relative to which modal evaluations are made should be representable in this way. (2) When such a transformation involves a contraction step – as in the case of evaluations expressed by counterfactual conditionals – the contraction is required to be one which minimizes loss of information relative to a constraint.

To appreciate the ramifications of these proposals for the so called problem of cotenability, consider a situation where $K_{X,t}$ contains the following sentences:

(a) All A's are B's.
(b) a is not A.
(c) a is not B.

Let X contemplate the optimal contraction of $K_{X,t}$ which removes (b) from his corpus. There are three contraction strategies to consider; (i) removing (a) as well as (b), (ii) removing (c) as well as (b) and (iii) removing all three. Clearly (iii) yields a greater loss of information than the other two alternatives and should be favored only if the losses of information incurred by (i) and (ii) are roughly equal.

In a situation where (a) is considered to have great value in explanation, it will be considered to have considerable informational value. Hence, when (a) is lawlike, strategy (i) incurs a greater loss of information than (ii) and, hence, X will favor (or should favor) (ii).

In cases where (a) is considered an 'accidental' generalization, that appraisal reflects the low esteem in which (a) is held as a resource for explanation. Often surrendering it will not lead to a greater loss of

2 Of the many authors who have advanced views resembling the proposal advanced here, the positions most similar to mine seem to be found in Kyburg (1961), p. 239 and Mackie (1962).

173

informational value than surrendering (c) and sometimes it may lead to a smaller loss. When the loss suffered is the same from following (i) and (ii), (iii) is optimal. When the loss is greater from (ii), (i) is optimal.

Consider the contracted corpus K_1. Add 'a is A' to K_1 and form the deductive closure to yield K_2. Relative to K_2, evaluate the modality of 'a is B'.

When (a) is considered lawlike, the falsity of 'a is B' is not a serious possibility relative to K_2. When (a) is accidental, it will, in general, be a serious possibility.

Thus, when (a) is considered lawlike, X is entitled to say at t when his corpus is $K_{X,t}$ 'If a were A, it would be B'. If (a) is accidental for X, he is not entitled to say this but he is entitled to say 'If a were A, a could fail to be B'.

The critical step in the evaluation of cotenability in this case and in more general situations where cotenability of antecedent conditions is an issue comes at the step where a contraction strategy is adopted. The cotenable statements (i.e., the statements cotenable with the indicative of the antecedent of the counterfactual) are those items in $K_{X,t}$ which are not removed at the contraction step. Which items are removed and which are not depends on the relative corrigibility or vulnerability of items in $K_{X,t}$ given that the negation of the antecedent of the counterfactual is to be removed.

My contention is that such vulnerability to removal does *not* depend on evaluations of items in $K_{X,t}$ with respect to evidential support, probability, plausibility or the like. All items in $K_{X,t}$ are, from X's point of view at t, part of his evidence and, hence, have full evidential support. He assigns them all credal probability 1. For him, they are all certain. There is no basis for X to discriminate between the sentences in $K_{X,t}$ with respect to the considerations just mentioned.

Hence, cotenability is not to be analyzed within the framework of an account of evidential support, inductive logic, plausibility or the like. It is loss of informational value which is critical to vulnerability to removal and, hence, to cotenability.[3]

The account of subjunctive conditionals briefly outlined here indicates the sense in which lawlike generalizations support counterfactual conditionals.

3 This is the main difference between my account of counterfactuals and the view contained in J. L. Mackie's excellent discussion in Mackie (1962). If X's full beliefs of the moment constitute his evidence or knowledge, he cannot discriminate between causal laws and accidental generalizations in his corpus with respect to the evidence supporting them. Hence, he cannot account for the relative vulnerability of accidental generalizations to removal in terms of deficiency in evidential support. Mackie appears to think otherwise. Apparently, X's full beliefs at the moment do not serve as his standard for serious possibility and, hence, as his evidence according to Mackie's view. Because I differ from Mackie on this point, I have modified his account of counterfactuals in the manner indicated.

In Lewis (1973), David Lewis offers what he takes to be a decisive counterinstance to Mackie's view. Lewis considers a 'moderate Warrenite' who suspends judgement as to whether Oswald killed Kennedy, somebody else did or no one did. (See Lewis, 1973, pp. 70–2.) He is, nonetheless, a Warrenite because he assigns high credal probability to the first alternative. According to Lewis, he assigns low probability to the remaining two alternatives but more to someone else's killing Kennedy than to the hypothesis that no one else does.

No doubt some moderate Warrenites might assign credal probabilities in the manner described by Lewis. But I could equally well imagine probabilistically moderate Warrenites assigning higher credal probability to the hypothesis that no one killed Kennedy than to the hypothesis that somebody else did.

Lewis invites us to consider the result of adding the statement 'Oswald did not kill Kennedy' to the moderate Warrenite's corpus of full beliefs. When the moderate Warrenite has views such as those attributed to him by Lewis, he should, according to conditionalization, assign high probability to 'somebody other than Oswald killed Kennedy' and very low probability to 'No one killed Kennedy'. ('Oswald killed Kennedy', of course, receives probability 0.) Lewis argues that Mackie's analysis recommends that the following counterfactual be legitimately assertible by the moderate Warrenite: 'If Oswald had not killed Kennedy, somebody else would have'. Lewis goes on to claim that this is 'just backward from the truth' and that Mackie's analysis leads to untenable results.

There are three glaring defects in Lewis' argument:

(1) Lewis distorts Mackie's analysis of counterfactuals and constructs his criticism by appealing to the distorted analysis rather than to the view Mackie actually endorses. Mackie quite clearly indicates that when someone legitimately asserts a counterfactual, he believes the truth of the negation of the indicative version of the antecedent. When the agent does not assume this but is in a state of suspense regarding the antecedent, he may assert an 'open conditional' but not a counterfactual. Mackie explicitly recognizes important differences between the two (e.g., with respect to what conditionals accidental generalizations support). Lewis has elected to ignore Mackie's clear statements on this score. Had he attended to Mackie's view, he would have appreciated the fact that, for Mackie, the probabilistically moderate Warrenite is not in a position to affirm a counterfactual at all. Rather an open conditional would be appropriate. Perhaps, the moderate Warrenite might say, 'Should it turn out that Oswald did not kill Kennedy, then someone else must have done so' or 'If Oswald did not kill Kennedy, somebody else did'. Lewis (1973), p. 3 seems to endorse this result.

(2) Even if we overlook Lewis' distortion, he seems to think that when the antecedent is added to the stock of beliefs, the conditional is assertible if the probability of the consequence relative to the new stock of beliefs is sufficiently high. The naivety of this view is well documented in the literature and deserves no further comment. Even if high probability were necessary, it can scarcely be sufficient.

(3) Finally, even if we ignore the second point along with the first, it remains the case that Lewis obtains his allegedly objectionable consequence from a characterization of a probabilistically moderate Warrenite which is by no means the only one envisageable. I have identified above a sort of probabilistically moderate Warrenite whose beliefs are such that, on Lewis' interpretation of Mackie, that individual would be justified in asserting the counterfactual Lewis thinks appropriate. Of course, the other sort of Warrenite would be entitled to assert the counterfactual Lewis thinks backward from the truth. What does this prove except that Lewis is one sort of probabilisitically moderate Warrenite and not another?

I suspect that lurking behind Lewis' discussion of Mackie is the following worry: Consider the convinced Warrenite. Should he assert 'If Oswald had not killed Kennedy, somebody else would have?' In the text, I described a scenario where the committed Warrenite should do so. I suspect that it is a scenario that most committed Warrenites should fit. Yet, those same Warrenites should be prepared to assert 'If Oswald had not killed Kennedy, Kennedy would have been reelected for a second term'. This may seem incoherent. Surely those who lust after a logic of counterfactuals and who wish to use modal semantics will wish to regard the legitimate assertibility of these two counterfactuals by convinced Warrenites as untenable. But, as I explained in the text, there is no incoherence, once obvious considerations of context are taken into account. Perhaps, we should keep our lust for a logic of counterfactuals in check.

175

If X accepts a lawlike generalization into his corpus, he then has a license for making the sorts of conditional modal appraisals linguistically expressed by means of counterfactual conditionals of certain kinds. Other statements can also support counterfactual conditionals. In particular, knowledge of singular disposition statements such as 'This glass is fragile' and singular chance statements such as 'This coin has a 0.5 chance of landing heads and a 0.5 chance of landing tails' often legitimate counterfactual modal appraisals. In the following discussion, disposition statements and chance statements and the modal appraisals they support will be considered.

4

An explicit disposition predicate is one of the form 'is disposed to R when S'd'. I shall abbreviate this sort of predicate in the form '$D(R/S)$...'. 'Is fragile', 'is elastic', 'has temperature k' and the like are not explicit disposition predicates – even though we may be prepared to accord them dispositional status. In the subsequent discussion, I shall focus on explicit disposition predicates.

Singular disposition statements such as '$D(R/S)a$' predicate of some object or system a some feature which a is said to possess 'objectively' – i.e., independent of persons or their propositional attitudes (except of course when the disposition predicates are alleged to describe propositional attitudes or other states of persons). Moreover, the truth of such statements is alleged to be linked in some way or another with the test behavior of objects asserted to have the dispositions in question. Indeed, it is tempting to seek necessary and sufficient truth conditions for singular disposition statements in terms of claims about test behavior. If one succumbs to this temptation, it appears plausible that such truth conditions cannot be given except in modal terms – e.g., in terms of some suitably constructed subjunctive conditionals.

On the analysis of subjunctive conditionals I have proposed, however, such conditionals are construed epistemologically whereas singular disposition statements are not plausibly construed this way. Either we should reject efforts to give truth conditions for disposition statements in modal terms or we should embrace a more realistic construal of modal statements and move down the primrose path of modal semantics realistically interpreted.

Needless to say, I favor the former alternative. I do so not merely because I find realistically interpreted modal semantics obscure. My chief complaint is that it contributes nothing of value to understanding how knowledge of the truth of disposition statements contributes to the evaluation of hypotheses about test behavior with respect to modality in the sense which I claim is of primary relevance to deliberation and inquiry. I do not maintain that one cannot use modal semantics to furnish such an account but merely that it functions gratuitously in this connection. For the purposes of serious inquiry and deliberation one can do without it. To be sure, armed with modal semantics one can raise problems which cannot be raised without it. However, I have not seen any indication that the problems generated are of vital importance to scientific inquiry or to practical deliberation. In Neurath's phrase, realistic modal semantics is a type of *verdoppelte Metaphysik* mimicking gratuitously the epistemic modalities which are of relevance in inquiry and deliberation.

This gratuitousness is apparent in the case of disposition statements. To bring this out I shall offer an outline of how knowledge of disposition statements affords a basis for epistemically construed appraisals of modality for hypotheses about test behavior.

Suppose X writes down in a book some discourse reporting the contents of his current corpus. In the text, he writes the following sentence:

(1) Da.

(1) is a singular statement 'a is a D', In addition, X might wish to write an ancillary comment in a footnote. To do this, he might append an asterisk to (1) as follows:

(1*) Da^*.

At the bottom of the page, X writes the following footnote:

(2)* '(x) (if Dx, then whenever x S's, x R's)' is true and lawlike.

Here 'S' describes a kind of trial and 'R' a kind of result.

The text and footnote reveal some information about the content of X's corpus $K_{X,t}$. Both (1) and the generalization mentioned in (2) are in $K_{X,t}$. Relative to $K_{X,t}$, therefore, it is not a serious possibility that a be subjected to a trial of kind S and fail to respond in manner R.

Suppose that, instead of writing (2) as a footnote, X were to write an abbreviated version of it which everyone will understand as follows:

(2*) $*(R/S)$.

X could economize on space still further by rewriting (1*) as follows:

(1') $D(R/S)a$.

The expression '(R/S)' is now used as an index on the predicate 'is a D' and points to a marginal comment which readers will be able to supply without X actually having to write it down. I suggest that the apparent structure of explicit disposition predicate is to be construed as an index pointing to a marginal comment in the manner just indicated.

On this construal, the singular disposition statement is a truth value bearing statement in L. When X affirms it sincerely, we may suppose that (1) is in X's corpus $K_{X,t}$. Moreover, the index '(R/S)' indicates that X's corpus in L_1 (the metalanguage for L) contains the statement that the sentence quoted

177

in (2) is true and that it is lawlike for X. That the generalization is lawlike for X indicates that the general sentence is not easily vulnerable to removal from his corpus.

Under these circumstances, the analysis of counterfactuals given previously legitimates X's asserting 'If a were subjected to a trial of kind S (during the period when a is D), it would respond in manner R'. Hence, X's knowledge that a is D supports the appraisal of modality expressed by the counterfactual.

This approach does appear to give an adequate account of how knowledge of dispositionality furnishes a basis for appraisals of epistemic modality of the sort relevant for inquiry and deliberation. Moreover, it does so without appeal to modal semantics realistically construed. I contend that it gives all the 'understanding' of the connection of dispositionality and test behavior that can be reasonably required.

It may be objected that this account fails to give truth conditions for disposition statements (or satisfaction conditions for disposition predicates) in terms of test behavior. In my view, there is no advantage to specifying such truth conditions if the price is embracing a realistically construed modal semantics. Offering such truth or satisfaction conditions contributes nothing to our understanding of how knowledge of the truth of disposition statements regulates our assessment of hypotheses about test behavior with respect to serious possibility which is not already furnished by the reduction sentence mentioned in the marginal comment (2). We need nothing more in the way of a semantics for the disposition predicate than the stipulation that '$D(R/S)\ldots$' is true of x if and only if x is a $D(R/S)$.

Some authors complain that one should not countenance an infinity of primitive predicates on the grounds that one cannot learn a language containing so many such predicates. My view of disposition predicates countenances a countable number of such predicates. But it seems plainly false that one cannot acquire a competence for using such an infinity of primitives in inquiry and deliberation. My quasi-genetic account of explicit disposition predicates furnishes an effective procedure for generating an infinity of such primitives from predicates describing test behavior and, at the same time, furnishes an instruction for filling in the marginal gloss associated with each such predicate. I do not claim accuracy for my account of genesis; but it does suggest one way in which an infinity of primitives can be learned.

Why do we countenance the introduction of disposition predicates in the first place? According to a proposal advanced by Sidney Morgenbesser and myself, they serve as place holders for alternative descriptions of the objects of which they are predicated (Levi and Morgenbesser, 1964, Levi, 1967a, ch. XIV).

This does not mean that disposition predicates are dummy predicates and that, as a consequence, disposition statements lack truth values. To assert of some object that it is disposed to break into small pieces when dropped is to describe that object correctly or incorrectly as the case may be. However, if the assertion of the disposition statement is intended as part of an explanation, the explanation is not fully adequate in the sense that it is recognized as an appropriate project for further research to seek replacements for the disposition predicate in its explanatory role.

Thus one may lamely explain why a water glass broke when dropped by noting that it was fragile – i.e., disposed to break when dropped. The marginal comment affirms the truth of 'All objects disposed to break when dropped break when dropped' and evaluates the generalization as lawlike. A feeble covering law explanation has been offered. It is feeble not because the generalization is analytic. (It is not analytic.) It is feeble because what is desired is explanation invoking laws containing explanatorily more satisfactory predicates. Because the investigator may not be in a position at the moment to offer satisfactory explanations of the required type, explanation by appeal to disposition is made as a stopgap measure and expresses a recognition that inquiry to identify more satisfactory sorts of explanation is worth pursuing.

I am not assuming that standards for adequate, deep or fundamental explanation and the predicates which should occur in them can be specified which are mandatory on all scientific investigators at all times. Standards of adequate explanation are relative to commitments to research programs which are themselves open to revision in the course of scientific inquiry. However, I am supposing that at any given time, investigators will be committed to some more or less clear view of what is to count as fully satisfactory or fundamental explanation such that there is no point in engaging in further inquiry in order to improve upon it (although there may be good reasons to pursue further inquiry on other grounds – e.g., to explain phenomena not as yet explained at all).

In many contexts, disposition terms – especially explicit disposition terms – do not meet the standards for terms to be used in fundamental explanation adopted at the time. But investigators may, nonetheless, rest content with such explanations for the moment recognizing the need for further investigation. It is in this sense alone that disposition predicates are to be construed as placeholders. This view is quite compatible with maintaining that disposition statements have truth values and that dispositions are, therefore, real.

Often disposition predicates – especially those which are not explicitly dispositional – become so well integrated into an explanatory theory that they are regarded as perfectly satisfactory for purposes of fundamental explanation. Since whether this is the case or not depends critically on the standards for satisfactory explanation embedded in a research program, controversies over the merits of rival research programs can be manifested in controversies over the placeholding status of certain disposition predicates.

179

Be that as it may, I am not committed to the view that for purposes of satisfactory explanation, disposition predicates should be replaced by descriptions of their microstructural bases. That condition may be imposed by some research programs in some domains; but it should not be imposed unconditionally.

One final comment. True singular disposition statements like 'a is disposed to R when S'd' are not laws. The generalization mentioned in the marginal comment alluded to by the index is a law. That is why explanation by disposition may be considered a feeble sort of covering law explanation. However, the singular disposition statement itself is not a covering law (Levi, 1969e).

5

Consider a simple singular statement of objective probability, statistical probability or chance such as 'The chance of heads on a toss of coin a with tossing device b equals 0.5 and the chance of tails is also equal to 0.5'. Such statements assert a certain sort of predicate true of an object or system (chance set up) just as singular disposition statements do. Moreover, the predication has some sort of relevance to the test behavior of the object or chance set up. Understanding of the predicate requires clarification of how knowledge of chance statements in which the predicate occurs contributes to assessments of hypotheses about test behavior with respect to modality and credal probability.

As in the case of explicit disposition predicates, chance predicates have indices pointing to marginal comments in abbreviated form. In the case of chance predicates, the indices contain three items: (a) a predicate describing events as trials of some kind S, (b) a specification of a family of predicates describing events as responses of different sorts of trials of kind S and (c) a specification of a family of probability distributions over the field of predicates generated by the family of predicates (or sample space) specified in (b). If exactly one distribution is specified for the sample space, the chance predicate is 'simple'. Otherwise it is composite.

In the case of the statement cited above, there is some small controversy as to whether the chance set up of which the chance predicate is predicated is coin a or a system of which coin a and tossing device b are parts (or, alternatively, whether the chance predicate is a two place predicate true of the pair (a, b)). If the first view is adopted, the predicate describing the kind of trial – namely, 'is a toss of coin a with tossing device b' occurs in the chance statement cited above with 'a' in referentially transparent position and 'b' in referentially opaque position. This prevents quantification into the position of 'b'. If the chance set up is taken to be the pair (a, b), both 'a' and 'b' occur in transparent positions.

In my opinion, we can be tolerant about this matter and allow L to have explicit chance predicates of both varieties and, indeed, to provide for as much variable polyadicity of this sort as is necessary. Fortunately, decisions concerning these matters have at most marginal relevance for the concerns of primary interest here – namely, an understanding of how knowledge of chances contributes to modal and credal probability evaluations in deliberation and inquiry. They are relevant only when we wish to formulate general statements containing chance predicates such as 'All pairs of coins and tossing devices furnished by the Hohokus Novelty Company yield heads on a toss with a chance of 0.5 and tails with a chance of 0.5'. The problem of interest here, however, is how knowledge of instantiations of such generalizations contributes to evaluations of hypotheses about test behavior.

In the case of explicit disposition predicates, the index alludes to a marginal comment which does explain how knowledge of disposition contributes to evaluations of modality of hypotheses about test behavior. The indices appended to chance predicates contribute in the same way to explaining how knowledge of chances contributes to evaluations of hypotheses about test behavior both with respect to modality and credal probability. The most important issue to be faced in coming to grips with the concept of chance is the specification of the contents of the marginal comment.

I pointed out that in the case of disposition predicates, the marginal comment fails to specify necessary and sufficient satisfaction conditions for the disposition predicate in terms of test behavior. Nonetheless, the comment provides an adequate depiction of how knowledge of disposition contributes to evaluation of the modality of hypotheses about test behavior. It does so by providing a necessary (but not sufficient) satisfaction condition for the disposition predicate.

The marginal comment for simple chance predicates also provides necessary but not sufficient satisfaction conditions in terms of test behavior. Thus, in the case of the chance statement about the coin, the following reduction sentences are true and lawlike (or so the marginal comment says):

(3) (x) (if x is D, then whenever x is tossed it will land heads up or tails up).

(4) (x) (if x is D, then whenever x is tossed it will not land both heads up and tails up).

Thus, the singular chance statement serves, in part, as a singular disposition statement. It states that the chance set up has a disposition to yield one and only one of the types of response specified by the sample space on a trial of the kind cited in the marginal comment.

If this were all there was to the marginal gloss, however, there would be small point in introducing chance predicates in addition to disposition predicates into L.

The peculiarity of chance predicates is that knowledge of chances is supposed to provide us not only appraisals of hypotheses with respect to

181

modality but with respect to credal probability as well. The hypotheses so appraised are, of course, hypotheses about test behavior. Thus, in the case of coin a, we wish to be able to evaluate the credal probability of the hypothesis that coin a will land heads on a toss with device b at some time t, that it will land heads r out of n times in a sequence of n such tosses, etc. Comments like (3) and (4) are not enough to indicate how knowledge of chances can provide such evaluations. These reduction sentences are mentioned in the marginal comment for 'coin a has a 0.4 chance of heads on a toss with b and a 0.6 chance of tails' just as they are in the marginal comment for the chance statement cited previously. Yet, presumably knowledge of the truth of the latter chance statement warrants different evaluations of outcomes of tosses with respect to credal probability than knowledge of the former does.

The specification of principles for assigning credal probabilities to hypotheses about outcomes of trials on the basis of knowledge of chances is the problem of formulating a principle of direct inference or a 'frequency principle' as Hacking has called it (Hacking, 1965, p. 135). Constructing an adequate formulation of such a principle is by no means free from controversy and the resolution of these controversies has important ramifications for inferences from knowledge of test behavior to evaluations of credal probabilities of hypotheses about chances. No matter how the problem of direct inference is formulated, it lies at the heart of all statistical inference. An adequate understanding of direct inference is a *conditio sine qua non* for understanding chance or statistical probability and its uses in scientific inquiry. Moreover, when principles of direct inference are supplemented by an account of how new information about outcomes of trials can be added to X's corpus on the basis of knowledge of chances and an account of legitimate inference from knowledge of test behavior to credal judgements (and knowledge) about chances, we obtain a basic understanding of the concept of chance. Little else is required.

6

The thesis I wish to advance (I have advanced it before in slightly different ways) is that the comment in the marginal gloss for a chance predicate which specifies the rule of direct inference for that predicate cannot be derived from any truth value bearing statement or from some metalinguistic comment affirming the truth and lawlikeness of some truth value bearing statement (Levi, 1967a, p. 200, and 1969e). No matter what true and lawlike sentences are mentioned in the marginal gloss additional to statements like (3) and (4), they will not suffice to yield an adequate rule of direct inference.

This is not so in the case of disposition statements. The reduction sentence (2) together with the information that set up a is a D entails that whenever a is S'd it R's. Hence, if the disposition statement is in X's corpus $K_{X,t}$, his evaluation of the possibility of a S'ing without R'ing is decided. In the case of direct inference from chance statements, no reduction sentence – not even when one allows for probability implications rather than material implications – will suffice to yield a rule of direct inference.

Consider, for example, an urn U whose contents consist of 50 coins with a 0.4 chance of landing heads on a toss and a 0.6 chance of landing tails and 50 coins with a 0.6 chance of landing heads on a toss and a 0.4 chance of landing tails. Let a trial of kind S on u be the selection of a coin from u'at random' – i.e., according to some procedure which yields 0.4 coins with a chance equal to their proportion in u – and tossing the coin picked. The chance of heads on a trial of kind S is 0.5. Let a trial of kind T be a trial of kind S which results in a 0.4 coin being tossed. The chance of heads on a trial of kind T is equal to 0.4.

Obviously, X can know at t both that the chance of heads on a trial of kind S on set up u is 0.5 and that the chance of heads on a trial of kind T on set up u is 0.4.

Given that X has such knowledge, consider the following two cases:

Case 1: X knows that a given trial is of kind S and that is the strongest information X knows true of the trial.

Case 2: X knows that a given trial is not only of kind S but is also of kind T and that is the strongest information X knows true of the trial.

In the first case, it seems clear that X should assign a credal probability of 0.5 to the hypothesis that the coin drawn will land heads. In case 2, he should assign credal probability of 0.4 to that hypothesis. The problem of direct inference is to formulate criteria which explain why these plausible prescriptions are legitimate in these cases and which are competent to handle other questions of direct inference.

I am not concerned in this essay to present a view of direct inference. One point, however, deserves to be emphasized. The differences between case 1 and case 2 which are relevant are differences in X's knowledge in the two cases. Moreover, what X knows in case 2 does not contradict what he knows in case 1. X's corpus in case 2 is an expansion of his corpus in case 1.

Consequently, even if reduction sentences or other truth value bearing statements are mentioned in the marginal glosses and these statements do provide some link between the truth of chance statements and test behavior, such information cannot suffice to account for how knowledge of chances contributes to determining credal probabilities. We would have to supplement such reduction sentences with nontruth value bearing principles of direct inference anyhow.

This observation applies not only to principles of direct inference regulating how assignment of credal probability should be controlled by knowledge of chances but also the conclusions one should add to one's corpus of knowledge concerning test behavior on the basis of knowledge of chances.

Because I have felt all along that the only urgent questions concerning the understanding of the concept of chance and its relation to test behavior are the question of direct inference and the companion question of inverse inference, I have adopted the view that attempts to give a semantics for chance or statistical probability statements which would link chances with test behavior are both gratuitous and diversionary.

Consider, for example, the view of von Mises. Von Mises may be interpreted (I think) as construing chance predicates in terms of explicit disposition predicates. The trial explicitly cited in the chance predicate (e.g., 'is a toss of coin a') is not the trial in the explicit disposition. The trial explicitly cited in the latter would be an infinite 'random' sequence of trials of the kind cited in the chance predicate – e.g., 'is an infinite sequence of tosses of coin a which meet conditions of randomness'.

Von Mises apparently thought that the appropriate reduction sentence would specify that if the chance of an R on a trial of kind S equals r then in any infinite random sequence of trials of kind S the limit of relative frequency of R's is r. Von Mises' view is obviously untenable on its face. It is, of course, vacuously true that if coin a has a 0.5 chance of landing heads on a toss then whenever it is tossed an infinite number of times in a random sequence, it will land heads in the limit with a relative frequency equal to 0.5. The truth is vacuous because the coin will never be tossed that number of times. Notice, however, that the reduction sentence is not plausibly taken to be lawlike. It surely does not support a counterfactual. If X adds to his corpus containing the information that coin a has a 0.5 chance of landing heads the further information that it is tossed an infinite number of times, he will or should consider it seriously possible that it will lands heads every time.

But quite aside from this obvious point (well known to von Mises but ignored by him on the grounds that his view was perfectly consistent – a curious response to make), it is clear that von Mises' approach contributes nothing to the solution of the problem of direct inference or, for that matter, inverse inference. I do not mean to suggest that no solution could, in principle, be proposed compatible with von Mises' approach. To the contrary, I am suggesting that the problem of direct inference can be handled more or less completely ignoring whether one has given a semantics for chance statements in terms of test behavior or at least partially done so by means of reduction sentences or has dropped all pretenses at providing such full or partial interpretations and has treated the chance predicate as a primitive predicate in L (as I have proposed doing) for which no necessary and sufficient satisfaction conditions can be offered in terms of test behavior and not even useful necessary conditions via reduction sentences can be provided.

Because it seems to me that the question of providing a semantics for chance statements has philosophical importance only insofar as it bears on the role of the concept of chance in scientific inquiry and because it is clear that an understanding of the concept of chance in scientific inquiry is to be gained through a good grasp of direct and inverse inference, it seems to me

184

that the question of providing a semantics for chance predicates ought to be dropped as a gratuitous and diversionary enterprise. Of course, I do not mean to deny that chance statements have truth values; but the semantics needed to acknowledge this can be gained by treating chance predicates as primitive predicates in an extensional first order object language true or false of chance set ups. We can establish the credentials of chance statements as meaningful truth value bearing statements by giving an account of how knowledge of test behavior bears on acquiring knowledge of chance and how knowledge of chance bears on acquiring knowledge of test behavior.

I suppose one can treat von Mises' proposed interpretation of chance as a harmless little exercise in model building rather irrelevant to the important questions pertaining to the understanding of chance but harmless nonetheless. Historically, however, it does not seem to me that von Mises' ideas have been harmless. They have, to say the least, been diversionary. Serious energies have been devoted to clarifying von Mises' concept of a random sequence in order to spell out a consistent version of von Mises' conception of a collective. It has been thought that this formal exercise has considerable importance for the understanding of the concept of chance. This is, in my opinion, flatly wrong and the supposition to the contrary is an illustration of the diversionary character of such efforts to give a semantics for chance in terms of test behavior.

In recent years, an alternative to von Mises has been widely discussed – a so called 'propensity' interpretation of chance. I myself have been guilty of styling my own view a qualified propensity interpretation. I wish to emphasize now that all I meant by this is that I wished to treat chance predicates as primitives and to refuse to offer a semantics for chance predicates in terms of test behavior. Indeed, although I meant to suggest a certain analogy between chance predicates and disposition predicates in that both sorts of predicates should be taken as primitive, I meant to deny that reduction sentences could serve to illuminate the connections between chance and test behavior in the way they can illuminate the connections between disposition and test behavior.

In recent years, a blizzard of diverse propensity interpretations have been produced which are focused on issues as gratuitously diversionary as was the von Mises' approach. In various ways, these approaches argue that truth values bearing and lawlike reduction sentences can be supplied for statistical disposition predicates although they differ among themselves concerning how this is to be done. The most intelligent approach of this sort is to be found in Mellor (1971).[4] According to Mellor, an appropriate reduction

4 I mean to exclude Hacking (1965) from the blizzard of propensity theories as I mean to exclude myself. Mellor's discussion of propensities, displays, and chances is developed in ch. 4 of Mellor (1971). The criticisms I offer here are elaborations on criticisms already advanced in Levi (1973b).

sentence for the predicate 'has a propensity of 0.5 for landing heads on a toss and a propensity of 0.5 for landing tails' runs roughly as follows:

(5) Every object bearing the propensity is such that whenever it is tossed, it 'displays' a chance distribution of 0.5 for heads and 0.5 for tails.

According to Mellor, the propensity is a disposition predicate like 'is fragile'. The peculiarity is that the predicate describing the test outcome is a probability display predicate.

Mellor makes reference to an alternative view which replaces the notion of a display by that of a tendency.[5] The reduction sentence then reads as follows:

(6) Every object bearing the propensity is such that whenever it is tossed, it tends with a strength of 0.5 to land heads and tends with a strength of 0.5 to land tails.

Proposals such as these and variants on them seem to me as objectionable as the von Mises' approach. Indeed, they seem to me to be a backward step. Like the von Mises' approach, these proposals invoke reduction sentences which contribute nothing to giving an account of either direct inference or inverse inference. These problems, which are of paramount importance to the understanding of the connection between chance and test behavior, can be handled just as well without invoking such reduction sentences. But not only are the reduction sentences introduced gratuitously, their introduction is at least as diversionary as is the von Mises' approach; for the concept of a probability display is at least as obscure as the concept of chance whose meaning it is designed to clarify. So is the connective for probabilistic tendency. Efforts to clarify these ideas by introducing an extended possible worlds semantics supplemented by probability measures over such worlds and becoming enmeshed in the niceties of working out such schemes contributes nothing here to what is required for clarity – to wit, an account of direct and of inverse inference.

These obscurantist diversions are supplemented by controversies concerning whether probability dispositions are long run relative frequency dispositions or single case dispositions and whether or not the truth of chance statements precludes determinism.

By insisting on the construal of chance predicates as primitive predicates (*vis à vis* descriptions of test behavior) in the manner outlined previously, I mean to emphasize the gratuitous, diversionary, and obscurantist character

---

5 Mellor (1971), pp. 68–70 rejects the tendency analysis on the grounds that the concept of tendency needs as much analysis as the concept of chance itself. Mellor is, no doubt, right. What I find puzzling is the notion that clarity is advanced by introducing the notion of a display. But be that as it may, disputes between those favoring tendencies and those favoring displays are precisely the sorts of diversionary controversies which give propensity interpretations a bad name.

of such 'interpretations' and to insist on the fundamental importance of providing an account of direct inference to the understanding of the conception of chance or objective probability.

This does not mean that there is nothing to be said regarding the long run or the single case. But what has to be said should be said in connection with direct inference. Thus, I am prepared to recognize as perfectly intelligible objective chance statements of the following sort:

The chance of heads on a toss of coin a is 0.5.

The chance of heads on a toss of coin a by Isaac Levi in 705 Philosophy Hall at 12:00, March 11, 1976 is 0.5.

The chance of 100 heads in 200 tosses of coin a is $(200!/100! \, 100!)0.5^{200}$.

Given knowledge of any one or all of these chance statements, the problem of critical importance is to ascertain what credal probability X should assign to hypotheses about outcomes of the trials specified given knowledge that on an appropriate occasion such a trial has occurred. Does this make me a long run relative frequency propensity theorist as Henry Kyburg has claimed[6] or am I a single case propensity theorist? I do not know how to answer this question. Nor do I care.

It may be objected that chance statements support subjunctive conditionals and that the sorts of subjunctives they support reveal something about their meaning. In a sense that is quite true. But since, on my view, subjunctive conditionals are expressions of conditional modal appraisal construed epistemologically whereas chance statements are truth value bearing statements of objective probability, we should not attempt to give

6 Kyburg (1974a), pp. 374–5. Kyburg and others have also classified Hacking as a 'long run relative frequency disposition' advocate apparently on the grounds that Hacking has used the terms 'chance' and 'frequency in the long run' interchangeably and when emphasizing the misleading character of the latter term points to the fact that chance concerns what the long run relative frequency would be were a sequence of trials conducted (Hacking (1965), p. 10). But if I understand Hacking correctly, he maintains that if X knows that the chance of heads on a toss of a is 0.999 999, he should endorse the claim that were a tossed once and only once it would land heads. I shall let Hacking speak for himself, but in my view the controversy over whether chances are long run dispositions or single case dispositions is another example of a dispute which gives propensity interpretations a bad name. I might add that I do not recognize the positions attributed to me by Kyburg on pp. 374–5 under the categories 'Nature of Disposition' and 'Semantics' and would qualify his attribution of views to me under 'Empirical meaningfulness' and 'application problem' by noting that I have always thought that the problem of direct inference involved both a principle for assigning credal probabilities to hypotheses about test behavior on the basis of knowledge of chances and a rule for inductive acceptance like rule A and that a rule of the latter sort requires a rule of the former type. I have, however, often called the latter sort of rule a rule of direct inference rather than applying that description to the former sort of rule as I do here. I trust that this lack of consistency in terminology is not taken to reflect an inconsistency in viewpoint. See Levi (1967a), ch. XV. In spite of these inaccuracies of attribution, Kyburg's discussion ends with a critique of other propensity views in agreement with the one I am advancing here and advanced in Levi (1973b).

truth conditions for chance statements in terms of the subjunctive conditionals any more than we should do so in the case of disposition statements. Indeed, the matter is even more complicated in the case of chance statements than in the case of disposition statements.

Consider, for example, the following (abbreviated) chance statement schema:

(7) The chance of r heads on n tosses of coin a for $0 \leq r \leq n$ is equal to $n!/r!(n-r)!0.5^n$.

(7) can plausibly be said to support the following counterfactual in most contexts:

(8) If coin a were to be tossed n times, it would land heads approximately 50 % of the time.

By the same token, however, (7) also plausibly supports the following counterfactual:

(9) If coin a were to be tossed n times, it could land heads every time (even when n is very large).

(8) and (9) appear to conflict as appraisals of counterfactual modality. I doubt whether this conflict can be adequately accounted for by means of the apparatus proposed in David Lewis (1973) – although, perhaps, he could supplement his approach in a manner which would resolve the conflict.

An epistemological approach of the sort I am proposing has easier going here.

Suppose that $K_{X,t}$ contains (7) plus the information that the coin has not been tossed n times and, hence, has not landed heads r times in n tosses for any value of r from 0 to 1. By contracting to K_1 and expanding to K_2 through adding the information that the coin has been tossed n times, one is then in a position to evaluate modality relative to K_2 in the manner indicated previously. Relative to K_2, it is a serious possibility that the coin will land heads every time. According to this appraisal, X can legitimately affirm (9) but cannot legitimately affirm (8).

On the other hand, suppose X considers the expansion of K_2 which is optimal relative to the question which asks what the relative frequency of heads in the n tosses is. To obtain the optimal expansion yielding a new corpus K_3, X would first have to ascertain his credal state for the alternative hypotheses concerning the precise value of r/n. This requires invoking a principle of direct inference relative to K_2. Under suitable circumstances, the distribution of credal probability over the alternative hypotheses should conform to the binomial distribution specified in (7).

According to criteria for expansion I have proposed elsewhere (Levi, 1967a, pp. 219–25) (these criteria were formulated as principles of acceptance and rejection), K_3 would entail the falsity of all exact estimates of r/n

except those falling within a small interval around 0.5. Hence, relative to K_3, the hypothesis that the coin lands heads every time is not a serious possibility.

If we now evaluate counterfactual modalities relative to K_3 rather than K_2, X is entitled to affirm (8) and should not affirm (9). Thus, the apparent conflict in the counterfactuals supported by the chance statement (7) is seen to be due to an ambiguity which has to be resolved in the context.

Of course, once the subjunctives supported by chance statements are construed epistemologically in the manner I favor, it becomes apparent that the understanding of the sense in which (8) is supported by (7) cannot be understood itself without a closer examination of direct inference. It is only through an account of how, via direct inference, credal probabilities are assigned to hypotheses about relative frequency relative to K_2 that the evaluation of the expansion step to K_3 can be made. Once more we see that propensity theorists should not rest satisfied with analyses of chance in terms of subjunctive conditionals but should confront the question of direct inference head on.

<h1 style="text-align:center">7</h1>

It is a common practice among philosophers to treat chance statements as a sort of covering law. It is easy to see how such an idea can get started. In a finite domain where the set of A's, non-A's, B's and non-B's are all nonempty, the sentence 'All A's are B's' is equivalent to '100 % of A's are B's' and 'No A's are B's' is equivalent to '0 % of A's are B's'. In such a domain, statements of the form '$100r$ % of A's are B's' for values of r between 0 and 1 look like an intermediate sort of generalization.

Statements of chance are not, however, frequency statements. 'The chance of a trial of kind S yielding a result of kind $R = r$' has the terms 'is a trial of kind S' and 'yields a result of kind R' in nonextensional contexts. On the other hand '$100r$ % of trials of kind S yield results of kind R' has these same terms in extensional contexts. Nor can the chance statement be paraphrased by affirming the truth and lawlikeness of some sentence in which these terms occur extensionally.

These considerations and other elaborations on them establish the untenability of giving truth conditions for chance statements in terms of statements of relative frequency. They do not, of course, preclude construing chance statements as dispositional statements where the test outcomes are described as the occurrence of events of some kind with appropriate relative frequencies. Hence, they do not preclude views such as that I have attributed to von Mises. Nor do they preclude the other propensity interpretations of chance to which I have alluded.

What they do show, however, is that statements of chance are not covering laws any more than singular disposition statements are.

189

This in itself does not preclude regarding so-called inductive statistical explanation as covering law explanation. If suitable reduction sentences are available linking chance with test behavior, these reduction sentences can be taken to be the required covering laws. I have been arguing, however, that no such reduction sentences can be constructed which illuminate the connections between chance and test behavior. If I am right in rejecting reduction sentences involving introductions of probability displays or probability tendencies for this purpose, I fail to see how such reduction sentences can play a useful role as covering laws in explanation.

As I have stated elsewhere (Levi, 1969e), the surrogates for covering laws in 'inductive statistical' explanation should be rules for direct inference (of both the kinds which warrant assignments of credal probabilities and which warrant inductive expansions). Such rules of inference are not, however, covering laws. There are no covering laws to be had.

8

Throughout this discussion, I have been preaching the centrality of the problem of direct inference (and of inverse inference) for the understanding of chance. I have, however, said little about the problem of direct inference itself. I hope to consider the matter in greater detail on other occasions. However, in closing I would like to cite two views alternative to the one I have been advocating which are not, in my view, diversionary and which do deserve serious attention. One such view is that advanced by de Finetti who has insisted on the metaphysical obscurity of any notion of objective chance and has proposed dispensing with it and, as a consequence, has not seen the problem of direct inference as a serious problem altogether. Henry Kyburg has also favored dispensing with objective chance. However, unlike de Finetti, Kyburg believes that legitimate direct inferences can be mandated from knowledge of frequencies under suitable conditions. Kyburg does not favor interpreting (i.e., giving truth conditions) for chance statements in terms of statements of relative frequency. That view seems untenable and Kyburg knows it. Kyburg proposes a view according to which extensional frequency statements substitute for statements of objective chance in so-called 'statistical syllogisms'. On his view, what I and others take to be statements of objective chance are to be construed epistemologically.[7] The

---

7 Kyburg (1961), pp. 248–53 contains a discussion of five probability statements which I favor construing as objective non-epistemological statements of chance. Insofar as Kyburg and I disagree over the interpretation of 'probability', a major difference concerns whether contexts illustrated by these five examples are to be analyzed epistemologically or as statements of objective chance. However, a close examination of Kyburg's epistemological analysis reveals that its adequacy does, indeed, depend upon whether his effort to legitimize direct inference from knowledge of frequencies in lieu of knowledge of chances can succeed. Hence, the central dispute between us concerns direct inference.

particular analysis he offers presupposes that direct inference from suitable knowledge of frequencies is sometimes legitimate so that his epistemological interpretation of chance statements stands or falls with his own view of direct inference.

I believe that Kyburg's view is mistaken and shall attempt to explain my reasons elsewhere (Levi, 1977a). But whether he is right or wrong, the points under dispute are of considerable philosophical importance. They are of interest precisely because they concern the topics of direct and inverse inference and the role of probability judgement in scientific inquiry and practical deliberation.

13
Direct inference[†]

Many writers who recognize the intelligibility and importance of statements about statistical probabilities, or *chances*, as Ian Hacking calls them, also acknowledge that some account should be given of how rational agent X should assign weights, personal probabilities, or credal probabilities to hypotheses about outcomes of trials X knows to have taken place, given knowledge of the chances of outcomes of that kind occurring on trials of that kind. Thus, if X knows that coin a is to be tossed and also knows that the chance of coin a landing heads on a toss is 0.5 and if this is all the relevant information that X knows to be true, he should assign a degree of credal probability equal to 0.5 to the hypothesis that coin a will land heads up on the toss.

Inference of this sort is sometimes called *direct inference*. It is of critical importance to have an adequate account of the conditions under which various sorts of direct inference are or are not legitimate. Direct inference provides an important link between knowledge of objective probability and personal or credal probability judgements concerning test behavior of 'chance setups'. Furthermore, views concerning direct inference are critical to accounts of inverse inference from knowledge of data concerning test behavior to credal judgements concerning statistical hypotheses.

Hans Reichenbach pioneered attempts to formulate a principle of direct inference – at least, in recent times (Reichenbach, 1949, pp. 372–8 and 1936, pp. 312–19). He failed, however, to formulate criteria comprehensive enough to handle all cases that might arise. Indeed, to my knowledge, no one except Henry Kyburg has seriously attempted to do so. For the past decade and a half, Kyburg has been identifying the main issues pertaining to direct inference, has ably argued for a solution to the problems that arise, and has attempted to bring his positive account to bear on major issues in statistical theory.[1] It is unfortunate that his proposals are so rarely discussed. It is an

---

[†] Reprinted from *The Journal of Philosophy* v. 74 (1977), pp. 5–29.
1 (Kyburg, 1961) and (Kyburg, 1974a) are the two major works where Kyburg elaborates in detail on his approach to direct inference and its significance. For the purposes of this discussion, it may be useful to consult as well (Kyburg, 1970).

outright scandal that many authors continue to write about direct inference (especially in connection with statistical explanation) as if the problems raised by Kyburg did not exist.

I write, however, not to praise Kyburg but to criticize him. In my opinion, Kyburg's account of direct inference is fundamentally wrong. The error, moreover, is not restricted to his account. It is to be found in Reichenbach's proposals as well. The error is connected with Kyburg's method of handling the misleadingly labeled 'problem of the reference class'. In this paper, I shall attempt to identify the error and elaborate briefly on its significance.

1

There is important controversy, not always recognized for what it is, concerning the content of the premises accepted by X in his corpus of knowledge on the basis of which he is justified in making judgements of credal probability via direct inference (or via a 'statistical syllogism').

According to one view, to make a direct inference, X should accept in his corpus two types of premises: a major premise of the form

(1) The chance of an outcome R occurring on a trial of kind S on a chance setup a equals r (or falls in some specific interval from r_* to r^*)[2]

and

(2) a minor premise asserting that event e is a trial of kind S on chance setup a.

On the basis of information of this sort and provided that X does not know other information that frustrates the inference, X should assign a degree of personal or credal probability to the hypothesis that e results in an event of kind R, which equals r (or some subinterval of the interval from r_* to r^*).

---

2 The expressions 'r', 'r_*', and 'r^*' should be standard designators for real numbers. This qualification prevents a paradox discussed by David Miller in (Miller, 1966). Miller himself is aware of the solution, as he indicates in (Miller, 1968). Miller credits Popper with the observation and with the charge that qualifications of the sort I am introducing are *ad hoc* and have no precedent in mathematics. We, however, are concerned with statistics, where the distinction does, indeed, have a precedent. It is embedded in the distinction between simple and composite statistical hypotheses. This distinction is relevant not only to direct inference but to views that take the notion of likelihood to be of critical importance. Thus, the distinction does have precedent in statistical theory. I do not pretend that this response will satisfy Miller; but it should suffice to induce those worried about Miller's paradox to consider a family of serious problems concerning direct inference. And, as Miller himself will concede, the restriction imposed does seem to disarm the threatened contradiction.

An alternative approach substitutes for the major premise (1) a statement of the following form:

(1′) The percentage of trials of kind S that result in events of kind R equals r (or falls in some specific interval from r_* to r^*).

The statements (1) and (1′) are obviously different. Chance or statistical-probability statements are not equivalent to percentage or frequency statements.

In the first place, chance statements may be true even though no trials of kind S are conducted on setup a or, for that matter, on any other chance setup. Frequency or percentage statements like (1′) are true only if the set of S's is non-empty.

Furthermore, the predicates 'S' and 'R' that occur in statements like (1) occur in non-extensional contexts, whereas such predicates occur in statements like (1′) in extensional contexts.

Consider a coin-producing machine b that produces coins with a 0.4 chance of landing heads on a toss or coins with a 0.6 chance of landing heads on a toss when a button is pressed. The chance of obtaining an outcome of the first kind on a pressing of the button is 0.5, and the chance is the same for yielding an outcome of the second kind. Let 'S' be true of trials that are tossings of coins obtained from the machine by pressing the button. 'T' describes trials that are tossings of coins having a 0.4 chance of landing heads on a toss obtained from the machine by pressing the button. 'R' describes trials that result in a coin landing heads up.

All events of kind T are of kind S in virtue of the characterization just given. It can happen, moreover, that all S's are T's. That is to say, it may prove to be the case that all tosses of coins obtained from the machine are tosses of 0.4 coins. Suppose that is the case.

Even when this is the case, the following two statements are true:

(3) The chance of an R on a trial of kind $S = 0.5$.
(4) The chance of an R on a trial of kind $T = 0.4$.

Yet, the percentage of trials of kind S that are R's must be identical with the percentage of trials of kind T that are R's.

These objections cannot be avoided by restricting the frequency statements involved in the interpretation of chance statements to those specifying relative frequencies in very large sequences of trials or to those specifying limits of relative frequencies in infinitely long sequences of trials.

Thus, chance statements ought to be carefully distinguished from statements of percentages or frequencies. This does not preclude claiming that statements of type (1) often support subjunctive conditionals concerning relative frequencies of results in sequences of trials of kind S. Thus, (1) will sometimes support a claim that, if trials of kind S were repeated on a a large number of times, the relative frequency of R's would approximate r.

We cannot, however, suppose that this observation contributes to the clarification of the connection between the truth of statements like (1) and the test behavior of chances setups on long sequences of repeated trials.

In the first place, although there seems to be sense in which (1) supports 'If trials of kind S were repeated on a a large number of times, the relative frequency would approximate r'', there is also a sense in which (1) supports the opposite claim that the relative frequency of R's could deviate substantially from r.

The source of the difficulty, in my opinion, is that there is no true lawlike sentence which, together with (1) and the statement that a trial of kind S is repeated on a a large number of times, entails that R will occur with a relative frequency close to r. In this sense, the relative frequency of R's could deviate from r quite substantially on a large number of trials of kind S. On the other hand, under suitable circumstances, knowledge of (1) and of the fact that a large number of repetitions of trials of kind S are to be made, warrants being 'practically certain' that the relative frequency will be close to r.

Thus, in order to clarify the sense in which (1) supports the subjunctive affirming approximation to r, we need to explain the conditions under which knowledge of (1) and the fact that a large sequence of trials of kind S are to be conducted warrants practical certainty that the relative frequency will be close to r. This in turn requires clarification of the conditions under which direct inference is legitimate.

Thus, if we attempt to clarify the respects in which chance is related to relative frequency of results of some kind on repeated trials by appealing to the fact that sometimes statements like (1) support subjunctive conditionals affirming approximations of relative frequencies to the chances specified, we cannot rest there. We must replace the account based on support of subjunctive conditionals by an account of direct inference. An account of how chance statement (1) supports a subjunctive conditional statement about frequencies presupposes an antecedent understanding of direct inference.[3]

Whatever one might say about frequency interpretations of chance which resort to subjunctive conditionals, it remains obvious that statements of chance like (1) are not equivalent to corresponding percentage statements like (1').

Bruno de Finetti, among others, regards the concept of chance or statistical probability as a piece of metaphysical moonshine (de Finetti, 1963, pp. 141–2). He ignores, therefore, the problem of direct inference.

Kyburg agrees with de Finetti in discarding the concept of chance, or statistical probability. Like de Finetti, he does not countenance direct

---

3 For an excellent account of the relation between chance and relative frequency, see (Hacking, 1965, pp. 1–12). I outlined my own similar but independently developed view in (Levi, 1967a, pp. 190–204).

inference involving statements like (1). However, he does recognize – and, indeed, places great emphasis on – direct inference involving premises like (1').[4]

In effect, Kyburg advocates the 'functional replaceability' of chance statements by frequency statements in direct inference. He thereby avoids the untenable thesis that chance statements are to be interpreted as frequency statements. In this respect, his view represents an advance in clarity over the views of Reichenbach and Wesley Salmon, who seem to construe chance statements as asserting the existence of very long finite or infinitely long sequences of repetitions of trials of some kind.

2

Suppose X knows that 90 % of the Swedes living in 1975 are Protestants and that Petersen is such a Swede. Imagine that X knows nothing else about Petersen. On Kyburg's view, X should assign a degree of credence equal to 0.9 to the hypothesis that Petersen is a Protestant.

I see no compelling reason why rational X should be obliged to make a credence judgement of that sort on the basis of the knowledge given. X does not know whether the way in which Petersen came to be selected for presentation to him is or is not in some way biased in favor of selecting Swedish Catholics with a statistical probability, or chance, different from the frequency with which Catholics appear in the Swedish population as a whole. Given X's ignorance, no principle of reason compels him to violate Kyburg's recommendation. But no principle compels him to obey it either. This observation is not, of course, an objection to Kyburg's view, but rather an expression of disagreement. I shall offer my argued objection later. My immediate aim is to indicate an important difference between views that regard direct inference as legitimate only if it uses premises like (1) and views, like Kyburg's, that allow direct inference from major premises like (1').

For those who take chance seriously, in order for X to be justified in assigning a degree of credence equal to 0.9 to the hypothesis that Petersen is a Protestant on the basis of direct inference alone, X should know that Petersen has been selected from the Swedish population according to some procedure F and also know that the chance of obtaining a Protestant on selecting a Swede according to procedure F is equal to the percentage of Swedes who are Protestants. Given such information and the information that 90 % of Swedes are Protestants, X knows that the chance of obtaining a Protestant on a selection from the Swedish population according to F equals 0.9. This is the premise of kind (1) needed in a chance-based direct inference.

In practice, methods of selecting members of some population having the

---

4 I am freely translating Kyburg's presentation into my own jargon. I do not, however, believe that I am doing injustice to his intent.

required property involve using tables of random numbers or some stochastic device. Kyburg explicitly inveighs against the need for knowledge that Petersen is selected from the Swedish population at random.[5]

There is one further aspect of the example worth emphasizing. The chance of obtaining a Protestant on a selection from the Swedes of kind R equals r if and only if the percentage of Protestants among the Swedes equals r. In this case, the chance statement equals a percentage statement – counter to what was claimed previously. However, the percentage statement does not concern the percentage of selections from Swedes of type F that yield Protestants.

The chance setup involved in our example is the population of Swedes. This population is considered to be a whole of which individual Swedes are parts. It is a physical system on which trials can be conducted. The population of Swedes should not be confused with the set of Swedes. The chance of obtaining a Protestant on a selection of kind F from that population is a characteristic of the population. So is the percentage of Protestants in the population. It could be the case that the numerical value of the chance is identical with the numerical value of the frequency, so that the possession of a given chance property obtains if and only if the population has a given frequency of Protestants.

In the case of chance setups like coins, the chance of obtaining heads on a toss cannot be readily equated with some condition satisfied by the coin specifiable in terms of frequencies. The coin is not a population. It is not like an urn containing balls. The coin's chance of landing heads on a toss could, indeed, depend on the distribution of mass over the coin. In that case, a necessary and sufficient condition for the attribution of a chance to a coin may be its possession of one sort of distribution of mass rather than another. The physical characteristics of the coin function in such cases as analogues of percentages in the case of populations and sampling from them.

Thus, sometimes, chance statements can be equated with statements of frequency. However, this is by no means universally the case – even when we are considering sampling from populations (Levi, 1967a, pp. 202–3).

5 See both books. For Kyburg, the problem of defining 'is a random member of' is the problem of choosing a reference class for direct inference. Given this definition, Kyburg defines 'probability' in his epistemological sense. In this context, he explicitly rejects approaches that regard randomness as a condition met by methods for selecting individuals from a population. Such views presuppose a concept of probability and, hence, cannot be used to define probability, as Kyburg aims to do.

   Hacking (1965, pp. 118–32) approaches random sampling from a radically different point of view. With the exception of a passage on p. 128 where Hacking seems to slip into agreement with Kyburg, Hacking's analysis of random sampling presents cogently the point of view of someone who recognizes knowledge of chances rather than frequencies to be critical in direct inference. (I am grateful to Teddy Seidenfeld for pointing out to me the passage on p. 128 where Hacking seems to contradict what ought, in my opinion, to be his view.)

As I have said, Kyburg will have none of this. For him, percentage statements alone serve as major premises in direct inference. Often the percentage statements will speak of percentages of outcomes of some kind in a set of trials of some kind. But they need not do so. If X knows that Petersen is a Swede and knows nothing about his mode of selection from the population of Swedes, the 'reference class' to be used in direct inference (i.e., the set within which percentages of objects or events of various kinds are of concern in direct inference) will be the set of Swedes, and not the set of selections of type F from the Swedish population.

3

Let X know that $\%(B; A) = [r_*, r^*]$ – i.e., that the percentage of A's that are B's falls in the interval from $100r_*$ to $100r^*$ where $r_* \leqq r^*$. X also knows that the object or event i is a member of A.

Suppose further that X does not know of any narrower reference class to which i belongs and does not know of any broader (i.e., more inclusive) reference class to which i belongs such that $[r_*, r^*]$ spans the interval in which X knows the percentage of B's in that broader class to belong. Under such conditions, Kyburg would recommend assigning to the hypothesis that i is a B the degree of credence $[r_*, r^*]$.

Unlike most authors who discuss assignments of credal-probability values to hypotheses on the basis of knowledge or evidence, Kyburg allows interval-valued credal or personal-probability values. This feature distinguishes him, in particular, from authors like Reichenbach who are concerned with principles of direct inference for assigning credal probabilities (*weights*, in Reichenbach's terminology) to hypotheses on the basis of knowledge of frequencies or of chances. Kyburg's approach can be viewed as an attempt to generalize Reichenbach's proposal to cover cases where credence assignments might appropriately be supposed to be interval-valued. Indeed, in cases where $r_* = r^*$, Kyburg's approach and Reichenbach's coincide.

Suppose that X knows that i is both A and C. He knows that $\%(B; A) = r$ and $\%(B; C) = s$. ($s \neq r$.) He does not, however, know the percentage of B's among objects that are both A's and C's. According to Reichenbach, who considered this sort of case, there is no narrowest reference class for which X has 'reliable statistics', and no degree of credence can be assigned to the hypothesis that i is a B (Reichenbach, 1938, 316–18).

In this case, Kyburg's intervalist approach allows him to reformulate Reichenbach's view without concluding that no degree of credence can be assigned.

It is true that X does not know the *precise* percentage of B's among those objects which are both A's and C's. But he does know that the percentage

198

falls somewhere between 0 and 100. On Kyburg's view, X should assign to the hypothesis that i is a B the degree of credence [0, 1]. The advantage of putting the matter in this way is that it allows us to recognize that precise degrees of credence and maximally indeterminate or 'undefined' degrees of credence are two extremes and that there are many intermediate kinds of credence judgement which ought also to be taken into account. Neither Reichenbach nor any of his later followers have taken such judgements seriously.

In the two examples just cited, X was obliged to base his credence judgement concerning the hypothesis that i is a B on frequency knowledge of B's in the narrowest reference class to which he knows i to belong. However, neither Reichenbach nor Kyburg requires this in all cases. I am not alluding to cases where X knows that the percentage of B's among the A and C's is the same as among the A's, so that the fact that i is a C can be ignored and one need not explicitly use the set of A and C's as the reference class. Consider, in contrast, a case where X knows that i is both A and C, knows that the percentage of B's among the A's equals r and that the percentage of B's among the C's also equals r (or falls in an interval spanning r), but knows of the percentage of B's among the A and C's only that it falls somewhere between 0 and 100. Both Kyburg and Reichenbach would recommend that X use A as the reference class, even though it is not the narrowest reference class to which X knows i to belong, and, for every narrower reference class to which X knows i to belong, X does not know that the percentage of B's is equal to r. Reichenbach would recommend A over A and C because it is the narrowest reference class (or one of the two) for which X has reliable statistics.

Kyburg's principle for selecting a reference class for use in direct inference is more complicated to state, but is a generalization of Reichenbach's recommendation covering all cases:

If X knows that i belongs to both A and C and if X does not know that A is a subset of C, then, if the narrowest interval in which X knows the percentage of B's among the A's to fall does not span and is not spanned by the narrowest interval in which X knows the percentage of B's among the C's to fall, A cannot be used as a reference set for assigning credence to the hypothesis asserting that i is a B.

Among those reference classes to which i is known to belong which are not precluded by the condition just cited, X should select for use in direct inference that reference set D such that the shortest interval in which X knows the percentage of B's among the D's to fall is the shortest.[6]

6 For a relatively clear formulation of Kyburg's principle, see Kyburg (1974a, pp. 222–8). Kyburg's principle also covers the fact that when X knows that i is a member of reference set A, the ordered pair (i, i) is a member of the Cartesian product $A \times A$, and kindred complications. I leave these out of account here; for they play no role in the discussion that follows.

Consider, for example, the case where X knows that 90 % of Swedes are Protestants and that Petersen has been selected in manner F from the Swedes. Suppose he also knows that n trials describable as selections from the Swedes in manner F have been made, but knows nothing about the percentage of Protestants obtained. In this case, X should assign 0.9 as his degree of credence to the hypothesis that Petersen is a Protestant. On the other hand, if X knows that 80 % of those selected in manner F from the Swedes are Protestants, X should use the set of those selected by procedure F as his reference set. His degree of credence for the hypothesis that Petersen is a Protestant should be 0.8.

Suppose that X's corpus K contains the following items of information:

(5) 90 % of Swedes are Protestants.
(6) Either 85 % of Swedish residents of Malmö or 91 % or 95 % are Protestants.
(7) Petersen is a Swedish resident of Malmö.

Let f_r assert that $100r$ % of Swedish residents of Malmö are Protestants. (6) is then equivalent to $f_{0.85} \vee f_{0.91} \vee f_{0.95}$. Let h assert that Petersen is a Protestant.

Kyburg's principle for regulating direct inference recommends that X should assign to h a degree of credence equal to 0.9; for, according to (6), X knows that the percentage of Swedish residents of Malmö who are Protestants falls in the interval from 0.85 to 0.95, which spans 90 %.

Notice that X knows that Petersen is a member of the set of individuals identical with Petersen, that this is the narrowest reference set to which X knows Petersen to belong, and that X knows nothing about the percentage of Protestants in that set stronger than that it is either 0 or 100. Kyburg's rule of direct inference allows X to ignore this rather inconvenient information on the same grounds that it recommends that X ignore the information that Petersen resides in Malmö.

For advocates of the use of percentage statements like (1') as major premises in direct inference, Kyburg's move is of critical importance. If X were required to use the narrowest reference class to which he knew object i to belong, he would be obliged to use the set whose only member is i. Before finding out whether i is a B, X knows only that the percentage of B's in that set is either 0 or 100. Hence, X's degree of credence would be the interval $[0, 1]$.

Insofar as we rely on direct inference based on major premises asserting frequencies and on such inference alone to determine credence, I contend that we should always use the narrowest reference class and that the degree of credence that i is a B should be $[0, 1]$. Endorsing this claim is a roundabout way of denying that useful results can be reached via direct inference when the major premise is not a statement of chance.

I shall not now offer a proof of this conclusion. I shall, instead, show that

Kyburg's method for avoiding it conflicts with relatively noncontroversial conditions on how judgements of credence ought to be controlled by knowledge. As a preliminary to this argument, a brief summary will be given of these conditions.

4

At any time t, X's cognitive state is characterized by three factors: (1) a corpus of knowledge, (2) a confirmational commitment, and (3) a credal state.[7]

A confirmational commitment is a function C which takes as arguments potential corpora of knowledge and as values potential credal states. If $K_{X,t}$ is X's corpus at t, $C_{X,t}$ is his confirmational commitment at t, and $B_{X,t}$ is his credal state at t, the *principle of total knowledge* requires that $C_{X,t}(K_{X,t}) = B_{X,t}$.

A potential corpus expressible in L is a deductively closed set of sentences in L containing the 'urcorpus' UK for L. UK contains all logical truths expressible in L. I shall leave open what other items should be in UK, although I myself would consign set-theoretical and mathematical truths to the urcorpus.

The potential corpus $K_{X,t}$ adopted by X at t consists of all sentences in L that X is committed at t to holding as certainly true. Other potential corpora represent commitments as to what is certainly true that X could come to embrace if he revised his corpus at t. The urcorpus UK is the weakest commitment that X could legitimately have – at least within the framework I am proposing. Within that framework, items in the urcorpus are immune to removal and, in that sense, are incorrigible.

X's credal state $B_{X,t}$ is his system of personal or credal probability judgements at t.

X's confirmational commitment at t is his criterion for determining which credal state he should adopt if he were to adopt potential corpus K (which may differ from $K_{X,t}$) as his corpus.

Given a potential corpus K, $B = C(K)$ should be representable by a set of functions $Q(h; e)$ from sentences h and e in L, where e is consistent with K, to real numbers meeting the following conditions:

(1) *Consistency:* B is nonempty if and only if K is consistent.

(2) *Coherence:* Every Q-function in B is a probability measure relative to K.

Let e be some sentence or proposition consistent with K. Define $Q_e(h) = Q(h; e)$. If t is any sentence entailed by K (where K is consistent), $Q(h) = Q_t(h) = Q(h; t)$. This is the absolute or unconditional credal-probability function according to the given Q-function. Given the credal

---

7 The discussion in this section is a distillation of the contents of an already condensed paper, (Levi, 1974).

CHANCE AND SURPRISE

state B, B_e is the set of Q_e functions generated from the Q-functions in B. B_t is the set of unconditional Q-functions.

For fixed e, B_e is a convex set of Q_e-functions if and only if every weighted average of a finite subset of the set B_e is in B_e.

(3a) B_t is convex.

From (2) and (3a), it can be shown that, for e consistent with K but not necessarily entailed by it, where $Q(e)$ is positive for every Q-function in B, B_e is convex. Should some Q-functions be such that $Q(e) = 0$, this result is by no means guaranteed. However, we can consistently impose the requirement that B_e be convex.

(3b) *Convexity:* For e consistent with K, B_e is convex.

X's degree of credence for h given e at time t, $\mathrm{Cr}_{X,t}(h; e)$ shall be defined to be the set of values $Q(h; e)$ for Q-functions in $B_{X,t}$. Convexity guarantees that this function is interval-valued.[8]

When X's credal state contains a single Q-function, $\mathrm{Cr}_{X,t}(h; e)$ becomes numerically precise and, indeed, becomes a personal or credal probability function. Classical 'strict' Bayesians like Carnap, Ramsey, and de Finetti require of ideally rational agents that they endorse numerically precise credal states. They, in this way, strengthen the condition of convexity to a condition of *credal uniqueness*. Otherwise their requirements on credal states agree with mine. Thus, the conditions I have imposed are weaker than the traditional Bayesian requirements on credal rationality. The conditions I have proposed also agree with proposals made by B. O. Koopman, I. J. Good, C. A. B. Smith, F. Schick, and A. P. Dempster.[9] As already noted, Kyburg also uses interval-valued credence functions and might be prepared to endorse the conditions I have proposed.

Notice that two or more convex credal states can define the same interval-valued credence function. Since, as I have already illustrated elsewhere, differences in convex sets of Q-functions do make a significant difference in applications to decision making, characterizing credal states by means of interval-valued credence functions entails some loss of relevant information about the credal state. This point will not, however, loom large in the discussion here.

Inductive logic, as I shall understand it, imposes necessary conditions that a Q-function must satisfy in order to be a member of a potential credal state relative to a potential corpus of knowledge. Only one of the three principles

8 I have modified the statement of the convexity requirement to take care of ambiguities in my original formulation (Levi, 1974), which were brought to my attention in conversation with R. D. Luce. I hope to publish a proof elsewhere of the fact that, for cases where, for all Q-functions in B, $Q(e)$ is positive, if B_t is convex, then B_e is (see Levi, 1978a).
9 See (Levi, 1974) for references.

cited above – the principle of coherence – qualifies as a principle of inductive logic in that sense. For authors like de Finetti and Savage, it is the only principle of inductive logic. Many other authors disagree. One additional principle is often recognized – namely some sort of principle of direct inference.

I shall call those who favor de Finetti's view 'coherentists'. 'Objectivists' maintain that a complete inductive logic *IL* is given by the principle of coherence and a suitable principle of direct inference. Of course, there are many authors who contend that there are still other principles of inductive logic.

For any potential corpus K, there is a unique weakest credal state BIL_K – namely, the set of Q-functions eligible for membership in some credal state or other relative to K according to the complete inductive logic *IL*. $CIL(K)$ is that confirmational commitment which takes potential corpora as arguments and the weakest allowable credal states relative to given arguments as values. That confirmational commitment can appropriately be called the *logical* confirmational commitment.

Many authors insist that rational agents should always endorse the weakest credal state allowed by inductive logic relative to what they know. Carnap was a 'necessitarian' in this sense. So is Kyburg. I contend that Reichenbach, as well as Neyman and Pearson, can be interpreted in a manner that takes them to be necessitarians as well.

Carnap differs from the other authors mentioned with respect to what constitutes a complete inductive logic. He hoped to identify principles sufficiently powerful to single out a unique Q-function for each potential corpus. By way of contrast, the other authors cited are objectivists. Yet, like Carnap, they are necessitarians. Because they agree with Carnap on this point yet disagree with him concerning what constitutes a complete inductive logic, when they cannot justify assigning a numerically precise degree of credence to a hypothesis on the basis of the principles of coherence and direct inference alone, they insist that degrees of credal probability go undefined (which, on my translation, means that such probabilities are not numerically determinate).

X's confirmational commitment at t is, in effect, the criterion he endorses at t for evaluating revisions of his credal state due to changes in his corpus of knowledge. I have assumed that this commitment can be well defined for arbitrary potential corpora expressible in K. (The assumption is not as extravagant as it would be were X's confirmational commitment required to be numerically determinate for all potential corpora; but I will not elaborate on this point further here.)

Sometimes X might revise his credal state without changing his corpus at all. If he should do so, the revision should be seen as involving a deviation from the confirmational commitment he initially endorsed. Given his commitment $C_{X,t}$ and corpus $K_{X,t}$, X is committed to the credal state

CHANCE AND SURPRISE

$B_{X,t} = C_{X,t}(K_{X,t})$. If X shifts to a new credal state B while keeping $K_{X,t}$ constant, he clearly must have changed his mind as to the credal state he should endorse relative to $K_{X,t}$. Of course, X might change his confirmational commitment while revising his corpus. However, if X revises his credal state while keeping his corpus constant, he must have altered his commitment.

Rational men should not alter their confirmational commitments for revising credal states without good reason. On the other hand, they should not be so pigheaded as to keep the faith with the confirmational commitments they initially endorse should there be good reasons for revision. I shall not discuss the conditions under which X should or should not revise his commitment. I wish, however, to emphasize that I am not claiming that X's confirmational commitment is immune from revision.

Thus far, confirmational commitments have been characterized in such a way that no restrictions have been imposed on the credal state that should be adopted relative to K' given the credal state associated with corpus K. Yet, it is widely thought that some such dependencies do obtain. If K' is obtained from K by adding information e, the value $B = C(K)$ somehow imposes a constraint on the value $B' = C(K')$ – as long, of course, as the confirmational commitment is held fixed. The restrictions imposed on confirmational commitments so far have, in effect, constrained the domain and range of functions representing confirmational commitments. There is, however, one further condition on the structure of such functions concerning dependencies of the sort just mentioned which is widely endorsed.

Confirmational Conditionalization: Let K' be obtained from K by adding e consistent with K. Let $C(K) = B$ and $C(K') = B'$. For every Q-function in B, there is a Q'-function in B' such that $Q'(h;f) = Q(h;f \& e)$ when f is consistent with K'. Conversely, for every Q'-function in B', there is a Q-function in B such that $Q(h;f \& e) = Q(h;f)$.

Confirmational conditionalization can, perhaps, be best understood by considering the special case where $C(K)$ is single-membered for each value of K. In that case, the single Q'-function in B' is such that $Q(h; e \& f) = Q'(h;f)$ where the Q-function is the single Q-function in B.

During any period of time when X keeps his confirmational commitment constant, confirmational conditionalization implies that X should revise his credal state with changes in knowledge in accordance with a principle that I shall call *temporal credal conditionalization*. This principle is often called the 'principle of conditionalization' and is the basis upon which Bayes' theorem is used to obtain 'posterior' credal probabilities for hypotheses on the basis of data. Temporal credal conditionalization should be distinguished from confirmational conditionalization. If X shifts from confirmational commitment C to commitment C', temporal credal conditionalization will, in general, break down. (For example, this will happen if X changes his credal

204

state without revising his corpus.) However, both the old and the new commitment could conform to confirmational conditionalization. Necessitarians recommend that all rational agents endorse the same standard commitment CIL at all times. Confirmational commitments should not be revised. Hence, for necessitarians and anyone else who thinks that confirmational commitments are incorrigible, temporal credal conditionalization and confirmational conditionalization become equivalent.

I am not a necessitarian. In my opinion, confirmational commitments ought often to be subject to critical review and revision. For this reason, I reject temporal credal conditionalization as a condition obligatory on all legitimate revisions of credal states. Yet, in my opinion, confirmational conditionalization is an entirely plausible condition to be imposed on confirmational commitments. I shall not attempt to defend confirmational conditionalization here. It is important to note, however, that one can consistently reject temporal credal conditionalization while endorsing confirmational conditionalization.

Kyburg also rejects temporal credal conditionalization. On this point, we agree. But, as I understand him, he is a necessitarian. Hence, in rejecting temporal credal conditionalization, Kyburg is obliged to reject confirmational conditionalization as well.[10]

Aside from offering one or two illustrations designed to appeal to intuition in support of violating confirmational conditionalization, Kyburg offers no argument for his position (Kyburg, 1974a, pp. 287–8). Furthermore, his examples are far too bizarre for us to suppose that intuitions about them are going to be clear or nonidiosyncratic. If we are going to appeal to intuition or to presystematic precedent to support a conclusion, there should be at least some indication that it is widely endorsed. I am not concerned, however, to prove the cogency of confirmational conditionalization and the consequent untenability of Kyburg's rejection of it. My aim here is to show that violation of confirmational conditionalization is mandated by Kyburg's rule of direct inference if confirmational coherence is to be obeyed. Thus, Kyburg's account of direct inference stands or falls with his rejection of confirmational conditionalization (assuming that we hold fast to confirmational coherence).

In my opinion, this result constitutes the basis for a powerful objection to Kyburg's scheme and, indeed, to accounts of direct inference like that proposed by Reichenbach; for, although I shall not attempt to prove it here,

---

10 Once more I am translating freely. Kyburg discusses a notion of conditional 'epistemic' probability relative to a corpus K which can at least verbally be construed as the unconditional interval-valued degree of credence that X should assign to some hypothesis were he to add the condition e to his corpus (see Kyburg, 1974a, p. 287). If these conditional probabilities were construed as conditional credence in my sense, coherence would be violated. Kyburg, however, would be unhappy with such a result – so it seems (Kyburg, 1961). The more favorable interpretation is to construe him as allowing deviation from confirmational conditionalization. (I mean more favorable from his point of view.)

I have no serious doubt that confirmational conditionalization ought not to be violated. If I am right, X should always be obliged, counter to Kyburg and Reichenbach, to use the narrowest reference class to which he knows i to belong. If X remains an objectivist in the sense that he relies only on coherence and direct inference from frequency assumptions as principles of inductive logic and is a necessitarian to boot, the degrees of credence he assigns to conclusions of direct inferences will invariably be the unit interval from 0 to 1. In my opinion, this is just as it should be. The only direct inferences warranted from premises like (1′) without supplementation by premises like (1) are useless.

5

Let corpus K contain the sentences (5), (6), and (7) of section 3. According to Kyburg's principle of direct inference, the appropriate reference class to use in this case for determining the credence of h (i.e., 'Petersen is a Protestant') is the set of Swedes. This is so even though X knows that Petersen is also a resident of Malmö. Hence, every Q-function according to X's credal state at t when X's corpus is K should meet the following condition:

(a) $\qquad\qquad\qquad\qquad Q(h) = 0.9$

Suppose X were to add to his corpus K the information that $f_{0.85} \vee f_{0.91}$ — i.e., that the percentage of Swedish residents of Malmö who are Protestants is either 85 or 91. Once more the percentage is known by X only up to an interval that spans 0.9. Relative to the expanded corpus, X should continue to use the reference class of Swedes. His set of Q-functions should all assign to h the value 0.9.

From X's point of view, when his corpus is K, this implication of Kyburg's view of direct inference implies that every Q-function in his credal state should satisfy the following condition:

(b) $\qquad\qquad\qquad Q(h; f_{0.85} \vee f_{0.91}) = 0.9$

The basis for (b) is Kyburg's prescription concerning credence values for h when X's corpus is strenthened by adding $f_{0.85} \vee f_{0.91}$ *plus the principle of confirmational conditionalization*. Because Kyburg himself rejects that principle, he would not see himself as obliged to endorse (b). However, those who do not reject confirmational conditionalization may wish to pursue the matter further.

The following results also follow from Kyburg's principle of direct inference and the principle of confirmational conditionalization:

(c) $\qquad\qquad Q(h; f_{0.85} \vee f_{0.95}) = 0.9$
(d) $\qquad\qquad Q(h; f_{0.85}) = 0.85$
(e) $\qquad\qquad Q(h; f_{0.91}) = 0.91$
(f) $\qquad\qquad Q(h; f_{0.95}) = 0.95$

206

Notice that (d), (e), and (f) reflect the fact that, if $f_{0.85}$ $(f_{0.91}$ or $f_{0.95})$ were added to K, the reference class that X should choose according to Kyburg becomes the set of Swedish residents of Malmö.

Conditions (a) to (f) must be satisfied by any Q-function in B if confirmational conditionalization and Kyburg's principle of direct inference are both to be satisfied.

I shall now show that no Q-function obeying the conditions of the calculus of probability can satisfy these conditions. Hence, if confirmational conditionalization and Kyburg's rule of direct inference are jointly satisfied, coherence is violated.

Assuming that coherence and consistency are sacrosanct, either conditionalization or the rule of direct inference must be sacrificed.

Let x and y be such that x & y is inconsistent with K. The calculus of probability implies that every Q-function in B satisfies the following condition:

$$Q(z; x \vee y) = Q(z; x)Q(x; x \vee y) + Q(z; y)Q(y; x \vee y)$$

Moreover, when $x \vee y$ is entailed by K, $Q(x; x \vee y) = Q(x)$. These facts and a little algebra yield the following results:

(g) $Q(h) = 0.9Q(f_{0.85} \vee f_{0.91}) + 0.95Q(f_{0.95})$ from (b) and (f)
            $= 0.9$ from (a)
(h) $Q(f_{0.95}) = 0$ from (g).

A similar argument establishes the following:

(i) $Q(f_{0.91}) = 0$

By the calculus of probability,

(j) $Q(f_{0.85}) = 1$
(k) $Q(h) = 0.85Q(f_{0.85}) + Q(h; f_{0.91} \vee f_{0.95})Q(f_{0.91} \vee f_{0.95})$
            $= 0.85 + 0$
            $= 0.85$

(k) contradicts (a).

It may be thought that trouble arises here not because of a conflict between confirmational conditionalization and Kyburg's rule of direct inference but because of an oversight in Kyburg's formulation of his rule. Relative to K, X knows that Petersen is a Swedish resident of Malmö. Moreover, he also knows that the percentage of Swedish residents of Malmö who are Protestants differs from the percentage of Swedes who are Protestants. In such a case, it seems strongly counterintuitive to recommend using the set of Swedes rather than the set of Swedish residents of Malmö as the reference class.

Consider the corpus K_1 exactly like K except that X now suspends judgement between $f_{0.85}$, $f_{0.9}$, and $f_{0.95}$. The reasoning that led to contradiction previously does not do so now. There is exactly one Q-function that satisfies all the conditions – to wit, that which assigns to $Q(f_{0.9})$ the value 1.

But this is absurd. I have not required that Q-functions be *regular* in the sense that, if a sentence is not entailed by the corpus, its Q-values should be less than 1. However, it would be extremely objectionable for a condition of inductive logic to require that Q-functions violate the condition of regularity. Perhaps inductive logic should avoid legislating one way or the other. Perhaps, inductive logic should legislate in favor of regularity. I am inclined toward the former view, but that is not the point about which I am now concerned. What is clear is that for inductive logic to legislate against regularity in a case where there are a finite number of exclusive and exhaustive alternatives relative to what X knows is blatantly absurd. If this is right, the amendment to Kyburg's proposal seems of little help.

In any case, this emended version of Kyburg's rule will not help with cases where X knows (as he always does) that i is a member of the set of objects identical with i.

Finally, it should be noted that the argument that leads to obligatory violation of regularity applies to Reichenbach's version of direct inference. The problem cannot be confined to Kyburg's theory. Indeed, we owe a debt of gratitude to Kyburg for having so clearly improved the level of discussion of the problem of choosing a reference class for direct inference beyond the level at which Reichenbach had left it; in consequence the conflict between confirmational conditionalization and certain views of direct inference typically based on the thesis that the major premise of a direct inference is a frequency statement has been rendered accessible to critical scrutiny.

As I have said, I shall not attempt to demonstrate to the unconvinced that violation of the principle of confirmational conditionalization is a fatal objection to Kyburg's approach to direct inference (and to Reichenbach's). Instead, I shall conclude this paper with a brief indication of how direct inference based on chance assumptions rather than frequency assumptions can yield useful results via direct inference without violating confirmational conditionalization, direct inference, or coherence.

6

When direct inference based on knowledge of chances or statistical probabilities rather than on frequencies is considered, we can no longer speak of the problem of selecting a reference class. There is a corresponding problem of selecting one of the descriptions known to be true of the trial event to use in direct inference. The difference derives from the fact that the term 'S' occurs non-extensionally in 'The chance of a result R on a trial of kind S on a equals r'.

One could, nonetheless, formulate an analogue of Kyburg's principle of direct inference for cases where the major premise is a chance assumption. Moreover, Kyburg's rule leads to conflict with confirmational conditionalization even when it is so modified.

However, if, in order to avoid such conflict, X is required to employ the strongest description he knows to be true of the trial on a, he need not necessarily be compelled to assign to the hypothesis that the trial event results in an event of kind R the degree of credence $[0, 1]$. It is, indeed, true that, if X knows that event e is a trial of kind S, he also knows that event e is an S identical with e. However, the chance of obtaining a result R on a trial of kind S identical with e can be some value different from 0 and 1. Indeed, it can be the same as the chance of obtaining a result on a trial of kind S. That the event e is also correctly described as identical with e can be 'stochastically irrelevant' information. Thus if 'e' describes the event by identifying it as the toss at place p and time t, X's conviction that he can ignore the information that the event is identical with e may be a consequence of his general conviction that the spatiotemporal location of trials of kind S is stochastically irrelevant to their resulting in events of kind R.[11]

Someone may object that chances are undefined for results of kind R relative to trials of kind S occurring at place p and time t, on the ground that trials of that kind are not repeatable. I myself cannot find any basis for the requirement that trials relative to which chances are defined should be repeatable, other than that this requirement is needed in order to make sense of limit-of-relative-frequency interpretations of chance. Furthermore, there are plenty of cases where chances are defined relative to trials known not to be repeatable. Thus, the chance of Pepsi bottle b breaking into ten pieces when hit with a hammer, may be defined even though it is known that b can be hit with a hammer at most once. Of course, other bottles can be hit with a hammer; but this is of little help to frequentists. If X knows that the chance of b breaking into ten pieces when hit with a hammer is r, he cannot use Bernoulli's theorem to calculate a high probability that approximately $100r\%$ of bottles on which the trial of hitting with the hammer is repeated will break into ten pieces unless he also assumes that the chance of any other bottle subject to the test breaking into ten pieces on the trial is the same as that for bottle b. X may not know this. He may know the contrary. Yet, the chance statement concerning b will be well defined.

The dogma of repeatability is extremely well entrenched, and casting doubt on it will require more discussion than the previous paragraph affords.

11 Hacking (1965, p. 128) worries about a similar case, and says that, as long as 'there is no reason to suppose' that the chance of an R on a trial of kind S identical with e differs from the chance of an R on a trial of kind S in any significant way, we can ignore the extra information. Seidenfeld has observed that Hacking slips into a variant of Kyburg's position. What he should have said is that we have strong reason to suppose that the chances are the same or nearly so. Otherwise, Hacking has no reason for introducing a principle of irrelevance for the purpose of generating the fiducial argument (see note 5 above).

Fortunately, for the present purpose, it is unnecessary to undertake it here. If chances are undefined relative to descriptions of trials as of kind S identical with e, we can ignore such descriptions in direct inference without threat of contradiction of the sort generated for Kyburg's theory. The point I am concerned to make here is that, even if such chances are defined, they pose no threat of implying that credence assignments must always be maximally indeterminate.

To make the point in a form that will, I hope, undercut the issue of repeatability, let us suppose that the strongest information X knows about a given trial is that it is a toss of coin a by Sidney Morgenbesser. Trials of this kind are repeatable. It seems plausible that the chance of coin a landing heads on a trial of this kind is well defined. But X may be convinced that Morgenbesser has and will toss coin a once and only once. Hence, from X's point of view, the reference class of tosses of a by Morgenbesser contains exactly one event, and the percentage of such tosses landing heads must be either 0 or 100. Yet the chance of heads on such a trial can be some value between 0 and 1, and, indeed, can be equal to the chance of heads on a toss of coin a. If X knows that the fact that the toss is by Morgenbesser is stochastically irrelevant, he can ignore that information in direct inference and base the inference on his knowledge of the chance of heads on a toss of coin a.

Thus, if X is obliged to use the strongest description known to be true of the trial event, he will sometimes avoid assigning indeterminate credence values to hypotheses about the outcome. If, on the other hand, X based his assignment of credence on frequency rather than chance assumptions and used the strongest information available to him concerning the reference class to which the trial event belonged, his credence judgements would be indeterminate.

Of course, occasions will arise where chance-based direct inference will fail to be superior to frequency-based direct inference in this regard. However, depending on X's knowledge, it will sometimes be better and it will never be worse. In this sense, the pressure to endorse a Kyburgian rule of direct inference is less when the major premises of direct inference are chance statements than when they are frequency statements. The conflict with confirmational conditionalization generated by Kyburgian rules poses greater problems for those who replace chance by frequency in direct inference than it does for those who reject such approaches.

Were de Finetti correct and chance an obnoxious metaphysical concept, these considerations suggest that he would also be right in denying the existence of any useful principle of direct inference altogether (which he does, at least by implication). I think, however, that de Finetti is wrong about direct inference. So does Kyburg. But Kyburg agrees with de Finetti (at least by implication) with regard to chance. For this reason, he is led to reject confirmational conditionalization. In my opinion, both de Finetti and

Kyburg ought to reconsider the excessively rigorous standards by which they judge the intelligibility of the concept of chance. The alternatives seem far less acceptable.

7

Perhaps the most important ramification of the conclusions reached here for applications in science is that the selection of control groups in experimentation 'at random' is not the *conditio sine qua non* of scientific experimentation which it is widely taken to be.

I shall not, however, discuss the question of randomization here. In closing, I shall consider briefly another problem of critical concern to those who have sought to develop ways of evaluating posterior credal probabilities for hypotheses relative to data when the prior credal probabilities are extremely indeterminate. This problem is very pressing for objectivist necessitarians, as will become apparent in the course of the discussion. R. A. Fisher proposed an account of how this can be done via so-called 'fiducial arguments'.[12] In recent years, Kyburg and Hacking have offered alternative reconstructions of Fisher's arguments.[13] Their reconstructions are not equivalent, even though both can claim some authority in the writings of Fisher himself. Kyburg's account is based on his view of direct inference. Hacking, as I understand him, insists on chance assumptions rather than frequency statements as major premises of direct inference and does not endorse Kyburg's methods. At least tacitly, Hacking's conception of direct inference resembles the conception I am advocating here.

Let X's corpus K_3 contain the assumption $f_{0.4} \vee f_{0.6}$, where f_r asserts that the chance of heads on a toss of coin a equals r. X also knows that coin a is tossed.

An event is of kind G if and only if it is a case of a landing heads up on a toss when $f_{0.6}$ is true or of a landing tails up when $f_{0.4}$ is true. The chance of a result of kind G on a toss of coin a is 0.6, regardless of whether $f_{0.6}$ or $f_{0.4}$ is true. Hence X should know that chance to be 0.6.

Let h assert that coin a lands heads on the toss taking place, and let g assert that the result of the toss is an event of kind G.

---

12 Fisher first introduced fiducial arguments by that name in (Fisher, 1930). For a later statement, see (Fisher, 1959, pp. 51–7, 114–24). In the later work, Fisher attaches fundamental importance in fiducial reasoning to the role of 'recognizable' sets in a manner which suggests that his understanding of fiducial inference is closer to the reconstruction offered by Kyburg than to that introduced by Hacking.
13 Hacking's reconstruction is given in (Hacking, 1965, ch. ix). Kyburg's is embedded in his account of direct inference. See, however, (Kyburg, 1974a, ch. 14). The example I am using is due to Hacking's ingenuity. He succeeded in illustrating fiducial inferences by means of examples from which irrelevant mathematical trappings have been removed, so that the logical features of the argument could be isolated for critical inspection.

Every function Q_3 in X's credal state B_3 meets the condition that $Q_3(g) = 0.6$. What about $Q_3(g; h)$?

If for every Q_3-function $Q_3(g; h) = Q_3(g)$, it will then follow, via confirmational conditionalization, that X's degree of credence for g should he find out that the coin has landed heads should be the same as it was before he found out that h was true. But it is clear that $Q_3(g; h) = Q_3(f_{0.6}; h)$. Hence, if the information that the coin has landed heads fails to alter X's credal state regarding whether it resulted in an event of kind G, X can use the information that the coin has landed heads to assign 0.6 as the degree of credence to the hypothesis $h_{0.6}$ that the chance of heads on a toss of coin a equals 0.6. Assigning credence in this way is an example of fiducial reasoning.[14]

Notice that the chance of obtaining a G on a toss of coin a that lands heads is 0 if $h_{0.4}$ is true and is 1 if $h_{0.6}$ is true. Hence, the smallest interval within which X knows that chance to fall is the interval from 0 to 1. This interval spans the value of the chance of a G on a toss of coin a. Hence, by the modification of Kyburg's rule suitable to direct inference from chance assumptions, the appropriate description of trials to use is the description of the trial as a toss of coin a when X adds to his corpus K_3 the information that the toss has landed heads. Thus, confirmational conditionalization and this rule lead to the result that $Q_3(g; h) = Q_3(h)$ and to a vindication of fiducial reasoning.

But confirmational conditionalization and Kyburgian rules of direct inference contradict coherence and consistency. For this reason, I contend that Kyburgian rules should be rejected. Hence, Kyburg's reconstruction of the fiducial argument is questionable on precisely the same grounds that his account of direct inference is.

Hacking's approach is different. He does not argue for the condition $Q_3(g; h) = Q_3(g)$ by an appeal exclusively to the principle of direct inference (which he calls 'the frequency principle'). At least by implication, he agrees with the position taken here that Kyburgian inferences are illegitimate. However, Hacking introduces a principle of inductive logic (of the 'logic of inductive support' in his terminology) additional to coherence and direct inference which can be invoked in the example just discussed to obtain the desired fiducial result. It can be demonstrated in the case of this example that Hacking's principle of irrelevance entails that, relative to K_3 before X's finding out that coin a has landed heads up, $Q_3(f_{0.4}) = Q_3(f_{0.6}) = 0.5$ for

---

14 In (Seidenfeld, 1979b), Seidenfeld has shown that inconsistencies can be generated using fiducial arguments reconstructed along lines consonant with Hacking's reconstruction. It appears that Hacking's principle of irrelevance is inconsistent with coherence, direct inference (for chance-based statistical syllogisms), and confirmational conditionalization. Seidenfeld's argument does not preclude permitting judgements of irrelevance to be made on some occasions where Hacking's principle mandates them. It does prohibit making all judgements mandated by Hacking's principle.

every Q_3 function in B_3 (Hacking, 1965, 141–3). At least this must be so if confirmational conditionalization is to be obeyed. This leads to no contradiction here. But it is, to say the least, debatable whether such a condition should be mandated on credal states relative to K_3 by inductive logic.[15]

I am not suggesting that rational men should be prohibited from adopting such credal states. But inductive logic should not obligate them to do so. In cases where X's corpus is K_3, the weakest credal state for $f_{0.4}$ and $f_{0.6}$ would often allow all assignments of Q_3 values from 0 to 1 to $f_{0.6}$. As a good objectivist with regard to inductive logic, I claim that no principle of inductive logic should be invoked other than coherence and direct inference.

On the other hand, I am not a necessitarian. I do not think that rational agents should be obliged to endorse the weakest credal state relative to what they know according to inductive logic. Thus, X is allowed by inductive logic to adopt the credal state Hacking's principle of irrelevance obliges him to endorse. In spite of the rough agreement between Hacking's views and mine concerning the notion of chance and the evaluation of direct inferences, we differ as to whether Hacking's principle of irrelevance is a principle of permission or obligation. This is not a trivial matter.

Were Kyburg's account of direct inference acceptable, he would have succeeded in mandating the legitimacy of fiducial arguments by inductive logic alone – where inductive logic consists of the principles of coherence and direct inference alone, as objectivists require. An objectivist inductive logic of the sort which so many statisticians might have found palatable would enable even a necessitarian to make useful inferences not only from chance or frequency to test behavior but from test behavior to chance or frequency. Indeed, Kyburg's recent book indicates how powerful an approach of that sort can be; for, as I have indicated, he has no qualms about rejecting confirmational conditionalization and has employed the reconstruction of the fiducial argument just attributed to him as the foundation of an account of inverse inference for statistical theory.

Thus, to reject Kyburg's account of direct inference does generate costs for those who would endorse objectivism and necessitarianism. Hacking, as we have seen, gives up objectivism. I prefer abandoning necessitarianism. I do not pretend to have resolved these controversies here. However, I do hope that a critical issue relevant to these matters has been isolated for further examination.

---

15 Objectivist necessitarians may bite the bullet and conclude that nothing can be learned from the data via Bayes' theorem without denying the legitimacy of confirmational conditionalization. They could attempt to focus attention on situations where data can be used to guide policy without treating the data as knowledge or evidence. This, as I understand it, is the gist of the Neyman–Pearson–Wald approach. Elaboration and sustained critique of this view cannot be undertaken here.

14
Potential surprise: its role in inference and decision making[†]

G. L. S. Shackle published *Expectation in Economics* in 1949.[1] That essay introduces potential surprise in determining the expectations controlling decision making in general and the decisions of investors and other agents in the market place in particular.

In this paper, I shall attempt to do the following:

(*i*) Reformulate an account of Shackle's theory of potential surprise along lines similar to those I first followed in 1966.

(*ii*) Explain the application of this account of potential surprise I suggested in (Levi, 1967*a*, chs. VIII and IX).[2]

(*iii*) Outline Shackle's decision theory and the role of potential surprise in that theory and evaluate Shackle's theory from the vantage point of the decision theory I favor.

(*iv*) Compare Shackle's theory of potential surprise with L. J. Cohen's measures of inductive support and inductive probability (Cohen, 1970 and 1977) and G. Shafer's belief and support functions (Shafer, 1976).

My aim will be to show that Shackle's ideas merit serious attention from philosophers but that the domain of application of greatest interest is not the one he intended.

1 Credal states

At time *t*, I suppose that ideally situated agent X is in a cognitive state representable by a *corpus of knowledge* $K_{X,t}$ and a *credal state* $B_{X,t}$.[3]

† Reprinted from *Applications of Inductive Logic*, edited by L. J. Cohen and M. Hesse, Clarendon, Oxford (1980), pp. 1–27 with additional material taken from 'Support and Surprise, L. J. Cohen's View of Inductive Probability', reprinted with permission of the editor from *British Journal for Philosophy of Science*, v. 30 (1979), pp. 279–92.
1 Shackle (1949). A more recent account is found in Shackle (1961).
2 An earlier account is found in Levi (1966*a*) and a more recent discussion in Levi (1972*a*, pp. 213–36).
3 For further details see Levi (1974, 1976*a*, and 1977*a*).

X's corpus of knowledge (expressible in regimented language L) is representable by a set of sentences in L containing all logical truths, set-theoretical truths, and any other items expressible in L consigned to an incorrigible uncorpus UK. In addition to containing UK, the corpus is deductively closed.

X's corpus serves as X's standard for serious possibility at time t. h is seriously possible according to X at t if and only if h is consistent with X's corpus at t.

X's credal state at t is representable by a set of functions each member of which is of the form $Q(h; e)$ where both h and e are in L and e is consistent with X's corpus at t. The set $B_{X,t}$ is non-empty; each Q-function in $B_{X,t}$ obeys the requirements of the calculus of probabilities relative to $K_{X,t}$; and $B_{X,t}$ satisfies a convexity requirement.

Strict Bayesians insist that X's credal state should contain exactly one Q-function. Sometimes they will acknowledge that X will find it difficult to determine what his Q-function is. However, an ideally rational agent will be committed to exactly one such function.

B. O. Koopman (1940), I. J. Good (1962), C. A. B. Smith (1961), and H. E. Kyburg (1961) all abandoned strict Bayesianism in favor of an approach allowing credal states representable by the largest sets of Q-functions compatible with specifications of upper and lower probabilities for sentences in L.

More recently, A. P. Dempster (1967) has investigated a more restricted class of credal states but one still broader than that allowed by strict Bayesians.

According to such *intervalist* views, credal states can be represented by specifying a lower probability function $Q(h; e)$; for the upper probability $\overline{Q}(h; e)$ should equal $1 - Q(h; e)$. Given the identification of $Q(h; e)$, intervalists recommend adopting as credal state the largest convex set of Q-functions obeying the calculus of probabilities and agreeing with $Q(h; e)$ and $\overline{Q}(h; e)$. If the only credal states allowed are of this kind, specifying lower probabilities suffices as a complete characterization of the credal state.

I have argued elsewhere (Levi, 1974) that we should not be so restrictive, but should permit several non-empty convex sets of Q-functions – obeying the requirements of the calculus of probabilities and compatible with the same interval-valued specifications – to be credal states.

The point is of some importance.

Strict Bayesians have thought that degrees of belief could be represented by unique Q-functions representing the credal states of rational agents. Those who have doubted the strict Bayesian doctrine have not despaired of proposing numerical representations of degrees of belief. Intervalists can represent credal states by lower probability functions. As has been known for a long time, these lower probability functions do not behave like probability measures. I am not familiar with anyone who has suggested in print that such lower probability measures be interpreted as degrees of belief. However, G. Shafer has proposed measures of degrees of belief which he explicitly acknowledges to have the same formal properties as Dempster's measures of lower probability. As will be explained later, Shafer appears to interpret Dempster's formalism differently from how Dempster intended.

In any case, such interpretations of lower probabilities as degrees of belief are precluded by my approach according to which a lower probability function cannot characterize X's credal state completely.

2 Degrees of belief and disbelief

Strict Bayesians sometimes regard the Q-function representing X's credal state as measuring degrees of belief in various hypotheses. I noted how intervalists could (but in practice do not) represent degrees of belief by lower credal-probability functions.

The interesting point to notice is that neither representation captures what appears to be the conception of degree of belief and degree of disbelief which is dominant presystematically.

In presystematic discourse, to say that X believes that h to a positive degree is to assert that X believes that h. To claim that X disbelieves that h to a positive degree implies that X disbelieves that h (i.e., believes $\sim h$). Finally, when X believes that h to a 0 degree and disbelieves that h to a 0 degree, he suspends judgement as to the truth of h.

On this understanding, X assigns maximum degrees of belief to hypotheses when he is certain of their truth so that they belong to his corpus. However, he can assign minimum 0 degree of belief to a hypotheses even though he is not certain that it is false. Similarly, X may assign a positive degree of belief to h even when he is not certain that h is true.

No function obeying the requirements of the calculus of probabilities can represent such degrees of belief. Consequently, strict Bayesian conceptions of degrees of belief are automatically violated.

Unlike lower probability functions, measures of the sort under consideration are *acceptance-based*. They presuppose that in addition to what X accepts as evidence in his corpus $K_{X,t}$, X accepts as true additional hypotheses whose falsity is consistent with $K_{X,t}$. Recall that X's corpus of knowledge or evidence consists of all hypotheses X is committed to accepting as certainly true and not possibly false – i.e., to accepting as evidential in subsequent deliberations and inquiries. If X assigns a positive degree of belief to h even though he is not certain that h is true, X must accept h (i.e., in some sense, believe that h) even though he does not accept h as evidence at the time.

Shackle's measure of potential surprise is intended by him as a measure of degrees of disbelief in an acceptance- (or rejection-) based sense (Shackle, 1961, ch. IX).

216

3 Four kinds of ignorance

To elaborate on the distinctions just made, it may be helpful to explain four different senses in which X may be said to be ignorant concerning rival hypotheses.

X is *modally ignorant* concerning $h_1, h_2, \ldots, h_n$ if and only if each of the h_i's is consistent with $K_{X,t}$ and $K_{X,t}$ entails that at least and at most one of the h_i's is true. In that event, all of these hypotheses are serious possibilities according to X at t and he is not certain as to which of them is true.

Given a set U of hypotheses concerning which X is modally ignorant at t, X is *Laplace ignorant* concerning the elements of U if and only if every Q-function in $B_{X,t}$ satisfies the condition that $Q(h_i) = Q(h_j)$ for every h_i and h_j in U. (For simplicity, I consider only finite U.)

X is *probabilistically ignorant* with respect to U if and only if every Q-distribution over the elements of U is represented in $B_{X,t}$ (with the implication that $Q(h_i) = 0$ for every h_i in U).

Given a set U of hypotheses with respect to which X is modally ignorant, X is *modally ignorant in the extreme* concerning the members of U if and only if no disjunction of a proper subset of elements of U is accepted as true without being accepted as evidence. That is to say, no disjunction of a proper subset of U is assigned a positive acceptance-based degree of belief and no such disjunction is assigned a positive degree of disbelief (i.e., of potential surprise).

Modal ignorance is presupposed by the other three kinds of ignorance. Laplace ignorance is the plaything of strict Bayesians. Those unencumbered by the dogmas of strict Bayesianism are not likely to take it seriously. Conceptions of probabilistic ignorance are discussed by Smith, Kyburg, and Dempster. Extreme modal ignorance is discussed by Shackle and, so it appears, by (Shafer, 1976, pp. 22–4).[4]

Thus, we have an abundance of conceptions of ignorance. Are they in competition with one another? Or do they possess different uses in inquiry and deliberation? Answers to these questions go hand in glove with clarification of the conceptions of credal state and acceptance-based measures of degrees of belief.

4 Caution-dependent acceptance rules

Let K be X's corpus of evidence (I omit subscripts whenever convenient). I suppose K is deductively closed, contains the urcorpus UK and is consistent.

---

4 K. Arrow and L. Hurwicz take note of Shackle's conception of extreme modal ignorance in (Arrow and Hurwicz, 1972). They appear to confuse it with probabilistic ignorance. Shafer may be doing the same thing. I claim that probabilistic ignorance implies modal ignorance in the extreme sense but not conversely. I discuss the four kinds of ignorance in (Levi, 1977c, pp. 745–56).

U is a set of hypotheses with respect to which X is modally ignorant. $D(U)$ is the set of hypotheses equivalent given K to disjunctions of subsets of elements of U.

Let R_k be an acceptance rule relative to K and U. It specifies the set of elements of $D(U)$ which are merely accepted.

Suppose that R_k belongs to a family of such rules indexed by values of k ranging from a maximum (which I shall fix at 1) to a minimum (set at 0). The family of rules is *caution-dependent* if and only if for every g in $D(U)$ there is a value $k(g)$ of k such that $k(g) = 0$ if g is inconsistent with K and otherwise $k(g)$ is the maximum value of k for which R_k fails to reject g (i.e., fails to recommend acceptance of $\sim g$) and where g is unrejected for all smaller values of k.

To illustrate, suppose U consists of a null hypothesis H_0 and its rival H_1 where both are simple statistical hypotheses. Suppose the rule is to pick a significance level and pick a test so that the power is maximized. If a sample point falls in the critical region, reject H_0 and otherwise reject nothing. Let the significance level range from 50 % to 0 %. The resulting family of rules specifies for each outcome of experiment what the set of accepted hypotheses will be and does so in a manner satisfying requirements of caution-dependence. I do not endorse this rule but pending later discussion, it can serve to illustrate the idea.

Given a caution-dependent family of acceptance rules, a corpus K, an ultimate partition U, and set of hypotheses $D(U)$, $b(h) =$ the degree of belief that $h = d(\sim h) =$ the degree of disbelief that $\sim h$.

$$b(h) = d(\sim h) = 1 - k(\sim h).$$

When $b(h)$ is equal to 0, h is not accepted according to any of the rules in the caution-dependent family. It is in this sense that it is not accepted as true. If $b(h) > 0$, h is accepted according to all rules for which $k > k(\sim h) = 1 - b(\sim h)$.

Thus, if we are given the values of the belief function $b(h)$ for all h in $D(U)$, we can recover the result of applying the caution-dependent family of acceptance rules through the equation $k(h) = 1 - d(h) = 1 - b(\sim h)$.

The parameter k for the caution-dependent family of acceptance rules represents the degree of boldness (or degree of caution) entailed in using R_k. The higher the value of k, the bolder the rule. X's degree of belief is positive if there is some sufficiently high level of boldness at which h is accepted ($\sim h$ is rejected) according to rules in the family.

Neither Shackle, Shafer, nor Cohen explicitly introduce caution-dependent rules to explicate their ideas of belief and disbelief (or inductive probability in Cohen's case). However, any acceptance-based measures of degrees of belief may be seen to generate results of employing members of a sequence of caution-dependent acceptance rules. In this sense, all these authors are tacitly committed to such rules.

218

The connection between acceptance-based degrees of belief and caution-dependent families of acceptance rules is a useful one; for any clue we might find as to the intended meaning and application of acceptance based on degrees of belief may shed light on the corresponding notion of acceptance. Conversely any clarity we may have regarding acceptance may illuminate our understanding of degrees of belief.

5 Cogency

Let MK_k be the set of sentences in $D(U)$ accepted according to R_k where R_k is a member of a caution-dependent family of acceptance rules.

R_k is *feebly cogent* if and only if it satisfies the following conditions:

(1) K is deductively closed and consistent and MK_k contains K.
(2) If $\sim h$ is in K, h is not in MK_k.
(3) If h is in MK_k, so are all logical consequences of K and h.

R_k is *piecemeal cogent* if and only if it is feebly cogent and satisfies the following:

(4) If h is in MK_k, $\sim h$ is not in MK_k.

R_k is *deductively cogent* if and only if it is piecemeal cogent and satisfies the following:

(3*) MK_k is deductively closed.

We can show that measures of degrees of belief derived from a caution-dependent family of acceptance rules must satisfy the following theorems.
If the family of rules is feebly cogent,

B1: If $k \vdash \sim g$, $b(g) = 0$ and $d(g) = 1$.
B2: If $K \vdash g$, $b(g) = 1$ and $d(g) = 0$.
B3: If $K, h \vdash g$, $b(h) \leqq b(g)$ and $d(\sim h) \leqq d(\sim g)$.

If the family is piecemeal cogent as well,

B4: Given a set of elements of $D(U)$ exclusive and exhaustive relative to K, at most one member of the set bears positive b-value and at most one member of the set of negations of members of the set bears positive d-value.

If, in addition, the caution-dependent family is deductively cogent, B3 and B4 may be strengthened as follows:

B3*: $b(h \mathrel{\&} g) = \min(b(h), b(g))$ and $d(h \vee g) = (d(h), d(g))$.
B4*: Given the set of exclusive and exhaustive alternatives relative to K specified in B4, at least one member bears 0 d-value and the negation of at least one member bears 0 b-value. B4 continues to hold.

219

6 Potential surprise

Shackle imposes conditions B1, B2, B3*, and B4* on d-functions – i.e., measures of potential surprise.[5] I propose interpreting Shackle as being committed by implication to families of deductively cogent and caution-dependent acceptance rules. I offered this interpretation of Shackle's view in 1966 and, setting minor adjustments to one side, see no reason to change the proposal today.

Why should acceptance rules be deductively cogent? Alternatively, why should potential surprise conform to Shackle's requirements? I believe presystematic precedent strongly supports this view. X's degree of belief that h & g should equal the smallest of $b(h)$ and $b(g)$ as Shackle's theory requires. This idea is so intuitively compelling that instructors offering popular discussions of probability as a measure of degree of belief must go to some lengths to overwhelm qualms concerning the multiplication theorem.

But intuition is not decisive here. Whether probabilities are degrees of belief or not, credal probabilities have a useful role to play in deliberation and inquiry. Given X's credal state and some decision problem confronting him, X should restrict his choice of an option to members of that subset of feasible options bearing maximum expected utility relative to computations of expected utility employing some Q-function from X's credal state. That is to say, either X should restrict his choice of this set of E-admissible options or find some way of deferring choice between E-admissible options pending further deliberation.

I do not care to argue the matter here; but I have no doubt strict Bayesians are mistaken in requiring rational agents to adopt credal states representable by single Q-functions. Even so, indeterminate appraisals of hypotheses with respect to credal probability play a critical role in the evaluation of the admissibility of hypotheses.

The challenge is to find a use for measures of potential surprise and cognate measures of degrees of belief which have some important use in deliberation and inquiry.

There are two reasons for this:

(1) Bayesians have been skeptical of inductive acceptance rules. By implication they must be skeptical of acceptance-based measures of degrees of belief and disbelief (potential surprise). They challenge those who are friends of acceptance to identify a use for acceptance rules.

(2) Friends of acceptance disagree among themselves concerning the properties acceptance should have; and such disagreements are not likely to

---

5 Shackle (1961), ch. X, especially axioms (2), (4), (6), and (9). Axiom (1) does not conform precisely to my characterization of degrees of belief. (See also p. 73.) However, the characterization on p. 71 does conform to mine. I suspect Shackle considers two senses of 'belief'. Degrees of belief in the sense in which $b(h) = d(\sim h)$ and a belief state for h represented by the pair $(d(h), d(\sim h))$.

220

be resolved by an appeal to intuition. I suggest that a more promising avenue of attack is to consider the intended applications of acceptance rules.

In my opinion there is a useful sense of acceptance which argues decisively in favor of acceptance rules (for that sense of acceptance) satisfying requirements of deductive cogency.

Suppose X seeks to revise his body of knowledge K via induction by adding new information supplying an answer to some question. Adoption of the answer should result in a shift from K to a new corpus K^* which is consistent and closed. K^* should be obtained from K by adding some hypothesis in $D(U)$ and forming the deductive closure.

The deductive closure requirement on the corpus of knowledge or evidence is an expression of the function of X's corpus as a standard for serious possibility and the idea that, when we ignore limitations on X's capacity for making computations and on his memory, his standard should be represented by the set of all hypotheses whose falsity is not seriously possible according to X's point of view.

Prior to adopting a potential answer to his question and changing his corpus, X might contemplate the inductive expansion strategies recommended by various rules for inductive expansion which differ from one another in the way members of a family of caution-dependent acceptance rules do. He can identify the optimal expansion strategy according to each rule R_k in the family.

Some hypotheses will not be added to K no matter what value of the parameter k is used. Others will be added for some values of k but not for others. Thus, relative to X's initial corpus K, X can evaluate hypotheses in $D(U)$ by specifying those rules licensing their addition to the body of evidence and those rules which fail to license their addition. In this manner, both a b-function and a d-function can be defined.

To decide which hypotheses to add to K involves determining a level of boldness k and accepting all hypotheses into the evidence which are licensed by the rule with that value of the index k. *But to fix on a value of k is equivalent to determining how high the acceptance-based degree of belief relative to K should be before a hypothesis may be added to K and become evidence in its own right.* To do this is tantamount to determining whether inquiry into the truth value of the hypothesis h ought to continue or the matter settled by adding h (or $\sim h$) to the body of evidence.

This is the understanding of the matter I had in (Levi, 1967a, chs. VIII and IX).[6] But on that understanding, it is plain that the caution-dependent family of acceptance rules should be deductively cogent; for the purpose of such a family of rules is to evaluate in a preliminary manner various

---

6 See also Levi (1972, pp. 213–36). In those essays, I suggest that surprise and belief-measures capture an aspect of Keynes's conception of weight of argument. The reader should check those references for elaboration.

potential expansion strategies leading to the revision of the corpus of knowledge. Given the function of a body of knowledge as a standard for serious possibility, the deductive cogency requirement becomes compelling.

Thus, if it is ever legitimate to revise a corpus of knowledge (understood as a standard for serious possibility) via inductive expansion, there is room for the conception of potential surprise to play a useful role in the evaluation of expansion strategies. Moreover, the measures of potential surprise to be employed should have the formal properties Shackle claimed they should have.

Can plausible caution-dependent and deductively cogent acceptance rules be constructed? I shall suggest two candidates. The first is derived from a proposal of I. Hacking's (1965, pp. 89–91)[7] which eschews appeal to probability in favor of likelihood in deciding which elements of U to reject.

Hacking$_k$: Let the elements of U be simple chance hypotheses and let K consist of background knowledge b, data e concerning the outcome of an experiment and the deductive consequences thereof. The likelihoods of all elements of U on e are given. h^* bears maximum likelihood relative to e and h_i is another element of U. h_i is rejected ($\sim h_i$ accepted) if and only if $L(h_i; e)/L(h^*; e) < k$. g in $D(U)$ is accepted if and only if g is equivalent to the disjunction of elements of a subset of U such that all elements of U not in that set are rejected.

Hacking$_k$ is deductively cogent and caution-dependent. One can define b-functions and d-functions relative to Hacking$_k$. Thus, one need not appeal explicitly to probability measures in determining degrees of potential surprise that have the desired formal properties. Whether such rules are otherwise adequate is, of course, another story.

On the other hand, there is no obstacle to using credal probability to determine surprise. I myself favor caution-dependent families of deductively cogent rules which are based on credal probability in the following manner:

Levi$_k$: Let the credal state be B and consider all unconditional Q-distributions over elements of U allowed by B. Let $\mathfrak{M}$ be another convex set of probability distributions (called M-distributions) over elements of U. These are the information-determining probability functions. Reject h_i in U if and only if for every Q-function in B and M-function in $\mathfrak{M}$, $Q(h_i) < kM(h_i)$. Accept g in $D(U)$ if and only if $\sim g$ is equivalent given K to a disjunction of rejected elements of U.

In Levi (1967a and 1967b),[8] I took B and $\mathfrak{M}$ to be single-membered. In Levi (1967a) I required the single M-function to assign equal values to all elements of U. This last requirement was abandoned in 'Information and Inference' and now that I have constructed an alternative to strict Bayesian dogma. I no longer assume that B and $\mathfrak{M}$ are single-membered. Yet, the

7 Rule B in Levi (1966a, p. 115) is an alternative likelihood-based rule. Hacking's suggestion and mine were proposed quite independently of one another.
8 Levi$_k$ is first proposed in Levi (1972, p. 230).

more general Levi$_k$ provides a deductively cogent acceptance-rule for each value of k. Measures of potential surprise satisfying Shackle's requirements can be constructed relative to these rules.

7 Deviation from deductive cogency

According to a widely held view, h should be accepted relative to corpus K if and only if the credal probability that h relative to K is sufficiently high. I suspect this view is based on a confusion of credal probability with acceptance-based degrees of belief (b-measure); for if the acceptance-based degree of belief is sufficiently high and other contextual factors are right, h should be added to X's corpus via induction.

Be that as it may, many authors insist that high probability is sufficient for acceptance and H. E. Kyburg has generalized this view to apply to cases where credal probability goes indeterminate by insisting that the lower probability $Q(h)$ be sufficiently high (Kyburg, 1961).

Kyburg$_k$: Let $m = k/2$ where k, as usual, ranges from 0 to 1. Accept g in $D(U)$ if and only if $Q(g) > 1 - m$. Reject g in $D(U)$ if and only if $1 - Q(\sim g) = \overline{Q}(g) < m$.

Consider the set of acceptance rules obtained by modifying Kyburg$_k$ through equating m with k so that m ranges from 0 to 1. This too is a probability-based and caution-dependent set of acceptance rules. I shall call it *Shafer$_k$*.

According to Shafer$_k$, $b(h) = Q(h)$ and $d(h) = b(\sim h) = Q(\sim h) = 1 - \overline{Q}(h)$ (Shafer, 1976, p. 43).

Thus, the measures of degrees of belief generated by Shafer$_k$ coincide with measures of lower credal probability. The family of acceptance rules is feebly cogent and, hence the b-functions and d-functions are constrained to conform to B1, B2, and B3 but not necessarily B4, B3*, or B4*.

Kyburg has never introduced b-functions or d-functions generated by Kyburg$_k$. He has, however, endorsed rules from this family for acceptance. He has not intended his acceptance rules as rules for the preliminary appraisal of potential strategies for inductive expansion of the evidential corpus as I have done.

Thus, it is entertainable that Kyburg and I do not disagree over issues of deductive closure as I once thought we did; for Kyburg's conception of acceptance and the function acceptance performs within his epistemological program appears to be different from the function of mere acceptance within my framework.

Furthermore, a great many authors have thought of accepting a hypothesis as tantamount to assigning it a high credal probability. Kyburg has generalized the idea so that it applies in cases where credal states are not representable by unique Q-functions.

Nonetheless, I find Kyburg's conception difficult to evaluate. If Kyburg meant by acceptance what I mean, he could not plausibly remain faithful to a high probability rule; for such a rule fails to be deductively cogent. On the other hand, if he does not mean what I mean by 'acceptance', what does he mean? Why should we not dispense with the notion of acceptance altogether and rest content with the corpus of knowledge (and the cognate notion of acceptance as evidence) and the credal state? Perhaps there is an answer other than one based on an appeal to intuition. Kyburg's intuitions and mine seem to clash so strongly here, I have not found appeal to either his intuitions or mine very helpful.

Unlike Kyburg, Shafer never discusses acceptance rules explicitly; but he does investigate measures of degrees of belief or support and measures of degrees of disbelief. Moreover, his measures exhibit the formal properties of measures satisfying B1, B2, and B3 and, in addition, his b-functions are explicitly acknowledged by Shafer to be formally similar to lower probability functions.

Thus, *if* Shafer's b-functions are acceptance-based measures of degrees of belief, they are generated by the family Shafer$_k$. Indeed, Shafer's b-functions are determined by the family Shafer$_k$ for those cases where the credal states meet the requirements imposed by Dempster.

On this construal, the difficulties confronting Kyburg face Shafer along with some additional ones. Shafer$_k$ consists of acceptance rules which are not even piecemeal cogent. Furthermore, although Kyburg's theory belongs to a tradition which considers high probability as warranting acceptance, Shafer's theory implies that any positive probability – no matter how low – warrants acceptance.

Both of these results are bizarre enough to render Shafer's idea difficult to swallow. One wonders here even more than in Kyburg's case why the talk of degrees of belief, disbelief, and support is not eliminated altogether in favor of representations in terms of the credal state with its upper and lower probabilities.

It is clear, however, that Shafer wants to resist that interpretation. He is quite anxious to acknowledge his debt to Dempster. Yet, he seeks a 'reinterpretation of Dempster's work, a reinterpretation that identifies his "lower probabilities" as epistemic probabilities or degrees of belief, takes the rule for combining such degrees of belief as fundamental, and abandons the idea that they arise as lower bounds over classes of Bayesian probabilities' (Shafer, 1976, p. ix).

Thus, Shafer wishes to retain Dempster's formalism but with a new interpretation. Moreover, Shafer does construe his 'epistemic probabilities' or 'degrees of belief' in a manner often suggesting an acceptance-based interpretation. If X assigns 0 degree of belief to h and also to $\sim h$, X is ignorant as to the truth of h and, in a sense in which X neither believes that h nor that $\sim h$ and has no warrant for believing either alternative. When X has evidence supporting h, Shafer seems to suggest that he has a warrant for believing that h to a positive degree.

Reading Shafer's idea as an effort to reinterpret Dempster's theory in terms of some acceptance-based conception of degrees of belief is reinforced by his brief discussion of L. J. Cohen's account of inductive support and Shackle's account of potential surprise (Shafer, 1976, pp. 223–6). He incorrectly identifies Cohen's measure of inductive support as satisfying B1, B2, B3*, and B4* and correctly contends that Shackle's measures obey the same requirements.

Shafer contends that Shackle's measures are special cases of measures in the family he is studying. He has a name for them. They form the family of 'consonant' support functions. He complains that both Cohen and Shackle fail to take into account the phenomenon of dissonance.

It is easy to share the desire of these scholars to ban the appearance of conflict from our assessment of evidence and our allocation of belief. But in the light of what we have learned, the ambition of doing so must be deemed unrealistic. The occurrence of outright conflict in our evidence should and does discomfit us; it prompts us to reexamine both our evidence and the assumptions that underlie our frame of discernment with a view to removing that dissonance. But this effort does not always bear fruit – at least not quickly. And using all the evidence means using evidence that is embarrassingly conflicting (Shafer, 1976, pp. 225–6).

An inspection of Shafer's examples of conflict or dissonance (Shafer, 1976, pp. 84–5) reveals that what he has in mind are situations where X might have a corpus obtained by adding to the urcorpus the proposition e_1 & e_2 and forming the deductive closure. Relative to K_1, obtained by adding e_1 to UK and forming the closure, X is justified in accepting h and all its consequences. Relative to K_2, obtained by adding e_2, X is justified in accepting g contrary to h together with the consequences including $\sim h$.

e_1 and e_2 are not inconsistent with each other but they conflict in the sense that when taken separately they warrant incompatible conclusions.

This notion of conflict, which presupposes a conception of acceptance or warranted acceptance, is not itself embarrassing or difficult. Its presence need not prompt us to re-examine our evidence as Shafer suggests. Neither Cohen nor Shackle ever denied the presence of such conflict or dissonance in data.

Shafer thinks otherwise because he wishes his measures of degrees of belief or support to satisfy two demands: (i) they should be acceptance-based; and (ii) where the total evidence exhibits dissonance, all hypotheses receiving positive support from part of the evidence when taken by itself should be assigned positive support (and, hence, should be believed to a positive degree) when the evidence is pooled.[9]

9 In (Shafer, 1976, ch. 4) Shafer assumes this for separable support-functions. Some qualification of no importance for the points under consideration in this discussion should be introduced to obtain Shafer's general theory. See chs. 7 and 9.

Once this pair of requirements is insisted upon, dissonance does create trouble; for now two incompatible hypotheses must be positively believed and, hence, accepted whenever dissonance is present. Shackle would surely object to this and so would Kyburg. Even Shafer allows that such conflict would and should 'discomfit' us.

Shafer suggests that we should undertake efforts to remedy the situation; but the conflict cannot be eliminated by adding new evidence but only by getting rid of some of the old. And Shafer does state that we should 'reexamine' dissonant evidence. The only thing which prevents getting rid of conflicting evidence is that our effort to do so does not always 'bear fruit' – whatever that means.

I submit it is a bizarre theory which implies that, whenever we have two bits of data e_1 and e_2 each of which supports contrary hypotheses when taken in isolation from each other, we should undertake efforts to remove one of the bits from our evidence!

To escape the predicament Shafer acknowledges himself to be in (without appreciating how troublesome it is for his theory) Shafer could surrender the idea that degrees of belief are acceptance-based; but this move can raise anew the problem of giving an interpretation different from Dempster's for Dempster's formalism.

The alternative is to give up (ii). To be sure, (ii) is part of an answer to an important question. If e_1 warrants positively believing that h when e_1 is the total evidence, and e_2 warrants believing that g when e_2 is the total evidence, and h and g are contraries, what attitude should X adopt when his total evidence is e_1 & e_2? This is one of the questions Shafer seeks to answer in discussing the problem of 'combining evidence' (Shafer, 1976, ch. 3).[10]

My contention is that, whatever the correct solution of the problem may be, it is not to be found in recommending that rational men believe both hypotheses to a positive degree (as (ii) requires). e_1 & e_2 may warrant believing that h, or it may warrant believing that g, or it may warrant refusing to believe either. It cannot justify believing both h and g. In at least one important sense, recommending this is recommending inconsistency. I stop short of saying this because feebly cogent acceptance rules still prevent believing that h & g even when h is believed and g is believed. To me that is small comfort, not be enhanced by euphemisms like 'dissonance'.

Thus, Shafer's claim that Shackle's theory is less general than his because it fails to acknowledge the phenomenon of dissonance is a mare's nest of

10 Both Shafer and Hacking (1974, pp. 113–23) see their problem as one investigated by J. Bernoulli in *Ars Conjectandi*. I have read this book in German so that perhaps some nuance in the original has escaped me. But the discussion in part IV to which Shafer and Hacking allude suggests to me that they have both misread Bernoulli. Bernoulli is far from clear, but he is obviously concerned with situations where one can only in part satisfy the requirements fulfilled according to Huygens' analysis (incorporated as part I of the *Ars Conjectandi*) and he is exploring ways and means to characterize indeterminate probability judgements which then ensue. This, however, is a construal of his own theory which Shafer disavows.

confusion. I do not think Shackle handled the question of combining evidence any more adequately than Shafer has; but at least his insistence on measures of belief and disbelief grounded on deductively cogent acceptance rules exhibits a good grip on common sense lacking in Shafer's discussion.

8 Combining evidence

The source of Shafer's confusion seems to reside in his assumption that the b-distribution over the elements of $D(U)$ relative to e_1 & e_2 should be uniquely determined by (1) U relative to background knowledge, (2) the b-distribution over $D(U)$ relative to e_1, and (3) the b-distribution over $D(U)$ relative to e_2.

If Levi$_k$ is used to determine b-values, the b-function relative to e_1 & e_2 is determined by (a) the partition U, (b) the credal state relative to e_1 & e_2, and (c) the set $\mathfrak{M}$ of information determining M-functions.

Given (a) and the credal state relative to e_1, the credal state relative to e_1 & e_2 required by (b) may be obtained by a suitably formulated principle of conditionalization. From the system of M-functions relative to e_1, one can also compute the set $\mathfrak{M}$ relative to e_1 & e_2 required by (c).

But the b-distribution relative to e_1 & e_2 will not be uniquely determined by (1), (2), and (3).

To illustrate let U consist of h_1, h_2, and h_3. Let there be exactly one M-function assigning each element of U the value $\frac{1}{3}$.

Case 1: The strictly Bayesian credal state relative to e_1 assigns the three elements of U the values 0.5, 0.4, 0.1 respectively. Relative to e_2 the assignment is 0.1, 0.1, 0.8 and relative to e_1 & e_2 it is 0.6, 0.3, 0.1. The three sets of d-values for elements of U are 0, 0, 0.7; 0.7, 0.7, 0; and 0, 0.1, 0.7.

Case 2: The credal states relative to e_1, e_2, and e_1 & e_2 are 0.45, 0.45, 0.1; 0.1, 0.1, 0.8; and 0.3, 0.6, 0.1. The corresponding triples of d-values are 0, 0, 0.7; 0.7, 0.7, 0; and 0.1, 0, 0.7.

The d-function for e_1 is the same in both cases as is the d-function for e_2. Yet the d-function for e_1 & e_2 in case 1 differs from that in case 2. Shafer's requirements are violated.

Of course, this result is obtained using Levi$_k$. But similar results could be obtained using Kyburg$_k$ or Hacking$_k$. We are capable, therefore, of constructing acceptance rules which account for combining evidence but not in a manner meeting Shafer's requirements. Shafer nowhere explains why the principles for combining evidence should satisfy his requirements. Once we direct attention to the identification of acceptance rules underlying acceptance-based measures of degrees of belief and disbelief, the temptation to embrace Shafer's requirements dissipates.

Like Shafer, Shackle also was concerned to account for the revision of surprise values with new data. This particular aspect of his theory has caused him more technical difficulty than any other ingredient in his account of potential surprise. He has had to modify the principles he used for revision of surprise to accommodate trenchant criticism. Shackle's revised approach requires considering surprise relative to e_1 & e_2 as a function of the surprise of h & e_2 relative to e_1 and the surprise of e_2 relative to e_1, and even this revised approach has been subject to what, in my opinion, is telling criticism (Shackle, 1961, p. 80, axiom (7) and its variants, pp. 82–3, and ch. XXIV). On my reconstruction, Shackle's account can be no more satisfactory than Shafer's.

The source of Shackle's difficulty, like the source of Shafer's is his failure to attend to the implications of dealing with acceptance-based notions of degrees of belief and disbelief and, in particular, his failure to attend to the way acceptance rules control the question of revising b-values and d-values in the light of new data.

9 Decision making under uncertainty

X assumes he faces a decision problem where he must choose at least and at most one option from the set α. He knows that at least and at most one hypothesis (state of nature) from the set Ω is true and that if he chooses $A_i \in \alpha$ when $h_j \in \Omega$ is true, o_{ij} is true.

Under these conditions, every Q-function in X's credal state B must meet the requirement that $Q(o_{ij}; A_i \text{ is chosen}) = Q(h_j; A_i \text{ is chosen})$ for every i and j.

I shall discuss decision problems of this kind where the states of nature are *credally* or *probabilistically* independent of the states of nature. That is to say, for every i and j, $Q(h_j; A_i \text{ is chosen}) = Q(h_i)$.

Suppose X evaluates the o_{ij}'s relative to his goals and values in terms of a utility function $u(o_{ij}) = u_{ij}$ unique up to a linear transformation.

$E(A_i/Q) =$ the *expected utility* of A_i according to the function Q in B and is equal to $\sum Q(h_j)u_{ij}$ where the sum is over all the h_j's in Ω.

A_i in α is *optimal* relative to Q in B if and only if $E(A_i/Q)$ is a maximum for all options in α. A_i is *E-admissible* relative to B for the decision-problem under consideration if and only if A_i is optimal relative to some Q in B.

The decision problem is, in the terminology of Luce and Raiffa (Luce and Raiffa, 1958, pp. 275–8) a decision problem *under risk* if and only if the credal state B contains exactly one Q-distribution over the states of nature in Ω. Luce and Raiffa contrast this kind of problem with decision making *under uncertainty*. I suggest that this kind of problem may be represented as one where B allows all Q-distributions over the states of nature in Ω which satisfy the requirements of the calculus of probabilities.

We may also envisage decision problems belonging to neither category. In such cases, the credal state allows some convex subset of the set of all distributions over Ω although the set is not a unit set.

Most writers concede that in decision making under risk, all and only *E*-admissible options are admissible – i.e., legitimately chosen by rational X.

Difficulties arise, however, when the credal state fails to single out a unique Q-distribution. Those devoted to strict Bayesian doctrine insist that appearances are deceiving and that rational X should be (or even is) committed to a single-membered credal state at all times and is, therefore, always facing a decision problem under risk. Others rightly question this dogma.

Typically only situations where the decision problem is under uncertainty are considered although, in my view, intermediate cases are the most realistic ones. In decision making under uncertainty, every feasible option is E-admissible unless dominated by some other feasible option. Consequently, efforts are made to discriminate among the E-admissible options by invoking some additional criterion such as some variant of a minimax or maximin rule or the Hurwicz optimism–pessimism criterion (Luce and Raiffa, 1958, pp. 278–86).

It has been customary to think of decision making under risk and decision making under uncertainty as being regulated by distinct decision theories. On the view I propose, this is not the case. In both kinds of decision making, E-admissibility is taken to be necessary and not sufficient for admissibility. To be sure, most students of decision making under risk regard E-admissibility as sufficient in that case for admissibility. I suggest amending that view. When two or more options are optimal with respect to expected utility, other criteria may be invoked to decide between them just as when, in decision making under uncertainty, other criteria are invoked to decide between the abundance of E-admissible options.

This simple modification in outlook yields several advantages.

(1) We have some hope of giving a unified account of decision making where the same principles govern decision making under risk and under uncertainty and without pretending that all decision making is under risk.

(2) This general account extends in an obvious and natural way to the intermediate cases between risk and uncertainty.

(3) We can see the fallacy in some of the standard objections to decision criteria such as maximin.

This last point is worth explaining. Advocates of maximin are alleged to be urging decision makers to behave as if they are confronting a hostile nature in a zero-sum two-person game. That analogy may be useful for identifying formal similarities between decision making under uncertainty and zero-sum two-person games; but it can also be misleading. In decision making under uncertainty, the decision maker makes no assumption as to which state of nature is 'most likely' to be true. He has no definite view of the probabilities of the states of nature. He is probabilistically ignorant concerning the states of nature and, hence, is neither optimistic nor pessimistic.

In using maximin, X is not deciding on a new and more determinate credal state relative to which to maximize expected utility. Rather he is

CHANCE AND SURPRISE

invoking a new criterion different from and supplementary to expected utility to decide between options which have already passed the test of expected utility. Because so many options have passed the test of expected utility, considerations additional to expected utility have to be invoked to decide between them. Maximiners invoke considerations of security. It is sheer confusion to suppose that when X chooses an E-admissible option which bears maximum security among all E-admissible options, he regards himself as modifying his credal state so that it is restricted to Q-distributions which render that particular option optimal.[11]

Some authors object to maximin because it ignores all but the worst possible outcomes of each option. This objection is symptomatic of the confusion just noted. All possible outcomes have been taken into account in assessing E-admissibility. But the appeal to expected utility has failed to discriminate finely enough and other criteria are being invoked. It is not surprising if these criteria take other factors into account different from those invoked in appraising expected utility.

Several criteria have been proposed for decision making under uncertainty which could be generalized in the manner I am suggesting and which could be defended against Bayesian question-begging in the manner I have indicated in the case of maximin. It is far from obvious which of these alternatives should be favored. I have no decisive argument for my position but I think a carefully but weakly formulated maximin principle (or, better still, a leximin principle) is most suitable. The following familiar phenomenon may help motivate acceptance of this viewpoint.

I recall reading in the papers in the summer of 1973 that British bookmakers were prepared to offer odds of 2 to 1 that Nixon would not be impeached while offering 1 to 3 odds that he would be impeached. Assuming utility linear in money, this practice does not coincide with the Bayesian theory. Bayesians can explain the phenomenon away. Bookmakers are out for a profit and, in any case, utility is not linear in money.

There is another way to account for the spread in the odds. We might suppose that the bookmakers adopted a credal state assigning the hypothesis that Nixon will not be impeached a lower probability of $\frac{2}{3}$ and an upper probability of $\frac{3}{4}$. Assuming utility linear with money, a bet at 5 to 2 odds on Nixon's not being impeached would have been E-admissible among the pair of options consisting of offering the gamble and refusing to do so. So would refusing the gamble. The refusal to offer the odds derives from the fact that offering the gamble bears lower security than refusing to do so. The maximin solution is to refuse the gamble. On the other hand, for odds less than 2 to 1, the gamble is uniquely E-admissible. Even though refusing the gamble bears a higher security level, the gamble is chosen. For similar

11 L. J. Savage (1954, p. 206) seems to acknowledge this point.

230

reasons, a gamble on Nixon's being impeached would be accepted at odds lower than 1 to 3.

This rationalization of the behavior is not the only one available as I have already acknowledged. But it is as cogent as the rival accounts and suggests a bias in favor of maximin as the criterion to use to arbitrate between E-admissible options. I offer it as an elementary illustration of behavior in conformity with the theory I favor.

10 Shackle's decision theory

Shackle has been interpreted as addressing the question of decision making under uncertainty. Shackle is, indeed, investigating decision problems where X's credal state contains more than one Q-distribution over the states of nature. But if potential surprise is related to credence in the manner suggested by $Levi_k$, Shackle's proposals cover more than decision making under uncertainty. According to $Levi_k$, if all Q-distributions conforming to the calculus of probabilities are in B, every state of nature in Ω bears 0 potential surprise. However, all states of nature can bear 0 potential surprise even when probabilistic ignorance does not obtain. Moreover, there are cases of partial indeterminacy where some states of nature bear positive surprise. Shackle clearly intends to cover some situations where some states of nature bear positive surprise. On my reconstruction, Shackle does intend to cover more than decision making under uncertainty.

What Shackle fails to do, however, is to restrict the domain of applicability of his criteria to options which are E-admissible – i.e., which pass the test of expected utility. I have already registered my disagreement and shall not belabor the point any further. I shall proceed with this exposition under the assumption that credence is related to surprise via $Levi_k$ and that Shackle's decision-principles are designed to apply to E-admissible options.

In order to understand Shackle's decision criterion,[12] we need a notion additional to potential surprise. I shall use a modification of Shackle's notion of an ascendancy function. Consider a real-valued function $A(x, y)$ where x ranges over the utility values u_{ij} and y ranges over the values of $d(h_j)$ or, more generally, over any pair (x, y) where x is a utility and y a surprise value even though that pair is not realized in the agent's decision matrix. $A(x, y)$ is the *ascendancy value* X would assign to the utility x were it associated with potential surprise y.

The A-function represents an aspect of X's cognitive and valuation state additional to those aspects captured by the credal state, the utility function and the assignment of degrees of potential surprise. To explain it further, we shall have to consider Shackle's conception of its role in decision making.

---

12 For the mature account of Shackle's theory, see (Shackle, 1961, part III).

Before doing that, however, mention should be made of some very weak conditions imposed on A-functions.

Values of the A-function can be determined by reference to a designated number n, the range of utility numbers, and a function $f(d)$ whose arguments are surprise numbers from 0 to 1 and which is a strictly decreasing positive function of d such that $f(0) = 1$.

$$A(u, d) = f(d)u + n(1 - f(d)).$$

Thus when $d = 0$, $A(u, d) = u$ and otherwise is a positive linear transformation of u (where the transformation depends on the value of d). If, instead of u, $u' = au + b$ is used as the utility function, $n' = an + b$ and $A'(u', d) = aA(u, d) + b$.

The designated value n represents that utility such that for every pair of surprise values d and d', $A(u, d) = A(u, d')$. Shackle regards n as the value (I, not he, call it utility) of a 'neutral' outcome. That is the value the agent X places on his circumstances from his viewpoint when reaching a decision. From X's viewpoint, utility numbers greater than n represent values of situations which are improvements over his current situation as he sees it and utilities less than n represent situations worse than this.

The A-function is a sort of extended and modified utility function. It reduces the value of prospects bearing utility greater than n as they become more surprising and increases the values of prospects bearing utility less than n as they become less surprising.

Let A_i be E-admissible. For each o_{ij}, there is a definite utility u_{ij} and surprise value $d(h_j)$. Hence, for each o_{ij}, $A(u_{ij}, d(h_j))$ is defined. Let $\underline{A}_i$ be the least of these values and $\bar{A}_i$ be the greatest. Thus, with each E-admissible option, we can associate a pair of A-values $(\underline{A}_i, \bar{A}_i)$.

We finally come to the last exogenous variable in Shackle's theory. Shackle assumes the agent has a 'gambler's indifference map' for such pairs of values. He makes no assumptions about the indifference curves except that they conform to the requirements for an ordering and obey usual convexity conditions.

Shackle then recommends that the agent pick that option (from the set of E-admissible options, so I am assuming) which is on the highest indifference curve (or one of those on a highest indifference curve).

Shortly after Shackle wrote *Expectation in Economics*, L. Hurwicz[13] proposed a criterion similar to Shackle's.

According to Hurwicz, for each (E-admissible) A_i, one should identify the value of utility $\underline{u}_i$ which is a minimum and the value $\bar{u}_i$ which is a maximum and plot indifference curves for pairs $(\underline{u}_i, \bar{u}_i)$. Hurwicz assumed that the

---

13 L. Hurwicz (1951) as summarized in Luce and Raiffa (1958, pp. 282–4). The relation between Hurwicz and Shackle is discussed in Ozga (1965, pp. 269–72). In Arrow and Hurwicz (1972, pp. 1–11), a weaker position closer to Shackle's is adopted.

indifference curves are linear implying that there is some real number α between 0 and 1 such that an option A_i is on the indifference curve characterized by $\alpha \bar{u}_i + (1 - \alpha)u_i = r$. The agent should maximize r.

Hurwicz's proposal is a special case of Shackle's. If indifference curves for ascendancy pairs are linear and $f(d) = 1$ for all values of d rather than being a strictly decreasing function, Shackle's theory becomes Hurwicz's.

Moreover, in those cases where all states of nature bear 0 potential surprise, as they must in decision making under uncertainty, A-values coincide with u-values. Given the linearity assumption on the indifference map, Shackle's theory once more become Hurwicz's.

Hurwicz's theory was intended for decision-making under uncertainty. Shackle's theory preceded his by a few years and, moreover, is more general in several respects.

Maximin criteria are special cases of the Hurwicz's theory when $\alpha = 0$. This is so in Shackle's theory as well. However, the injunction is maximizing the minimum A-value rather than the minimum u-value. However, in cases where all states of nature bear 0 surprise, this difference disappears.

I have already registered my preference for some form of maximin (or, perhaps, leximin) criterion for the purpose of evaluating rival E-admissible options. I am inclined to think that there is no need to modify such criteria in order to take into account potential surprise and A-values.

I have no utterly decisive arguments against Shackle's decision theory; but I suspect the strongest motivation for it derives from Shackle's view of potential surprise as serving as a rival to credal probability as a measure of uncertainty.

Now I readily concede that, as a rule, credal states will fail to be numerically determinate and, moreover, E-admissibility, in general, fails to be sufficient for admissibility. But decision criteria such as Shackle's, if cogent at all, are to be invoked only after considerations of expected utility have failed to render a verdict. In resisting the dogmatism of Bayesianism, we should not ignore its insights.

If that is so, potential surprise should not be construed a rival to credal probability. Its function in decision making – if it has such a function – should be understood differently from the functioning of credal probability in computing expectations.

But there's the rub! Shackle utilizes surprise measures in decision making in a manner resembling the use of credal probability in computing expectations. An expected utility is a sum of products where each product is of a utility and a probability. Shackle avoids using sums. But his decision theory, in effect, introduces 'expectation elements' which are products of utilities and functions of surprise values. These are exactly what A-values are. These A-values are ways of discounting utilities in terms of surprise just as the more familiar expectation elements are ways of discounting utilities in terms of probability.

But in testing for E-admissibility, such a discounting process has been undertaken. I find it doubtful that we should discount a second time using surprise rather than probability. I confess that my discomfort is nothing more than that – namely a sense of discomfort. I have no decisive argument against Shackle's idea.

Whether my reservations are well taken or not, it has been shown that the role of potential surprise in Shackle's decision theory need not be construed as rival to that of credal probability but as supplementary. This in itself is a significant correction of what appears to have been Shackle's own view of the matter.

Furthermore, even if Shackle's own proposed use of measures of potential surprise in decision theory is misguided, the concept of potential surprise has other uses in connection with the appraisal of rival potential answers being considered for addition via induction to a body of knowledge.

Thus, there are at least two entertainable domains of application for measures of potential surprise. Neither of these are rival to applications of credal probability measures. Both types of application merit further consideration.

11 Applications to economics

Shackle completed his doctoral dissertation in 1936 and published it in 1938 (Shackle, 1938). It undertook to provide a dynamic model for the business cycle compatible with Keynesian ideas including the multiplier by appealing to changes in investors' expectations. By Shackle's own testimony, work on this idea provided some of the impetus for his efforts to develop a theory of decision making taking expectations and uncertainties into account.[14]

I am unqualified to pass judgement on Shackle's ideas about the business cycle. Although Shackle clearly was one of the early proponents of a model of the business cycle to take Keynesian (and neo-Wicksellian) ideas into account, this aspect of his work is rarely discussed in the economics literature.

On the other hand, other elements of his work have been discussed. I refer, in particular, to his efforts to apply his account of decision making to the problem of choosing investment portfolios. Once more neither space nor my qualifications warrant my discussing the technical particulars of his applications of his theory to problems of economics.

One point, however, is worth mentioning. I have already commented on the difficulties Shackle faced in providing an account of how surprise values change in the light of new data. Yet, Shackle persisted in attempting to construct such an account. The reason seems to have been that he was

14 See the introduction to the second edition of Shackle (1938).

concerned to provide an account of how changes in investors' expectations control developments in a business cycle. He sought to do this by appealing to a surprise-based decision theory of the sort we described together with a model of how surprise values should change with changes in data.

Shackle emphatically denied that one could predict the behavior of investors or explain their behavior without reference to their cognitive attitudes and their desires. In every way he could, he emphasized the 'freedom' of such decision makers.

Shackle did not preclude explanation of the behavior of investors; but he did insist that adequate explanation required appeal to epistemic and affective attitudes. Indeed, to the extent that one could in advance make assumptions about the subjective states of economic agents, one could predict their behavior.

Shackle thought of his decision theory as a framework for such explanation and prediction. But the theory is not free of all normative components. Shackle disclaims the intention of constructing a theory of rational decision making or rational belief and disbelief. But in developing his account of potential surprise, he defends some of the key conditions on surprise functions by insisting that some ways of making assignments are 'logical' and others 'illogical'.

Shackle apparently sought a system of conditions on potential surprise which he thought men, if they are 'logical' would conform to. He also thought that men do conform to a good degree of approximation. He also thought men have ascendancy functions meeting his conditions and, at least implicitly, that they are committed to gambler's indifference maps. But he left those factors relatively unstructured so that his apparatus would be flexible enough to model widely different kinds of behavior.

Shackle is to be admired for his interest and concern for the application of his decision theory. For my part, I have been more inclined to consider his ideas in the context of a normative account of belief and decision making and shy away from dealing with explanatory or predictive applications. Shackle's emphasis on the importance of deliberation due to the circumstance of human freedom suggests that he would not be indifferent to this concern.

12 Cohen on inductive support and inductive probability

L. J. Cohen in his recent book (Cohen, 1977) has introduced a measure of 'inductive probability' having the formal properties of Shackle-like measures of degrees of belief (b-functions). Moreover, Cohen has followed my interpretation of Shackle-like measures as indices of weights of argument sufficient for the termination of inquiry and the addition of new information into evidence.

This pleasant agreement with my proposed reconstruction of Shackle's idea is enhanced by Cohen's contribution to the discussion. Cohen contends that inductive probability (b-value) has properties rendering it useful in clarifying certain kinds of reasoning in Anglo-American law. I regret to say that I lack the competence to make an independent judgement as to the merits of Cohen's proposals; but his discussion promises to extend the reach of Shackle's ideas to an important new domain.

There are some important differences between Cohen's approach to the application of Shackle's measures and my own. He seeks to restrict the domain of scientific applications of his measures of inductive probability (Shackle b-measures) in such a way as to render their use parasitic on applications of measures of inductive support he introduced in his earlier book (Cohen, 1970). According to Cohen, establishing this link ties applications of inductive probability to the Baconian method of relevant variables in scientific inquiry.

Inductive support is the measure Shafer wrongly identified as a Shackle measure. I have not been able to construct a useful application for Cohen's idea of inductive support. I think the link he alleges to hold between inductive support and inductive probability in his sense is expendable and that Cohen's concern to retain the link has led him to restrict the scope of applicability of his measures of inductive probability unnecessarily. In saying this, I do not think I am rejecting the 'Baconian' emphasis on the need to control for relevant variables in well-designed experimentation.

According to Cohen, when designing tests of a universal generalization of the form '$(x)(Rx \supset Sx)$', attempts should be made to control for all the relevant variables. This requirement presupposes that we already have background information stipulating which factors or variables are relevant. The first variable v_1 specifies whether R occurs or not. The remaining variables $v_2, v_3, \ldots, v_n$ take *variants* as values. Cohen supposes that for each variable v_i ($i > 1$), there is a normal variant N_i and abnormal variants $V_{i1}, V_{i2}, \ldots, V_{im_i}$.[15]

Cohen claims that if the experimenter does not control for the variable v_i, his attempt to determine whether in the presence of R an S occurs will be restricted to cases where N_i is the prevailing circumstance. Consequently, a positive result will show only that all R's under that normal circumstance are S's and, if it fails, that none are. To test the hypothesis that all R's are S's, we should, insofar as feasible, test for all abnormal variants of v_i as well. To do so is to control for the variable v_i.

Cohen is correct in claiming that the experimenter should control for relevant variables; but I have one small reservation even at this level. I

---

15 I have modified Cohen's terminology slightly. I find it convenient to use 'variant' to cover both normal and abnormal cases. Cohen restricts 'variant' to abnormal cases. When no variant in his sense (abnormal variant in mine) is present, Cohen says the situation is normal with respect to the variable (Cohen, 1977, p. 136).

would have thought that if the experimenter failed to control for the factor v_i, he could not guarantee that N_i – the normal variant – would be present. Indeed, in failing to control, he may never find out what variant of v_i is present. And, in many cases, it is obscure to me what the distinction between normal and abnormal variants is. Yet, *modulo* this reservation, I agree with Cohen we should control for relevant variables and that we generally assume in advance of experimentation what the relevant variables are.

According to Cohen, Baconian method requires more than this. Cohen contends that the relevant variables are ranked with respect to what Cohen calls 'falsificatory potential' based also on background information culled from the testing of generalizations belonging to the same category as the generalization under scrutiny.

The variable v_2 bears highest falsificatory potential. Whatever it means, it implies that the generalization could be falsified by a combination of circumstances (i.e., a specification of variants for all relevant variables) where an abnormal variant of v_2 is present and the variants of all variables for $i > 2$ are normal even if a fully normal combination of circumstances never falsifies the generalization.

On the other hand, a combination of circumstances where v_3 has an abnormal variant but all other variables including v_2 are normal cannot yield a result in the presence of an R different from what ensues when v_2 is abnormal as well as v_3. That is why v_3 bears less falsificatory potential than v_2.

Similar remarks apply *mutatis mutandis* concerning the relation between v_4 and the preceding variables. Thus, the n variables are ranked with respect to falsificatory potential.[16]

This ranking of relevant variables yields a ranking of relevant combinations of circumstances or variants with respect to falsificatory potential. The combination with the greatest falsificatory potential is the one where R is realized and all variants of other relevant variables are normal. Consider any case where R is realized, v_2 has an abnormal variant and all other variants are normal. Such combinations of circumstances belong at the

---

16 Cohen fails to state this assumption explicitly; but it is crucial to the situations he considers typical of experimental science (i.e., excluding the allegedly remote cases he discusses in (Cohen, 1977, pp. 144–5)). Let the generalization '$(x)(Rx \supset Sx)$' pass the first three tests in a Cohen hierarchy. R has been realized in the presence of normal variants for all relevant v_is where $i > 1$. R has been realized in the presence of all possible cases of abnormal variants of v_2 where the variants for all other v_is are normal. R has been realized in the presence of all possible combinations of abnormal variants of v_2 and v_3 where variants for all v_is where $i > 3$ are normal. For all these cases, the generalization passes. In (Cohen, 1977, p. 185), Cohen clearly implies that in a case such as this, the data fully support 'Every R unaccompanied by an abnormal variant of a variable for $i > 3$ is S'. I take it that Cohen means to preclude falsification by a situation where the only abnormal variant (other than the presence of an R) is the occurrence of an abnormal variant of v_3. But this is exactly the assumption I attribute to Cohen.

second highest level of falsificatory potential. The procedure reiterates until all variables have abnormal variants.[17]

If there is a combination where the variant of v_3 is abnormal and the other variants including that for v_2 are normal, the falsificatory potential of that combination can be no different than that for a combination where v_2 is abnormal and so is v_3.

Thus, Cohen thinks that if one is about to test '$(x)(Rx \supset Sx)$', it is to be expected given the background knowledge that, if the generalization is falsifiable at all, it will be more easily falsified (in some sense of 'easier') by a combination of circumstances bearing high falsificatory potential than by one bearing low falsificatory potential. It is not clear whether Cohen is claiming that the probability of falsification (in a classical sense) conditional on realizing an instance of R in the presence of a combination with high falsificatory potential is greater than the probability of such falsification conditional on the presence of a combination with low falsificatory potential. Perhaps the comparison involves some other mode of appraising what is to be expected. I suspect that Cohen does mean probability in some sense conforming to the requirements of classical calculus; for the evidence he allows for falsificatory potential comes from records of the frequencies with which other generalizations belonging to the category to which the generalization under investigation belongs have been falsified by various combinations of circumstances.

In any case, according to Cohen, in testing '$(x)(Rx \supset Sx)$' highest priority should be given to controlling for variables with high falsificatory potential. Given that the generalization passes test controlling for variables of this sort, it may then be desirable to test for variables of lesser relevance (falsificatory potential) as well.

When experimentation incurs costs and one is not able to test for all relevant variables, it is understandable how a ranking of relevant variables with respect to falsificatory potential could be useful. But we can still control for relevant variables subject to cost constraints even if there is no ranking to help in selecting variables to control. Thus, ranking with respect to relevance is not essential to methods of controlled experimentation. This point is important; for Cohen insists, for reasons obscure to me, that controlled experimentation requires such a ranking and that those who do not understand this have no sympathy for the Baconian tradition.

Consider now cases where the agent is able to control for all relevant variables. In such contexts, it is utterly unclear to me what importance the

---

17 Cohen does not call this induced ranking of combinations of circumstances a ranking with respect to 'falsificatory potential'. Only ranking of relevant variables is alleged to be with respect to falsificatory potential. I think my extension of his terminology suggestive and fair; but nothing much hinges on it. What is crucial is that his ranking of relevant variables and tests generates a ranking of combinations of circumstances. The significance of the ranking will emerge subsequently.

ranking with respect to falsificatory potential has. Its role in providing a way to select variables to control disappears.

Cohen disagrees. Suppose that '$(x)(Rx \supset Sx)$' passes a test controlling for no relevant variables so that all variants are normal. The generalization has been tested for circumstances bearing highest falsificatory potential and has passed. It would be tested more severely, if it passed a test for all possible combinations of circumstances at the next level down of falsificatory potential. Passing the first test reveals that the generalization has a modicum of 'ability to resist falsification' (Cohen, 1977, p. 140); passing the second test in addition to the first reveals a still greater ability. Needless to say, tests of greater severity entail controlling more variables in the hierarchy.

If there are n relevant variables, there are n tests in the sequence. Suppose the generalization has been subjected to all of them and has passed the first i of them and failed the $i + 1$st. According to Cohen, the generalization bears a degree of inductive support equal to i/n. What this means is that the generalization has an ability to resist falsification of degree i/n. Cohen's index of inductive support cannot be a credal probability and it cannot be a b-measure; for a hypothesis receives positive support even when the evidence entails its falsity.

To conclude from this feature of Cohen's notion of support that it has no value would be wrong. It is fair, however, to ask for an explanation of the use of Cohen's measure in deliberation and inquiry.

One possible use is as a summary of information concerning the results of batteries of tests meeting the rather special conditions Cohen imposes on such tests.

Observe, however, that the summary provided by reports on inductive support is highly selective of the information available. Why and for what purpose should we retain the information conveyed by a report of inductive support rather than other information about the results of testing?

Cohen does offer an answer in (Cohen, 1977). Inductive support can be used to determine inductive probability – i.e., b-values.

Suppose an agent X knows that an event of kind R is about to occur and is interested in whether an event of kind S will ensue. He knows which variables are relevant for S in the presence of R and can order them with respect to falsificatory potential (for '$(x)(Rx \supset Sx)$'). He knows the results of a complete battery of tests. Hence, he knows for each possible combination of relevant circumstances whether R's are invariably followed by S's or not. What X does *not* know is which possible combination of relevant circumstances is present. Thus, he does not know whether all variants of all relevant variables are normal or, if some are abnormal, which are.

Under these very special circumstances, Cohen claims that X should assign a degree of inductive probability to the hypothesis that an S will ensue equal to the inductive support assigned the generalization '$(x)(Rx \supset Sx)$'.

According to Cohen, the reason we are entitled to link inductive

239

probabilities of inferences from R's to S's with the inductive support for '$(x)(Rx \supset Sx)$' in this way is that inductive support is an index of the reliability of the generalization in the sense in which reliability is ability to resist falsification.

In some sense of 'reliable', the reliability of such a generalization controls the degree of confidence with which one may legitimately infer the occurrence of an S from information that an R has or is about to occur. However, in the sense in which Cohen takes the generalization to be reliability, this link does not hold.

Let the generalization be supported to the $(n-1)/n$ degree. This means that the generalization survives falsification under all relevant combinations of circumstances except some combination or combinations bearing minimum falsificatory potential. Even so, these circumstances do falsify the generalization and X knows them to be not-S inducing in the presence of R.

If X knew such a not-S-inducing combination of circumstances to be present, he should be certain that an S will not occur and, if he knew that the combination did not obtain, he should be certain that an S will occur. But we suppose X to be in suspense. His degree of confidence of acceptance (b-value or inductive probability) that an S will occur should be equal to the potential surprise he assigns the hypothesis that an S will not occur. Given the background, that d-value is equal to the d-value assigned the disjunction of hypotheses asserting that a combination of circumstances which is not-S inducing obtains; and this d-value is equal to the d-value assigned the disjunct bearing a minimum d-value.

All of this follows strictly from the theory of inductive probability endorsed by Cohen when its scope of applicability is extended from hypotheses about the results of the occurrence of an R to hypotheses about the unknown combination of relevant variables. Surely, given his Baconian commitment, Cohen will agree that X's judgements concerning the occurrence of an S depend critically on his judgements concerning the combination of relevant circumstances which obtains.

In our example, if X is to assign a high inductive probability (b-value) to the hypothesis that an S will occur because the inductive support for the generalization is so high, he should be obliged to assign a high d-value to the hypothesis that not-S inducing circumstances are present because these circumstances have low falsificatory potential. More generally the ranking of combinations of circumstances with respect to falsificatory potential should tend in the opposite direction from the ranking of these combinations with respect to potential surprise.

However, Cohen's characterization of falsificatory potential furnishes no basis for assuming that if combination of circumstances a bears greater falsificatory potential than combination b, $d(b) \geq d(a)$. I conjecture that Cohen has confused two senses of normality or abnormality. In one sense, circumstances normally present are to be expected to obtain more than circumstances not normally present. But in Cohen's theory, normal circumstances are those bearing maximum falsificatory potential regardless of how likely it is that they obtain (and this is so whether 'likely' means 'probably' in a sense conforming to the classical calculus or in the sense of Cohen's 'inductive probability'). I suspect that Cohen has moved illicitly from the second sense to the first in establishing his link between inductive probability and inductive support.

Cohen's link could be preserved by restricting the scope of applicability of his account of inductive probability still more narrowly than it already is – namely to cases where normality in both senses correlate well. But I doubt whether there will be much scope for Cohen's proposals under those circumstances. In any case, the restriction is gratuitous. As long as some appropriate caution-dependent family of deductively cogent acceptance rules is available for use in assigning d-values and b-values to hypotheses about the combination of relevant circumstances, we do not need to rely on reference to inductive support to assign inductive probabilities to inferences from R's to S's.

Furthermore, we can employ caution-dependent families of deductively cogent acceptance rules to reach conclusions pertaining to which of rival theoretical hypotheses is true, in estimating the value of a parameter and in other situations not readily represented as involving inference from R's to S's. To be sure, some sort of inductive acceptance or rejection rules must be countenanced; but Cohen does not object to this. Identification of adequate families of rules remains a matter of controversy; but it is demonstrable that as long as adequate families should satisfy requirements of deductive cogency, d-functions and b-functions will behave like Shackle measures and will be interpretable as measures of weight of argument. We do not have to claim to have settled all problems to claim to have settled some of them.

Thus, Cohen has hobbled his account of inductive probability by linking it so closely to his measures of inductive support. The theory of inductive probability or degrees of confidence of acceptance has a life of its own independent of Cohen's theory of inductive support. It is a good thing this is so; for the Shackle-like measures characterize interesting features of evidence and hypotheses in deliberation and inquiry. Cohen has succeeded in identifying many of these features; and he has broken new ground by exploring applications in legal contexts. I suggest we separate his important contributions to the appreciation of Shackle's ideas from his views concerning inductive support whose status and importance remain obscure.

13 Conclusion

Contemporary literature on scientific inquiry contains an abundance of proposals for ways to appraise hypotheses. We have more measures of belief, support, corroboration, and the like than anyone can hope to take seriously.

It is important to be able to identify the intended domains of application and the significance of the intended applications so that a clear idea can be had as to which measures have established worth and which still stand in need of vindication.

In my opinion, the contributions of G. L. S. Shackle to the study of non-additive measures of degrees of belief or support continue to be the most important ones in the literature. Shackle himself has suggested interesting applications; and there are others which he himself did not explicitly consider.

I do not mean to suggest that potential surprise should be assigned as central a place in the epistemic polity as the concept of credal probability or the more general notion of a credal state. We should not, however, let the verbal posturings of simplistic probabilism blind us to the virtues of Shackle's contribution.

Part IV

Decision making

15

Newcomb's many problems†

1

Robert Nozick (1969) attributes to William Newcomb a certain conundrum about rational choice. According to Nozick, the puzzle has fundamental significance for a theory of rational choice.

Suppose X is faced with the following predicament. Two boxes lie before him. One box contains $1000 whereas the other contains $1 000 000 ($M$) or nothing depending on whether hypothesis H_1 or H_2 is true. (These two hypotheses or 'states of nature' will be explained shortly.) X has two options: A_1 which is taking what is in the second box alone and A_2 which is taking what is in both boxes.

Prior to X's making a decision, a being (to be called 'Newcomb's demon') predicts X's choice. Newcomb's demon predicts that X will choose A_1 if and only if the demon places M in the second box and predicts that X will choose A_2 if and only if the demon places nothing in the second box. X knows all of this. Hence, we can let H_1 represent the statement that M is in the second box or, equivalently, that the being predicts that X will choose A_1. Similarly, H_2 represents the assertion that the being places nothing in the second box or, equivalently, that the being predicts that X will choose A_2. X's decision matrix looks like this:

	H_1	H_2
A_1	M	$0
A_2	$1000 + M	$1000

X knows that Newcomb's demon is a highly reliable predictor of X's choices or, more generally, of the choices of agents confronted with choice situations of the sort just described. On the other hand, the demon is not perfectly infallible.

Nozick considers the questions as to how X should choose under the circumstances. He introduces two arguments one of which favors choosing

† Reprinted with permission of the publisher from *Theory and Decision* v. 6 (1975), pp. 161–75.
Copyright © 1975 by D. Reidel Publishing Company, Dordrecht, Holland.

A_1 (Nozick's first argument) and one of which favors choosing A_2 (Nozick's second argument).

Nozick's first argument: Since Newcomb's demon is an almost perfectly reliable predictor of X's choices in problems of the sort under consideration, the probability of the demon predicting that X will choose A_1 (i.e., of H_1 being true) conditional on X's choosing A_1 should be very high. Similarly, the probability of H_2 conditional on X's choosing A_2 should also be high. Hence, X is almost certain of obtaining \$$M$ if he chooses A_1 and is almost certain of obtaining \$1000 if he chooses A_2. Clearly he should choose A_1. This argument can be put more formally – provided we assume utility to be linear in money – by saying that the expected utility of A_1 is $p(H_1; A_1)M$ and the expected utility of A_2 is $p(H_1; A_2)(1000 + M) + p(H_2; A_2)(1000) = 1000 + M - p(H_2; A_2)M$.

Since by the first argument both $p(H_1; A_1)$ and $p(H_2; A_2)$ are near 1, the expected utility of A_1 is almost M and of A_2 is almost 1000.

Nozick's second argument: When X makes his decision, Newcomb's demon has already made his prediction and has, depending on which prediction he had made, placed \$$M$ in the second box or refrained from doing so. The truth values of H_1 and H_2 are, in Nozick's words, 'fixed and determined'. Nothing X can do will alter this circumstance. His choice will have no casual effect on whether \$$M$ is in the second box or not.

If H_1 is true and there is \$$M$ in the second box, X will be better off choosing A_2; for he will then receive \$$M$ + \$1000 rather than \$$M$. If, on the other hand, H_2 is true, by choosing A_2 he will receive \$1000 rather than nothing. Thus option A_2 dominates option A_1 in the sense that no matter which state of nature is true, X will be better off choosing A_2 than choosing A_1. X should, therefore, choose A_2.

Nozick reports that those he has interrogated on the matter have thought the solution to the problem to be obvious. However, they divide almost evenly on whether X should choose A_1 or A_2.

As Nozick sees the situation, the first argument appeals to the principle of maximizing expected utility whereas the second appeals to the 'dominance principle'. In many contexts, the prescriptions of the two principles do not conflict. This is so, for example, in situations where $p(H_1; A_1) = p(H_1; A_2) = p(H_1)$ so that states of nature are probabilistically independent of the option chosen. Conflict can arise, however, when, as in the case under consideration, the states of nature fail to be probabilistically independent of the options chosen. The question which concerns Nozick is which of the two principles is legislative under these circumstances.[1]

1 Formulations of the principle of maximizing expected utility and the dominance principle are given in Nozick (1969, p. 118). Nozick and R. C. Jeffrey independently noticed the possibility of divergence between these two principles (Nozick and Jeffrey, 1965).

   Some authors seem to have thought that the dominance principle could be used as a condition of adequacy for any acceptable theory of rational choice. It seemed as though

Nozick's proposed resolution of the problem is that the principle of maximizing expected utility ought to be legislative in all cases except those where the truth values of the hypotheses characterizing states of nature are 'fixed and determined' prior to the agent's making a decision. Consequently, he favors choosing A_2 rather than A_1.

My own view can be summarized as follows:

(*i*) Nozick's first argument invoking the principle of maximizing expected utility is fallacious.

(*ii*) The decision problem facing X is not described in sufficient detail to invoke the principle of maximizing expected utility in order to recommend a choice.

(*iii*) The principles invoked by Nozick in buttressing his second argument lead to untenable consequences.

(*iv*) Thus, Nozick's second argument does not establish a rival to the principle of maximizing expected utility in situations where states of nature are fixed and determined. On the other hand, given Nozick's description of Newcomb's problem, the principle of maximizing expected utility cannot furnish a definite prescription as to what X should do. For some versions of the problem, A_1 should be chosen and for others A_2 should be chosen.

(*v*) Suppose, however, that X lacks the extra information required in order to invoke the principle of maximizing expected utility. This problem with the principle is a familiar one and has nothing to do with whether states of nature are fixed and determined or not. Among the many proposals which have been made for situations where the probabilities required for applying the principle of maximizing expected utility cannot be determined, a familiar one is the maximin principle. This principle favors choosing A_2.

Given the obscurities in Nozick's engaging presentation of Newcomb's problem, it is understandable why men might differ as to what X should do.

2

If Newcomb's demon were perfectly infallible, then, whenever he made a prediction of X's choice in contexts of choice of the sort described above (or of the choices of other agents in relevantly similar predicaments), his prediction would be true. Consequently, his prediction would be true regardless of whether he predicted that X chooses A_1 or X chooses A_2.

On the assumption that Newcomb's demon is nearly but not perfectly infallible, we can conclude that the probability of the demon predicting

adopting the dominance principle begged no questions between those theories which rely on probabilities assigned to states of nature and those which do not. The analyses of Nozick and Jeffrey undermine such views. Their contributions, therefore, furnish an important insight into the theory of rational choice.

247

correctly conditional on his making a prediction is very high. That is to say, $p(A_1 \ \& \ H_1 \lor A_2 \ \& \ H_2) = p(A_1; H_1)p(H_1) + p(A_2; H_2)p(H_2)$ is very high. $(p(H_2) = 1 - p(H_1))$; for the probabilities are conditional on the demon making some prediction about the agent's choices. This condition can be met without our being able to claim that the probability of the demon's predicting correctly is high regardless of whether he predicted that X chooses A_1 or chooses A_2. At least one of the two probabilities $p(A_1; H_1)$ and $p(A_2; H_2)$ must be high. However, it need not be the case that both are. Nonetheless, it seems clear that Nozick's intent in presenting the problem is to suppose that Newcomb's demon is nearly infallible in the strong sense that both $p(A_1; H_1)$ and $p(A_2; H_2)$ are both high – i.e., nearly equal to 1. In the subsequent discussion, I shall assume they are both equal to 0.9. When these conditional probabilities are both high and equal to each other, it follows that $p(A_1 \ \& \ H_1 \lor A_2 \ \& \ H_2)$ is also very high – indeed, equal to the common value of the two conditional probabilities.

Care should be taken, however, not to confuse the conditional probabilities $p(A_1; H_1)$ and $p(A_2; H_2)$ which are conditional probabilities of X's choosing an option given that the demon predicts it with the conditional probabilities $p(H_1; A_1)$ and $p(H_2; A_2)$ which are the conditional probabilities of the demon's predicting X's choosing an option given that X chooses that option. Assuming that the first two conditional probabilities are high, it does *not* follow that the second two conditional probabilities are both high. To see this consider the following three cases where X might have obtained statistics concerning the past performance of Newcomb's demon in predicting choices of agents faced with predicaments similar in all relevant respects to the one X is currently facing.

Case 1

	Predicts choice of second box	Predicts choice of both boxes
Chooses second box	900 000	10
Chooses both boxes	100 000	90

Case 2

	Predicts choice of second box	Predicts choice of both boxes
Chooses second box	495 045	55 005
Chooses both boxes	55 005	495 045

Case 3

	Predicts choice of second box	Predicts choice of both boxes
Chooses second box	90	100 000
Chooses both boxes	10	900 000

To simplify, suppose X is justified in assigning probabilities equal to the relative frequencies revealed in these tables. Nothing relevant to this discussion is distorted by proceeding in this way. Given the simplifying assumption, the following table states the pertinent probabilities for each of the three cases:

	$p(A_1; H_1)$	$p(A_2; H_2)$	$p(H_1; A_1)$	$p(H_2; A_2)$	$p(H_1)$
Case 1	0.9	0.9	0.999 988 8	0.000 899 1	0.999 900 0
Case 2	0.9	0.9	0.900 000 0	0.900 000 0	0.500 000 0
Case 3	0.9	0.9	0.000 899 1	0.999 988 8	0.000 099 9

All three cases represent situations where Newcomb's demon is nearly perfect as a predictor of X's choices and where the specification of the decision problem is precisely met. The demon is just as infallible a predictor in cases 1 and 3 as he is in case 2. The chief difference between the cases is that in case 1 the demon predicts that the agent will choose A_1 on almost every occasion when he makes a prediction; in case 2, he makes such a prediction only 50 % of the time; and in case 3 he makes that prediction only rarely.

Because of this difference in the probability with which the demon predicts that the agent will choose A_1, in case 1, $p(H_1; A_1)$ is high and $p(H_2; A_2)$ is low; in case 2, $p(H_1; A_1)$ and $p(H_2; A_2)$ are both high and equal; and, in case 3, $p(H_1; A_1)$ is low and $p(H_2; A_2)$ is high.

In presenting his first argument, however, which purports to show that X should choose A_1, Nozick fallaciously concludes from the fact that Newcomb's demon is nearly infallible as a predictor that both $p(H_1; A_1)$ and $p(H_2; A_2)$ are very high. This is so in case 2 but not in cases 1 and 3 even though the demon is just as reliable a predictor of X's choices in cases 1 and 3 as he is in case 2.

As Nozick sees the matter, the first argument invokes the principle of maximizing expected utility to justify choosing A_1. In general, the computation of expected utility uses the probabilities of the states of nature (i.e., H_1 and H_2) conditional on X choosing the option whose expected utility is being evaluated. Thus the expected utility of the first option is $p(H_1; A_1)M + p(H_2; A_1)0$ and the expected utility of the second option is $p(H_1; A_2)(M + 1000) + p(H_2; A_2)1000$.

Thus, Nozick's fallacious inference is crucial to the first argument. Without it, the case of choosing A_1 collapses. Indeed, assuming that utility is linear with money, in cases 1 and 3, the principle of maximizing expected utility favors choosing A_2. A_1 is favored only in case 2.

We may conclude, therefore, not only that Nozick's first argument is invalid but that, from the point of view of someone committed to using the principle of maximizing expected utility, no recommendation can be made

249

concerning what X should do without filling in more details concerning X's predicament than Nozick has done.[2]

This result is relevant to the statistics which Nozick has collected concerning reactions to Newcomb's problem. A partisan of the principle of maximizing expected utility can explain the division of opinion as due to the incomplete specification of the problem. I shall return to this point at the end of the paper.

3

Whereas Nozick's first argument attempts to justify choosing A_1 on the grounds that choosing A_1 maximizes expected utility, his second argument attempts to justify choosing A_2 on the grounds that A_2 dominates A_1 under circumstances where choosing the dominant option is appropriate.

According to Nozick's second argument, when X comes to choose between A_1 and A_2, Newcomb's demon has already made his prediction and has either placed the million dollars in the second box or failed to do so. X's choice will have no influence on whether H_1 or H_2 is true. Hence, so Nozick argues, X should consider that no matter whether H_1 or H_2 is true, he will be better off choosing A_2.

According to Nozick, the second argument suggest that X should use the 'dominance principle' in choosing between the two options because the states of nature are fixed and determined before X makes a choice. The first argument, on the other hand, invokes the principle of maximizing expected utility. Nozick erroneously holds that the options recommended will be different. This is not true. In cases 1 and 3, invoking the principle of maximizing expected utility leads to the same conclusion as invoking the dominance principle. Only in case 2 is there disagreement.

Thus, if Nozick's second argument has any legitimacy, it shows that when the states of nature are fixed and determined, (a) the principle of maximizing expected utility is not to be used and (b) the dominance principle is to be used. This, at any rate, is the position which Nozick seems to take.

Suppose, however, that X faces a 'revised version' of the decision problem we have considered (which shall now be called the 'authorized version') where the states of nature are fixed and determined before X makes a choice but where no option dominates any other.

To illustrate, let X have the same options as before – to wit, picking the second box (A_1) and picking both boxes (A_2). Newcomb's demon predicts his choice beforehand and predicts correctly with a 0.9 probability – i.e., $p(A_1; H_1) = p(A_2; H_2) = 0.9$.

---

2 In a shrewd discussion of Nozick's paper, Maya Bar-Hillel and Avishai Margalit (1972) conclude in favor of choosing A_1 as per the first argument. Although I sympathize with much of what they have to say about Nozick's second argument, they too have committed the fallacy ingredient in the first argument.

If the demon predicts that X will choose A_1 (state of nature H_1), he places $\$M$ in the second box. However, in the unlikely event that he makes this prediction and X actually chooses A_2, the demon exacts a penalty of $\$1500$ from X so that X's net return is $\$M-\$500$. Otherwise the payoff matrix is precisely as before.

Unlike the authorized version where A_2 dominates A_1 the revised version contains no option which is dominated by any other. Hence, the dominance principle cannot render a verdict between the two options. Yet, as is true in the authorized version, the states of nature are fixed and determined before X can make a choice. This is so whether the probabilities are as in case 1, case 2 or case 3.

	H_1	H_2
A_1	$\$M$	$\$0$
A_2	$\$M-\$500$	$\$1000$

It is crucial to Nozick's second argument that he deny the applicability of the principle of maximizing expected utility to the revised version. As he elaborates his argument, employing the principle of maximizing expected utility (where the probabilities used to compute expectations are probabilities of the states of nature conditional on choosing given options) he presupposes that the agent regards his choice as having a causal influence on which state of nature holds. Such causal efficacy does not obtain in the revised version any more than it does in the authorized version. Nozick should, therefore, forbid maximizing expected utility in the revised version as well as the authorized version.

Consider now the typical and allegedly nonproblematical cases where states of nature are probabilistically independent of the options chosen. This would hold if our examples were $p(H_1; A_1) = p(H_1; A_2) = p(H_1)$. These cases, like the authorized and revised versions, are situations where states of nature are causally independent of the options chosen. The states of nature are, in this sense, fixed and determined. Clearly, Nozick should deny, in the case of probabilistic independence, that the principle of maximizing expected utility is applicable. Yet, Nozick explicitly endorses the contrary view. By doing so, he undermines his second argument.

There is, however, a way to save Nozick's second argument from this difficulty. The principle of maximizing expected utility requires the computation of expected utility for an option where the probabilities used to compute expected utilities are probabilities of states of nature *conditional on the choice of the option whose expected utility is being evaluated*. It is this version of the principle whose application, Nozick alleges, presupposes the causal efficacy of choice on which state of nature obtains.

Notice, however, that expected utilities could be computed relative to the *unconditional* probabilities of the states of nature. When states of nature are probabilistically independent of the choice of an option, the computation of expected utility comes out exactly the same no matter which system of probabilities is used to compute expected utility. Moreover, whatever might be said when conditional probabilities are used, computing expected utilities with the aid of unconditional probabilities does not presuppose causal efficacy. Thus, Nozick could have argued that when states of nature are causally independent of the choice of option, the unconditional probabilities are to be used to compute the expected utilities to be maximized. When causal dependence obtains, conditional probabilities are to be used.

Had Nozick adopted this approach, he could have retained his analysis of cases where probabilistic independence obtains. Moreover, in the authorized version, the dominating option A_2 would have been favored as Nozick's second argument requires. Finally, in the revised version, A_1 would be favored in case 1 whereas A_2 would be recommended in the other two cases.

Thus, Nozick's second argument can be made consistent with his endorsing the principle of maximizing expected utility for situations where probabilistic independence obtains. Moreover, the principle regulating choice which emerges can be applied not only to the authorized version but to situations like the revised version where no option dominates any other.

This analysis suggests how misleading Nozick's own presentation is. He claims that the problem posed by Newcomb reveals a clash between two principles of choice: the principle of maximizing expected utility and the dominance principle. Even if we concede, for the sake of the argument, that a clash between two principles is exemplified, Nozick's statement of the two principles cannot be right. The dominance principle is not legislative in situations where no option dominates another. (To say that in such cases all options are admissible will often lead to clearly absurd prescriptions.) If there is a clash between principles of choice, it is between two versions of the principle of maximizing expected utility. At least this is so as long as we concede to Nozick that (*i*) when states of nature are probabilistically independent of choice, expected utility is to be maximized and (*ii*) when states of nature are probabilistically dependent and causally dependent, expected utility is to be maximized.

I have proposed one way of formulating the clash. It is between two ways of computing utility to be used in implementing the injunction to maximize expected utility.

Although Nozick himself does not make any such proposal, he does attempt to come to grips with situations like the revised version where no option dominates any other. It turns out that his proposal can be generalized to cover all cases where states of nature are fixed and determined whether they are like the authorized version, the revised version or are situations where states of nature are probabilistically independent of the options chosen. Although this generalization furnishes the identical prescriptions when states of nature are probabilistically independent of choice and when we are dealing with problems like the authorized version, it differs from the first proposal in situations like the revised version. Thus, it turns out that there are at least two ways (and, indeed, infinitely many more) in which we can provide a systematic underpinning for Nozick's second argument. For the sake of completeness, I shall attempt to motivate and formulate this second proposal which is more in keeping with the views actually expressed by Nozick than the first proposal is. Afterwards I shall offer what seem to me decisive arguments against both proposals and the infinitely many variants on them.

When there are two options and two states of nature as in our examples, the unconditional probability $p(H_1) = p(H_1; A_1)p(A_1) + p(H_1; A_2)p(A_2)$ where $p(A_2) = 1 - p(A_1)$. Thus, the unconditional probability $p(H_1)$ is a weighted average of the conditional probabilities of the states of nature. (This holds, of course, even if there are more than two options.)

According to my first proposal, the weights to be attached to the conditional probabilities in order to obtain a probability distribution for the states of nature to be used in computing expected utilities are, in effect, the unconditional probabilities assigned to the hypotheses as to which option is to be chosen. Suppose, however, that we do not regard this particular method of weighting as privileged.

When states of nature are probabilistically independent of the option chosen, $p(H_1; A_1) = p(H_1; A_2)$. Hence, no matter how weights are assigned (provided that they are positive and sum to 1), the probability distribution obtained for the states of nature will be the unconditional probability distribution as is the case when the weights are $p(A_1)$ and $p(A_2)$.

This is not so when probabilistic dependence obtains. However, in the authorized version, no matter which system of weights is adopted, the dominating option will bear maximum expected utility.

This leaves only the revised version to consider. Here the choice of weights does matter. My first proposal favors choosing $p(A_1)$ and $p(A_2)$. Nozick's proposal for the revised version stipulates, in effect, that any choice of a system of weights would be arbitrary. He suggests that if an option bears maximum expected utility no matter which system of weights is employed, it should be chosen. Otherwise, he leaves the matter undecided.[3] Clearly, he could have formulated this procedure to apply not only to situations like the revised version but to all situations where states of nature are fixed and

3 My formulation of Nozick's approach differs from his but is equivalent to it when only two options and two states of nature are available. When three or more options are feasible, Nozick demurs at giving a characterization of his principle. I suspect, however, that he would not definitely reject my proposal (Nozick, 1969, p. 133 and note 18, p. 145).

determined. The recommendations for the authorized version and for situations where states of nature are probabilistically independent would be the same as those prescribed by my first proposal. Differences emerge only in connection with the revised version. My proposal and his recommend A_1 in case 1. They both recommend A_2 in case 3. In case 2, my proposal favors A_2 whereas his leaves the verdict between the two options unrendered.

Thus, we now have two principles which could be consistently proposed to cover all cases where states of nature are fixed and determined and which could be used as a systematic underpinning for the second argument. It should be apparent, moreover, that there are infinite variations on these principles which achieve the same result.

Fortunately, we need not worry ourselves about which of these principles is best. All of them are unacceptable. By showing this to be the case, a compelling case is made, I believe, for rejecting Nozick's second argument.

In reconstructing the theoretical underpinnings of Nozick's second argument, pains have been taken to appeal to verdicts concerning rational choice which Nozick himself acknowledges to be sound. I have shown how his endorsement of the principle of maximizing expected utility in situations where states of nature are probabilistically independent can be made consistent with his endorsement of the dominating option in the authorized version and his general contention concerning the way the question of causal efficacy is relevant to rational choice.

One consideration, however, has been left out. Suppose that X confronts either the authorized or the revised version decision problem in a situation where he assumes at the outset that Newcomb's demon is perfectly infallible. In that event, $p(A_1; H_1) = p(A_2; H_2) = 1$ and $p(H_1; A_1) = p(H_2; A_2) = 1$. Once more we have a case where states of nature are fixed and determined even though they are probabilistically dependent on the choice of option. (For example, $p(H_1)$ could equal 0.5 in which case $p(A_2)$ would equal 0.5 as well.)

In his essay, Nozick often appeals to examples where the verdict of presystematic judgement varies from person to person (at least so it would seem). Here, however, we have a case where we can expect widespread consensus as to what X should do. Nozick himself agrees that X should choose A_1.

This is precisely the prescription favored by the principle that expected utility be maximized relative to the probabilities of states of nature conditional on the choice of option. If, however, my proposal that expected utility be maximized relative to unconditional probabilities is used, A_2 will be recommended both in the revised and authorized versions. If we follow my reconstruction of Nozick's suggestion, A_2 is favored in the authorized version. In the revised version, no verdict can be rendered. The verdict in favor of A_2 remains for the authorized version relative to every other variant in the family. The revised version will be handled differently by different variants.

254

These results are absurd. Nozick himself agrees. But instead of regarding them as decisive evidence that maximizing expected utility relative to conditional probabilities does not presuppose causal efficacy and that it is irrelevant to the legitimacy of applying this principle whether states of nature are fixed and determined or not, Nozick treats the case where Newcomb's demon is perfectly infallible as an anomaly demanding further clarification (Nozick, 1969, pp. 140–1).

The case of perfect infallibility is no mere anomaly.[4] The verdict which Nozick agrees is clearly required in that case is straightforwardly inconsistent with the point of view underlying Nozick's second argument in two respects:

(a) Nozick's second argument presupposes that maximizing expected utility using probabilities of states of nature conditional on the choice of an option implies that the choice of an option is causally relevant as to which state of nature obtains. This presupposition is flatly contradicted by the case of perfect infallibility. In that case, we do not argue in favor of choosing A_1 by saying that in choosing A_1 X makes H_1 true and in choosing A_2 he makes H_2 true. What is claimed is that, given the background information, that X chooses A_1 is conclusive evidence for the truth of H_1. Similarly, the truth of H_2 is conclusively supported by the evidence that X chooses A_2. No claim of causal efficacy is in any way implied.

Once this is recognized, the validity of Nozick's second argument is decisively undermined. In choosing A_1, X does not 'cause it to be more probable that' H_1 is true. It is true that his choosing A_1 is positively relevant evidence for the truth of H_1.

(b) When the case of perfect infallibility is left out of account, we have shown that there are many principles which might be held to apply to all situations where states of nature are causally independent of the choice of option and which, in the case of probabilistic dependence, deviate from the dictates of the principle of maximizing expected utility relative to conditional probabilities. But as we have seen, all of these principles founder on the case of perfect infallibility.

In the light of these considerations, it seems to me that Nozick's second argument and the approach he builds on it are indefensible.

4

Given that Nozick's second argument fails to limit the scope of the principle of maximizing expected utility using probabilities for states of nature conditional on the options chosen, let us assume that, whenever it is feasible to apply this principle, it should be applied. How does this help us in connection with the authorized version of the Newcomb problem?

4 Bar-Hillel and Margalit agree with me on this (1972, p. 300).

In section 2 I demonstrated that maximizing expected utility does not help furnish a recommendation as to what X should do. The trouble is that Newcomb's problem has not been spelled out in sufficient detail to indicate whether it is a variant of case 1, case 2, or case 3. Without such specification, the principle of maximizing expected utility can furnish no answer.

Perhaps, this is all the help we need. There is no paradox. There is no problem. There is a family of problems each with its own solution. Hence, there is no unique solution.

This conclusion is too pat. Suppose that X faces Newcomb's problem and does not himself know whether he is facing a variant of case 1, case 2, or case 3. That is to say, he is not in a position to specify precise numerical values for $p(H_1; A_1)$ and $p(H_2; A_2)$. When X's probability judgements are indeterminate, X cannot apply the principle of maximizing expected utility to reach a verdict.

This difficulty with the principle of maximizing expected utility is, of course, a familiar one and can arise in situations which lack the peculiarities of Newcomb's problem. Nonetheless, it is fair to ask what X should do when his probability judgements are indeterminate.

Many authors have suggested that X should pick an option which is a maximin solution to his problem. In the authorized version, this means picking A_2. This solution is favored by maximin for the revised version as well.[5]

Thus, we have discovered a new argument for choosing A_2 as Nozick's second argument recommends. When X's situation is neither case 1, case 2, nor case 3 but his probability judgements are indeterminate, invoking maximin favors A_2. Of course, this line of thought has nothing to do with whether states of nature are fixed and determined. In any case, Nozick has nowhere indicated that this situation (which might be called 'case 4') is the one he was thinking of rather than cases 1, 2, or 3. I think we have a right to be bewildered!

5 This prescription is, of course, controversial. I have endorsed it elsewhere (Levi, 1974, pp. 411–12).

16

Conflict and social agency*†

Formal analogies between criteria for rational individual decision making and group or social decision making have been evident to many authors ever since Plato exploited analogies between the organization of the soul and the state in the *Republic* in expounding his conception of Justice. Nonetheless, there is a widespread reluctance to acknowledge the existence of groups and institutions as agents. This leads to some bizarre juxtapositions.

Thus, neoclassical economists are not noted for their sympathy with notions of group mind. Yet, in expounding the theory of consumer demand, families are often allowed to qualify as consumers. Such consumers are taken, ideally at least, to be maximizers of their preferences or valuations, subject to budgetary constraints. Given the indifference maps representing the consumer's preferences and the budgetary constraints, demand curves are derived. Such analysis is not restricted to persons, but is intended to apply to any consumer, including a family. Families make choices from accessible commodity bundles, given budgetary constraints. They are taken to be rational preference maximizers like individual consumers and to have preferences representable by indifference maps. In this context, no distinction between individual and social decision making is drawn.

Not only are corporations often qualified legally to be persons; but corporations and other business firms are taken in both positive and normative theory to make decisions relative to information available to them and to be subject to criticism depending on whether the decisions are intelligent given their aims.

It is well known that the high priest of Hacking's 'heyday of ideas,' Thomas Hobbes, spoke of the endowments and actions of the 'sovereign' in a manner neutral with respect to whether the sovereign was a person,

* Work related to this essay began while I was a fellow of the National Endowment of the Humanities and associate fellow of Darwin College, Cambridge University. This work has received subsequent partial support from the National Science Foundation. I have benefited from written comments by Amartya Sen and extended discussions with Paul Lyon. John Watkins and Ned McClennen have repeatedly reminded me of the importance of phenomena like that exhibited in the Allais paradox. They were right.
† Reprinted from *The Journal of Philosophy* v. 79 (1982), pp. 231–47.

parliament, or citizenry. His individualism did not prevent him from discussing group agency.

The best known effort in recent years to apply canons of rational choice to social entities is that of Kenneth Arrow. According to Arrow, appropriate social groups are to be represented as seeking to maximize the welfare of their citizens or, more accurately, to maximize some increasing function of the welfares of their citizens. Arrow's concern and the concern of the participants in the debate that followed his justly celebrated *Social Choice and Individual Values* focused chiefly on the relations that do or should obtain between the valuations made by the individual citizens, whose interests are to be promoted by society as represented by rankings of the 'social states' or options some subset of which are feasible for society, and the social evaluation or preference ranking as represented by another weak ordering of the same social states.

Among the social institutions to which Arrow thought his approach might apply are included markets in which producers and consumers exchange goods leading to social states in which goods are allocated to individuals in certain ways and committees where decisions are taken according to some voting mechanism.

J. M. Buchanan (1964, p. 117) has complained against Arrow that 'Voting and the market, as decision-making mechanisms, have evolved from, and are based upon an acceptance of, the philosophy of individualism which presumes no social entity'. He complains because he thinks that Arrow is committed to the existence of such social entities when Arrow assumes that the rationality of decision-making mechanisms such as voting or the market should be assessed in terms of whether social preference is maximized where social preference induces a weak ordering over the feasible social states. Because Arrow flouts individualism in this manner, his approach is deeply flawed at the very outset.

One response to Buchanan's objection is to reject individualism. That is to say, one might concede that social groups are sometimes agents in the sense that they make choices to promote given ends and that their evaluations of options and the choices they make may be assessed for rationality.

Buchanan, however, thinks that Arrow cannot, given his other commitments, do so consistently, as the following passage reveals:

Rationality or irrationality as an attribute of the social group implies the imputation to that group of an organic existence apart from that of its individual components. If the social group is so considered, questions may be raised relative to the wisdom or unwisdom of this organic being. But does not the very attempt to examine such rationality in terms of individual values introduce logical inconsistency at the outset? Can the rationality of the social organism be evaluated in accordance with any value ordering other than its own?

The whole problem seems best considered as one of the 'either-or' variety. We may adopt the philosophical bases of individualism in which the individual is the only entity possessing ends or values. In this case no question of social or collective rationality may be raised. A social value scale as such simply does not exist. Alternatively, we may adopt some variant of the organic philosophical assumptions in which the collectivity is an independent entity possessing its own value ordering. It is legitimate to test the rationality or irrationality of this entity only against this value ordering (Buchanan, 1964, p. 116).

Thus, according to Buchanan, there is nothing inconsistent or incoherent in attributing 'organic existence' or agency to a social group such as a corporation. Such an agent may be understood to be making decisions in a manner that seeks to promote its values. Buchanan's own metaphysical predilections are in favor of individualism. He does not acknowledge institutional agents – especially in the case of groups participating in market exchange or committee voting. But his criticism of Arrow is not directed primarily to the issue of the 'organic existence' of social groups.

His charge is that Arrow's project suffers from incoherence. He claims that the 'very attempt' to examine the rationality of group decision making 'in terms of individual values' introduces 'logical inconsistency' at the very start.

According to Buchanan, Arrow is not incoherent in attributing social preference rankings of social states to social groups. That is in keeping with the view of social groups as having 'organic existence' apart from that of their members. The 'logical inconsistency' emerges when Arrow seeks to represent social preference as a function of the preferences of citizens for the same social states. Since Arrow must do this if he is to relate his analysis to markets or committees who take decisions by voting, Arrow can apply his theory to these cases only at the cost of 'logical inconsistency'.

Buchanan's critique of Arrow raises two distinct issues:

(1) Should we attribute rationality to social groups?
(2) When we do attribute rationality to social groups, may we consistently allow social preference to be a function of individual preference?

We have already observed that even students of market economies attribute beliefs, desires, goals, values, and choices to families and to firms and, of course, government agents (which may be bureaus rather than bureaucrats) as well as to persons. No doubt the mechanisms whereby the decisions taken by such social agents are to be explained typically involve reference to the behaviors of and, indeed, sometimes the decisions taken by individual agents (and by other social agents). Perhaps group choices are redescribable as complex processes involving no other choices than those of persons. But this need not detract from the reality of such group choices any more than the redescribability of individual choices as complex neurophysical processes detracts from the reality of individual choices. Nor should redescribability in itself preclude the propriety of subjecting social choice to canons of rationality any more than it should preclude the propriety of subjecting individual choice to the very same canons.

When we focus on characterizations of social groups in terms of their beliefs, goals, choices, and other such propositional attitudes, we are no more concerned with the underlying mechanisms than we are when we use such characterizations of human agents or, for that matter, of automata. Perhaps differences in the 'hardware' should make a difference in the view we take of the principles of rational preference, belief, valuation, and choice; but, unless a decisive case is advanced that this should be so, it seems sensible to seek an account of rational choice, belief, preference, and valuation which is indifferent to whether the agent is human or not and, if not, whether it is automaton, animal, angelic, or social.

The ontological sensibilities of some may be offended by speaking of groups as agents. But if they are prepared to attribute beliefs, values, and choices to groups as well as to individual humans and to think that such values, beliefs, and choices ought to be judged by the same principles of rationality as are applied to human agents, they are recognizing such social entities as agents in the only sense that matters here.

Arrow's own response to the critiques of Buchanan and of I. M. D. Little is curious in this respect. He contends that he was concerned with rules for arriving at social decisions which 'may be agreed upon for reasons of convenience and necessity without its outcomes being treated as evaluations by anyone in particular' (Arrow, 1963, p. 106).

Arrow appears quite anxious to disavow commitment to group minds or social groups as organic beings. Yet, according to his account of social choice, groups do choose one from among a set of feasible social states in an environment and, if rational, do so in a manner that is optimal relative to a social preference which weakly orders the social states. In this connection, he cites with approval a comment by Karl Popper: 'Not a few doctrines which are metaphysical, and thus certainly philosophical, can be interpreted as hypostatizations of methodological rules' (Popper, 1959, p. 55). Thus, for Arrow, in social choice we have choice without a choosing subject and preference without a preferring subject, just as, for Popper, in science we have knowledge without a knowing subject.

I sympathize with the response of C. R. Plott to Arrow's maneuver when he declares that it is 'operationally' difficult to distinguish efforts motivated from Arrow's point of view from efforts motivated from points of view that treat society as an organic entity (Plott, 1973, p. 1078). Plott's operationalist rhetoric is questionable; but it is irrelevant to the core of his observation. Any system, whether it is animal, vegetable, or mineral, whether it is an automaton, a human, or a group of automata or humans, can qualify as an agent for the purpose of discussing rational choice (which is the context in which Plott discusses Arrow's views) provided that choices, beliefs, preferences, values, and goals are ascribable to the system and provided that it is appropriate to urge conformity to norms of rational preference, belief, and choice.

To say this does not imply that all social groups act as agents or that those which do do so all the time. However, we cannot claim more for animals, automata, or even human beings. I have characterized agenthood in terms of the propriety of criticism from the vantage point of norms of rational choice. I do not have any independently specifiable criteria for determining such propriety; but we do not need any to appreciate the hard core of Plott's insight, which is that when qualms about group minds are construed as an objection to attributing agency to social groups, then talk about social preference and social choice should be avoided – at least in any sense in which such preference and choice is subject to critical scrutiny by norms of rationality. Arrow and those who follow him cannot have their cake and eat it. Retreating to the third world is no more acceptable in discussions of social choice than it is in discussions of the growth of knowledge.[1]

To this extent, Plott's view coincides with Buchanan's – and quite rightly so. But Arrow need not have denied agency to social groups. Indeed, given his position, he should have done precisely the opposite. Moreover, in doing so, he could still have defended himself against the main thrust of Buchanan's criticism, to which we now turn.

Recall that the second and critical step in Buchanan's critique of Arrow is his denial that social preferences (if there are social organisms having them) can coherently be made to depend on individual values. Buchanan thinks it a 'logical inconsistency' to 'attempt to examine such [social] rationality in terms of individual values' (p. 116). Clearly he is thinking of social agents who maximize values in a manner independent of the interests of the citizens or subjects. Social agents are to be thought of as promoting their own interests just as individuals are to be thought of as promoting their own personal concerns.

Some social institutions undoubtedly seek to promote their own selfish interests just as individuals do. Social agents, like human agents, can be selfish or, if other-directed, can be directed toward other social agents. But just as, at least on some occasions, human agents can seek to promote the interests and welfare of other human agents, so too, social institutions can seek to promote the interests of human agents who are somehow related to the social agents in question as citizens are. If there is no logical inconsistency in the one case, there should be none in the other.

Thus, it is not incoherent to regard a society that allocates commodity bundles through a market mechanism as an agent. The market mechanism

---

1 I have advocated thinking of knowing subjects as comprising institutions such as scientific communities as well as persons for some time, but most recently and explicitly in Levi (1980a, 1.1–1.5).

in operation provides a procedure whereby the society makes certain kinds of social choices. We may ask two questions about the way such choices are made: (*a*) Are the choices made in a manner maximizing some social preference? (*b*) If the answer is affirmative, are the social preferences dependent on the interests of the participants in the market?

Arrow's impossibility theorem presupposes that affirmative answers may be given to both questions but then goes on to assert that the dependency of social preference on the preferences of citizens cannot jointly satisfy several important conditions.

Perhaps, as Buchanan suggests, there is nothing disturbing about this result as it applies to the use by society of markets as choice mechanisms for the distribution of commodities to consumers. In any case, whether there is or is not something troublesome about Arrow's result, the trouble arises (if it does) for any social agency seeking to maximize social preferences aimed at promoting individual welfares and not just for such agencies that seek such ends through the use of market mechanisms.

Moreover, to declare that Arrow's result misses the mark because social groups cannot be taken coherently to be maximizers of social preferences depending on individual values is in no way to neutralize the impact of Arrow's theorem. Buchanan to the contrary notwithstanding, nothing in logic prevents our taking social groups to be agents of the sort that seek to maximize just such preferences. Blanket refusal to attribute agency of this kind to social groups as practiced by Buchanan is conceptual stonewalling which places roadblocks in the path of inquiry.[2]

Insisting that social institutions should sometimes be recognized to be agents does not entail insensitivity to the differences between persons and social institutions – especially the morally relevant differences. Neither an unborn human fetus nor someone in coma is an agent subject to critical control according to canons of rational choice. Yet, they are clearly objects of moral concern; and some apparently are prepared to insist that they be treated with the same moral respect as is to be accorded other human beings. Conversely, attributing agency to animals, automata, or social institutions does not entail granting such agents the same moral concern and respect we accord human agents.

Agency is undoubtedly a morally relevant trait; but it is one among many. We should not be deterred from scrutinizing the decisions and aims of

---

2 It should be noted in passing that Arrow's formalism for social choice can be applied to the evaluations of the options of a person seeking (perhaps because of moral conviction) to promote the welfares of others. Hence, even if Buchanan had (counter, in my view, to fact) been right about social agency, Arrow's analysis would still retain important applicability. I do not seek, however, to defend the applicability of Arrow's analysis in general. My concern has been with those contexts where governmental, corporate, or other institutional policies are considered.

institutions with the aid of canons of rationality because of moral scruples any more than we should be prevented from doing so by metaphysical dogma.

Nonetheless, some justifiable skepticism remains concerning Arrow's assumption that social groups are representable, at least on some occasions, as maximizers of social preferences. Society is presented with a choice between social states belonging to some subset S of a domain U of entertainable social states. According to Arrow, society has a system of preferences which induces a weak ordering of the elements of U. Society's evaluation of the elements of S is the restriction of that weak ordering over U to the elements of S.

Society is taken to have as its goal the objective of promoting the values or welfares of its 'citizens', where the 'welfares' of the citizens are representable by weak orderings of the elements of U (and, hence, of S) – each citizen being assigned an ordering.

The individual valuations are usually different rankings over the same social states. Hence, to maximize according to one of these rankings is incompatible with maximizing according to another. In this way, social agents, like personal agents, often face decision problems where the agent is committed to promoting different values which conflict in the way they rank the feasible options.

Both in the first edition and even more so in the second edition of *Social Choice and Individual Values*, Arrow insists that the evaluation of social states or options society ought to use in determining which options are admissible should be a weak ordering of the options or social states and that the admissible set should be restricted to those which are optimal relative to that weak ordering.

Thus, Arrow presupposes as a condition or rational choice that conflicts of value be resolved prior to choice. Hence, he sees the problem presented to him as focused on resolving the conflict between the evaluations for the several citizens according to some rule which determines, for each 'profile' of individual values, a social preference ranking that weakly orders the domain U.

It is well known, of course, how widespread the view is that rational individual decision making ought to maximize preferences. By 'preference' here, I do not necessarily mean a ranking of alternatives with respect to anticipated satisfactions. The individual may have taken into account moral, political, economic, cognitive, and aesthetic values in making a ranking. But precisely because he may do so and because these diverse desiderata can lead to conflicting rankings of the same alternatives when employed in isolation from one another, the requirement that preferences be maximized relative to a single ranking presupposes that such conflicts be resolved prior to choice.

Even moral theorists, who feign to dispense with the notion that rational agents should maximize preferences in the generous sense just indicated in favor of approaches grounded on principles of obligation and permission, share the same outlook. In the first place, if, in a given context of choice, a particular option is held to be obligatory, it is presumably ranked over the other alternatives and in this sense preferred over them. Second, if moral principles conflict, appeal is typically made to second-order principles that arbitrate and prescribe which options among those feasible are morally (or legally) admissible. For the most part, so I suggest, decision theorists and moralists agree that, to be rational or coherent at the moment of choice, an individual agent should have ironed out all conflicts at the moment of choice, or, if not, we should regard his choice as itself constituting an expression of his resolution of the conflict.

Arrow's view of rational social choice is no different, in this respect, from received notions of rational individual decision making.

On the other hand, insofar as there is some reason for skepticism concerning the propriety of mandating that conflicts be resolved prior to choice in the context of individual decision making, it becomes at least entertainable that such skepticism should be endorsed in connection with social decision making as well.[3] Objection to the requirement that society maximize preferences represented by a weak ordering of social options along these lines should not be confused with objections, like Buchanan's, which are grounded on preconceptions concerning when one can and when one cannot attribute agency to social institutions. This skepticism derives from doubt concerning the conditions on rational choice, whether the agent is individual or social.

The issue is not whether preferences, values, and goals do or do not come into conflict. Nor is it whether it is rational for an agent to suffer from conflict in his values. That value conflict occurs and confronts even rational agents is widely acknowledged. What is questionable is whether rational agents should have resolved all conflicts when fixing on a decision, so that they can claim that the option chosen is for the best, all things considered. The dominant view is that rationality prohibits decision making under unresolved conflict. I mean to reject this view.

According to strict Bayesians, ideally rational agents maximize expected utility. To determine expected utilities for feasible options, however, the agent must be in a position to make judgements of probability enabling him to assign probability numbers to hypotheses concerning 'consequences' of his options conditional on his implementing them and utility numbers (unique up to positive affine transformation) to these hypotheses. In this way, the agent's evaluation of his feasible options in terms of expected utility would be free of any conflict.

3 K. O. May argued essentially along these lines in May (1954, pp. 1–13).

A common source of skepticism about strict Bayesian doctrine concerns the grounds on which probability numbers are to be assigned. Often it seems that, given the available evidence and background knowledge, there is no warrant for favoring one system of probability judgements over another. Personalist Bayesians advocate picking a system of judgements out of one's hat, often covering up the arbitrariness of the procedure with a display of rhetoric and a reminder that one's judgements must at least be coherent. Others follow in the footsteps of Harold Jeffreys and Rudolf Carnap by seeking objective criteria for constraining probability judgement. Typically they stumble into inconsistency or obscurantism.[4]

The great statisticians, R. A. Fisher, Jerzy Neyman, and Abraham Wald, who pioneered in the 1920s, 30s, and 40s what were to become the dominant approaches to statistical theory in the postwar period, sought to avoid both paths. They thought that, when there was no warrant for making definite probability judgements, one should avoid making them – counter to the advice of personalist Bayesians. And they denied that one could devise an inductive logic so strong as to justify numerically definite probability judgements in every situation. They sought methods that either bypassed the need to use Bayes' theorem or displaced it. And Neyman and Wald, both of whom thought that statistical theory ought to be viewed as a branch of a theory of decision making, sought ways and means of making decisions under conditions where the injunction to maximize expected utility cannot be obeyed because probability information is lacking.

These authors insisted that it is better to remain in a state of unresolved conflict – i.e., in suspense – concerning how to make probability judgements than to resolve such conflict arbitrarily or to introduce principles of inductive logic of questionable merit. But when probability judgement is indeterminate in this manner, calculations of expected utility must also be indeterminate even if the utility information available is precise. Thus, one opinion might rank over another according to one probability distribution, and the ranking might go the other way according to another. If there is no warrant for favoring one distribution rather than the other, the agent should be in suspense not only as to the merits of the two distributions but also as to the merits of the rival ways of evaluating his feasible options with respect to expected utility. That is to say, he should remain in a state of unresolved conflict even when facing a decision. Neyman and Wald, among others, suggested criteria for evaluating feasible options to be used when consideration of expected utility fails to render a verdict – such as looking at security levels. I have sought to elaborate such an outlook myself elsewhere.[5]

4 For a beautifully clear exposition of the troubles with objective Bayesianism, see Seidenfeld (1979, pp. 413–40).
5 In greatest detail in Levi (1980a) and previously in Levi (1974, pp. 391–418).

265

Conflict in how an agent evaluates his options with respect to expected utility need not be engendered by indeterminacy in probability judgement. Conflict in how the agent evaluates the 'possible consequences' of his options (how he evaluates his 'utilities') can also generate conflict in the appraisal of options with respect to expected utility.

An interesting illustration of this is furnished by an example introduced into general discussion by Maurice Allais (1953, pp. 503–46). Mr Unsure-thing is presented with two different situations where he must choose between two options. In both situations a ball is to be selected from an urn containing 100 balls of which one is red, 89 white, and 10 are blue. In situation I, option A guarantees $1 000 000 regardless of the outcome of the draw. Choosing option B yields nothing if a red is drawn, $1 000 000 if a white is drawn, and $5 000 000 if a blue is drawn. In situation II, option C pays $1 000 000 if a red or blue is drawn and nothing otherwise, whereas option D pays nothing if a red or white is drawn and $5 000 000 if a blue is drawn.

In both situations I and II, the probabilities of possible outcomes are quite determinate. And so are the monetary payoffs. The following table sums up the pertinent information:

	1 Red	89 White	10 Blue
I			
A	$1 000 000	$1 000 000	$1 000 000
B	$0	$1 000 000	$5 000 000
II			
C	$1 000 000	$0	$1 000 000
D	$0	$0	$5 000 000

Notice that the only difference between the payoff matrices for situations I and II concerns the case where a white ball is drawn. In situation I, Unsurething receives a million whatever he does, and in situation II he receives nothing. According to the so-called 'sure-thing principle' enunciated by L. J. Savage (Savage, 1954, pp. 20–2) and implied by strict Bayesian doctrine, Unsurething should weakly prefer option A to option B in situation I if and only if he weakly prefers C to D in situation II.

Allais reports that the most frequent response concerning what Unsurething should do in the two situations among those who are prudent and are so regarded by others is that A be chosen in situation I and D in situation II (p. 527).

The attractiveness of this verdict is widely acknowledged, and even Savage conceded its pull (p. 103).

Although Allais's paper appeared before Savage's book, Allais does refer to another presentation of Savage's axioms and is quite clear that he thinks that the predominant response to the two predicaments just described is in violation of what was subsequently called the 'sure-thing principle'.[6]

The predominant response would, indeed, exhibit violation of the sure-thing principle were it the case that Unsurething's choice of A in situation I revealed his strict preference for A over B and his choice of D over C in situation II revealed his strict preference for D over C.

Allais himself declares that his own abstract definition of rationality entails that the set of feasible options should be weakly ordered, apparently so that the option chosen may be identified as optimal (Allais, 1953, p. 518 and p. 522). That is to say, Allais insists that to be rational an agent should be free of conflict as to how his options are to be ranked. And this assumption implies that the predominant response is in violation of the sure-thing principle.

Observe, however, that, if we reject Allais's assumption that rational agents resolve conflict in their choice, the predominant response no longer manifests violation of the sure-thing principle; for it is at least entertainable that Unsurething is in conflict as to how to rank A and B with respect to expected utility and likewise with respect to C and D. Such conflict cannot arise as a result of indeterminacy in probability judgement. The probabilities are numerically definite. But even if Unsurething prefers $5\,000\,000$ to $1\,000\,000$ to 0 and even if the marginal utility of money decreases at rates sufficient to guarantee that the difference in value between 0 and $1\,000\,000$ is greater than the difference between $1\,000\,000$ and $5\,000\,000$, Unsurething might be in conflict as to whether the ratio of the two differences is greater or less than $10/1$. And if he were in such conflict, then Unsurething would be in conflict also as to whether to rank A over B or B over A with respect to expected utility and would be in a similar conflict with regard to C and D.

Under these circumstances, Unsurething might choose A over B because the 'security level' or 'worst possible case' is better for A than for B. And he might choose D over C even though the security levels are the same because the second worst possible case is better for D than for C. In that event, Unsurething has chosen A over B without preferring A to B and has chosen D over C without preferring D to C. Of course, A beats B when considerations of security are taken into account, and D beats C according to the same factors. But Unsurething has invoked these criteria only because the conflict in his utilities prevents him from rendering a verdict concerning his options taking consideration of expected utility alone into account. Thus, he does not prefer

6 The proposed analysis of Allais's problem should be compared with the different approaches developed by D. Kahneman and A. Tversky (1979, pp. 263–92) and by P. Gärdenfors and N.-E. Sahlin (1982). Allais (1953) contains a characterization of Savage's 'axiom of independence' and on pp. 527–8 explicitly states that the example under consideration shows the 'pseudo-evident' character of Savage's axiom.

A to B and D to C 'all things considered' – at least not in a sense that yields a violation of the sure-thing principle.

In my opinion, the tradeoff between giving up the sure-thing principle and the requirement that rational choice be under unresolved conflict favors giving up the latter – counter to Allais's own conclusion.[7] Of course, strict Bayesians will refuse to abandon either condition, insisting that the predominant response to the Allais phenomenon illustrates how vulnerable to fallacy even the sanest of us are and how important it is for all of us to receive good training in Bayesian rationality.

The approach advocated here suggests that instruction in the Bayesian catechism is less than urgent and even, for some purposes, harmful. In particular, the predominant response to the Allais problem may prove to be the sensible response after all.

Given that Unsurething prefers more money to less and given that his utility function for money exhibits diminishing marginal utility of money, should he be required to decide whether the ratio of the differences in utility between receiving a million and receiving nothing and between receiving five million and receiving one million is greater than, equal to, or less than 10/1? Perhaps there are occasions where he may have other value commitments which can be invoked to justify some judgement on this matter. But it seems absurd to suppose that, to be rational, Unsurething must have sufficient other commitments which, together with analogues of principles of inductive logic for utility judgement, suffice to render a verdict. And it seems equally absurd to insist that, in the absence of such commitments, Unsurething should decide without justification in order to save his reason. He should be allowed to suspend judgement.

The conflict in value considered here concerns the rate at which the value of money increases with an increase in monetary payoff. But it is widely acknowledged that decision makers often face predicaments where there are conflicts in value deriving from commitments to different professional and social roles, different moral principles or aesthetic values. Such conflicts can induce on the same set of feasible options different weak orderings. It seems no more acceptable here to suppose that an agent will always be in a position to justify one resolution of the conflict over another before taking a decision than it is in Allais's problem. Sartre's example of the son torn between filial devotion to his mother and commitment to the Free French cause illustrates the point. Unlike Sartre however, I contend that it is quite as untenable to regard his decision as a resolution of the conflict as it is in Allais's problem.

7 H. Raiffa (1968, pp. 82–5) offers an interesting critique of Allais's example. He gives some striking arguments implying the untenability of the predominant response. These arguments presupposes that rational agents choose an option they most prefer according to a weak ordering representing their conflict-free valuation of the feasible options. Raiffa's arguments appear to me to be telling against someone like Allais who shares his assumption that rational choice ought to be free of unresolved conflict. Space does not permit detailed discussion of Raiffa's arguments here.

The son need not regard his decision to join the Resistance as for the best all things considered. He could and, perhaps, should see the conflict in his values as unresolved even though he had to take a decision. The fact that one conflict (in Allais's problem) is pecuniary and the other moral does not seem especially relevant.

I argued originally that conditions of rational belief, valuation, and decision ought to be applicable to all agents whether they are animal, automaton, human, or social. The discussion immediately preceding supports the contention that agents need not betray their rationality by taking decisions under unresolved conflict. The examples were taken from decision making by personal agents but, according to the first argument, ought to apply to social agents as well.

Ironically, Arrow's impossibility theorem itself offers a compelling case for concluding that social agents may retain their rationality while taking decisions under unresolved conflict just as personal agents do.

Arrow's requirement of nondictatorship on 'social welfare functions' that specify how conflicts between the values of the individual citizens are to be resolved in social preference precludes recommending that society follow the practice of resolving conflict by adopting the ranking of some designated citizen. And his proscription against appealing to interpersonal comparisons of values precludes adopting any other ranking compatible with Pareto conditions, 'independence' requirements, and the condition that the social welfare function be defined for all possible preference profiles.

The net effect of these Arrovian conditions is to rule out any potential resolution of the conflict between the welfares of different citizens from representing social preference.[8] That is to say, these conditions preclude society from resolving such conflict. Arrow gets a contradiction by insisting that society resolve conflict anyhow. But if it is conceded that decision making under unresolved conflict may be rational for social agents as it is for personal agents, Arrow's insistence on endorsing the requirements that, for any system of individual preferences or welfare rankings of the social states, a ranking representing social preference should be determined may be abandoned.

To be sure, the Arrovian result remains troublesome even when the requirement that social preferences be free of conflict is abandoned. It is one thing to say that society, like a person, may sometimes be justified in taking decisions without having resolved all conflicts. But it is quite another thing to impose conditions on social valuation which prevent resolution of any conflict.

8 These remarks are a rough characterization of the insight expressed in Luce and Raiffa (1958, pp. 343–5) in their discussion of how an argument due to Blackwell and Girshick (1954, p. 118) pertaining to individual choice under uncertainty could be adjusted to yield the Arrow impossibility theorem. Paul Lyon and Teddy Seidenfeld drew this to my attention independently of each other.

I, for one, remain unconvinced that interpersonal comparisons are always to be avoided. And, in certain classes of decision problems, society may be justified in adopting a dictatorial rule – or, at least, in restricting resolutions to preference rankings belonging to members of some oligarchy. Nonetheless, society often may lack a warrant for making interpersonal comparisons and for favoring the values of some privileged group of citizens. In such cases, society should be prohibited from adopting any ranking of the social states as a basis for maximizing behavior.

Thus, Buchanan is right at least to this extent. Society should not *always* be thought of as a preference-maximizing agent. But, counter to Buchanan, the trouble with Arrow's insistence that social choice maximize preference according to some social preference ranking is not that social institutions fail to qualify as agents whose choices are subject to critical assessment according to the same canons of rational valuation and choice applicable to persons. Social groups ought often to be treated as agents just as persons ought often to be treated as agents, and we should devise our approaches to rational choice with this in mind.[9] But just as personal agents may terminate deliberation and take decisions without having resolved the moral, political, economic, and aesthetic conflicts relevant to their predicaments, so too social agents committed to promoting the welfares of their clients or citizens might justifiably make decisions without settling on how to balance the competing interests of these clients.

It is often alleged that the chief difference between 'pure' or 'theoretical' scientific inquiry and practical deliberation is that in practice but not in science the need to make decisions deprives the deliberating agent of the luxury of remaining in suspense even when there is no warrant for settling outstanding issues one way or another. Curiously enough, some pragmatists (e.g., Charles Sanders Peirce) seemed quite prepared to accept such a dualism between theory and practice. An alternative pragmatist response is to assimilate theoretical inquiry somehow to practical deliberation in a manner that denies to pure research, as it does to practical deliberation, the opportunity for suspension of judgement. My own brand of pragmatism agrees that scientific inquiry is a goal-directed activity subject to the canons of criticism regulating all practical deliberation. But the need to take decisions (which, in my view, is as urgent in pure research as it is in practical deliberation) does not mandate or even excuse unjustified resolution of conflict or leaping to conclusions. My aim in this paper has been to indicate how this brand of pragmatism bears on 'rationality' assumptions built into the conditions that entail Arrow's impossibility theorem.

9 An important recent effort to develop decision theory applicable to both social and personal agents has been undertaken in (Lyon, 1980).

17
Liberty and welfare[†]

According to A. K. Sen, liberalism (or 'libertarianism' as he now prefers to call it (Sen, 1976, p. 218)), permits each individual in society 'the freedom to determine at least one social choice, for example having his own walls pink rather than white, other things remaining the same for him and the rest of society' (Sen, 1970b, p. 153).

Sen contends that the value involving individual liberty illustrated by this example imposes a constraint on social welfare functions – i.e., rules which specify a ranking of social states with respect to whether they serve the general welfare better or worse given information about the preferences of individual members of society for these social states or their welfare levels in these social states. This constraint 'represents a value involving individual liberty that many people would subscribe to' regardless of whether it captures all aspects of the presystematic usage of the terms 'liberalism' or 'libertarianism' (Sen, 1970, p. 153, note 1).

Sen's condition L asserts that each citizen ought to have his preference ranking of at least one pair of social states determine the social ranking of the same pair of states with respect to welfare (Sen, 1970, p. 153).

P. Bernholz pointed out that libertarians do not concede individuals rights to determine the social ranking of social states but to determine aspects of social states (Bernholz, 1974, pp. 100–1). P. Gärdenfors has recently combined Bernholz's observation with R. Nozick's suggestion that granting rights to individuals cedes to them the ability to constrain the domain of social choice to a given class of social states (Gärdenfors, 1978, and Nozick, 1974, pp. 165–6).

In his interesting discussion of Nozick's idea, Sen points to an ambiguity in the interpretation of a social ordering. He suggests that a social ordering can be construed 'to be purely a mechanism for choice' or as 'reflecting a view of social welfare' (Sen, 1976, pp. 229–31).

In the following discussion, I shall distinguish between a mechanism for social choice, a standard for social value, and a view of social welfare.

Mechanisms for social choice are to be understood to be institutionally

[†] Reprinted from *Utilitarianism and Beyond*, edited by Amartya Sen and Bernard Williams, Cambridge University Press (1982), pp. 239–49.

sanctioned procedures for selecting social states. Liberalism or libertarianism is a doctrine recommending the imposition of constraints on social choice mechanisms. Instead of having social states selected by some special panel, rights holders make choices concerning *aspects* of social states over which they hold socially sanctioned rights in accordance with their personal preferences. Through their choices, these aspects of the social state are determined. Either the result is the determination of the total social state (in all relevant respects) or something is left for a governmental agency or agencies to determine. To simplify the discussion, I shall suppose that under a libertarian social choice mechanism the social state is totally determined by the decisions of the rights holders over the domains to which they hold rights.

In debating the merits of different social choice mechanisms, we should consider the social states selected by the use of these mechanisms relative to different contexts of social choice where the sets of feasible options or social states vary. Presumably it is a mark in favor of a choice mechanism when it chooses states which are best among those available when best options exist and it is a mark against the mechanism when it chooses inferior states when best options exist.

To make assessments of this sort requires some standard of social value which evaluates social states with respect to whether they are better or worse. Such a standard need not provide a complete ordering of the states in any feasible set. It need not guarantee that there be at least one best option in a feasible set. Nor need it be assumed that such a standard must rank social states as better or worse according to how well they promote social welfare. A view of social welfare may be endorsed as a standard of social value. Whoever does so may be called a *social-welfarist*.

Views of social welfare are representable by social welfare functions which by definition do completely order social states with respect to social welfare as a function of the preferences or welfares of the individual members of society. Different views of social welfare correspond to different types of constraint on social welfare functions. Of course, one can entertain a view of social welfare without being prepared to advocate its use as a standard of social value to be employed in assessing the admissibility of feasible options in contexts of social choice. But such views of social welfare play no clear role in policy making. To be a social-welfarist (of one of the many varieties entertainable) one should be ready to appraise the admissibility of options in problems of social choice using a social welfare function as a standard of social value and, to this extent, to appraise the legitimacy of social choice mechanisms.[1]

---

1 Social-welfarism should be distinguished from what Sen has called 'welfarism'.

    Both welfarism and social-welfarism are 'outcome moralities'. Moreover, welfarism according to Sen requires a standard of value representable by a social welfare function. Hence, welfarism is a species of social-welfarism in my sense.

    But there are types of social-welfarism which are not welfaristic in Sen's sense. Anyone who

Non-social-welfarists may be divided into two categories. Some non-social-welfarists commit themselves in advance to a non-social-welfarist standard of social value and appraise choice mechanisms in terms of how well they promote the values licensed by the standard. If the 'fit' is poor, they will propose tinkering with the choice mechanism rather than the standard of value.

Other non-social-welfarists proceed in the opposite manner. If the fit is poor, they will leave the choice mechanism intact and revise the standard of social value.

Of course, non-social-welfarists might fail to belong strictly in either category but, when the fit between choice mechanism and standard of social value breaks down too badly may, depending on the type of breakdown, tamper with one or the other or with both. My own inclination is to favor a view of this sort.

In any case, Nozick, Gärdenfors, and recently F. Schick[2] have argued that application of a social choice mechanism should not be evaluated in terms of

endorses a standard of social value representable by a Social Welfare function is a social-welfarist. Sen imposes additional constraints on the social welfare function. In section 8 of (Sen, 1977), Sen requires that a welfarist social welfare function obey strong neutrality. In (Sen, 1979, p. 468), he requires conformity with the Pareto principle as well. In this last cited paper, Sen contrasts welfarism with weak Paretianism which endorses social welfare functions obeying the weak Pareto principle. He acknowledges that weak Paretianism belongs in the same family of views as welfarism, it can violate strong neutrality and, hence, may fail to be welfarist in the strict sense (or one of the two strict senses) employed by Sen.

My 'social-welfarism' is intended as a generic term covering Sen's welfarism as well as weak Paretianism.

I contend that a standard of value appraising the goodness of states has ramifications for the appraisal of feasible options as admissible or inadmissible. I have just tried to indicate briefly what I think some of these ramifications are. They fall short of what Sen calls a 'consequentialist' view (Sen, 1979, p. 464).

2 Schick's statements (Schick, 1980) are quite explicit on this point. He contends that liberals (i.e., libertarians) focus on the distribution of goods rather than on the maximization of welfare, where goods are understood to endow their possessors with control over some aspects of the social state. He points out that a ranking of alternative distributions of goods so construed is not to be confused with a social welfare ranking. Social welfare functions and the rankings they induce are not excluded from consideration (although the purpose they serve in the formation of policy remains obscure). However, Schick explicitly denies that liberals rank distributions of goods in terms of their efficiency in promoting welfare and concludes that one can consistently impose the Pareto principle P on social welfare functions and over the entire domain of social states while remaining a liberal. This is so because constraints on social welfare functions have no bearing on the evaluation of the justness and fairness of alternative distributions of goods.

I think this way of formulating the matter is somewhat less misleading than the Gärdenfors–Nozick approach according to which the social welfare function is defined on those states which remain after rights holders have exercised their rights and excluded others. I doubt whether any issue of substance is involved.

It should also be mentioned that those rugged libertarians I have identified seem to reject any evaluation of a system of rights by reference to the efficiency of the system in promoting the goodness of social states in any other sense of goodness than one which takes the endowment with rights as a measure of goodness.

its efficacy in promoting social welfare. So they are clearly non-social-welfarists. But their views seem stronger than that. They insist that the rights of individuals are somehow fundamental in the appraisal of choice mechanisms. I conjecture that they endorse variants of non-social-welfarist libertarianism which require modification of the standard of social value when its fit with libertarian choice mechanisms turns out to be poor. Whatever the precise views of these authors might be, however, I shall consider anyone who endorses such a position a *rugged libertarian.*

It is important to keep in mind that libertarianism (whether rugged, social-welfaristic or of some non-social-welfaristic alternative to rugged libertarianism) is distinguished by the constraints it advocates for mechanisms of social choice. On the assumption that ideally such a mechanism should select states which are admissible relative to some standard for social valuation, a libertarian view of the social choice mechanism has ramifications for the standard of social valuation to be adopted; but unless libertarianism is combined with social welfarism, libertarianism imposes no constraints on social welfare functions.[3]

Sen does not characterize libertarianism as imposing constraints on the social choice mechanism. His condition L is understood as a constraint on social welfare functions; and he correctly establishes the incompatibility of condition L with the weak Pareto principle.

A logomachy over the correct use of 'libertarianism' would be futile. But it seems fairly non-controversial that under normal circumstances a person should have the right to sleep on his back or on his belly. What is non-controversial in this claim is that no institutional procedures be adopted which prevent anyone from sleeping as they choose and that sanctions be adopted prohibiting others from interfering with such choice. Thus, what is non-controversial is a view of mechanisms for social choice and not a view of social welfare. Hence, Sen may call his condition L a libertarian principle if he likes; but that does not establish that L represents 'a value involving

---

3 Some liberals or libertarians who are by no means social-welfaristic in their conception of the goodness of social states have clearly been opposed to rugged libertarianism. This was clearly true of John Dewey in the 1930s and 1940s who attacked those defenders of property rights who did so in the name of freedom. Dewey thought that the systems of property rights being defended were not effective in maximizing more 'liberty' for individuals. It is clear that Dewey did not mean, by liberty for individuals, legally sanctioned rights but a character attribute which individuals may or may not lack – a capacity to realise one's 'potentialities'. Nor did he mean welfare in the sense in which Sen and I are using that term. But like social-welfarists and in opposition to rugged libertarians he was concerned to pick and choose among systems of institutionalized rights in terms of how well they promoted good social consequences. I think it is to be regretted that the recent discussion has tended to polarize around the opposition between social-welfarist libertarians and rugged libertarians. Other forms of libertarianism are worth examining. I do not, of course, think that any of the authors I have mentioned would disagree. (See Dewey, 1946, especially chs. 9 and 10.)

individual liberty' of the sort illustrated by the fairly non-controversial view that a person should have a right to sleep on his back or his belly as he chooses.

On the other hand, Sen's thesis is not refuted either. The question to be settled is whether a commitment to a libertarian mechanism for social choice presupposes a version of L as a constraint on social welfare functions. If the answer is in the affirmative, Sen's condition L represents 'a value involving individual liberty' even if one is a libertarian in the sense in which libertarianism imposes constraints on mechanisms for social choice.

We have already seen that libertarianism does have ramifications for standards of social value. On the other hand, unless the standard of social value adopted is social-welfaristic, libertarianism has no implications for social welfare functions. Rugged libertarians are not committed in virtue of their libertarianism to any particular view of social welfare and, hence, are not committed to condition L.

On the other hand, it is at least entertainable that a commitment to social-welfarist libertarianism incurs a commitment to condition L as a constraint on social welfare functions used as standards of social value. If so, Sen's arguments will have established that a welfarist libertarian cannot endorse a social welfare function as a standard of social value conforming to the weak Pareto principle P and the condition of unrestricted domain U.

Social-welfarist libertarianism does not entail a commitment to L. Moreover, the constraints which are entailed are compatible with principle P and, counter to what Bernholz suggests, with U as well (Bernholz, 1974, p. 100).

Social-welfarist libertarianism does presuppose, however, that the preferences of rights holders over *disjunctions* of social states are related to social preference over social states in certain ways. But these constraints may be met by restricting the beliefs rights holders have about the behavior of other rights holders and not their preferences over social states.

If these observations are sound, it is perfectly possible to be a paretian, social-welfarist libertarian. This possibility does not derive from any flaw in Sen's proof that commitment to his condition L cannot be consistently embraced along with commitment to conditions U and P on social welfare functions. It is based on the fact that condition L is not a necessary presupposition of social-welfarist libertarianism and that the presuppositions which are necessary do not preclude satisfaction of conditions U and P.

Bernholz and Gärdenfors have both correctly emphasized that if agent X possesses a right, the right concerns some aspect of social states (Bernholz, 1974, pp. 100 ff., and Gärdenfors, 1978). The social choice mechanism does not secure for X the power to determine social states but only some aspect of such states. When X exercises his right, he does not choose a social state but chooses one of several alternative determinations of an aspect of social states.[4]

Thus, if X has the right to choose the color of his walls, he is not entitled by his choice of a color for his walls to determine the complete social state (including, for example, the color of Y's walls).

This applies, of course, to the rights granted agents as part of the social choice mechanism.

In response to Berholz on his point, Sen alleges that his remarks 'would seem to be based on a misunderstanding of the type of space on which these preferences are to be formulated. Given the rest of the world Ω, Jack's choice over the "measure" of sleeping on his back and that of sleeping on his belly *is* a choice over two "social states"' (Sen, 1976, p. 228).

It is true that if Jack knew the condition Ω of the rest of the world or social state, his choice of sleeping on his back over sleeping on his belly (or vice versa) would be a choice of one social state over another. But when Jack makes his decision, the 'rest of the world Ω' is not given to him. What Jack chooses to be true is that the social state be described correctly by 'Jack sleeps on his back and (either Ω_1 or Ω_2 or ... or Ω_n)' over the state described by 'Jack sleeps on his belly and (either Ω_1 or Ω_2 or ... or Ω_n).' It is true that when Jack makes his decision and when all other rights holders make their decisions and when the other institutional agencies make whatever residual decisions are required, a social state may be fully determined. But the decisions of other rights holders and of the other social agencies are not given to Jack (at least not necessarily). What he chooses to be true in exercising his rights is that a disjunction of social states be true without choosing true that one of the disjuncts be true.

To illustrate, let us use Sen's well-known example. a and b each have the right to read or not to read *Lady Chatterley's Lover*. The following matrix gives the utility payoffs to the two parties in each of the four possible social states:

	Rb	$\sim Rb$
Ra	(1, 4)	(3, 3)
$\sim Ra$	(2, 2)	(4, 1)

a has the right to choose Ra or $\sim Ra$. But choosing Ra (i.e., choosing that Ra be true) is equivalent to choosing Ra & Rb or Ra & $\sim Rb$. It is choosing that a disjunction of social states be true but not that one particular social state be true. The same applies *mutatis mutandis* to a's other option.

4 Gärdenfors makes a distinction between exercising a right and failing to do so. X may fail to exercise his right to have his walls painted white by not deciding at all – e.g., by letting the color be decided by some agency or by a lottery. I find it preferable to say that X did make a choice and did exercise his right by choosing to have the color selected by an agency or lottery. On the view I favor, a right is characterized as a legally or socially sanctioned set of options from which the agent is free (legally or socially) to choose at least one and is constrained to choose at most one. Other circumstances beyond legal or social control may cut down the space of options further. The right need not be characterized by actually listing

To be sure, if a knew that Rb obtains, his choosing that Ra be true would be equivalent to his choosing that Ra & Rb. But even if it is true that Rb, if a does not know this, a's decision is not that Ra & Rb be true but that Ra & Rb or Ra & $\sim Rb$ be true.

That is to say, this is so if we are thinking of choice in the sense in which choice is the outcome of deliberation where the agent adopts an option he judges admissible with respect to his preferences.

Thus, if a does not know b's decision, his decision whether to read or not to read the book will be based on his preference over the pair of options represented by the two disjunctions of social states cited above. His preferences over any pair of social states will be relevant only insofar as that preference determines or contributes to determining his preference over the pair of disjunctions of social states. It is a's preference over the disjunctions which ought to control his choices. Since the same thing obtains for b, it is apparent that whether or not the net effect of choices made by a and b is an optimal social choice of a social state depends upon how the preferences of rights holders over appropriate pairs of disjunctions of social states relate to social preferences of social states. The decisiveness of a's preferences over the pair Ra & Rb, $\sim Ra$ & Rb or the pair Ra & $\sim Rb$, $\sim Ra$ & $\sim Rb$ for the social ranking has nothing to do with this.

Thus, suppose the social ranking is Ra & $\sim Rb$, Ra & Rb, $\sim Ra$ & Rb, $\sim Ra$ & $\sim Rb$. The Pareto principle P is satisfied. a prefers $\sim Ra$ & Rb to Ra & Rb. But social preference is in the opposite direction. a prefers $\sim Ra$ & Rb to Ra & $\sim Rb$. Again society prefers the opposite. a's preference over the appropriate pairs of social states is not decisive for society.

Does this mean that a lacks the rights to decide whether to read or not to read the book in accordance with a's preferences for these two options? Not at all. Is it possible that a's preferences for the two options available to him can induce him to choose in a manner which does not prevent a socially optimal choice of a social state? Clearly if a prefers to read the book rather than not, his choice will not prevent a socially optimal social state from being selected.

What needs to be shown now is that a's preferences for disjunctions of states (and b's preferences for disjunctions) can be so constrained that the socially optimal state is selected by their choosing in accordance with their preferences within the framework of rights and that this can be done without imposing any constraint ruling out possible congeries of individual preference profiles for social states in violation of condition U or modifying the

---

the set of options but may be described in some more general way (such as having the right to decide the color of one's walls). But any choice with regard to the issue is an exercise of the right. This mode of representation may not conform to common legal or political categories; but I do not see that it prejudices any issues critical to the present discussion. I suspect it would simplify the formal articulation of the issues as compared with the proposals made by Gärdenfors. But I do not undertake such formalization here.

Pareto condition *P* on social welfare functions. Constraints may be necessary on preferences over disjunctions of social states. That is obvious. But such constraints ought not to be construed as restrictions on preferences over social states.

Bernholz has correctly observed that decision problems like those faced by *a* and by *b* are decision problems under uncertainty (Bernholz, 1974, p. 101). If the numbers assigned his values represent cardinal utilities unique up to a positive linear transformation and, if conditional on his reading *Lady Chatterley's Lover* he has numerically definite probability assignments for *Rb* and ~*Rb* and corresponding assignments conditional on his not reading the book, expected utilities can be computed for *a*'s two options and his preferences determined accordingly.

Notice that even if the utility function for the social states representing *a*'s preferences remains fixed, *a*'s preferences for the two options open to him in virtue of his rights can be modified by changes in his probability judgements (which I shall call his *credal state*) unless each disjunct in one disjunction is preferred over every disjunct in the other – a condition not met in our example. In our example, *a*'s preferences for the social states are such that ~*Ra* dominates *Ra* relative to the two states *Rb* and ~*Rb* but does not superdominate it.[5] Hence, by assigning a probability near 1 to ~*Rb* conditional on *a*'s choosing to read the book and a probability near 1 to *Rb* conditional on *a*'s choosing not to read the book, *a* can be in a credal state where he prefers reading to not reading – in the sense of preference which should dictate his choice when exercising his rights.

This observation does not depend upon the assumption that preferences are represented by a utility function unique up to a positive linear transformation and probabilities by a unique probability function. I have suggested elsewhere that an agent's preferences may be represented by a set of utility functions and his credal state by a set of probability functions.[6] Both sets should be non-empty but the former need not be restricted to positive linear transformations of a given utility function and the latter need not be a unit set.

An option among the set feasible for the agent is *E-admissible* if and only if it ranks highest in expected utility relative to one permissible utility function in the set of utility functions representing the agent's preferences and to a probability function in the set representing the credal state. Ignoring some special complications, the agent's choice of an option should be restricted to maximin (or, perhaps better, leximin) solutions from among the E-admissible options.

In our example, if *a*'s credal state is sufficiently indeterminate, both options will be E-admissible. He should then choose not to read because that

5 This terminology is due to E. McClennen.
6 Levi (1974), pp. 391–418. A more articulate version appears in Levi (1980*a*).

is the maximin solution even though he does not rank that option preferable with respect to expected utility. If b's credal state is similarly indeterminate, he will choose to read not because it is preferable to not reading but because it bears the superior security level.

When the credal states of the two rights holders are of this kind, the social state chosen will, prisoner's-dilemma-like, be Pareto dominated by another social state. Although the exercise of rights leads neither to violation of condition U nor of condition P on social welfare functions, the choice mechanism based on the grant of rights to a and b fails to lead to the maximization of welfare.

Social-welfarists will find such situations unpleasant and seek remedies. But they need not restrict the rights of a and b, modify the social welfare function, violate P, or prohibit a and b from ranking the social states the way they do.

It is enough to seek to promote conditions under which a and b will have credal states that, given their individual preferences for the social states, will lead to preferences over disjunctions of social states that will induce the determination of a social state which is optimal with respect to welfare. Thus, a should be persuaded to assign near certainty to b's choosing not to read conditional on a's reading and near certainty to b's choosing to read conditional on a's not reading. Under these circumstances, a acquires a sharp preference for reading over not reading. Similar adjustment in b's credal state secures that b prefers not reading to reading leading to a welfare maximizing solution.

Making such adjustments requires no violation of conditions U or P on social welfare functions. It requires no modification of the rights built into the mechanism for social choice. It does require an alteration in the climate of trust, and ability of individuals to communicate with one another and to negotiate cooperative solutions.[7]

Situations can arise where a rights holder prefers one option over all others granted by his right and no modification of his credal state can induce a legitimate modification of his preferences over the options (which are disjunctions of social states). This can happen when one option super-dominates all others. That is to say, the rights holder prefers any social state which is a disjunct in that option to every social state which is a disjunct in a rival option.

Social-welfarist libertarians must, in such cases, restrict the social welfare function to one which assigns maximum welfare to at least one social state

---

7 Libertarians who, like Dewey, are neither rugged nor welfaristic libertarians may be prepared to modify individual preferences in order to induce behavior in rights holders conducive to maximizing whatever it is they regard as good where these preferences are over social states. The point I am now making, however, is that such maneuvers are not necessary in the case of welfarist libertarians in the narrow sense and may not be for other sorts of libertarians either.

which is a disjunct in the option which is superdominating for the rights holder (or at least ensure that no other option bears greater social welfare).

This is the only sense in which the preferences of a rights holder over social states constrains the social ranking for a social-welfarist libertarian. This constraint is far weaker than Sen's L or L'.

It is not news that libertarians, whether they are welfarists or, like John Dewey, prize liberty because it promotes some other sort of good, often insist that liberties be integrated in an organization of institutions in such a way 'that men's "ultimate" values – their consciences, their sense of meaning of life, their personal dignity – do not become elements of public conflict' (Frankel, 1958, p. 83). If they are social-welfarists, they would also promote institutional arrangements providing for negotiation over conflicting values (whether 'ultimate' or not) so that welfare may be promoted without depriving anyone of their rights.

It is not always possible to ensure social and institutional arrangements which will induce rights holders to adjust their beliefs so that it is rational for them to exercise their rights in a cooperative manner. And sometimes doing so will conflict with requirements of intellectual integrity. We may be reluctant to persuade rights holders to adjust their credal states in ways which run counter to common sense or the best scientific evidence available solely for the sake of promoting welfare maximizing solutions to social decision problems through the exercise of rights.

Any libertarian who contends that a given system of liberties is justifiably integrated into a social choice mechanism because it leads to or tends to lead to social states maximizing some sort of good – whether it is social welfare or something else – runs the risk that economic, social, and other relevant conditions may not be conducive to the use of such a choice mechanism. Such libertarians (whether social-welfarist or not) may have to reconsider the system of rights they defend. Under these circumstances, only radical forms of rugged libertarianism advocated by those ready to modify the standard of social value in order to save the choice mechanism and the system of liberties it embodies may oppose advocates of radical reform of the choice mechanism without discomfort.

But social-welfarists are not precluded on any logical or conceptual grounds from endorsing libertarianism while remaining loyal to paretianism and the condition of unrestricted domain. Whatever difficulties social-welfarism may face, they must be sought elsewhere.

Bibliography of Isaac Levi

1958

Review of Roy Harrod, *Foundations of Inductive Logic*, *Journal of Philosophy* **55**, 209–12.

1959

(a) 'Putnam's Three Truth Values', *Philosophical Studies* **10**, 65–9.
(b) Translation of R. Carnap, 'The Old and the New Logic', in *Logical Positivism* (ed. by A. J. Ayer) (Free Press).

1960

(a) 'Must the Scientist Make Value Judgments?', *Journal of Philosophy* **57**, 345–57.
(b) Translation of A. Meinong, 'The Theory of Objects', in R. M. Chisholm (ed.), *Realism and the Background of Phenomenology* (Free Press) (with D. B. Terrell and R. M. Chisholm).

1961

(a) 'Decision Theory and Confirmation', *Journal of Philosophy* **58**, 614–25.
(b) Review of *Minnesota Studies in Philosophy of Science, Vol. II*, *Journal of Philosophy* **58**, 241–8.
(c) Review of Danto and Morgenbesser (eds.), *Philosophy of Science* and E. H. Madden (ed.), *The Structure of Scientific Thought*, *Journal of Philosophy* **58**, 387–90.
(d) Review of A. Rapaport, *Fights, Games and Debates*, *Harvard Educational Review* **31**, 477–9.

1962

'On the Seriousness of Mistakes', *Philosophy of Science* **29**, 47–65.

1963

(a) 'Corroboration and Rules of Acceptance', *British Journal for the Philosophy of Science* **13**, 307–13.
(b) Review of H. Leblanc, *Statistical and Inductive Probabilities*, *Journal of Philosophy* **59**, 21–5.
(c) Contribution to *Harper's Encyclopedia of Science*.

1964

(a) 'Belief.and Action', *The Monist* **48**, 306–16.
(b) 'Belief and Disposition', *American Philosophical Quarterly* **1**, 221–32 (with Sidney Morgenbesser).
(c) 'Utility and Acceptance of Hypotheses', *Voice of America Forum Lectures, Philosophy of Science Series*, No. 2.

1965

(a) 'Deductive Cogency in Inductive Inference', *Journal of Philosophy* **62**, 68–77.
(b) 'Hacking Salmon on Induction', *Journal of Philosophy* **63**, 481–7.

1966

(a) 'On Potential Surprise', *Ratio* **8**, 107–29.
(b) 'Recent Work in Probability and Induction' (reviews of books by I. J. Good, I. Hacking, R. C. Jeffrey, and H. Törnebohm), *Synthese* **16**, 234–44.

1967

(a) *Gambling with Truth* (A. Knopf, New York) (reissued in paperback without revision in 1973 by MIT Press).
(b) 'Probability Kinematics', *British Journal for the Philosophy of Science* **18**, 197–209.
(c) 'Information and Inference', *Synthese* **17**, 369–91.

1968

(a) Review of J. Hintikka and P. Suppes (eds.), *Aspects of Inductive Logic*, *British Journal for the Philosophy of Science* **19**.
(b) Review of W. Salmon, *The Foundations of Scientific Inference*, *British Journal for the Philosophy of Science* **19**, 259–61.

1969

(a) 'Confirmation, Linguistic Invariance and Conceptual Innovation', *Synthese* **20**, 48–55.
(b) 'If Jones Only Knew More', *British Journal for the Philosophy of Science* **20**, 153–9.
(c) 'Induction and the Aims of Inquiry', *Philosophy, Science and Method, Essays in Honor of Ernest Nagel*, ed. by S. Morgenbesser, P. Suppes, and M. White (St. Martin's Press), pp. 92–111.
(d) Review of *The Problem of Inductive Logic*, ed. by I. Lakatos, *Synthese* **20**, 143–8.
(e) 'Are Statistical Hypotheses Covering Laws?', *Synthese* **20**, 297–307.

1970

'Probability and Evidence', *Induction, Acceptance and Rational Belief*, ed. by M. Swain (Reidel, Dordrecht), pp. 134–56.

1971

(a) 'Certainty, Probability and Correction of Evidence', *Nous* **5**, 299–312.
(b) 'Truth, Content and Ties', *Journal of Philosophy* **68**, 865–76.

1972

(a) 'Potential Surprise in the Context of Inquiry', in *Uncertainty and Expectations in Economics: Essays in Honor of G. L. S. Shackle*, ed. by C. F. Carter and J. L. Ford (Blackwell, Oxford), pp. 213–36.

(b) Invited Comments on Churchman (pp. 87–94) and on Braithwaite (pp. 56–61). *Science, Decision and Value*, ed. by J. Leach, R. Butts, and G. Peirce (Reidel, Dordrecht).

1973

(a) 'But Fair to Chance', *Journal of Philosophy* **70**, 52–5.
(b) Review of D. H. Mellor, *The Matter of Chance, Philosophical Review* **82**, 524–30.

1974

'On Indeterminate Probabilities', *Journal of Philosophy* **71**, 391–418.

1975

'Newcomb's Many Problems', *Theory and Decision* **6**, 161–75.

1976

(a) 'Acceptance Revisited', in *Local Induction*, ed. by R. Bogdan (Reidel, Dordrecht), pp. 1–71.
(b) 'A Paradox for the Birds', in *Essays in Memory of Imre Lakatos*, ed. by R. S. Cohen *et al.* (Reidel, Dordrecht), pp. 371–8.

1977

(a) 'Direct Inference', *The Journal of Philosophy* **74**, 5–29.
(b) 'Subjunctives, Dispositions and Chances', *Synthese* **34**, 423–55.
(c) 'Four Types of Ignorance', *Social Research* **44**, 745–56.
(d) 'Epistemic Utility and the Evaluation of Experiments', *Philosophy of Science* **44**, 368–86.

1978

(a) 'Irrelevance', *Foundations and Applications of Decision Theory*, ed. by Hooker, Leach, and McLennen, Vol. 1 (Reidel, Dordrecht), pp. 263–75.
(b) 'Coherence, Regularity and Conditional Probability', *Theory and Decision* **9**, 1–15.
(c) 'Confirmational Conditionalization', *Journal of Philosophy* **75**, 730–37.
(d) Reprint of (1964b) and of (1977b) in *Dispositions*, ed. by R. Tuomela (Reidel, Dordrecht).

1979

(a) Translation of (1967a) into Japanese (Kinokuniya Book Store, Tokyo).
(b) 'Inductive Appraisal', *Current Research in Philosophy of Science*, ed. by P. D. Asquith and H. E. Kyburg (PSA, East Lansing, Mich.), pp. 339–51.
(c) 'Serious Possibility', *Essays in Honour of Jaakko Hintikka* (Reidel, Dordrecht), pp. 219–36.
(d) 'Abduction and Demands for Information', *The Logic and Epistemology of Scientific Change*, ed. by I. Niiniluoto and R. Tuomela (North Holland for Societas Philosophica Fennica, Amsterdam), pp. 405–29.
(e) 'Support and Surprise: L. J. Cohen's View of Inductive Probability', *British Journal for the Philosophy of Science* **30**, 279–92.

1980

(a) The Enterprise of Knowledge: An Essay on Knowledge, Credal Probability and Chance (MIT, Cambridge, Mass.).

(b) 'Induction as Self Correcting According to Peirce', Science, Belief and Behaviour, Essays in honour of R. B. Braithwaite, ed. by D. H. Mellor (Cambridge), pp. 127–40.

(c) 'Potential Surprise: Its Role in Inference and Decision-Making', Applications of Inductive Logic, ed. by L. J. Cohen and M. Hesse (Clarendon, Oxford), pp. 1–27. Also replies to comments by P. Teller, H. E. Kyburg, R. G. Swinburne, and L. J. Cohen and comments on papers by R. Giere, J. Dorling, J. E. Adler, and R. Bogdan.

(d) 'Incognisables', Synthese **45**, 413–27.

1981

(a) 'On Assessing Accident Risks in U.S. Commercial Nuclear Power Plants', Social Research **48**.

(b) 'Should Bayesians sometimes neglect base rates?' The Behavioral and Brain Sciences **4**, pp. 342–3.

(c) Comment on 'On Some Statistical Paradoxes and Non-conglomerability' by Bruce Hill, Trabajos de Investigacion Operativa Y Estadistica **32**, pp. 135–41.

(d) 'Direct Inference and Confirmational Conditionalization,' Philosophy of Science **48**, pp. 532–52.

(e) 'Escape from Boredom: Edification according to Rorty', Canadian Journal of Philosophy **11**, pp. 589–601.

1982

(a) Review of Theory and Evidence by Clark Glymour, The Philosophical Review **91**, pp. 124–8.

(b) 'Liberty and Welfare', in Utilitarianism and Beyond ed. by A. Sen and B. Williams, Cambridge University Press, pp. 239–49.

(c) 'Self Profile' (pp. 181–216) and 'Replies' (pp. 293–305) in Profiles of Henry E. Kyburg, Jr. and Isaac Levi ed. by R. Bogdan, Dordrecht: Reidel.

(d) 'Dissonance and Consistency according to Shackle and Shafer', PSA 1978 **2**, pp. 466–75.

(e) 'Conflict and Social Agency', Journal of Philosophy **79**, pp. 231–47.

(f) 'A Note on Newcombmania', Journal of Philosophy **79**, pp. 337–42.

(g) 'Ignorance, Probability and Rational Choice', Synthese **53**, pp. 387–417.

(h) Review of A. W. Burks, Chance, Cause, Reason: an Inquiry into the Nature of Scientific Evidence, Nous **16**, pp. 619–22.

1983

(a) Review of Studies in Inductive Logic and Proability v. 2 ed. by R. C. Jeffrey, The Philosophical Review **92**, pp. 116–21.

(b) 'Truth, Fallibility and the Growth of Knowledge', Language, Logic and Method ed. by R. S. Cohen and M. Wartofsky, Reidel, pp. 153–4 followed by comments by I. Scheffler and A. Margalit and replies.

(c) 'Information and Error', The Behavioral and Brain Sciences **6**, pp. 74–5.

(d) 'Consonance, Dissonance and Evidentiary Mechanisms', in Evidentiary Value: Philosophical, Judicial and Psychological Aspects of a theory ed. by P. Gärdenfors, B. Hansson, and N.-E. Sahlin, Lund: Gleerups, pp. 27–43.

Bibliography

Allais, M. (1953), 'Le Comportement de l'Homme Rationnel Devant le Risque: Critique des Postulats et Axiomes de l'Ecole Americaine', *Econometrica* **21**, pp. 503–46.

Arrow, K. (1963), *Social Choice and Individual Values*, 2nd ed. New York: Wiley.

—— and Hurwicz, L. (1972), 'Decision Making under Ignorance, in (Carter and Ford, 1972), pp. 1–11.

Ayer, A. J. (1957), 'The Conception of Probability as a Logical Relation', in *Observation and Interpretation in the Philosophy in the Philosophy of Physics*, ed. by S. Körner, New York: Dover, pp. 12–17 and discussion pp. 18–30.

Bar-Hillel, Y., Carnap, R., and Popper, K. R. (1955–7), Discussion Notes in *British Journal for Philosophy of Science* **6**, pp. 155–63 and **7**, pp. 243–56.

Bar-Hillel, M. and Margalit, A. (1972), 'Newcomb's Paradox Revisited', *British Journal for the Philosophy of Science* **13**, pp. 295–303.

Bernholz, P. (1976), 'Is a Paretian Liberal Really Possible?' *Public Choice* **20**, pp. 99–107.

Blackwell, D. and Girshick, M. A. (1954), *Theory of Games and Statistical Decisions*, New York: Wiley.

Braithwaite, R. B. (1953), *Scientific Explanation*, Cambridge University Press.

Buchanan, J. M. (1964), 'Social Choice, Democracy and Free Markets', *Journal of Political Economy*, pp. 334–43.

Carnap, R. (1945–6), 'Remarks on Induction and Truth', *Philosophy and Phenomenological Research* **6**, pp. 590–602.

—— (1950), *Logical Foundations of Probability*, University of Chicago, 2nd ed. 1962.

—— (1960), 'The Aim of Inductive Logic', *Logic, Methodology and Philosophy of Science* ed. by E. Nagel, P. Suppes, and A. Tarski, Stanford University Press, pp. 302–18.

Carter, C. F. and Ford, J. L. (1972), *Uncertainty and Expectation in Economics: Essays in Honor of G. L. S. Shackle*, Oxford: Blackwell.

Chernoff, H. and Moses, L. (1959), *Elementary Decision Theory*, New York: Wiley.

Chisholm, R. M. (1957), *Perceiving: A Philosophical Study*, Cornell University Press.

Churchman, C. W. (1948), *Theory of Experimental Inference*, New York: MacMillan.

—— (1956), 'Science and Decision Making,' *Philosophy of Science* **33**, pp. 247–9.

Cohen, L. J. (1970), *The Implications of Induction*, London: Methuen.

—— (1977), *The Probable and the Provable*, Oxford: Clarendon Press.

De Finetti, B. (1963), 'Foresight: Its Logical Laws, Its Subjective Sources,' in H. Kyburg and H. Smokler (eds.) *Studies in Subjective Probability*, New York: Wiley, pp. 93–158.

Dempster, A. P. (1967), 'Upper and Lower Probabilities Induced by a Multivalued Mapping,' *Annals of Mathematical Statistics* **38**, pp. 325–39.

Dewey, J. (1938), *Logic: The Theory of Inquiry*, New York: Holt.
—— (1946), *The Problems of Men*, New York: Philosophical Library.
Dewey, J. and Tufts, J. (1932), *Ethics*, New York: Holt.
Edwards, A. L. (1946), *Statistical Analysis for Students of Psychology and Education*, New York: Rinehart.
Ehrenfest-Afanassyewa, T. (1958), 'On the Use of "Probability" in Physics', *American Journal of Physics* **26**, pp. 388–92.
Fisher, R. A. (1930), 'Inverse Probability,' *Proceedings of the Cambridge Philosophical Society* **26**, pp. 528–35.
—— (1959), *Statistical Methods and Scientific Inference*, 2nd ed. New York: Hafner.
Frankel, C. (1958), *The Case for Modern Man*, Boston: Beacon Press.
Gärdenfors, P. (1978), 'Rights, Games and Social Choice', (mimeo.).
—— and Sahlin, N.-E. (1982), 'Decision Making with Unreliable Probabilities', *Synthese* **53**, pp. 361–86.
Good, I. J. (1962), 'Subjective Probability as a Measure of a Non-Measurable Set', *Logic, Methodology and Philosophy of Science* ed. by P. Suppes, E. Nagel, and A. Tarski, Stanford University Press, pp. 319–29.
—— (1967), 'On the Principle of Total Evidence', *British Journal for the Philosophy of Science* **17**, pp. 319–21.
Goosens, W. K. (1976), 'A Critique of Epistemic Utilities', *Local Induction* ed. by R. Bogdan, Reidel, pp. 93–113.
Hacking, I. (1965). *The Logic of Statistical Inference*, Cambridge University Press.
—— (1967), Review of Levi (1967a), *Synthese* **17**, pp. 494–8.
—— (1974), 'Combined Evidence', *Logical and Semantic Analysis* ed. by S. Stenlund, Reidel, pp. 113–23.
Harsanyi, J. (1955), 'Cardinal Welfare, Individualistic Ethics and Interpersonal Comparisons of Utility', *Journal of Political Economy* **73**, pp. 309–21. Reprinted in Harsanyi (1976), pp. 6–23.
—— (1975), 'Can the Maximin Principle Serve as a Basis for Morality? A Critique of John Rawls's Theory', *American Political Science Review* 69, pp. 594–606. Reprinted in Harsanyi (1976), pp. 37–63.
—— (1976), *Essays in Ethics, Social Behavior and Scientific Explanation*, Dordrecht: Reidel.
Hempel, C. G. (1949), Review of Churchman (1948), *Journal of Philosophy* **46**, p. 560.
—— (1960), 'Inductive Inconsistencies', *Synthese* **12**, pp. 439–69.
—— (1962), 'Deductive-Nomological vs. Statistical Explanation', *Minnesota Studies in the Philosophy of Science* **3**, pp. 98–169.
Hilpinen, R. (1968), *Rules of Acceptance and Inductive Logic*, Amsterdam: North Holland.
Hintikka, J. (1962). *Knowledge and Belief*, Cornell University Press.
Hintikka, J. and Pietarinen, J. (1966), 'Semantic Information and Inductive Logic', *Aspects of Inductive Logic* ed. by J. Hintikka and P. Suppes, North Holland, pp. 96–112.
Hurwicz, L. (1951), *Optimality Criteria for Decision Making Under Ignorance*, Cowles Commission Discussion Paper: Statistics #370.
Jeffrey, R. C. (1956), 'Valuation and Acceptance of Scientific Hypotheses', *Philosophy of Science* **33**, pp. 237–46.
—— (1965), *The Logic of Decision*, New York: McGraw Hill.
—— (1968), Review of Levi (1967a), *Journal of Philosophy* **65**, pp. 313–22.

Kahneman, D. and Tversky, A. (1979), 'Prospect Theory', *Econometrica* **47**, pp. 263–92.

Koopman, B. O. (1940), 'The Bases of Probability', *Bulletin of the American Mathematical Society* **46**, pp. 763–74.

Kyburg, H. E. (1961), *Probability and the Logic of Rational Belief*, Wesleyan University Press.

—— (1963), 'A Further Note on Rationality and Consistency', *Journal of Philosophy* **60**, pp. 463–5.

—— (1970), 'More on Maximal Specificity', *Philosophy of Science* **37**, pp. 295–300.

—— (1974a), *The Logical Foundations of Statistical Inference*, Reidel.

—— (1974b), 'Propensities and Probabilities', *British Journal for the Philosophy of Science* **25**, pp. 358–78.

Lehrer, K. (1964), 'Knowledge and Probability', *Journal of Philosophy* **61**, pp. 368–72.

Lewis, D. (1973), *Counterfactuals*, Harvard University Press.

Lewis, H. W. (1980), 'The Safety of Fission Reactors', *Scientific American* **242**, pp. 53–65.

Luce, R. D. and Raiffa, H. (1958), *Games and Decisions*, Wiley.

Lyon, P. (1980), *Preference Aggregation*, Doctoral dissertation, Washington University, St. Louis.

Mackie, J. L. (1962), 'Counterfactuals and Causal Laws', *Analytical Philosophy* ed. by R. Butler, Oxford: pp. 66–80.

Martin, R. M. (1959), *Towards a Systematic Pragmatics*, North Holland.

May, K. O. (1974), 'Intransitivity, Utility and the Aggregation of Preference Patterns', *Econometrica* **22**, pp. 1–13.

Mellor, D. H. (1971), *The Matter of Chance*, Cambridge University Press.

Michalos, A. (1966), 'Estimated Utility and Corroboration,' *British Journal for the Philosophy of Science* **16**, pp. 327–31.

Miller, D. (1966), 'A Paradox of Information', *British Journal for the Philosophy of Science* **17**, pp. 144–7.

—— (1968), 'The Straight and Narrow Rule of Induction', *British Journal for the Philosophy of Science* **19**, pp. 145–52.

Neyman, J. (1942), 'Basic Ideas and Some Recent Results of the Theory of Testing Statistical Hypotheses', *Journal of the Royal Statistical Society* **105**, pp. 292–327.

—— (1950), *A First Course in Probability*, H. Holt & Co.

—— and Pearson, E. S. (1932–3), 'The Testing of Statistical Hypotheses in Relations to Probabilities a priori', *Proceedings of the Cambridge Philosophical Society* **29**, pp. 492–510.

Niiniluoto, I. (1975), 'Inquiries, Problems and Questions; Remarks on Local Induction', *Local Induction* ed. by R. J. Bogdan, Reidel, pp. 263–96.

Nozick, R. (1963), *The Normative Theory of Rational Choice*, Doctoral dissertation, Princeton University.

—— (1969), 'Newcomb's Problem and Two Principles of Choice', *Essays in Honor of Carl G. Hempel* ed. by N. Rescher, Reidel, pp. 114–46.

—— (1974), *Anarchy, State and Utopia*, New York: Basic Books.

Ozga, S. A. (1965), *Expectations in Economic Theory*, London: Weidenfeld and Nicolson.

Peirce, C. S. (1931), *Collected Papers* v. 1, Harvard University Press.

—— (1950), *The Philosophy of Peirce* ed. by J. Buchler, Harcourt Brace.

Plott, C. R. (1973), 'Path Independence, Rationality and Social Choice', *Econometrica* **41**, 1075–91.

287

Popper, K. R. (1959), *The Logic of Scientific Discovery*, London: Hutchinson.
—— (1962), *Conjectures and Refutations*, New York: Basic Books.
Quine, W. V. (1960), *Word and Object*, New York: Wiley and MIT.
—— (1966), *The Ways of Paradox*, New York: Random House.
—— and Ullian, J. (1970), *The Web of Belief*, New York: Random House.
Raiffa, H. (1968), *Decision Analysis*, Addison Wesley.
Rasmussen *et al*. (1975), *Reactor Safety Study, An Assessment of Accident Risks in U.S. Commercial Power Plants:* Appendixes 1 and 2, Washington: Nuclear Regulatory Commission.
Rawls, J. (1971), *A Theory of Justice*, Harvard University Press.
Reichenbach, H. (1938), *Experience and Prediction*, University of Chicago Press.
—— (1949), *The Theory of Probability*, Berkeley: University of California Press.
Rorty, R. (1980), *Philosophy and the Mirror of Nature*, Oxford: Blackwell.
Rudner, R. (1953), 'The Scientist Qua Scientist Makes Value Judgements', *Philosophy of Science* **20**, pp. 1–4.
Savage, L. J. (1954), *The Foundations of Statistics*, New York: Wiley.
Schick, F. (1970), 'Three Logics of Belief', *Induction, Acceptance and Rational Belief* ed. by M. Swain, Reidel, pp. 6–26.
Schick, R. (1980), 'Welfare, Rights and Fairness', *Science, Belief and Behavior: Essays in honour of R. B. Braithwaite* ed. by D. H. Mellor, Cambridge University Press, pp. 203–16.
Seidenfeld, T. (1979*a*), 'Why I am not an Objective Bayesian', *Theory and Decision* **11**, 413–40.
—— (1979*b*), *Philosophical Problems of Statistical Inference: Learning from R. A. Fisher*, Reidel.
Sen, A. K. (1970), 'The Impossibility of a Paretian Liberal', *Journal of Political Economy*, **78**, pp. 152–7.
—— (1976), 'Liberty, Unanimity and Rights', *Economica* **43**, pp. 217–46.
—— (1977), 'On Weights and Measures: Informational Constraints in Social Welfare Analysis', *Econometrica* **45**, pp. 1539–72.
—— (1979), 'Utilitarianism and Welfarism', *Journal of Philosophy* **76**, pp. 463–89.
Shackle, G. L. S. (1949), *Expectations in Economics*, Cambridge University Press, 2nd ed. 1952.
—— (1961), *Decision, Order and Time in Human Affairs*, Cambridge University Press, 2nd ed. 1969.
—— (1938), *Expectations, Investment and Income*, Oxford: Clarendon, 2nd enlarged edition, 1968.
Shafer, G. (1976), *A Mathematical Theory of Evidence*, Princeton University Press.
Sleigh, R. C. (1964), 'A Note on some Epistemic Principles of Chisholm and Martin', *Journal of Philosophy* **61**, pp. 216–18.
Smith, C. A. B. (1961), 'Consistency in Statistical Inference and Decision' (with discussion), *Journal of the Royal Statistical Society* Ser. B. **23**, pp. 1–25.
von Neumann, J. and Morgenstern, O. (1947), *Theory of Games and Economic Behavior*, Princeton University Press.
Wald, A. (1950), *Statistical Decision Functions*, New York: Wiley.
Whittaker, E. (1960), *A History of the Theories of Aether and Electricity* v. 1, New York: Harper.

Index of names

Index of subjects

Abduction, 92–6, 120–2.

Acceptance, xii, xiv, 3, 15, 35, 88; and high probability, xii, 22, 43–5, 223–4; and maximizing probability, 58; and the seriousness of mistakes, 4–6; as evidence, xiv, 45, 88; as strongest via induction, xii, 45–6, 54, 93; mere, xiv; tentative, 51n.

Acceptance rules, caution dependent famiy of, 217–19; caution dependent family of deductively cogent, 219n., 222; feebly cogent, 219, 224–6; piecemeal cogent, 219, 223–4; deductively cogent and relative to ultimate partition, 48–50.

Agent, 87.

Allais paradox, xivi, 257n., 266–9.

Arrow's impossibility theorem, 269–70.

Ascendancy value, 231–4.

Avoidance of error and seriousness of mistakes, xi, 4, 5, 79–82, 98, 117–22, 143, 158.

Background knowledge and observation, 71–5.

Bayes method, 35, 36, 41, 53.

Bayesianism, xvi, 91–2, 128–31, 133, 147, 265–9; strict, 147–8, 202, 215–17, and sure thing principle, 265–9.

Belief, degrees of, 135; acceptance based, 216, 218–19; probabilistic, 215–16; as lower probabilities, 215–16.

Boredom, 146.

Caution (boldness), xi, xii, 22–5, 30–2, 60–4, 77–8, 98–9, 142n.

Chance (statistical or objective probability), 180–2, 192; and covering laws, 189–90; and direct inference, 182–4; and dispositions, 180–2; and frequency, 192–6; and propensity interpretation, 185n., 185–6; single case and long run, 187–9, 193n.

Cognitive state, 87–92.

Cognitive values (see epistemic utility).

Cognitive goal, 15.

Combining evidence, 226–8.

Commitment and living up to a commitment, 147–8.

Conceptual change, 140.

Conditionalization, 149; confirmational, 149, 204, 206–8; inverse temporal credal, 149, 204; temporal credal, 149, 204.

Confirmation, 20n., 34; degrees of, 9–10, 15.

Confirmational commitment, 89, 148–9, 201; and credibility, 166n.

Confirmational tenacity, 90.

Conflict between values, x.

Consistency and possibility, 148–51.

Content, 36, 39, 41, 43, 65–7.

Contractarianism and states of ignorance, 133–4.

Contraction, 90, 116, 122–5, 149, 169; and corrigibility, 124–5; and eliminating inconsistency, 123–4, 123n.; and giving a hearing to a worthy hypothesis, 124; and minimizing loss of information, 123, 169.

Corpus of Knowledge, 88, 113–15, 148, 167–8, 201.

Corrigibilism, xiv–xvii, 112–13, 116, 124–5; and fallibilism, 112–13, 116–27, 168; and truth as an ultimate or a proximate aim, 126–7.

Corrigibility, grades of, 122.

Corroboration, 20n., 34–41.

Credal state, 89, 147–8, 120, 214–16; and credal coherence, 201, 206–8; and credal consistency, 201, 206–8; and credal convexity, 202; and credal uniqueness, 202; indeterminate, 98, 132.

Decision making, cognitive, x, 142, 144–5; under uncertainty, 228–31; open ended decision problem, 6–8.

Deductive closure, xii, 44–5, 88, 113–15, 148.

Deductive cogency, 44–5, 88.

Direct inference, 182–4, 192–213.

Dispositions, 176–80; as placeholders, 178–80; explicit, 176, 178–80.

293